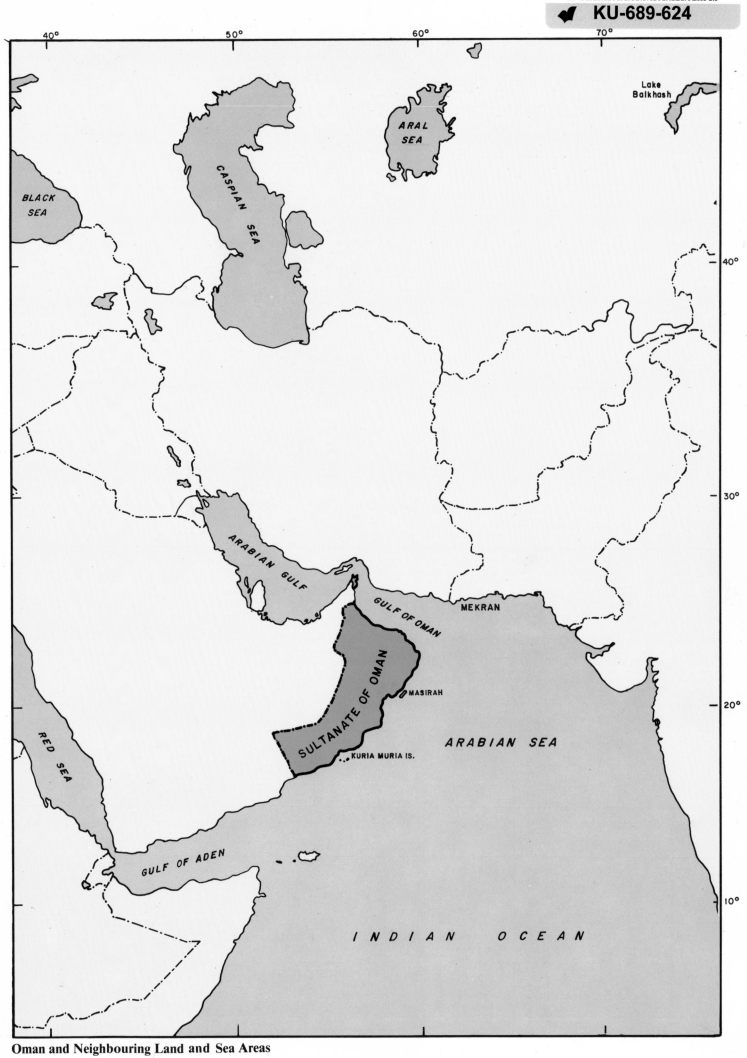

**Oman and Neighbouring Land and Sea Areas**

MWWoodcock

# THE
# BIRDS OF OMAN

Michael Gallagher
Martin W. Woodcock

QUARTET BOOKS
LONDON   MELBOURNE   NEW YORK

# The Holy Qur'an

'Have they not considered the birds above them opening and closing their wings.
Nothing supports them but the All Merciful.
He observes all things.'

Sura 67, verse 19.

THIS VOLUME IS DEDICATED TO HIS MAJESTY SULTAN QABOOS BIN SAID,
WHOSE INSPIRATION, SUPPORT AND ENCOURAGEMENT MADE ITS PREPARATION POSSIBLE,
AND BY WHOSE PERSONAL INTEREST, INITIATIVE AND FORESIGHT,
THE FAUNA OF THE SULTANATE HAS BECOME MORE WIDELY
UNDERSTOOD AND PROTECTED.

*Author's note:*
The text of this volume was completed in 1979 and early 1980,
but some additional information was included up to June 1980.
The author would be pleased to receive notification of any changes
that appear necessary; these should be sent to him c/o the publisher.

First published by Quartet Books Limited 1980
A member of the Namara Group
27/29 Goodge Street, London W1P 1FD
Copyright © text and colour photographs by Michael Gallagher, 1980
Illustrations © Quartet Books Limited, 1980
Designed by Namara Features Limited
Photoset by BSC Typesetting Limited, London
Printed in Great Britain by Lund Humphries, Bradford
Bound in Great Britain by Leighton-Straker Bookbinding Company Limited, London
ISBN 0 7043 2216 1

# Contents

Foreword by His Majesty
Sultan Qaboos bin Said, Sultan of Oman

بِسْمِ اللهِ الرَّحْمٰنِ الرَّحِيمِ

FOREWORD BY
## HIS MAJESTY SULTAN QABOOS BIN SAID
## SULTAN OF OMAN

*In our endeavours to develop the natural resources of Oman we must not forget that one mark of civilisation is the regard men bestow on wild things.*

*This volume shows us that among the wild things of our country are a very large number of different species of birds which find living space in the diverse geographical zones of Oman – high mountains, sea shores, desert steppe, grasslands and woodlands. The conservation of these natural wildlife habitats in harmony with the development of our resources is essential.*

*Some of the birds we see in Oman are residents and some are visitors who seek food and shelter here while they pass on their long journeys to and from their breeding grounds; yet others, like the Sooty Falcon, come here from places far away to raise their young in our country. All of them are of God's creation and by His grace given to us to cherish and protect as part of our heritage.*

*In the past men persecuted and killed some species of birds, either because they regarded them as enemies or because they or their eggs were easy to hunt for food. The Arabian Ostrich was hunted so much that it is now extinct; only petrified eggs are sometimes found as evidence that this magnificent flightless bird once lived in our desert areas. The Houbara Bustard is another desert species which has in some places been hunted almost to extinction; with wise conservation measures enforced throughout its range this bird can yet be saved. The eagles are another group of birds often persecuted by man in the mistaken belief that they regularly feed on livestock, whereas, when their habits are closely studied, we find that more often they feed on lizards and snakes, small wild mammals and on carrion, thus helping to prevent some creatures from becoming too numerous and helping to keep the country clean. By the intelligent study of wild creatures we can learn to understand the vital importance to us of their place in the world which we share with them.*

*It is our belief that 'The Birds of Oman' will open a door, especially for the youth of our country, through which the reader may enter, perhaps for the first time, into a new and exciting world where he or she can help to discover yet more about the birds of our land. The book is also a welcome work of international importance filling as it does a long felt need by ornithologists for an up-to-date guide to the birds of Eastern Arabia.*

*We wish to thank the author and the artist, and all the many other people who contributed reports of their observations, for producing this scholarly and artistic work.*

Muscat Palace

August 1980

QABOOS BIN SAID

قصر العلم

# Introduction

Wild birds are a fascination and source of interest to an increasing number of people, and nowhere in the Arabian Peninsula is that hobby and interest stimulated more than in the Sultanate of Oman. Here is a country, often thought to be entirely desert by those not fortunate enough to visit it, which in reality has perennial streams, lakes, woodland and mountains, as well as sand and rock desert, and thus has many different bird habitats.

The variety of species of bird found here is due largely to Oman's zoologically unique position at the junction of three of the great biogeographical realms of the world, and it has many representatives from each of them. Still little studied zoologically, the Sultanate offers much to interest bird-watchers and field naturalists, but there has long been a need for a comprehensive guide to all the birds which occur.

The present volume has been prepared to meet this need, and in this Introduction some details of its scope and content are given for the convenience of the reader.

The aim has been to provide, for the first time, an authoritative work on the birds of the region, with an illustration of every species and a compact, informative text, which will be of use both to the beginner and to the more experienced bird-watcher and field naturalist.

*Scope*

All species which definitely occur in Oman, and at sea in Oman's waters, are dealt with in the text, and are included in the Check List (Appendix 1). Species discovered too late for inclusion in the main text are named in Appendix 2.

Great care has been taken to assess the accuracy of the reported observations. When there has been any doubt about an observer's identification, for example when full field notes were not available for consideration in support of a claim of a species new or scarce in Oman, a cautious treatment has been adopted. Species reported without conclusive evidence are omitted from the Check List but included in Appendix 3 (as not yet accepted) or Appendix 4 (if escaped captive birds), and some are mentioned in the text, usually within square brackets.

*Illustrations*

These are based on the artist's field experience and his notes and sketches of many of the species, on the preserved skins of birds kindly lent by the British Museum (Natural History), and on photographs taken by the artist and author in Oman. Observers will appreciate that it is not possible to depict every important phase of a bird's growth and changes in plumage, nor every aspect of the individual bird's behaviour; due allowance should be made for this and for the many slight variations which occur in nature. Notes on some variations to be expected are included in the accompanying text.

To assist readers, similar birds have been grouped together on the plates, involving slight departures from the usual sequence. Changes in sequence also became necessary when birds (such as Bewick's Swan and the Common Crane) were found for the first time in Oman during the compilation of this volume.

Field-work and other researches during the preparation of this volume have led to changes in the list of birds known to occur and requiring illustration. Re-painting has been necessary to take account of some new records, while others are too recent for the species concerned to be incorporated in the illustrations. On the other hand, some birds are shown although they have not yet been proved to occur in the wild in Oman; these include some, such as the White-tailed Eagle, which have definitely occurred very near Oman's borders, and others which resemble species found in Oman and which have caused confusion in the past.

*Maps*

There are four different maps on the endpapers; these indicate Oman's importance in zoogeographical terms, and show most of the important features within and around the Sultanate. In the first map, 'Biogeographic Realms of the World' the biogeographers' speculative and very broad groupings of the terrestrial flora and fauna are shown. Though birds are certainly not necessarily confined to these regions, the differences between the composition of the bird fauna in each region are noticeable; similarly, some oceanic birds belong to particular areas of Oceania. There are differing opinions as to where the boundaries of the Palaearctic, Afrotropical (Ethiopian) and Indomalayan (Oriental) regions meet, but Professor Udvardy (Udvardy 1965, on which our map is broadly based) shows all Arabia as lying within the first region.

(**Note:** The maps are not authorities for the delineation of international boundaries.)

*Descriptive text*

The text accompanying the illustrations is in the following sequence:

Family, with a brief note of the characteristics and behaviour common to most members

Names, world distribution and status in Oman

Length of bird, as a comparative guide, from tip of bill to tip of tail when fully stretched

Description, with comparative notes on similar species

Behaviour, including habitat, flight, food, nesting and voice when in Oman.

*Sequence and nomenclature*

With some exceptions, the scientific and most vernacular names and their sequence follow Voous (1977) and Cramp and Simmons (1977), and the names of the sub-species (geographical races) follow Vaurie (1959, 1965). Some vernacular names in common use in Oman have been retained, for example Little Green Heron *Butorides striatus* and Palm Dove *Streptopelia senegalensis*. Dr G. P. Hekstra (in Hekstra 1973 and in personal communication) has been followed in the treatment of owls of the genus *Otus*.

The array of different English and Arabic popular names for the same species in different parts of the world makes an 'international language' imperative, and the Latin or latinised names of genera and species help meet this need. Professor Voous has introduced some recent alterations to these in his list, but the list has been welcomed by ornithologists as offering a basis of stability which should prevail for many years.

In the descriptive text, mention is sometimes made of the races which occur in Oman. Though these are not always included in guides, it seems important to include them here (when it is certain which occur in Oman) because some of these races differ markedly from others which readers may know in other countries. For example, the Swift *Apus apus* is represented usually by the eastern form *pekinensis*, which is paler and a little smaller than the nominate race of Europe, and is liable to be confused with the Pallid Swift *A. p. pallidus*; the Little Green Bee-eater *Merops orientalis* in Arabia is distinctly more golden on the crown and more blue on the face than the African forms; the Nightingale *Luscinia megarhynchos* and Scops Owl *Otus scops* are two of the many which are represented by paler, greyer races than in Europe; whilst the male Black Redstart *Phoenicurus ochruros phoenicuroides* is very unlike the western forms.

4

*Distribution*

The breeding range of each species generally follows Vaurie (1959, 1965), and is given in a brief word-picture, from west to east and north to south. When a species is migratory the farthest country normally reached after breeding is mentioned. Geographical terms have been simplified: thus 'Eurasia' means Europe and Asia; 'Near East' is the region from Egypt and Sinai to Syria; 'Asia Minor' is Turkey and the neighbouring parts; 'Middle East' is Arabia and Iraq to the Arabian (Persian) Gulf; 'SW Asia' or 'SW Russia' is the USSR near its borders with Iran and Turkey; 'India' means the whole sub-continent and 'N India' includes Baluchistan, Pakistan, Bangladesh (and usually Afghanistan); 'E Asia' includes the east coast; 'SE Asia' includes Malaysia and islands reaching towards the SW Pacific and 'Australasia'; the latter is Australia, New Zealand and neighbouring islands.

In describing the distribution in Oman, the term 'N Oman' includes the Musandam region and Masirah Island unless the text makes a distinction. The term 'Dhofar' is the southern province north to near the centre of the central desert plateau, unless restricted in the text to the 'Dhofar mountains'.

*Sources, status and behaviour in Oman*

The brief status of each species in Oman given in the text and abbreviated in Appendix 1 is based upon unpublished reports made during the last twenty-two years by many observers, whose kindness in making them available the author is pleased to acknowledge; it is also based upon museum specimens, upon the rather sparse literature of the last 140 years and upon the author's field-work while preparing this volume. The dates of occurrence are inclusive.

An indication of the abundance of the species is given, though insufficient is known of some and there are considerable annual variations in some migrants. The terms used, such as 'scarce', 'uncommon', 'common', etc., will give a general indication, but it is not possible to quantify them; other terms are explained in the Glossary.

Where possible, an indication of the song and of other distinctive calls of the species is given in a written form. Observers will differ widely on how they would write some calls, and much also depends upon the accentuation and 'pronunciation' of the sounds. However, the method used here will probably be more intelligible to the layman than sound spectrographs and sonograms.

Conditions for observing birds have improved immeasurably since 1976 in Dhofar and since 1970 in the rest of Oman. Yet the Sultanate is still relatively little known ornithologically, and, despite recent field studies and the discovery of species new to the Oman list and of 'new' behaviour in familiar birds, many basic queries persist. Furthermore, some of our species, such as the Socotra Cormorant *Phalacrocorax nigrogularis*, Crab Plover *Dromas ardeola* and White-cheeked Tern *Sterna repressa*, have never been fully studied anywhere in their world range.

That there is still so much to learn about our birds gives the hobby of bird-watching in the Sultanate a special dimension and excitement which everyone may share.

## ACKNOWLEDGEMENTS

The completion of this volume would not have been possible without the support of many people, and the author and the artist wish to thank them all unreservedly.

Particular appreciation is due to His Majesty Sultan Qaboos bin Said, his ministers and staff, who have been actively interested in the work and have offered much assistance and encouragement; and to the people of Oman, who have been unfailingly helpful and hospitable during field studies.

Mr R. H. Daly OBE, Adviser for the Conservation of the Environment in Oman, provided the idea and inspiration for this volume and the opportunity and facilities to prepare it.

Mrs F. E. Warr researched the literature and museum specimens, maintained records of reports of birds in Oman for use in this and subsequent publications, and commented on some drafts. Dr D. A. Scott gave close collaboration from 1979, and helped improve a draft of the text.

The Trustees, Mr I. C. J. Galbraith and the staff of the British Museum (Natural History) provided assistance and facilities for study. Mr Humayun Abdulali and Mr R. B. Grubh gave helpful information about specimens in the collection of the Bombay Natural History Society. Dr David L. Harrison of the Harrison Zoological Museum provided facilities for study.

Mr F. B. Gill of the Academy of Natural Sciences, Philadelphia, and Professor C. G. Sibley of Yale University, provided details of the Wm. K. Carpenter collection.

Suggestions, and comments on parts of earlier drafts, were offered by Dr R. S. Bailey, Dr W. R. P. Bourne, Mr A. A. Brockett, Mr D. Goodwin, Dr G. P. Hekstra, Mr T. C. Hoopes, Mr R. S. Hunter, Dr R. M. Lawton, Dr J. F. Monk, Dr D. G. Reade, Mr T. D. Rogers, Lt. H. Samuel and Dr M. P. Searle.

Mr M. C. Jennings provided notes of some Saudi Arabian birds. Mr T. Samuel and Mr T. Thomson drew the maps.

Facilities for field studies, particularly transport, were provided by the Diwan of H.M. for Protocol, the Ministry of Diwan Affairs, the Ministry of Defence and the Sultan of Oman's land, air and naval forces; by H. M. the Sultan's Royal Flight, by the Air Wing of the Royal Oman Police and by Petroleum Development (Oman) Limited.

The British Trust for Ornithology, and others named in Appendix 5, provided ringing data.

Mrs Pamela Craig, Mrs Linda Fling and Mrs Lilian James accurately typed the several drafts. Mrs. Jean Maund prepared the index.

The Publishers, particularly Mr Naim I. Attallah, Mr G. Grant, Miss Janet Law and Mr R. Trevelion, have given great encouragement.

In addition to reports in the literature, the author has been fortunate in being able to draw upon unpublished notes made during the last twenty-two years and generously provided by:

M. StC. Baddeley, R. S. Bailey, G. C. Band, D. G. Barnes, T. Bavelaar, S. M. Brogan and Mrs C. M. O. Brogan, M. R. Brown, A. Bruyn, D. H. Butcher, Mrs R. N. L. Butler, B. Bywater; J. R. L. Carter, J. Castree, P. W. G. Chilman, L. Clark, T. Coates, M. Conway, P. F. S. Cornelius, L. Cornwallis; R. H. Daly, W. H. Davidson, J. E. Davies, Miss A. De Young, R. Dinnin, D. A. Diskin, B. Drost, A. Dunsire; J. Elven, H. E. Ennion, B. Etheridge, H. F. Everard; C. J. Feare, J. A. C. Forbes, D. Foster; M. J. Gilbert, J. Goddard, M. R. Goodfellow, A. C. G. Gordon, C. M. Greaves, C. I. Griffiths, K. M. Guichard; I. Hall, K. I. R. Halley, D. Halstead, David L. Harrison, D. Harvey, W. R. Harvey, A. W. A. Hazeldine, A. J. Heasman, W. D. Heber Percy, W. Heimbach, K. Heron, M. J. Holman, R. A. Honeywell, P. J. Hoon, T. C. Hoopes, M. D. Howell-Davies, H. Howarth, J. A. Hume, Mrs M. Huxtable; D. H. Insall; J. E. Jany, P. J. F. Jeans, M. C. Jennings, P. H. Jones, H. Jungius; R. King, C. G. Kirkpatrick, M. D. Kyrle Pope; J. M. Lapthorne, A. D. Lewis, Adrian Lewis; D. P. Mallon, N. Marks, C. C. Maxwell, D. Meade, E. N. T. Morris, W. F. J. Mörzer Bruijns, S. Moult, P. N. Munton; J. R. Neighbour; J. Oddos, D. N. Ogram; R. J. Parker, W. J. B. Peat, C. A. Pomeroy, A. Potterton, J. Prins; H. M. Sultan Qaboos bin Said; A. Radcliffe-Smith, P. H. Rathbone, M. G. T. Robb, T. D. Rogers, J. Ros, J. M. P. Ross, Royal Air Force Ornithological Society, Royal Naval Bird-watching Society; K. Salwegter, T. D. de Schneidauer, D. Schraer, I. M. Scoggins, D. A. Scott, M. P. Searle, C. J. Seton-Browne, D. Shepherd, J. Shrimplin, P. R. Sichel, D. M. Simpson, J. C. Sinclair, Mrs J. Slingsby, Mrs P. Smethurst, A. E. Smith, P. A. Smith, R. A. Smith, Mrs K. R. Smythe, M. R. Stanley-Price, W. Stanford, K. R. Stobbs and Mrs G. P. G. Stobbs, M. J. Strickland, D. Sweeney; W. Taylor, G. Tedbury, M. Templer, J. Thompson, S. Tibbett, R. J. S. Townend; J. H. Usher-Smith; F. J. Walker, G. P. Walker, H. Walter, A. J. Warr and Mrs F. E. Warr, J. Watts and Mrs A. L. Watts, W. Weitkowitz, R. P. Whitcombe, P. G. White, B. Whitehead, M. W. Woodcock, L. Woods, W. Wyper; G. E. Young.

6

**Plate I**   The falls below Wadi Darbat in the Dhofar mountains, under the low clouds of the south-west monsoon in summer, after exceptional rain. Among the breeding birds of the region are the Kestrel *Falco tinnunculus*, Arabian Red-legged Partridge *Alectoris melanocephala* and Abyssinian Sunbird *Nectarinia habessinica*.

overleaf:

**Plate II**   Wadi Sahtan, a typical water-course and a means of access to the foothills of Jabal Akhdar, northern Oman. The running water irrigates village cultivation and attracts many resident species, such as the Sand Partridge *Ammoperdix heyi* and Lichtenstein's Sandgrouse *Pterocles lichtensteinii*.

**Plate III**   The highest peak in eastern Arabia, Jabal Akhdar, the Green Mountain, has an altitude of nearly 3,000 metres. Large juniper trees of the endemic species *Juniperus macropoda* grow here. The Woodpigeon *Columba palumbus* and the Hume's Wheatear *Oenanthe alboniger* nest lower down.

# Oman-The Country

The Sultanate of Oman is a land of contrasting climate, land forms, vegetation and bird life, and it is this variety which is one of the many refreshing attractions that the country has to offer the field naturalist.

Oman lies on the flank of the great belt of arid deserts, known as the 'Saharo-Sindian', the 'Great Palaearctic Desert' and the 'Eremian Zone', which stretches from western Africa to China. However, Oman has a very favourable position along the eastern sea-board of the Arabian Peninsula, with its shore-line stretching for over 1,800 kilometres from the Arabian Gulf to the Arabian Sea. From the most northerly point at Greater Quoin Island (Jazirat as Salamah) at 26°30'N, except for a corridor of the United Arab Emirates (UAE) which lies between the Musandam region and northern Oman, the Sultanate stretches in a huge crescent south-westward to its southern border, where it reaches the most southerly point of 16°38'N on the coast. In over ten degrees of latitude and mostly within the tropics, it bridges much of the gap between the huge land masses of Asia and Africa.

## Climate

A study of the climate and its indirect effects upon the bird life is complicated by the size and latitudinal spread of the country and the varied physical parts of it, as well as by the lack of detailed records of some areas. The climate of the year has two distinct periods: the cool winter months (approximately late November to March) when northerly winds affect much of the country and most rain falls in northern Oman; and the hot summer (May to September), when a south-westerly monsoonal airflow affects the south in particular, and when precipitation is highest in the Dhofar mountains near the coast.

In winter cool, dry northerly winds predominate in Musandam and northern Oman, usually with high barometric pressures and clear skies. Occasional cold fronts between November and March cause widespread cloud and good rainfall on the Hajar mountains for two or three days, carrying over to the southern slopes in a high wind and on rare occasions causing snow on Jabal Akhdar. In Dhofar and elsewhere along the south-east coast the local winds become southerly during the day, but the northerly winds occasionally return.

In summer, though the winds at high altitude are still northerly, lower-level south-westerlies predominate, and in coastal Dhofar the effects are unique in Arabia. By May the south-west trade winds begin to blow across the Indian Ocean from about 10°N and reach the coast of Dhofar as the warm moist monsoon. Sluggish at first, the winds reach a peak of 20 to 30 knots in July and August, though less where they are in contact with the coast. The wind's friction tends to drag the sea surface with it, setting up a strong current from Somalia to west India. To compensate for this surface movement, deeper cold water wells up, particularly off Dhofar, and this, being 4° to 8°C cooler than the air passing over it, cools the air to dew-point. A bank of mist and ragged cloud then forms over the sea from eastern South Yemen to Sudh, and for 40 to 100 kilometres to the south. A temperature inversion prevents its dispersal, and a more stable cloud sheet forms over it at an altitude of between 600 and 1,520 metres.

Where the mountains of Dhofar face this wind, which is usually drawn inland by the sea breezes, the mist and cloud press against the mountains, riding up to the top of Jabal al Qara, though rarely over Jabal al Qamr or Jabal Samhan. Moisture is deposited by condensation on vegetation and on objects, by drizzle and by orographic rain. The intensity of the cloud varies daily, but it is dispersed by warmer ground temperatures when it reaches the northern desertic edge of the mountains and meets the hot dry monsoon wind coming overland from Africa.

The intensity and effects of the monsoon vary annually, and there has been a recent tendency for the rainfall to be below average. Additional rain occurs in the Dhofar mountains during cyclonic storms (Plate I). This combination of rains gives rise to the remarkable vegetation cover of coastal Dhofar and assists in re-charging the ground-water reserves. The cool wind and current continues to affect the coast as far as Ra's al Hadd and Masirah Island, and the effects are felt inland, for example over the Jiddat al Harasis.

Temperatures (see Table 1) are usually highest in May (at Salalah and Masirah) and June or July (at Muscat), the cool south-westerlies tending to prevent further increases in summer; the Capital Area, how-ever, is sheltered from these and much of the cool winter winds, and is the hottest coastal region.

**Table 1    Comparison of monthly averages of maximum and minimum daily temperatures °C**

|  | Jan | Feb | Mar | Apr | May | Jun | Jul | Aug | Sep | Oct | Nov | Dec | Year |
|---|---|---|---|---|---|---|---|---|---|---|---|---|---|
| **Maximum** | | | | | | | | | | | | | |
| Muscat: 24 years | 25.0 | 25.0 | 28.4 | 32.3 | 36.7 | **37.8** | 36.1 | 33.4 | 33.9 | 33.9 | 30.0 | 26.1 | 31.6 |
| Ra's al Hadd: 3 years | 25.0 | 25.6 | 30.0 | 32.8 | 37.3 | **37.8** | 33.9 | 33.9 | 32.8 | 31.7 | 28.9 | 26.1 | 31.1 |
| Fahud: 2 years | 26.1 | 28.9 | 33.9 | 34.5 | 41.7 | **46.1** | 43.9 | 42.3 | 40.6 | 36.7 | 31.7 | 28.4 | 36.1 |
| Masirah: 23 years (1943–65) | 25.5 | 26.5 | 29.6 | 32.7 | **35.3** | 34.2 | 31.0 | 30.2 | 30.0 | 31.0 | 28.8 | 26.6 | 30.1 |
| Salalah: 20 years (1946–65) | 27.2 | 28.2 | 29.7 | 31.3 | **32.4** | 31.7 | 28.0 | 26.8 | 29.0 | 30.6 | 30.4 | 28.4 | 29.5 |
| **Minimum** | | | | | | | | | | | | | |
| Muscat: 23 years | **18.9** | 19.5 | 22.2 | 25.6 | 30.0 | 31.0 | 30.6 | 28.9 | 28.4 | 26.7 | 22.8 | 20.0 | 25.6 |
| Ra's al Hadd: 3 years | **18.3** | 18.9 | 20.6 | 23.4 | 26.1 | 26.1 | 25.0 | 24.5 | 22.2 | 21.1 | 21.1 | 20.0 | 22.2 |
| Fahud: 2 years | **12.8** | 12.8 | 17.2 | 19.5 | 23.9 | 26.1 | 27.2 | 27.2 | 23.4 | 15.6 | 16.7 | 13.3 | 19.5 |
| Masirah: 12 years | **18.3** | 18.9 | 21.1 | 23.4 | 25.6 | 25.6 | 23.4 | 22.8 | 22.2 | 22.2 | 21.1 | 20.0 | 22.2 |
| Salalah: 20 years (1946–65) | **17.5** | 18.4 | 20.4 | 22.7 | 24.8 | 26.0 | 24.2 | 23.1 | 23.3 | 21.0 | 20.3 | 18.9 | 21.7 |

The interior plains, sand desert and central desert plateau have features of a continental climate. They are very hot in summer (over 50°C in the shade), with a low relative humidity (average minimum 23% in June). In winter they are comparatively cold, with high humidity and much dew then and at most times near the coast. However, occasional heavy rain-storms occur, mostly in summer as a result of the south-westerly winds meeting northerly winds.

The higher mountains are cooler than at lower elevations (as rising air normally cools at a minimum rate of 0.5°C per 100 metres when moist, faster when dry). At Saiq, on Jabal Akhdar at about 2,000 metres, extremes of temperature have been recorded of –3.5°C (in January) and 34.5°C (in July).

In spring and autumn, at the time of monsoon changes and of bird migration, varied light winds and calms occur. In April, and particularly in May, there is an increasing though variable southerly component in the surface wind. In autumn, the southerly surface winds still predominate, and it is not until November that northerlies re-assert themselves although above 1,000 to 2,000 metres the winds are mostly northerly throughout the year. It is at these times of changes that cyclones and cyclonic storms originate in the southern Bay of Bengal or south-eastern Arabian Sea. Some track westward, generally in May–June and October–November, towards or across the coast of Oman, on average once in three years (28 out of 63 cyclones in 75 years). A severe cyclone has occurred about once in nine years, usually in the vicinity of Salalah, but on occasions as far north as Masirah Island. Violent winds of over Force 12 Beaufort scale are then experienced, which suck up the lower layers of moist sea air in the swirling vortex, and cause thick cloud and very heavy rain; the effects are sometimes felt far inland, where flash and sheet flooding may occur. Whenever heavy rain does fall, the moisture in the atmosphere is often sufficient to generate more rainfall, and flood hazards increase. Cyclones are relatively rare from Muscat northwards and in the Gulf of Oman, occurring about once in fifty years.

10

# Rainfall and water resources

Rainfall is very uneven in its distribution, and in most parts of the Sultanate it is irregular and unpredictable in its timing and quantity. Some years are very dry, but in others the rainfall is well above average. Extended periods of complete drought can occur locally. The variations in annual amounts at Muscat are shown in Figure 1, and at Salalah airport in Figure 2. Taking the country as a whole, 1941–54 (except 1944) were dry years, but 1944, 1955–57, 1960–63 (except on Masirah in 1962) and 1970–72 were wet. The winter of 1976/77 was wet, but 1978 and 1979 were dry years.

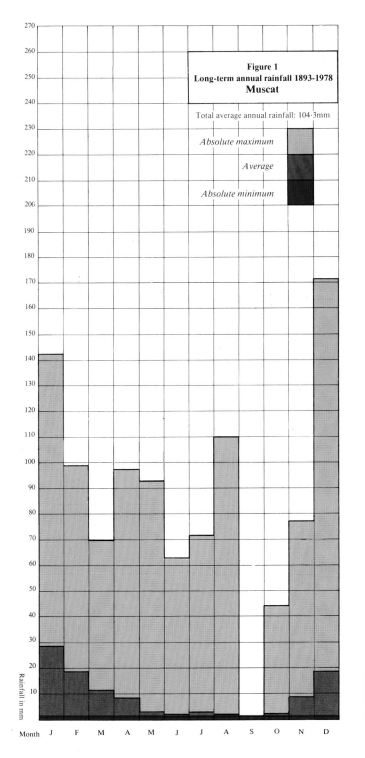

**Figure 1**
**Long-term annual rainfall 1893-1978**
**Muscat**

Total average annual rainfall: 104·3mm

*Absolute maximum*

*Average*

*Absolute minimum*

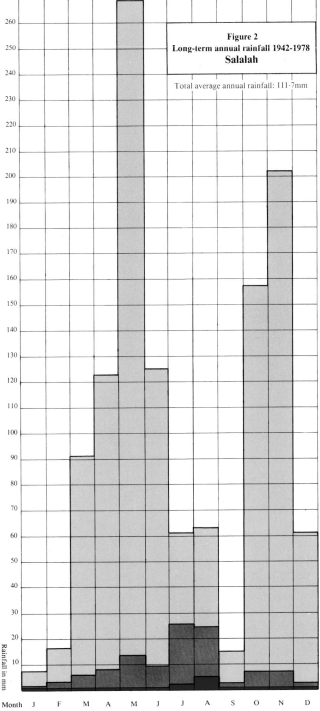

**Figure 2**
**Long-term annual rainfall 1942-1978**
**Salalah**

Total average annual rainfall: 111·7mm

**Plate IV** Typical of the sand and gravel plains of northern Oman, is Sayh Yakhukh, in the Sharqiya district, where the *Acacia tortilis* trees give the resemblance of savanna. The Desert Lesser Whitethroat *Sylvia curruca minula* occurs here in winter.

The average annual rainfall, based on available records of the Water Resources Department of the Ministry of Agriculture and Fisheries, can be summarized thus:

| | |
|---|---|
| Khasab, Musandam region: | 150 to 200mm (but 432mm fell in 1976) |
| Batinah: | nearly 100mm, mostly in winter |
| Muscat: | 104.3mm (300mm fell on 5 June 1890) (Figure 1) |
| Jabal Akhdar at 2,000m: | 300 to 350mm, mostly at night in winter and in afternoons in summer |
| Nizwa at 450m: | over 200mm |
| Interior desert and Masirah: | less than 50mm (430mm fell on Masirah on 13 June 1977) |
| Dhofar mountains: | 350 to 450mm, mostly from June to August but the equivalent of 500 to 650 has been estimated if an allowance is made for the condensation of mists. (In the wet spring of 1977 a fall of over 500mm was recorded in 24 hours) |
| Salalah airport: | 111.7mm, half of which falls in July and August (Figure 2). |

Rainfall is of itself not a true indicator of whether or not arid conditions prevail. Although a desert is sometimes defined as an area having an annual precipitation of less than 127mm, and semi-desert less than 380mm, what is important for life is the effectiveness of the rainfall. This effectiveness depends upon the type of ground on which the rain falls, the time of year, the nature of any soil present and the plants growing in it or which may germinate in it, the loss by transpiration, evaporation and run-off, and the availability of water remaining above or below ground.

When rains do occur in Oman, they may be torrential, running off rock, draining quickly into wadi systems (water-courses) and sometimes reaching the sea. More continuous rain may soak deeply into sand or alluvial

**Plate V** A view of the northern edge of the Wahiba Sands, showing temporary habitation and some vegetation. The Brown-necked Raven *Corvus ruficollis* is fairly common here.

deposits and be trapped when the surface dries out, for use over a long period; it will also soak into porous strata (aquifers). If the rain is early in the year, more plants will be able to make use of it than if it falls in the heat of summer. Evaporation rates are very high, particularly in summer and in strong winds. Losses by the transpiration from vegetation are correspondingly high, though limited by the special adaptive measures evolved by many desert plants.

Apart from rainfall, surface water occurs quite commonly in and near Oman's mountains as springs and as surface or sub-surface flows in some wadi systems. This comes from the aquifers, which are also tapped by aqueducts *(aflaj)*, hand-dug wells and bore-holes. Water in the form of the purified effluent from modern habitation is a very important source to birds in the desert environment.

## Physiographic regions

A look at Oman's physical geography or geomorphology, and at some of the vegetation which is to be found, will assist in an understanding of its different ecological zones and thus of the habitats available to birds. For convenience of description the following categories can be used, although none are homogeneous and other important situations can be found in most of the regions:

| | | | |
|---|---|---|---|
| A | Northern mountains | F | Mountains of Dhofar |
| B | Coastal plains | G | Coasts |
| C | Northern interior plains | H | Islands |
| D | Sand desert | I | Seas. |
| E | Central desert plateau | | |

13

## A  Northern mountains

The mountains of northern Oman commence in the Musandam peninsula and the Ru'us al Jibal ('Heads of the Mountains'), a thick limestone sequence which reaches an altitude of about 2,087 metres on Jabal Harim (Jabal Sayh). The north-eastern part has subsided, tilting under the sea, leaving an impressive coast-line of steep-sided islands and deep, drowned valleys. The mountainous character of this region is alleviated by plateaux, by deep, flat-bottomed wadis and by the fractured nature of some slopes, where there is natural scrub vegetation and some trees. Habitation and cultivation, some of it seasonal, are found in the relatively few places where water can be obtained or stored after the infrequent rains.

On the east coast near Bay'ah are a fault-line, a border with the UAE, and a corridor of coastal plains and headlands which extend southwards for nearly 80 kilometres to the next Oman border at Khatmat Malahah, at the southern tip of the mangrove-lined creek of Khawr Kalba (Khawr Za'ab).

The mountains, which continue southwards down the centre of this corridor, emerge to form the western and eastern Hajar ranges of northern Oman (Al Hajar al Gharbi and Al Hajar ash Sharqi), and these curl in a 500 kilometre-long arc to end near the coast below Ra's al Hadd. They are composed of rocks of many ages, the most obvious examples being the bleak grey-brown ophiolites such as those surrounding Muscat, and the grey to orange-coloured limestones which overlie the others in places.

Whereas the ophiolites have little vegetation except in wadis, the limestone mountains provide more soil and a more varied natural vegetation. In most of the gravel- and boulder-beds of the mountain wadis there are trees of *Zizyphus spinachristi (Sidr)*, *Prosopis cineraria* (synonymous with *spicigera*) *(Ghaf)* and some figs, especially *Ficus salicifolia*, though *Acacia* and bushes such as the toothbrush tree *Salvadora persica (Rak)* also occur. Villages, with date groves and other cultivation, are often found where water reaches the surface; the Oman oleander *Nerium mascatense (Habam)*, reeds, rushes and a tall grass also occur in places. These wadis are important lines of communication in a part of the country which is otherwise very difficult to traverse (Plate II).

Higher up on steep and arid slopes, cushions of the pale green, leafless *Euphorbia larica (Isbaq)* are a noticeable feature amongst a scattering of dwarf *Acacia,* tussock grasses and several other plants adapted to live here.

The huge tabular mass of fossiliferous limestones of Jabal Akhdar (or Jabal al Akhdar), the Green Mountain, is of particular interest. It forms the eastern part of the western Hajar mountains and reaches an altitude of about 3,000 metres on Jabal Sham, the highest peak in eastern Arabia. The sloping strata form limestone pavements, often unvegetated, which end abruptly in the irregular and precipitous northern face (Plate III). The slopes are disected by deep gorges, and the eastern flank dips steeply into the 'Sumail Gap'. On broken ground hardy tussock grasses and other small plants grow between a varied scattering of trees such as *Reptonia mascatensis (But),* wild olive *Olea africana ('Utm)* and *Sageritia spiciflora (Nimt)*. Above about 2,300 metres, large junipers of the endemic *Juniperus macropoda ('alan)* are a special feature of this impressive landscape. This vegetation plays an important part in binding the soil and assisting the penetration of rainfall and the recharging of the aquifers. In addition to its natural beauty the mountain provides an important refuge for endemic and relict species of animals and plants.

## B  Coastal plains

Plains occur along the coast wherever the mountains or plateaux do not reach the sea, and unless backed by mountains they are very arid. One of the most important is the Batinah; this slopes gently from the foothills of the western Hajar range towards the sea in broad gravel fans and sheets of dusty alluvium washed out of the mountains over a long period, and is 270 kilometres long and about 3 to 30 kilometres wide. The ubiquitous *Acacia tortilis (Samur)* is a feature of the vegetation and gives it a resemblance to African savanna; but the surface is dry and many other plants only appear for brief periods after heavy rain. In the more sandy parts *Ghaf* and *Rak* are present, as well as salt-tolerant scrub. Its fame, however, lies in the narrow strip of date palms and other cultivation just behind the sandy coast, and this is watered from wells.

**Plate VI** Fresh water and vegetation in the heart of the desert plateau, where it is a great attraction to migrant and resident birds. White Storks *Ciconia ciconia*, which visit the area in September, are present amongst the camels.

One of the drier coastal plains is Sahil al Jazir, which lies west-south-west of Ra's Madraka. Further southwards the Salalah plain extends for 50 kilometres from Rayzut to Taqah and lies between the Dhofar mountains and the coast; this is often covered in short grasses during the summer monsoon, and there is some cultivation, particularly of coconut-palms, fodder and vegetable crops, and some important creeks (described later under 'Coasts').

Further to the south-east the Ja'alan district reaches the sea from between the eastern Hajar mountains and the Wahiba sands. It has a semi-desert area of low hills, cultivated oases and many vegetated wadis draining eastwards to the sea.

### C  Northern interior plains

The northern interior plains lie between the foothills of the Hajar mountains and the sand desert or the desert plateau. The plains stretch from Buraimi in the Jaww district, southwards through the ridge of the Dhahirah and towns such as 'Ibri, Bahla and Nizwa. Another, in the Sharqiyah district, lies between the eastern Hajar and the Wahiba sands. Except where watered from streams, *aflaj* or wells at the foot of the hills, it is an arid region of gravel and sand, with little vegetation except small trees and scrub (Plate IV). Wadi-beds cross the area to drain into the sands or into saline depressions *(sabkha)* or 'playa' such as Umm as Samim, and southwards to the plateau, the Huqf and Ghubbat al Hashish (Bay of Grass).

### D  Sand desert

The sand desert occurs anywhere where blown sand accumulates in sufficient quantities to cover wide areas or to form dunes. Best known are the mobile dunes, some over 30 metres high, in the sand sea of the Empty

**Plate VII** The thickly wooded coastal cliffs of the Dhofar mountains, in the southern province of Oman, in September when the monsoon clouds have dispersed. A large variety of bird species pass through on their way towards Africa, including the Cuckoo *Cuculus canorus* and the Nightingale *Luscinia megarhynchos*.

Quarter (Ar Rub' al Khali), which reaches over Oman's western border with the Kingdom of Saudi Arabia. Amongst others are the Wahiba sands (Plate V) and those north of the Dhofar mountains, many with their own names. The general trend of many dunes is in parallel ridges *(seif)* in the direction of the prevailing wind, with level ground between. Other large areas are of the more complex *barkhan* dunes.

Although the crests and slip-faces of the mobile dunes are usually barren, *Calligonum crinatum (Arta)* grows as large bushes on the slopes, where *Tamarix* is also found. The tussocks of the sedge *Cyperus conglomoratus (Qsais)* grow widely and help anchor the dune sand. Lizards are fairly common, though most species are nocturnal; their presence indicates the availability of insect food even in the hottest season. Snakes, too, are present, some preying on lizards but others on small rodents.

In drainage lines and pans between dunes, clusters of *Ghaf* occur, occasionally with *Acacia* species, tangles of *Rak* and scattered bushes. Blown sand accumulates amongst the plants and offers refuge to the rodents and lizards, which retire to deep cool burrows in the heat of the day, emerging to feed at night, by which time the heat has penetrated to their burrows. Hares hide in forms beneath the bushes, and several other mammal species live on the edge of this desert and elsewhere in Oman.

At the foot of the dunes, and in many other situations in the country, a wealth of small annual plants will germinate after substantial rain, but unless prolonged by further rain will usually flower, seed and die within a few weeks. These green ephemeral carpets are of great importance to desert animals. The seeds of these plants will maintain their viability for many years in the dry sand. Equally important is the fact that dormant xerophytic plants will spring into life after prolonged rains and may remain green for more than a year without further rain; they survive not only on the moisture which becomes trapped in the lower layers of the sand but also on dews. This vegetation is soon invaded by numerous insects, many of which remain in the ground in a state of diapause during droughts.

16

**Plate VIII** An aerial view of part of the Dhofar mountains in October, showing settlements, tracks, hay and deep, wooded valleys. The Yellow-bellied Green Pigeon *Treron waalia*, the Spotted Eagle Owl *Bubo africanus milesi* and the Blackstart *Cercomela melanura* are three species of this unique region.

## E Central desert plateau

This plateau begins south of the town of Adam and stretches south-westwards, across the Negd north of the Dhofar mountains, towards the southern border of Oman. In general, it is a bleak area of rock, gravel and sand of low relief, but the infrequent rain-storms have marked out broad shallow sandy wadis, many of which trend inland to the dunes. Over large areas these drainage lines may be indicated, if at all, only by a scattering of *Ghaf* trees and scrub. In some wadis, such as Wadi Qitbit, there is often evidence of more sub-surface moisture, the variety of trees and the size and variety of other plants being greater than in superficially similar places, and there are large clumps of *Convolvulus hystrix*, *Crotalaria wissmanii*, *Heliotropium kotschyi*, the broom-like *Leptadenia pyrotechnica* and many others.

The Jiddat al Harasis, home of the Harasis tribe and the Oryx, is a limestone plateau of rock, gravel and sand, and is noted for its trees and other vegetation, for its numerous extensive depressions and for its wildlife. *Ghaf* and *Samur* are the predominant trees on the plain, but tangled clumps of *Acacia ehrenbergiana (Salam)* occur more frequently on hummocks in the depressions, where there is a rich variety of pasture plants such as the grass *Eleusine compressa* and the legume *Tephrosia apollinea*.

Al Huqf is at the edge of a saline depression between the Jidda and the coast of the Gulf of Masirah; and the Barr al Hikman is a dry, limestone plateau opposite Masirah Island. Water-holes are very scarce, but one is in the *Ghaf*- and date-lined wadi of Mugshin. More attractive to migratory birds are the outflows of hot sulphurous water from abandoned artesian wells at Fasad, Dawka, Montasar and Bir ba Shu'aythan (Muwaffaq), at most of which there is some vegetative cover, particularly of reeds, rushes and sedges (Plate VI). In Dhofar the vegetation of the desert plateau includes forms not found in the north, such as *Acacia nilotica* and a dwarf *Zizyphus*; however, groves of *Ghaf* trees still grow here in places.

17

**Plate IX** Part of the Qurm Nature Reserve, at the eastern end of the Batinah, near Muscat. The two tidal creeks and mangroves, with scrub behind, attract many birds. In the distance is Jazirat Fahl, where many Sooty Falcons *Falco concolor* nest in autumn and other species nest earlier in the year.

## F Mountains of Dhofar

The 290 kilometre-long chain of mountains, Jabal al Qamr, Jabal al Qara and Jabal Samhan, is composed mainly of limestone, overlying other strata which outcrop in places, and they have a maximum elevation of about 2,100 metres in Jabal Samhan. The region differs from the limestone mountains in the Musandam and northern Oman in the effects of the summer monsoon, the moisture from which has caused karst-type weathering, including the formation of caves and sink-holes, and the deposition of travertine or calcareous sinter and of soil from extensive vegetation. It also differs in the proportion of animals and plants with African affinities. The mountains have three main zones. Firstly, there are those with a southerly aspect which receive the full benefit of the moisture-laden mists of the monsoon; these are extraordinarily well vegetated and it is this vegetation which helps to condense the mists (Plate VII). Secondly, the semi-desert zone, which receives some moisture irregularly; and, thirdly, the spectacularly eroded desert regions sheltered from or out of range of this moisture. The mountains drain principally to north and south along very deep sinuous valleys and wadis, some containing perennial springs and pools; the southern wadis lead, usually by sub-surface flow, to coastal creeks of exceptional ornithological interest.

In the lower southern foothills are bushes of myrrh *Commiphora* species and *Jatropha* but, where some springs emerge and floods happen occasionally, there are many more trees and bushes, often growing in thickets. On the escarpment and steep wadi sides, where the incidence of orographic rainfall is at its greatest, is a discontinuous belt of broad-leaved woodland with bushes and creepers. *Delonix elata*, *Tamarindus indica*, *Cadaba longifolia*, *Croton conferta* are among the tree flora, but a little higher up almost pure stands of *Anogeissus dhofarica* (named in 1979) cover the steep slopes, in places in association with the evergreen shrub *Euclea schimperi*. On the southern part of Jabal al Qamr are plateaux of *Dodonea/Euclea* evergreen woodland, with man-made clearings for grass (Plate VIII). Certain of these plant species are endemic to Dhofar and confirm that the mountain region is biologically unique.

18

**Plate X** The mangrove-lined creek at Qurayat, south-east of Muscat, is backed by date gardens. The Goliath Heron *Ardea goliath* has been seen here in winter; it is also at present the most southerly breeding area in Oman of the House Crow *Corvus splendens*.

The woodland ceases near the rolling summit of Jabal al Qara and some hills of similar altitude, but some large fig-trees have survived clearance and occasional fires, and there are thickets of smaller trees and bushes in places. The distinctive feature of this part of the wet zone is the extensive covering of one metre-high grasses. Soon after the monsoon cloud clears in September these grasses turn to hay and the woodland takes on a bare grey-brown appearance, to be relieved only after occasional heavy rain-storms and the return of the monsoon.

The effects of the exceptional moisture of the monsoon mists normally cease in the upper parts of Jabal al Qamr, near the highest and northern part of Jabal al Qara, and in most of Jabal Samhan. Near the northern limit of the monsoon mists, clumps of *Euphorbia balsamifera*, *Aloes* and other hardy plants grow quite thickly, often in association with the wild olive *Olea africana*, and with short grasses between. When out of reach of regular monsoon mists, desertic conditions prevail; *Acacia* re-appears and the frankincense tree *Boswellia sacra*, for which Dhofar was famous, thrives (as it does in some drier sheltered wadis near Rayzut). The cliffs and slopes are rather bare, but in contrast the sandy or gravel beds of shallow depressions and deeper wadis have a number of small trees and bushes, including *Acacia*, *Ficus*, *Zizyphus* and *Moringa*, and at times a variety of smaller plants exist, several of them flowering in winter. Perennial spring-fed pools, often with many reeds, rushes and sedges, provide important oases in some of the northern wadis.

## G Coasts

Apart from the cliffs of the ria-coastline of north-eastern Musandam and some other parts, the coasts are mostly gently emergent, and of sand, gravel, shelf-reef and other rock. The sandy ground behind beaches and around creeks is normally well covered by salt-tolerant scrub bushes such as *Zygophyllum coccineum* (Harm), *Salsola* sp. *Suaeda* sp. *Haloxylon salicornicum* (Rimth) and perennial grasses, and there are some

19

**Plate XI** East Khawr, near Salalah, is a fine example of Oman's many creeks, and is usually sealed from the sea by a sand bar and is fairly fresh at the inland end. The Moorhen *Gallinula chloropus* breeds here, and visitors include the Cotton Teal *Nettapus coromandelianus* and the Pheasant-tailed Jacana *Hydrophasianus chirurgus*.

thickets of *Ghaf, Tamarix* and *Acacia* in places. Perhaps the most interesting feature of the coastline is the creeks *(khawr)*. These are the mouths of some wadis which flood occasionally. They may be shallow and surrounded by *sabkha*; or deep narrow channels lined with the dwarf mangrove *Avicennia marina* or with reeds, rushes and sedges. They may be strongly tidal, or temporarily sealed from the sea by a beach crest as lagoons until either a flood or a storm at sea bursts through. They may be saline, or partly fresh at the inland end when this is fed by sub-surface or very occasional surface flow. Many creeks exist along the Batinah, and in dry weather vary from small un-mapped pools to wide tidal creeks. Examples of mangrove creeks are at Liwa, the Qurm Nature Reserve near the Capital Area (Plate IX), and at Qurayat (Plate X). Along the coast south-east of Muscat, wadis emerge through narrow faults in some cliffs, with pools along part of their length, such as Wadi Shab, behind Tiwi. At some places between Muscat and Ra's al Hadd the creeks take the form of wide sheltered bays, some with patches of mangroves in parts of the extremities.

Extensive mud-flats are exposed within some creeks at low tide, such as at Ra's Sallan (at the mouth of Wadi Jizzi), at Sur and at Khawr Barr al Hikman. At the latter place and in the Ghubbat al Hashish the inshore mud-flats are extensive and are the most important wintering place for shore-birds in Oman.

In Dhofar the creeks or lagoons on the edge of the Salalah plain are often deep, well watered by sub-surface flow, with well vegetated margins and many fish and other freshwater and marine life, and are probably the best examples in Arabia (Plate XI). Khawr Salalah is a fine bird sanctuary.

20

**Plate XII** The island of Fanaku is one of the Quoin islands in the Straits of Hormuz. The Red-billed Tropicbird *Phaethon aethereus* and the Sooty Falcon *Falco concolor* both breed here.

## H  Islands

All the desert islands and islets of Oman are important as breeding places or potential breeding places for sea-birds, several of them also for marine turtles; with few exceptions, they have the characteristics of natural nature reserves and merit protection as such.

There are many steep-sided islands and rock stacks in the Musandam region, such as the Quoins (Plate XII). To the east of this region is Jazirat Umm al Faiyarin (or the 'Egg Mountain', *Ko Haig*). Off the Batinah at Ra's Suwadi is a group of limestone islands, and these form part of the same geological formation as the Daymaniyat islands (Jaza'ir Sabah) about 15 kilometres from the coast. Nearer Muscat, Jazirat Fahl, 'the Stallion', is conspicuous, and, further to the south-east, islands lie in Bandar al Jissah, in Bandar Khayran and off Ra's Abu Da'ud.

The largest island is Masirah, which is inhabited, and which has ornithologically important uninhabited islets near it. 100 kilometres south-west of Masirah and about 20 kilometres north-east of Duqm is the large rock islet of Jazirat Hamar an Nafur. The most southerly island group is the Kuria Muria off Dhofar, still inadequately explored zoologically; one, Al Halaniya, is partly inhabited. On some uninhabited islands scrub bushes, particularly salt-tolerant species near beaches, provide ground cover of importance to nesting birds.

21

*I Seas*

The currents in the Arabian Sea change with the monsoons. From October or November until January there is a westward drift, trending south-westerly down the coast of Oman; but from March or May this is reversed and a strong north-easterly current is set up. These currents are variable, but are most constant from June to August.

The seas are a source of food to Oman's resident sea-birds and an attraction to others to visit. The most important areas are where there is turbulence or up-welling, such as the shallow waters on or at the edge of the continental shelf, around some islands such as Masirah and in the cooler waters off Dhofar in summer. The deeper ocean is of less use for birds which fish by day because fish (except flying fish) are both scarce and patchy, but at night squid and other animals tend to come to the surface and provide prey for some pelagic birds.

There is little published information on the seasonal abundance of fish off Oman, though small fish appear to be most abundant during the cool winter and in spring. During summer off Dhofar the up-welling of cold water facilitates the growth of phytoplankton, zooplankton and organisms higher in the food chain, some of which become available to sea-birds. The production of fish may not be marked near the coast of Dhofar, except in shallow depths, as there is an inhibiting layer of water of high salinity and very low oxygen content between 30 and 70 metres depth.

---

No brief description, such as this, can hope to convey to the reader the full variety to be found within the Sultanate, the home of traditional Arab culture in an important part of the world. From the highest peaks of the Green Mountain, through deep gorges, streams and oasis cultivation, out to gravel plains and the rolling dunes of pure desert; or from lower wooded hills and grassy plains, to reed-lined creeks and desert islands set in a rich sea, one passes through many ecological zones, some of the greatest importance to birds in a predominantly desert environment, and many more of interest to the naturalist.

Progress in the development of the Sultanate will inevitably threaten some of these bird habitats, many of which are small, with communities of plants and animals which can be damaged easily, perhaps irrecoverably. However, with an understanding of the needs of the birds themselves, and of birds as indicators of the quality of the environment, needless disturbance will be avoided, and the country can retain both its beauty and its heritage of wildlife.

# Oman-The Birds

Most of the 372 species of birds known in Oman are of Palaearctic origin, though there are no relict species as there are in south-western Arabia. There are also Arabian endemic species, birds from India, from Africa, from the Indian Ocean and even from the Antarctic. Some are breeding residents, others visit for summer or for winter, but the majority are migrants between their breeding-grounds and winter quarters. The variety in Oman is one of the most interesting features of the country's bird life and helps to compensate for a lack of large numbers.

In this brief review it will be best to discuss separately the historical aspects of Oman's ornithology, the habitats available, the desert environment, the breeding and migration of land-birds, the sea-birds, and some aspects of the Indian and African connections.

## Historical note

What is now the Sultanate of Oman, and particularly the Kuria Muria islands and Dhofar (the southern province) was known to ancient traders, geographers and historians, but no useful accounts exist of the birds they saw. Zoological explorations, such as that by Dr Forskål and others to south-western Arabia in the eighteenth century A.D., and several to the Hadhramaut in the next century, never penetrated as far east as Dhofar.

Passing mention of the birds and guano of Jazirat Hamar an Nafur was made by Captain W. F. W. Owen in 1833 and 1857 and by Dr J. Anderson in 1896, though this rock islet was not visited by ornithologists until 1979.

The first detailed and published account of birds (in 1839–40 and 1841) comes from J. G. Hulton, who visited the Kuria Muria islands in 1835 and 1836 during surveys of Oman's coast. In reports of these surveys, which were commenced in 1833 and continued until 1846, mention is made of some birds seen, and the discoveries and literature of this period were summarised by Dr J. Anderson in 1896 and by J. G. Lorimer in 1915. Some reports of birds on the Kuria Muria islands were also made by R. W. Whish in 1860, and by F. von Heuglin in 1869–1873.

In December 1871 and possibly on other occasions, Dr W. T. Blanford, geologist and naturalist, visited Muscat and Ra's Musandam; and from 22 to 24 February 1872 A. O. Hume, Indian Civil Service and ornithologist, visited Muscat; both made small collections.

Colonel S. B. Miles was at Muscat for varying periods between 1872 and January 1888. He (or Surgeon Lt-Col. A. S. G. Jayakar) made collections of birds, which he presented to the British Museum (Natural History) from 1885, some possibly to Dr Blanford; but only a few are dated. He wrote several accounts of his travels, which include general references to birds; he visited Dhofar briefly in 1883 and 1884, but there is no proof that he collected there. Some of the specimens were reported on by S. Bowdler Sharpe in 1886.

Surgeon Lt-Col. Jayakar, who was at Muscat from about 1870 to 1900, collected birds and other specimens from about 1886 to 1898. He passed some to Colonel Miles, and some direct to the British Museum (Natural History) and to the Bombay Natural History Society; most are labelled 'Muscat', a name used then for much of the country as well as the capital, so that exact localities are uncertain. Major (later Sir) Percy Z. Cox,

British representative at Muscat from October 1899 to January 1904, made a collection of well-labelled bird skins which are now in the British Museum (Natural History).

Colonel R. Meinertzhagen, author of the classic work *Birds of Arabia* (1954), visited Muscat on 23 December 1913 and from 8 to 12 February 1914; he collected some specimens, now also in the British Museum (Natural History). Amongst residents interested in birds, Major A. R. Burton wrote a note on them which was published in 1918. In the winter of 1925/26 the geologist Dr G. M. Lees explored Oman; he was accompanied by J. M. Fernandez, who made a collection of bird skins which was reported on by N. B. (later Sir Norman) Kinnear of the British Museum (Natural History) in 1927.

In the winter of 1894/95 Mr and Mrs J. T. Bent explored parts of Dhofar and mentioned some birds seen. But it was not until B. S. Thomas visited Dhofar with Ali Muhammed in January and February 1930 that a collection was made there, and this was reported on by N. B. Kinnear in 1931.

The first of the more recent ornithological accounts was made by P. W. P. Browne in 1960 after visits to Dhofar and Masirah in June and September 1947. There is a report by C. Green in 1949 of some birds on Masirah. The accounts by W. Thesiger of his travels in Oman between 1945 and 1950 occasionally mention some birds seen.

Three birds were collected on Jabal Akhdar by Dr W. Wells Thoms in July 1951 and reported on by S. Dillon Ripley in the same year; and a small expedition, on behalf of the Academy of Natural Sciences of Philadelphia and the Peabody Museum, Yale, USA, collected bird specimens in northern Oman and Masirah between 15 December 1951 and 4 April 1952. K. M. Guichard made a collecting trip to northern Oman in January and February 1950. Dr David L. Harrison, the premier mammalogist of Arabia, collected near Buraimi between 28 August and 8 October 1953, and on the Batinah in 1967, for the Harrison Zoological Museum, Sevenoaks, England.

Major C. J. Seton-Browne and others were active on the northern Batinah from 1959 and made a collection between 1961 and 1968; with Dr J. G. Harrison he published in 1968 a review of the status and distribution of wildfowl in Oman.

A review of the literature concerning the sea-birds of the northern half of the Arabian Sea and the coast of south-east Arabia was published by Dr R. S. Bailey in 1966, after the International Indian Ocean Expedition in 1963–64; and Dr W. R. P. Bourne surveyed the ornithological work in the whole Indian Ocean in 1974.

Scientific interest in the birds of Oman and its seas had increased from 1954; more discoveries were made and more accounts were published. However, travel around the country was very difficult for political reasons, and it was not until 1958 that Jabal Akhdar could be visited again; the Musandam region and the rest of northern Oman were accessible from 1970, and Dhofar from 1976. Happily, the birds of the Sultanate can now be watched in most places without hindrance. From 1975 several expeditions and field studies have been completed, and more are planned in order to throw more light upon the birds, particularly in areas which are physically still difficult to reach.


**Habitats**

Most bird species have a fairly well-defined geographical range, and within its range each species lives by preference in a certain habitat. Each species is adapted to life within its habitat, and to coping with extremes in climate, to obtaining water or doing without it, to obtaining food, to breeding successfully, to avoiding or minimizing competition with other species and to avoiding predators. Many species may live within the same habitat, but competition between them has generally been reduced, if not entirely eliminated, by the special adaptations of each species to life in a particular niche within the habitat.

The adaptations, which include those of behaviour and morphology (form), have been evolved over a long period. They permit the avoidance of competition by such means as taking a different type of food, or a different size of the same food, or even the same food but obtained in a different manner, place, time or season. Even if species meet to take the same food, such as carrion, an order of feeding or 'peck order' is used to lessen direct competition. Little work has been done on the ecological separation of species in Oman and casual observations do not always disclose the differences. The Abyssinian and Palestine Sunbirds, for instance, sometimes feed in the same tree, apparently at the same flowers, but without evident competition; however, there may be subtle differences, associated perhaps with the difference in bill size, which could enable one to probe further and to take larger prey items than the other.

Within one habitat, for example the scrub and trees of the Qurm Nature Reserve near Muscat, a number of different species occupy separate niches. In March the House Crows are nesting in the largest trees and wandering to feed on carrion and scraps at neighbouring habitation. Palm Doves nest in the same and smaller trees on small airy twig platforms on partly-sheltered branches, feeding on seeds on the ground. The Little Green Bee-eaters, which perch on the trees, nest in burrows in the ground and feed by swooping on flying bees and other insects. The Yellow-vented Bulbuls build secure cup nests and feed on insects and small berries. The Graceful Warblers build domed nests in low scrub vegetation and forage for minuscule insects. The Purple Sunbirds build nests suspended from the inner branches of trees, and feed in trees and bushes on small insects and nectar taken in the specially adapted decurved bill with the long, partly-tubular tongue. The House Sparrows, building large straw nests, search widely in flocks for seeds and other items. The Arabian Babblers nest deep inside a thorn tree and feed more exclusively in or near cover, raiding palms for dates in summer and taking large invertebrates in co-operative hunting parties.

When migrants pass through or nest in a habitat they may find niches available to them, or they may conflict with resident species which defend their territory and drive the visitors off; the Red-tailed Wheatears, following the lines of foothills in northern Oman in autumn, are frequently chased by the resident Hume's Wheatears. With cooler winter weather and an increase in insect life, a habitat may be able to support more insectivorous species than at other times.

In the Qurm Nature Reserve, migrants may find several niches unoccupied. *Acrocephalus* and *Hippolais* warblers temporarily occupy their typical niches amongst the mangroves and other waterside vegetation, and in spring the Olivaceous Warblers burst into song and may breed; the Clamorous Reed Warblers are able to over-winter without conflict. The many smaller trees provide some insect food for passing *Sylvia* and *Phylloscopus* warblers, and Rufous Bush Robins feed on invertebrates on the ground below. The Spotted Flycatchers hawk insects flying between the bushes, whereas the swallows, martins and swifts generally hawk higher up and over damp ground and the beaches.

In the general description of the physiographic regions an indication has been given of the habitats available to birds in Oman. These habitats do not conform exactly to those regions, for the habitats form a mosaic across the country, and some species are therefore rather local in their distributions. In Table 2 an attempt has been made to categorize the most important habitat types and to show some of the resident and migrant species which nest in each; rather broad groupings have been chosen to avoid the proliferation of minor habitats or niches which actually occur. The population which is resident in a habitat throughout the year is that which can subsist in it during the worst time of the year; for example, resident birds of the lush woodland in coastal Dhofar in summer are those which can subsist there also in the poorer dry season, when other species must wander or migrate. No different mountain fauna (above, say 1,500 metres) exists on Jabal Akhdar, possibly because of its rather limited area and low rainfall, but the breeding season is later than at lower altitudes.

**Table 2    Habitats of breeding birds in Oman**

## 1  Mountains _____

*a  Cliffs*

Egyptian Vulture, Bonelli's Eagle, Kestrel, Barbary Falcon, Rock Dove, Woodpigeon (N), Pale Crag Martin, Hume's Wheatear (N), Brown-necked Raven, Fan-tailed Raven (D), Tristram's Grackle (D).

*b  Hillsides, rocky wadis*

Chukar (N), Arabian Red-legged Partridge, Sand Partridge, Lichtenstein's Sandgrouse, Palm Dove, Bruce's Scops Owl (N), Little Owl, Little Green Bee-eater, Indian Roller (N), Desert Lark, Long-billed Pipit, Yellow-vented Bulbul, Mourning Wheatear (D), Scrub Warbler, Arabian Babbler, Purple Sunbird (N), Abyssinian Sunbird (D), Palestine Sunbird (D), Yellow-throated Sparrow (N), Indian Silverbill (N), House Bunting.

*c  Woodland (D)*

Bonelli's Eagle, Arabian Red-legged Partridge, Palm Dove, Didric Cuckoo, Oriental Scops Owl, Spotted Eagle Owl, Grey-headed Kingfisher, Yellow-vented Bulbul, Blackstart, Graceful Warbler, Blanford's Warbler, African Paradise Flycatcher, Abyssinian Sunbird, Palestine Sunbird, White-breasted White-eye, Black-headed Bush Shrike, Rüppell's Weaver, African Silverbill, Golden-winged Grosbeak, Cinnamon-breasted Rock Bunting.

*d  Upland grassland (D)*

Singing Bush Lark, Crested Lark, Long-billed Pipit.

## 2  Coastal Plains _____

*a  Batinah (N)*

Grey Francolin, Collared Dove, Turtle Dove, Palm Dove, Rose-ringed Parakeet, Barn Owl, Bruce's Scops Owl, Little Green Bee-eater, Blue-cheeked Bee-eater, Bee-eater, Indian Roller, Hoopoe, Black-crowned Finch Lark, Hoopoe Lark, Crested Lark, Yellow-vented Bulbul, Graceful Warbler, Arabian Babbler, Purple Sunbird, Great Grey Shrike, House Crow, House Sparrow, Yellow-throated Sparrow, Indian Silverbill.

*b  Salalah (D)*

Collared Dove, Barn Owl, Little Green Bee-eater, Singing Bush Lark, Black-crowned Finch Lark, Crested Lark, Yellow-vented Bulbul, Graceful Warbler, Abyssinian Sunbird, Rüppell's Weaver, African Silverbill.

## 3  Desert and semi-desert _____

*a  Open sandy or stony desert*

Coronetted Sandgrouse, Spotted Sandgrouse, Chestnut-bellied Sandgrouse, Eagle Owl, Little Owl, Black-crowned Finch Lark, Dunn's Lark (D), Bar-tailed Desert Lark (D), Desert Lark, Hoopoe Lark.

*b  Desert with scrub and trees*

Long-legged Buzzard, Houbara, Little Green Bee-eater, Arabian Babbler, Great Grey Shrike, Brown-necked Raven.

*c  Prosopis woods and desert oases*

Grey Francolin (N), Palm Dove, Bruce's Scops Owl (N), Little Owl, Little Green Bee-eater, Crested Lark, Graceful Warbler, Purple Sunbird (N), Great Grey Shrike, House Sparrow (N).

## 4  Wetlands _____

*a  Inland pools and streams*

Little Grebe, Moorhen, Little Ringed Plover, Red-wattled Lapwing (N), Graceful Warbler.

*b  Mangroves (N)*

Little Green Heron, Western Reef Heron, Palm Dove, White-collared Kingfisher, Clamorous Reed Warbler, Booted Warbler, Purple Sunbird, House Crow.

*c  Creeks and lagoons*

Little Grebe, Moorhen, Kentish Plover, Red-wattled Lapwing (N), Graceful Warbler.

## 5 Coasts

*a  Coastal cliffs*

Red-billed Tropicbird, Sooty Falcon, Rock Dove, Pallid Swift, Pale Crag Martin, Tristram's Grackle (D).

*b  Islands*

Red-billed Tropicbird, Masked Booby (D), Socotra Cormorant (D), Little Green Heron, Western Reef Heron, Egyptian Vulture, Osprey, Sooty Falcon, Crab Plover (M), Sooty Gull, Crested Tern, Roseate Tern, White-cheeked Tern, Bridled Tern, Saunders' Little Tern (M), Common Noddy, Rock Dove, Pallid Swift.

---

N = northern Oman only    M = Masirah Island only    D = Dhofar only

---

## The desert environment

Birds which live in the hostile climate of the desert, and the scarcely less hostile semi-desert, must contend with extremes of dryness and heat; those in the open desert environment also require more natural protection from predators; all need to find food and several require water. Typically desert birds have become adapted to such life, both in their behaviour and in their morphological characteristics.

Much of the desert of Oman is made up of a mixture of true desert and of semi-desert environments, with scattered patches of better vegetation in the larger wadis, at springs and around human settlements. This has enabled a number of species of birds which are not strictly desert species to subsist in the desert regions. Thus species such as the Long-legged Buzzard, Barbary Falcon, Lichtenstein's Sandgrouse, Chestnut-bellied Sandgrouse and Pallid Swift may all be found in the deserts of Oman, although elsewhere in their world range they occur widely outside the desert.

The typically desert birds in Oman are listed in Table 3, in which it will be seen that all are inhabitants of the Great Palaearctic Desert.

### Table 3    Typically desert species in Oman

| Species | Arabian race | Status in Oman (see Appx 1) | World range of the species |
|---|---|---|---|
| Sooty Falcon | – | MB PM (W) | Libya, Red Sea, Arabian Coast |
| Sand Partridge | *intermedia* | BR | Nile to Arabia |
| Houbara | *macqueenii* | BR PM WV | W Sahara to Central Asia |
| Cream-coloured Courser | – | PM WV | W Sahara to NW India |
| Coronetted Sandgrouse | – | BR | W Sahara to NW India |
| Spotted Sandgrouse | – | BR | W Sahara to NW India |
| Black-crowned Finch Lark | *arenicolor* | BR PM WV | W Sahara to NW India |
| Dunn's Lark | *eremodites* | BR | W Sahara to Arabia |
| Bar-tailed Desert Lark | *arenicolor* | BR | W Sahara to NW India |
| Desert Lark | – | BR | W Sahara to NW India |
| Hoopoe Lark | – | BR | W Sahara to NW India |
| Pale Crag Martin | – | BR PM WV | W Sahara to NW India |
| Mourning Wheatear | *boscaweni* | BR | W Sahara to Iran |
| Hooded Wheatear | – | BR WV? | W Sahara to Iran |
| Hume's Wheatear | – | BR | N Oman to NW India |
| White-crowned Black Wheatear | – | ? | W Sahara to Arabia |
| Scrub Warbler | – | BR | W Sahara to NW India |
| Brown-necked Raven | – | BR | Cape Verde I to NW India |
| Trumpeter Finch | – | BR? | Canaries, Spain to NW India |
| House Bunting | – | BR PM WV | W Sahara to northern India |

*Water*

All animals need adequate water, which comes from free water, from water in the food and as a product of the metabolism of food within the body. Some birds, such as larks, wheatears, warblers, shrikes and babblers, do not need to drink if they have adequate succulent food. But others, particularly granivorous species such as sandgrouse, partridges, finches and buntings, must drink regularly, and thus need to keep within flying distance of free water. Others may drink if opportunity offers, and most are able to withstand a fair degree of dehydration. The few sources of free water available in the desert or semi-desert in Oman include some wadis, wells, cisterns, treated sewage at desert camps, dew and transpiration water on vegetation, and occasional surface rain-water; some sources in the desert are saline, which few land-birds can tolerate.

Sandgrouse often fly long distances to water, and they are able to carry water to the nest in the specially modified feathers of the breast and belly. Water may also be carried to the nest in the throats of some birds. Special measures have been evolved by desert birds to conserve water, the most important of these being the ability to excrete fairly concentrated waste matter. In the case of migrants over the desert, losses of water would be reduced by flying at high altitude or at night.

*Heat*

The shade temperature can give little idea of the enormous ambient temperature in the desert on a summer's day, where the usual lack of cloud means very high insolation and the bare ground becomes so heated that radiation continues long after sunset. Birds have no sweat glands, and to maintain a constant body temperature they must lose heat in several ways: by the evaporation of moisture from the surfaces of the respiratory system during panting; by gular flutter (the rapid vibration of the skin of the chin and throat, practised particularly by some sea-birds, herons, pigeons, owls and nightjars); by perching off the ground, where radiant heat is less and breezes may be felt; by feeding and drinking early and late in the day or at night; by resting in the shade of cliffs, rocks and vegetation and in caves; and by leaving the hottest parts in favour of cooler places, such as wadis and mountains (nomadism). Birds which are not adapted to desert life, such as falcons, owls, pigeons and swifts, may survive by living in caves.

Other cooling behaviour adopted by birds includes dangling the legs in flight, the erection of the feathers on the back, and the drooping of the wings at rest to permit air to reach the flanks and wing-pits. When water is available, some will lie in it or on damp vegetation or mud; and some sea-birds, such as the Bridled Terns nesting on desert islands, will dip their legs in the sea in flight.

*Plumage*

Most birds which live in warm dry areas are paler than related forms in humid regions (Gloger's Law). In the desert, the birds are characteristically very pale, but there are exceptions which have black in the plumage. The phenomenon of Gloger's Law and the exceptions to it have been discussed by many authors (e.g. Buxton 1923, Meinertzhagen 1954, Cloudsley-Thompson and Chadwick 1964, and Serventy 1971). The pallid colouration of most desert species has a distinct survival value in affording camouflage from predators; stationary birds, such as nesting sandgrouse and crouching Houbara, nightjars and desert larks are almost impossible to see by man or hawk. In the Desert Lark this cryptic colouration is particularly well developed, each population having evolved to match the colour of the ground on which it lives.

Crypsis may also be the explanation of the black colouration of some desert birds. Where the harsh sunlight casts deep shadows, the black has a protective effect in helping the bird to merge with or 'imitate' a shadow, for example the black-and-white wheatears on broken rocky slopes and Sooty Falcons on cliff ledges. In other species such as the Houbara, the sandgrouse, the Black-crowned Finch Lark and the Hoopoe Lark, the black (and some white) parts of the plumage are hidden when the bird crouches to avoid detection, but are conspicuous when the bird flies or displays. In this way the birds can strike a compromise between the need for crypsis to avoid detection by predators, and conspicuousness to signal to other individuals of the same species or to attract a mate.

*Other adaptations*

Typically desert birds need to be adaptable to changing conditions. Opportunism and nomadism allow them to take advantage of changes in the environment, such as the sudden appearance after rain of surface water and of vegetation and its associated insect life, and conversely to survive when such sources dry up and prolonged droughts occur. Some physical adaptations to life in deserts have already been mentioned; others include the long legs of several species such as the Long-legged Buzzard, Houbara, Cream-coloured Courser and Hoopoe Lark, the long decurved bills of the last two for obtaining food items deep in the sand, and the modification of the toes of some, such as the Houbara, to permit them to walk and run on soft ground.

## Breeding

A total of ninety-six species are known to breed in Oman, and a further eleven are thought to do so. Approximately three-quarters are resident, while the remainder are migrant breeders. Thirty-four species breed only in northern Oman, and twenty-five only in Dhofar (Table 4).

Table 4    Distribution of species breeding in Oman

|  | Sea-birds | | | Others | | | |
|  | N only | S only | N & S | N only | S only | N & S | Totals |
|---|---|---|---|---|---|---|---|
| Resident | – | 2 | 3 | 19 | 20 | 30 | 74 |
| Migrant | 2* | – | 3 | 13† | 3 | 1 | 22 |
| Totals | 2 | 2 | 6 | 32 | 23 | 31 | 96 |

*Includes Saunders' Little Tern, on Masirah only.    †Includes Crab Plover, on Jazirat Shaghaf near Masirah, only.

Most breed in the northern spring and summer; but Ospreys begin to breed in the winter or previous autumn, Red-billed Tropicbirds nest (perhaps exceptionally) in any month, and Socotra Cormorants and Sooty Falcons nest in late summer. In land-birds the onset of breeding is fairly regular for each species and is governed by the seasonal variation of daylight hours (Table 9), of temperature and also of food supply. In years of unusually good rain and vegetation, some birds will commence breeding earlier than usual, and some migrants may be encouraged to stop and breed. As a general rule, birds lay smaller clutches than related species in temperate or cool regions, and the clutch size may be reduced in lean years.

In the monsoon zone of Dhofar the breeding season of land-birds appears to be similar, despite the mist and damp from late June to September. However, in the Cinnamon-breasted Rock Bunting breeding activity seems to be concentrated before and after the monsoon; the detailed effects of the monsoon upon this and other Dhofar species deserve further study.

Only the largest eggs can survive prolonged exposure to the sun, and special measures are necessary to protect eggs from undue exposure. Some species in Oman nest in burrows, such as the Crab Plover, the Grey-headed Kingfisher and the bee-eaters; many others nest in holes, crevices and caves, or on sheltered ledges, or even on the eaves of houses (Palm Dove, Pale Crag Martin, House Sparrow); as in the burrows, there are less extreme diurnal ranges of temperature in such situations.

Tree-nesters obtain some benefit from the cooling effect of any breeze and from shelter from the sun by the foliage, but as most trees are themselves minimizing transpiratory water-losses by having small leaves this shelter is often minimal. Ground-nesters obtain some shelter by nesting on the shady north side of rocks and plants, or even under boulders. However, many have to contend with the direct rays of the sun, and in order to maintain an even temperature of eggs and chicks they must shield them and often stand over them; only in the cooler periods is the close brooding of chicks necessary. Birds are loathe to leave their eggs unshielded in the sun, and the Kentish Plover will partly cover the nest with sand before leaving it. Some White-cheeked Terns will deliberately wet the breast- and belly-feathers in the sea to return to the nest and cool the eggs. Sandgrouse, which nest on open ground in very hot situations, carry water in the feathers to their young.

## Migration of land-birds

One of the most remarkable features of bird life is the phenomenon of the regular annual migrations which many species make between their breeding-grounds and winter quarters. Every degree of migration is known in Oman, from purely local movements and dispersals after breeding to very long-distance migration. The origins of this behaviour are complex and ancient, but it enables birds to find and exploit the best opportunities both for breeding and for wintering. Thus migratory species can breed in areas which provide ideal conditions for reproduction and yet which could not support the species at other times of the year. Similarly, outside the breeding season they can take advantage of seasonal abundances of food in areas unsuitable for reproduction.

Migration out of Europe (the western Palaearctic region) in autumn is mainly southerly or south-westerly into Africa, though some species reach Africa by a clock-wise movement; and a few species of eastern origin such as the Blyth's Reed Warbler, Red-breasted Flycatcher, Rose-coloured Starling, Scarlet Rosefinch, and Rustic, Little, Yellow-breasted and Black-headed Buntings migrate south-eastwards towards the Indian sub-continent. Some of the latter occur in enormous numbers on migration through the Caspian region, Iran and Afghanistan and occur as regular passage migrants in Oman, while others which take a more northerly route occur in Oman only as vagrants.

For the breeding birds of western Asia, (the central Palaearctic region), the land mass and hence the potential wintering area to the south is very small, and the great majority must either migrate south-westwards over the Middle East to winter in Africa, or south-eastwards to India and beyond. In some species with a wide distribution across the Palaearctic, western populations migrate to Africa and eastern populations to India, for example the House Martin, Swallow, Yellow Wagtail, Reed Warbler and Lesser White-throat, which are found in both areas in winter. Most of these occur as regular passage migrants in Oman, but whether the birds are bound for Africa or India is not always clear.

The bulk of the birds breeding in eastern Asia migrate southwards to winter in the Indian sub-continent and south-east Asia. However, a number of species of western Palaearctic origin which have extended their ranges into the eastern Palaearctic continue to make the long passage south-westwards to winter only in Africa; these include the Nightjar, Redstart, Wheatear, Rock Thrush, Willow Warbler and Spotted Flycatcher. Even more unusual is the race *serratus* of the Jacobin (Pied Crested) Cuckoo, which breeds in northern India and is occasionally found in Oman during what is presumed to be passage to and from Africa.

The migration of many species in Oman, such as ducks and waders, is more obvious in autumn than in spring. This is very largely due to the greater numbers caused by the high proportion of young birds, as well as to their leisurely passage. Many passerines by contrast appear to be less numerous in autumn, probably because food is then more scarce and the surface winds contrary; the identification of feathers in the prey of Sooty Falcons in September shows that Rufous Bush Robins and others are probably just as numerous in autumn as in spring, but their passage is conducted without the pauses to feed which characterize their passage through Oman in spring, particularly in wet years.

In autumn the White Stork migrates, in parties totalling hundreds, high over the interior of Oman, through the Ja'alan district and Dhofar, and rings from dead birds indicate that many come from eastern Europe (Appendix 5); some are seen along the Batinah. They are rarely reported in spring, when the return passage is probably through western Arabia, where large numbers occur, an example of 'loop' migration.

Large numbers of wildfowl of some eighteen species were reported from the northern Batinah in the 1960s, most of them in autumn; as most of the ducks have a normal winter distribution in India but not in East Africa it was suggested (Seton-Browne and Harrison 1968) that the majority probably moved on in the direction of India; such numbers do not return on spring passage. However, of fifteen duck species occurring in Oman all but two (the Marbled Teal and Red-crested Pochard) reach Dhofar, most of them regularly, and at least six of them (the Wigeon, Teal, Mallard, Pintail, Garganey and Shoveler) have been noted in the desert, on Masirah or on the intervening mainland coast, indicating that some southerly passage does occur.

In the Musandam (an under-watched region) few migrants have been reported in autumn, and arrivals on the Batinah from over the sea confirm that many species over-fly or avoid the Musandam at that season. However, in spring small passerines, especially hirundines, wheatears, warblers and shrikes, are common at the pockets of vegetation in the Musandam.

Birds flying over Oman have no alternative but to cross the sea, mountains and desert. There is little direct evidence that they cross the Empty Quarter to reach Oman in autumn, and those migrants noted at water at Fasad, Dawka and Montasar may be following the border of the sands. However, it would be more natural for high-flying migrants to take direct routes across the apparent obstacles, and this may partly explain why more migrants, such as harriers, Nightingales, Cuckoos and Isabelline Shrikes, are seen in the Dhofar mountains and on the Salalah plain in autumn than are known in other parts of Oman; another factor is that the monsoon vegetation in coastal Dhofar will attract larger concentrations of birds than elsewhere.

Increasing evidence, gathered over many years from the water points in the Oman desert, shows that a wide variety of species, including Little Grebes, Great Cormorants, Little Bitterns, dabbling duck, nightjars, Rollers and small passerines, do regularly cross the desert in spring and autumn. That these are stragglers from major migrations that generally pass unnoticed is suggested by the 'falls', or sudden appearances of numbers of birds, which occasionally happen in mid-desert during periods of strong, unfavourable winds.

As mentioned when discussing climate, the surface winds seem generally favourable to spring passage, especially in May, but are contrary to autumn passage until November. However, birds travelling south-westwards in autumn would benefit from the southerly airflow above about 1,500 metres and thus above the south-west monsoon; this is probably another reason for the scarcity of passerine migrants in northern Oman at this season. In Africa, passage has been noted in autumn between 1,500 and 2,500 metres, with some over 3,000 metres, but the height of passage over Oman has not yet been studied.

Many species migrate at night, particularly the small passerines, setting off as light fades and dropping down in the morning when they sight favourable conditions or when they are halted by adverse weather or fatigue. 'Falls' of wheatears and shrikes in the Dhofar mountains are fairly common in autumn. Other species, such as the Swallow and some larks, travel by day, the latter often only in the morning. Some travel by night or day, or both, according to circumstances.

Some diurnal migrants fly low, following topographical features, or on a broad front. Large soaring birds, such as the White Stork and raptors, travel by making use of successive thermals, gliding fast in the required direction from the top of one thermal to near the base of the next; such migration is often invisible until, like the autumn arrivals of the Egyptian Vulture on the Batinah, or the White Stork in the Ja'alan district, they descend to rest. Autumn migrants near Muscat are generally fewer than on the northern Batinah, probably because birds which follow leading lines of the topography, such as the mountain range or the Batinah coast, break away and fly more direct when these lines no longer lead in the required direction; ducks, raptors, Collared Doves, hirundines and even waders have all been seen to turn southwards over or through the natural passes in Jabal Akhdar in autumn, and similarly the return passage of warblers up north-flowing wadis is a feature of spring migration near Jabal Akhdar.

Land-birds are sometimes seen at sea, such as Sooty Falcons, Egyptian Nightjars, bee-eaters, Hoopoes, wagtails, Swallows, Desert Wheatears, Starlings and even Grey Herons. Some of these may be regular trans-oceanic migrants, but some may be lost. At the appearance of a ship, birds will tend to change course to investigate it or to seek rest and refuge. Though their original course may not then be apparent to the observer on board, the occurrence of land-birds at sea will form valuable records. Some species, such as Hoopoes seen in autumn flying parallel to and within sight of the Batinah coast, may be attempting to avoid predators over land; unfortunately for the Hoopoe, it is a common prey of the Sooty Falcon. It is assumed that the Manchurian Red-footed Falcon, as well as the Jacobin Cuckoo, also regularly cross the Indian Ocean to Africa.

Winter visitors include long-distance migrants, such as some of the many species of waders which nest in the Arctic and sub-Arctic. Others come from India or from Iran (Table 6). Unless they find adequate conditions visitors wander or continue their southward movement by stages, often returning in a similar manner in early spring. Unusual visitors are sometimes found, such as Bewick's Swans, Eversmann's Redstarts, Ring Ouzels and other thrushes, possibly as the result of severe conditions on their normal wintering grounds. Non-breeding birds of several species dally in Oman over summer.

Other forms of migration may be mentioned briefly with a few examples. *Dispersive:* a general dispersal of birds, particularly young birds, away from the breeding-grounds after breeding, e.g. Little Green Bee-eaters and Long-billed Pipits. *Partial migration:* a directional movement of part of the population (particularly young birds and also often the adult females) after breeding, the other part being resident, e.g. Collared Doves breeding on the Batinah. *Irruptive:* irregular large-scale movements in response to severe food shortages, e.g. Wattled Starlings from Africa wandering into Arabia, presumably in search of food. *Altitudinal migration:* a local movement of birds down from mountain breeding-sites to lower elevations in winter, e.g. Woodpigeon and House Bunting.

**Sea-birds**

Although several species of sea-birds are present off the coast of Oman during winter, particularly around Masirah Island, the majority of species and the largest number of individuals are evident on spring and autumn passage and when breeding during the northern spring and summer. However, there are remarkable concentrations during the summer monsoon, particularly off Dhofar, of petrels, shearwaters and storm-petrels.

*Spring*

The spring migration starts, as it does for several species of land-bird, as a slight movement of winter visitors in January. Wintering Black-headed Gulls thin out, move northwards and replace the Slender-billed Gull as the most numerous gull of the Musandam by the end of February. Small numbers of Great Black-headed Gulls also move at this time, followed by large numbers of Herring Gulls and Sandwich Terns. The main passage of most species, including Sooty Gulls and White-cheeked, Bridled and Saunders' Little Terns, is in March and April. The Common Noddy arrives between May and July.

*Breeding*

Of the ten which breed in Oman (Table 5) six species or races are endemic to the northern Indian Ocean, and a seventh (the Crested Tern) is represented by the race *velox* which has an easterly but not a southerly extension. The status of the seven is shown here as 'breeding resident' or 'migrant breeder', but these are somewhat fine and arbitrary classifications as the distinction in some endemics is not always clear-cut, they could be called 'partial migrants'. For example, the Red-billed Tropicbird is present throughout the year at different places in coastal Oman, but is an offshore and pelagic species which wanders widely when not breeding. The Masked Booby is another 'resident' of the Arabian Sea, but with seasonal fluctuations of numbers on the Kuria Muria islands. The Sooty Gull and Crested Tern are present over winter, but in reduced numbers, which would indicate that the majority move out of Oman's waters; the winter birds may include visitors from the north as well as residents.

The Socotra Cormorant has one population which breeds in the Arabian Gulf in winter, and summers there and east to the Mekran coast. There is another which breeds on the Kuria Muria in summer (proved in 1977) and winters as far north as Masirah; this may be separate from or form part of the Gulf of Aden population.

The Common Noddy was discovered with eggs on the Daymaniyats in July 1978, but the record by von Heuglin (1869–73) of nesting on the Kuria Muria islands remains unconfirmed. The Persian Shearwater

**Table 5    Breeding sea-birds in Oman**

| Species | Race | Range | Status in Oman (see Appx 1) | Main breeding localities (and dates of first eggs) |
|---|---|---|---|---|
| Red-billed Tropicbird | *indicus* | N Indian Ocean | BR | Most islands (February or all year) |
| Masked Booby | *melanops* | N Indian Ocean | BR | KM (March) |
| Socotra Comorant | – | N Indian Ocean | | |
| | | Arabian Gulf | SV to Musandam | |
| | | SE Arabia | BR | KM (early July) |
| Sooty Gull | – | N Indian Ocean | BR MB PM | D, M, KM, (April) |
| Crested Tern | *velox* | N Indian Ocean to Bay of Bengal | BR MB PM | D, M, KM, (July) |
| Roseate Tern | ? | – | MB | D, M, (May) |
| White-cheeked Tern | – | N Indian Ocean | MB PM (w) | D, M, O,(May) |
| Bridled Tern | *fuligula* | N Indian Ocean | MB PM (w) | Q, UF, D, M, KM, (May) |
| Saunders' Little Tern | – | N Indian Ocean | MB PM | M (April) |
| Common (Brown) Noddy | – | Pantropical | MB | D (July), KM? |

| | | |
|---|---|---|
| D   = Daymaniyats | M = Masirah | Q   = Quoins |
| KM = Kuria Muria | O = Other islands | UF = Umm al Faiyarin |

*Puffinus lherminieri persicus* and the Jouanin's Petrel are also northern Indian Ocean endemics, but their breeding-grounds are unknown; the former may nest in the north in winter or in the south in summer, the latter may nest on the Kuria Muria or the mainland in summer. Individuals of the latter two species would require at least five months between prospecting for nest sites and the fledging of their young.

Although the breeding season for many species commences in March and April (Table 5) there is heavy disturbance and depredation of eggs and young on some islands. Replacement laying therefore continues into late summer for some birds, and even into October for Sooty Gulls; but the Saunders' Little Tern nests and departs early. The regular breeding season in Oman differs from that of birds in the southern and western Indian Ocean, which tend to breed for longer periods. The reason is likely to be that the Oman populations have become adapted to breeding in time to take advantage of the seasonal up-welling of cool, biologically rich water off Dhofar, and it also means that when this abundance of food declines there must be substantial migrations (Bailey 1966). However, the ecology of the sea-birds which breed off northern Oman in the same period, but which are presumably far less affected by the south-west monsoon, requires further study.

*Summer visitors*

Large concentrations of birds occur over the cool up-welling area off Dhofar, especially around the Kuria Muria and in lesser degree as far as Ra's al Hadd, an area studied during the International Indian Ocean Expedition in 1963–64 (Bailey 1966) and since watched briefly by several observers from Oman.

Persian Shearwaters move from winter quarters near the Straits of Hormuz and the Gulf of Aden from April, and the Jouanin's Petrels begin assembling a little earlier, until both species are very common off Dhofar from May to June. In April, Pale-footed Shearwaters begin to arrive from their breeding-grounds in Australia, and the Wilson's Storm-petrels from the Antarctic and sub-Antarctic, until from June to August the former are common and the latter abundant. Other southern or oceanic species reported off the southeast coast include the Wedge-tailed Shearwater, White-faced Storm-petrel and Black-bellied Storm-petrel. Red-billed Tropicbirds appear in large numbers around the Kuria Muria in the monsoon season, and Great Skuas (presumably a southern race of this bi-polar species), or McCormick's Skuas, are regular though uncommon summer visitors to Oman, particularly in the south. With the weakening of the monsoon, these visitors begin to disperse, the Pale-footed Shearwaters commencing in August.

*Autumn migration*

The autumn migration commences in July with the arrival of Herring Gulls, and by August and September there is a strong coastal passage of gulls and terns, the latter represented mainly by the Sandwich and White-cheeked Terns, which stop to feed *en route* and are parasitized by Pomerine, Arctic and Great Skuas. Bridled Terns disperse gradually.

By September, when the southerly winds off Ra's al Hadd have eased, the movement of mixed flocks of terns is unhindered, and there is also a steady flow of Sooty and Herring Gulls and some Bridled Terns. The passage of Slender-billed Gulls continues into November. During this season, occasional Sooty, Black-headed and Herring Gulls occur in the desert. Three Indian Skimmers appeared amongst Sandwich Terns near Muscat in August 1979 for three days, the first records for Arabia of this largely riverine species.

Red-necked Phalaropes begin to move south in July, and flocks move progressively further south off the coast of Oman, to winter widely at sea off Arabia until they begin a gradual return passage in spring. The movements of the Grey Phalarope are not so well-known because of the difficulty in separating it from the Red-necked Phalarope when both are in winter plumage.

The winter quarters of some migrants are not clear. While some move eastwards along the Mekran towards India, concentrations of others occur in the Red Sea and Gulf of Aden, and others move down the East African coast, and some probably go directly to the southern Indian Ocean.

## African and Indian connections

Arabia's land connection with Africa was broken one to two million years ago. The Straits of Hormuz between Musandam and Iran, which were reduced to a broad river valley 70,000 to 17,000 years before the present, were inundated by the return of the sea between 20,000 and 17,000 years ago, the sea reaching its present level only some 5,000 years ago. The sea divide between mainland Oman and Asia is now under 80 kilometres (40 kilometres between off-shore islands); that between south-western Arabia and Africa (Bab el-Mandeb) is under 25 kilometres. Such gaps would prevent the passage of only the weakest-flying birds.

The similarities between some genera of birds in Africa and India are close and provide evidence that their ranges were continuous across Arabia no longer than 6,000 years ago; however, some species shared between Africa and India are no longer present in Arabia, presumably as a consequence of the progressive desiccation of Arabia (Moreau 1966). Various climatic phases have occurred in the past, but probably at best there was only a little more rain and steppe or savanna vegetation across lowland Oman; nevertheless, this would have been sufficient to harbour some of the missing species.

If only the breeding species are considered, it is apparent that the present influence of the Indomalayan region is confined to northern Oman (Table 6), whereas the Afrotropical influence is restricted to Dhofar (Table 7). This is strikingly illustrated by the Palm Dove, with an African race occurring in Dhofar and an Indian race in northern Oman; and the similar separation of the two closely related silverbills. The Indomalayan and Afrotropical species which occur in Oman as vagrants, scarce passage migrants and winter visitors show a similar but less clear-cut separation, with most African vagrant species occurring in the south, and over half of the Indian occurring from Masirah northwards.

Fifteen Indian forms occur in Oman, eight as breeding species, and seven as vagrants, scarce passage migrants or scarce winter visitors (Table 6). All the breeding forms are confined as breeding species to northern Oman, where three, the Grey Francolin, Rose-ringed Parakeet and House Crow, were probably introduced originally.

The central desert plateau of Oman reaches the coast and must constitute at least a partial barrier to the gradual southward spread of these forms; however, the Palm Dove, Rose-ringed Parakeet, Indian Roller, Purple Sunbird and House Crow have all reached the latitude of Masirah, the Roller even on board ship off Socotra, and it is possible that individuals could reach Dhofar in autumn. As none have settled in Dhofar, it seems likely that the extension of the Indomalayan faunal element further south in Oman is further prevented by conditions there which are unsuitable for the species concerned.

All the breeding forms are identical to those occurring in north-western India. This would suggest either that these forms are recent colonists or that there is occasional gene-flow between the mainland of Asia and Oman.

Table 6    Indomalayan land-bird species in Oman

| Species | Race (and range) | Status in Oman (see Appx 1) | Remarks |
|---|---|---|---|
| **A Species which breed** | | | |
| Grey Francolin | *mecranensis* (NW India) | BR | N Oman (introduced?) |
| Red-wattled Lapwing | *aigneri* (Iraq to NW India, SW Russia) | BR PM | N Oman |
| Palm Dove | *cambayensis* (NW India) | BR PM | N Oman to Masirah; another race in Dhofar |
| Rose-ringed Parakeet | *borealis* (N India to SE China) | BR V | Batinah (introduced?), vagrant to Masirah |
| Indian Roller | – | BR PM WV | N Oman, vagrant to Masirah |
| Purple Sunbird | *brevirostris* (NW India) | BR | N Oman, vagrant to Masirah |
| House Crow | *zugmayeri* (NW India) or *zugmayeri×splendens* | BR | N Oman (introduced?), vagrant to Masirah |
| Indian Silverbill | – | BR | N Oman |
| **B Others** | | | |
| Indian Pond Heron | – | PM WV | N Oman, Masirah, Dhofar |
| Cotton Teal | – | WV (S) | Mostly in Dhofar |
| Pheasant-tailed Jacana | – | WV (S) | Mostly in Dhofar |
| White-breasted Waterhen | – | V | Once in Dhofar |
| Little Pratincole | – | V or PM WV | N Oman, Masirah, Dhofar |
| Red Turtle Dove | – | V | Once in Masirah |
| Koel | – | V | Masirah |

Twenty-six African species occur in Oman; sixteen of these are known to breed, a further four probably breed (the Lappet-faced Vulture, Spotted Thick-knee, Yellow-bellied Green Pigeon and African Paradise Flycatcher), and six occur as vagrants or scarce passage migrants (Table 7). All the breeding and probable breeding species are confined in Oman to the Dhofar mountains or the Salalah plain, and the majority are birds of woodland and grassland, the two habitats which occur nowhere else in Oman. All but five have an extensive range in Africa. The five exceptions, the Blanford's Warbler, Abyssinian Sunbird, White-breasted White-eye, Rüppell's Weaver and Golden-winged Grosbeak, have distributions centred on the Red Sea or Gulf of Aden, with very restricted ranges near the African coast, indicating perhaps an Arabian origin. Eleven of the breeding species each has a distinct Arabian race; this level of sub-specific differentiation would suggest that the African and Arabian populations have been separated for a considerable period. However, at least two species, the Didric Cuckoo and Grey-headed Kingfisher, migrate to winter in Africa, and the Singing Bush Lark (a migratory species within Africa) may also migrate from Oman after breeding.

There are seven species found in Oman which warrant special mention. Three are endemic to the Arabian peninsula: the Arabian Red-legged Partridge, Arabian Babbler and Tristram's Grackle. The first occurs from south-west Arabia to Dhofar, and again in Jabal Akhdar, to which it may have been introduced; the babbler is widespread southwards from Sinai and Palestine; and the grackle occurs from Sinai and Palestine, through western and southern Arabia, to southern Oman.

**Table 7    Afrotropical land-bird species in Oman**

| Species | Race in Dhofar | Status in Oman (see Appx 1) | Remarks |
|---|---|---|---|
| **A  Species which breed or may breed in Dhofar** | | | |
| Lappet-faced Vulture | – | WV BR? | |
| Verreaux's Eagle | – | BR | |
| Spotted Thick-knee (Dikkop) | *dodsoni* | BR? | Race also in E Africa |
| Yellow-bellied Green Pigeon | – | MB? | |
| Didric Cuckoo | – | MB | |
| Spotted Eagle Owl | *milesi* | BR | |
| Grey-headed Kingfisher | *semicerulea* | MB | |
| Singing Bush Lark | *simplex* | MB (W) | |
| Blackstart | *erlangeri* | BR | |
| Blanford's Warbler* | *leucomelaena* | BR or MB | |
| African Paradise Flycatcher | *harterti* | BR? | |
| Abyssinian Sunbird* | *hellmayri* | BR | |
| Palestine Sunbird | *osea* | BR | Race also in E and central Africa |
| White-breasted White-eye* | *arabs* | BR | |
| Black-headed Bush Shrike | *percivali* | BR | |
| Fan-tailed Raven | – | BR | |
| Rüppell's Weaver* | – | BR | |
| African Silverbill | *orientalis* | BR | Race also in E Africa |
| Golden-winged Grosbeak* | *percivali* | BR | |
| Cinnamon-breasted Rock Bunting | *arabica* | BR | |
| **B  Others** | | | |
| Black-headed Heron | – | V | |
| Abdim's Stork | – | V | |
| Sacred Ibis | – | V | |
| Namaqua Dove | – | V | |
| Nubian Nightjar | – | PM? | |
| Wattled Starling | – | V | Also to Masirah and desert |

*Restricted range in E Africa.

The other four species have unusual distributions and fit no special category. The first of these, the Crab Plover, has a breeding distribution from the upper Arabian Gulf, via the colony near Masirah, to the southern Red Sea, Gulf of Aden and Sri Lanka; it disperses to the coasts and islands of the Indian Ocean after breeding. The Jacobin Cuckoo probably migrates from northern India to winter in Africa, and has been mentioned above. The race of scops owl resident in Dhofar, *pamelae*, is now thought to be a race of the Oriental Scops Owl *Otus sunia*, and not of *O. scops*. The White-collared Kingfisher has its range mainly within the Indomalayan region, but there is an isolated resident population in Africa on the Red Sea, and in 1962 another was discovered in northern Oman and the adjacent UAE.

---

The variety of bird-life in the Sultanate of Oman will surprise many people, but with an awareness of the presence of the many species, and of their differing origins, behaviour and requirements, will come a still deeper appreciation of them. This brief discussion about the birds will have answered some questions; inevitably it will have raised many more. There are many aspects of bird-life in Oman, (and indeed in the whole of the Arabian Peninsula), which await exploration, and it is to the observers in Oman to whom the world's ornithologists will first turn for information.

# Observing Birds

The following notes on how to study birds in the field are addressed primarily to beginners, though it is hoped that some comments, especially those relating to local conditions, will prove helpful to experienced bird-watchers newly arrived in Oman.

Anyone who is interested in this increasingly popular and absorbing pastime – whether he or she has experience elsewhere or not – is highly recommended to try to find, at an early stage, other people who share the interest and who therefore may already have local experience. This may initially be done through questioning friends and acquaintances, but it may also be helpful to visit embassies or cultural centres, or enquire at the National Council for the Conservation of the Environment and Prevention of Pollution, Ruwi, or at the office of the Adviser for the Conservation of the Environment, PO Box 246, Muscat. Someone should soon be found who will be glad to show or advise on the best places to visit, and perhaps help with transport. Meeting others who share the same interest is helpful and stimulating, and soon widens one's scope, knowledge and interest. It is to the co-operative ventures of many observers that much is owed for our present knowledge of the status of the birds of Oman.

## Where and when

Bird species have their own life-styles and preferences for food and for places to find that food and shelter. They may frequent the thickest vegetation, or live on the open ocean, or in the air, on muddy shores or on rocky mountains. These are their preferred habitats or ecological zones, to which they are best adapted. They may search vegetation or the ground for invertebrate food or habitually fly after insects, plunge for sea-food, probe for small animals or live by preying upon other birds; there are many differences in behaviour which will give clues to an unknown bird's identity.

The variety of habits and habitats in Oman is wide, and something should be known of these in order to be able to find birds and appreciate their needs for survival. Some notes are given in preceding parts of this volume, and in the descriptive notes of each family and species. A glance at the bird 'diary' (Table 8) will indicate some of the activity to be expected in each month.

The best 'bird spots', the aim of most bird-watchers, are those at which numbers of individuals and species (or just one scarce species) may be found. If there is no guide or transport, it may be a matter of searching one's immediate neighbourhood for places of attraction to birds, such as gardens, natural vegetation, wadis and hill-sides. Working further afield, such places as creeks, sewage-treatment works and other sources of water, and areas of good vegetation may be discovered; some may be shown on maps, which are worth studying closely. Coasts, the sea and islands should not be neglected, and 'sea-watching' from a headland may be rewarding.

## How

How one observes birds is a matter of personal preference and circumstance, but certain techniques are necessary to achieve success. Birds are most active in the morning and evening, and many rest or shelter from the heat of the sun during the day; the most rewarding times to see them are therefore usually from before sunrise until 9 or 10, and again after 3 p.m.; and in order to see some marsh birds and Lichtenstein's Sandgrouse one needs to remain until after dusk. The amount of daylight available can be judged from Table 9. 'Nautical twilight' starts and ends at the first and last glimmer of light, when the sun's centre is 12° below the celestial horizon; 'civil twilight' begins and ends when the horizon first becomes indistinct or clear, when the sun's centre is 6° below the horizon.

## Table 8    A bird diary

Examples of some annual events in Oman

| January | February | March |
|---|---|---|
| Northerly move of wv/PM<br>e.g.<br>  ducks<br>  Short-toed Eagle<br>  Imperial Eagle<br>  waders<br>  Great Black-headed Gull<br>  Sand Martin<br>  Orphean Warbler<br>  thrushes<br><br>Arrival of some Socotra<br>  Cormorants from Gulf to<br>  Musandam<br><br>Nesting commences of<br>  Kestrel<br>  Grey Francolin (N)<br>  Palm Dove<br>  Pallid Swift<br>  Indian Roller (N)<br>  Graceful Warbler<br>  Purple Sunbird (N)<br>  Great Grey Shrike | Northerly passage<br>  increases<br><br>Departure of most late<br>  ducks<br>  waders<br><br>Nesting of many residents<br>e.g.<br>  Egyptian Vulture<br>  Long-legged Buzzard<br>  Bonelli's Eagle<br>  Moorhen<br>  Collared Dove<br>  Little Owl<br>  some larks<br>  Pale Crag Martin<br>  Yellow-vented Bulbul<br>  Hume's Wheatear (N)<br>  Brown-necked Raven<br>  Tristram's Grackle (D)<br>  House Sparrow (N)<br>  Indian Silverbill (N)<br>  Cinnamon-breasted Rock Bunting (D) | Passage continues<br><br>Arrival of Blue-cheeked<br>  Bee-eater<br><br>Nesting of<br>  Masked Booby (D)<br>  Little Green Heron<br>  other partridges<br>  Little Ringed Plover<br>  Kentish Plover<br>  Red-wattled Lapwing (N)<br>  Rock Dove<br>  Woodpigeon (N)<br>  some owls<br>  some larks<br>  Scrub Warbler<br>  Arabian Babbler<br>  House Crow (N)<br>  Rüppell's Weaver (D) |

| April | May | June |
|---|---|---|
| NE monsoon ceases<br><br>Peak northerly passage<br>  of many species<br>e.g.<br>  Red-necked Phalarope<br>  gulls<br>  terns<br>  cuckoos<br>  bee-eaters<br>  swallows<br>  passerine night-migrants<br><br>Southerly movement of<br>  Persian Shearwater<br><br>First arrivals of<br>  Pale-footed Shearwater<br>  Wilson's Storm-petrel<br>  Sooty Falcon<br>  Yellow-bellied Green Pigeon (D)<br>  Grey-headed Kingfisher (D)<br><br>Nesting commences of<br>  Little Grebe (D)<br>  Yellow-throated Sparrow (N)<br>  Western Reef Heron<br>  Blackstart (D)<br>  Crab Plover (M)<br>  Sooty Gull<br>  Turtle Dove (N)<br>  Singing Bush Lark (D) | Northerly passage of<br>  last migrants<br>e.g.<br>  nightjars<br>  Roller<br>  Rufous Bush Robin<br><br>Departure of last wvs<br>e.g.<br>  Kingfisher<br><br>Arrival of<br>  Didric Cuckoo (D)<br><br>Nesting commences of<br>  terns<br>  bee-eaters<br>  Grey-headed Kingfisher (D)<br>  Black-headed Bush Shrike (D) | Start of SW monsoon (D)<br><br>Some migrant stragglers<br><br>Some non-breeding birds<br><br>Nesting continues |

38

| July | August | September |
|---|---|---|
| Concentrations off Dhofar of<br>  shearwaters<br>  petrels<br>  Wilson's Storm-petrel<br><br>Post-breeding dispersal of<br>  Red-wattled Lapwing<br>  Blue-cheeked Bee-eater<br>  some Sooty Gulls<br><br>Arrivals of early PMS and WVS<br>e.g.<br>  herons<br>  Greater Flamingo<br>  Egyptian Vulture<br>  waders<br>  Herring Gull<br>  Whiskered Tern<br><br>Nesting commences of<br>  Socotra Cormorant (D)<br>  terns<br>  Sooty Falcon<br>  Common Noddy | Peak southerly passage<br>e.g.<br>  waders<br>  phalaropes<br>  terns<br>  pipits<br>  wagtails<br><br>Post-breeding dispersal of<br>  Crab Plover<br>  Collared Dove<br><br>Dispersal begins of<br>  Pale-footed Shearwater<br><br>Arrivals of first<br>  White Stork<br>  Houbara<br>  Kingfisher<br><br>Ospreys return to nest<br>  sites in Oman<br><br>Sooty Falcon – first chicks | Peak southerly passage<br>e.g.<br>  herons<br>  Ruff<br>  nightjars<br>  passerine night-migrants<br><br>SW monsoon ceases (D)<br><br>Dispersal of shearwaters, etc.<br><br>Arrival of early WVS<br>e.g.<br>  Great White Egret<br>  ducks<br>  Black-headed Gull<br>  White Wagtail<br>  Bluethroat<br>  Red-tailed Wheatear |

| October | November | December |
|---|---|---|
| Southerly passage continues<br>e.g.<br>  Lesser Kestrel<br>  Blue-cheeked<br>    Bee-eater<br>  Desert Wheatear<br><br>Arrival of more WVS<br>e.g.<br>  Great Cormorant<br>  ducks<br>  Sparrowhawk<br>  eagles<br>  Coot<br>  Pheasant-tailed<br>    Jacana<br>  Black Redstart<br>  Starling<br><br>Arrival of occasional vagrants<br>e.g.<br>  Koel<br>  Jacobin Cuckoo<br>  Brambling<br>  buntings<br><br>Dispersal of<br>  Socotra Cormorant (D)<br>  Didric Cuckoo (D)<br><br>Northerly passage of<br>  Persian Shearwater | NE monsoon commences<br><br>Passage of late migrants<br>e.g.<br>  Short-eared Owl<br><br>Arrival of more WVS<br>e.g.<br>  ducks<br>  eagles<br><br>Peak numbers of Egyptian Vulture<br><br>Dispersal of<br>  Sooty Falcon<br>  Grey-headed Kingfisher (D)<br><br>Nesting of<br>  Verreaux's Eagle (D) | Arrival of<br>  wintering thrushes<br>  occasional vagrants<br>e.g.<br>    Common Crane<br><br>Nesting of<br>  Osprey<br>  Fan-tailed Raven (D)<br>  more species in wet years |

N = northern Oman only      M = Masirah only      D = Dhofar only

**Table 9    Some times of twilight, sunrise and sunset**

| | Muscat | | | | Salalah | | | |
|---|---|---|---|---|---|---|---|---|
| | **21 Jan** | **21 Mar** | **21 Jun** | **21 Sep** | **21 Jan** | **21 Mar** | **21 Jun** | **21 Sep** |
| Nautical twilight | 05 59 | 05 21 | 04 22 | 05 06 | 06 08 | 05 42 | 04 59 | 05 26 |
| Civil twilight | 06 26 | 05 47 | 04 53 | 05 32 | 06 34 | 06 06 | 05 27 | 05 51 |
| Sunrise | 06 51 | 06 10 | 05 27 | 05 55 | 06 57 | 06 28 | 05 51 | 06 13 |
| Sunset | 17 43 | 18 17 | 18 57 | 18 02 | 18 13 | 18 35 | 19 00 | 18 20 |
| Civil twilight | 18 07 | 18 40 | 19 23 | 18 25 | 18 36 | 18 57 | 19 25 | 18 42 |
| Nautical twilight | 18 35 | 19 07 | 19 54 | 18 51 | 19 02 | 19 22 | 19 53 | 19 07 |

All times are 'local' to the nearest minute

To avoid alarming the birds which *may* be present, it is essential to approach slowly and silently, avoiding any sudden movement. If one is on foot, a slow walk round a likely bird spot may reveal all but the most secretive species. Companions can help by encircling the area from another direction, so that the birds disturbed by one observer may be better seen by another; or one person may advance while others observe.

However, to *observe* birds and their behaviour it will be necessary not to alert them to the observer's presence at all. A car can make a most useful mobile hide or blind, as birds may accept the arrival of a car if the passengers remain still and do not open and slam the doors; it usually pays to observe the birds (or watch for their presence) for a time before alighting. Longer periods of patient observation from a car (shielding the window behind the observer will add to his inconspicuousness), or from a natural or constructed static hide, may enable much more to be seen. Similarly, observations from a ship or small boat may enable one to get close to sea-birds.

A number of sites may be visited in the same day, so that a better idea of the total numbers of each bird species in the area can be gained. If a note is taken of these numbers on each occasion, regular visits to the same place will reveal the changing pattern during the year, which is another important way of discovering the status of the birds.

When an unknown bird is found, the observer should first try to decide, from its general size, shape and behaviour, what family it is; is it a thrush or a sparrow, a bee-eater or a roller? One's choice soon narrows to a few similar birds. Further patient observation will reveal more detail, and attention will be better focused if a sketch is made, however rough this is. Then refer to this volume, not only to the appearance, behaviour and calls of the likely species, but also to the probability of occurrence in this place and at this time of the year. For example, before deciding that a bird is an autumn Golden Plover, one should be aware that this is a scarce bird in Oman and that another rather similar species is more likely; a close look at the differences will then be necessary before the first species can be claimed with certainty. Snap judgements will lead to misleading errors and disappointments.

The observer should also be aware of other pitfalls. One is that plumage can vary within a species not only according to sex, age, the season and the amount of bleaching and wear, but also between individuals and apparently in different lights. Size is very difficult to judge, especially in the desert or on the open shore; direct comparison with a known species (particularly if nearby) is a great help and is better than guessing the size in inches.

The way a bird's plumage is marked makes more sense if one has an appreciation of the arrangement of the feathers, which do not cover the bird uniformly but in most species grow from definite tracts of skin. These tracts and other parts of the bird are named in the accompanying sketches. (Figure 3).

Many species may be identified by their call, which may be heard before the bird is seen. It will help to get to know the calls of the local resident species first, but the calls of migrants should not be neglected; to be alerted, for example, by the musical notes of bee-eaters sailing high overhead is an experience not to be missed.

Confirmation of breeding is worth obtaining, though naturally without disturbance to the birds or nest. If a nest is found, retire some distance and wait to see which species returns to it. The categories of breeding evidence, in use by the British Trust for Ornithology, are listed below:

### Possibly breeding
H    1    Species observed in breeding season in possible nesting HABITAT;
S    2    SINGING male(s) present (or breeding calls heard) in the breeding season.

### Probably breeding
P    3    PAIR observed in suitable nesting habitat in breeding season;
T    4    Permanent TERRITORY presumed through registration of territorial behaviour (song, etc.) on at least two different days, a week or more apart, at the same place;
D    5    DISPLAY and courtship;
N    6    Visiting probable NEST-SITE;
A    7    AGITATED behaviour or ANXIETY calls from adults;
I    8    Brood-patch on adult examined in the hand, indicating probably INCUBATING;
B    9    BUILDING nest or excavating nest-hole.

### Confirmed breeding
DD    10    DISTRACTION DISPLAY or injury-feigning;
UN    11    Recently USED NEST or eggshells found;
FL    12    Recently FLEDGED young (nidicolous species) or downy young (nidifugous species);
ON    13    Adults entering or leaving nest-site in circumstances indicating OCCUPIED NEST (including high nests or nest-holes, the contents of which cannot be seen) or adults seen sitting on the nest;
FY    14    Adults carrying FOOD for YOUNG, or faecal sac;
NE    15    NEST containing EGGS;
NY    16    NEST with YOUNG seen or heard.

## Binoculars

There are several aids to bird-watching which one may choose, but the two basic items are a pair of binoculars and a notebook.

Binoculars should be chosen carefully to give lasting pleasure in use. They should be light, easy to hold, and have a central focussing wheel. Above all they must give a clear and bright image. Clarity, and freedom from distortion of form and colour, will largely depend on the quality of the instrument (not necessarily the most expensive). Brightness will also depend upon the relationship between the magnification and the diameter of the large object lens; instruments with a high 'light value' will give the brightest image, as Table 10 shows.

**Table 10     Comparative figures for some popular sizes of binocular.**

| Magnification | Objective lens ø in mm. | 'Exit pupil' ø in mm. | Light value |
|---|---|---|---|
| 12 | 50 | 4.16 | 17 |
| 10 | 50 | 5 | 25 |
| 10 | 40 | 4 | 16 |
| 8.5 | 44 | 5.18 | 26.8 |
| 8 | 40 | 5 | 25 |
| 8 | 30 | 3.75 | 14.1 |
| 7 | 50 | 7.14 | 51 (a 'nightglass') |
| 6 | 30 | 5 | 25 |

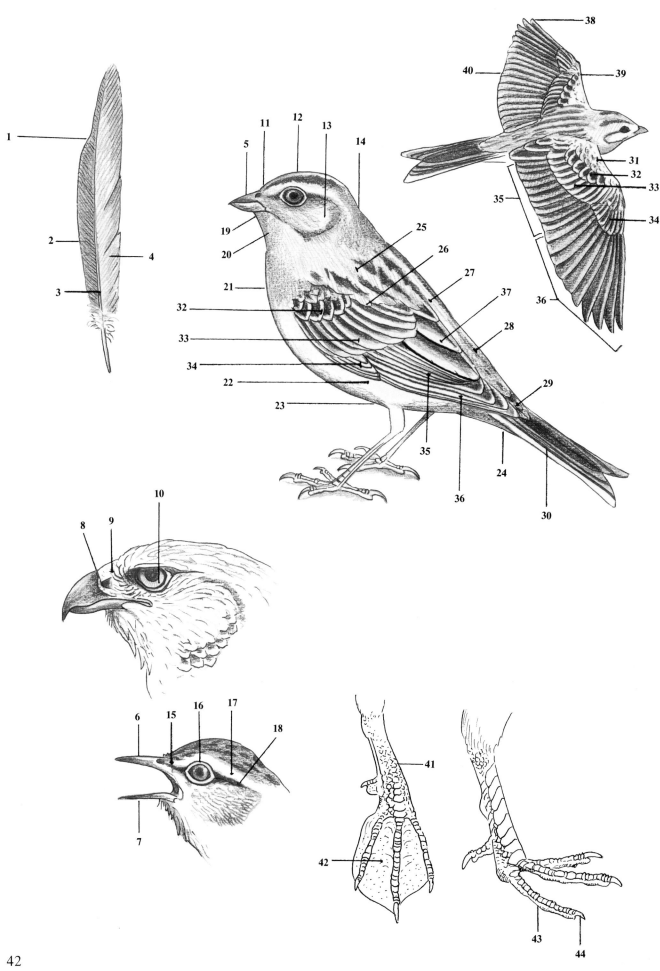

## Figure 3 Topography of a bird

(Other terms can be found in the Glossary)

1 **Emargination**
An indentation often found on the outer web of primary feathers; its position along the web can be an important identification feature in some small birds.

2 **Outer vane or web**

3 **Shaft**

4 **Inner vane or web**

5 **Bill**

6 **Upper mandible**
The hook on the bill of pelicans and some other birds is called the **nail.**

7 **Lower mandible**
The angle near the tip in such birds as gulls is called the **gonys.**

8 **Nostril**
Nostrils may be exposed, or covered by bristles or feathers. They may be set in a shallow depression, as in many small birds, or in a raised tube on the bill as in shearwaters and petrels.

9 **Cere**
The soft base of the upper mandible, naked in birds of prey, and swollen and called the **operculum** in pigeons.

10 **Iris**
The coloured part of the eye around the black pupil.

11 **Forehead**

12 **Crown**
The feathers are sometimes elongated to form a crest.

13 **Ear-coverts**

14 **Nape**

15 **Lores**
In some birds such as flycatchers and nightjars the bristles which spread out from this area around the base of the bill are called **rictal bristles.**

16 **Eye-ring**
This is a narrow ring of small feathers, often pale or white, sometimes incomplete, found in many birds. Note that the eyelids of some birds such as raptors and pigeons may be swollen or brightly coloured, and in others such as bulbuls there may be a wattle round the eye.

17 **Supercilium**
A streak above the eye, usually pale.

18 **Eye-stripe**
Streak 'through' the eye, usually dark.

19 **Chin**

20 **Throat**

21 **Breast**

22 **Flanks**
Often concealed under the edge of the closed wing in small birds, but may be conspicuously patterned and overlap the closed wing, as in partridges.

23 **Belly**

24 **Under tail-coverts**
Usually lie flat under the base of the tail.

25 **Mantle**

26 **Scapulars**
A group of dull, sometimes prominent feathers arising from the shoulder and overlapping the closed wing and **tertials.**

27 **Back**

28 **Rump**

29 **Upper tail-coverts**
May almost reach the tip of the tail, e.g. in some partridges.

30 **Tail**
The tail-feathers are properly called **rectrices.**

31 **Lesser wing-coverts**

32 **Median wing-coverts**
Sometimes have paler tips and/or dark centres, the tips forming a wing-bar. They overlie the bases of the next group.

33 **Greater wing-coverts**
May also have pale tips; they overlie the bases of the secondaries.

34 **Primary coverts**
There is another small group of feathers, usually inconspicuous, on the leading edge of the wing, known as the **alula** or the **bastard wing.**

35 **Secondaries**
The flight-feathers which form the rear margin of the open wing. The inner ones may be conspicuously lengthened and coloured, as in some ducks; in small birds such as larks they overlie the tip of the closed wing; these are numbered separately as **tertials** in this list. In ducks the secondaries are often brightly coloured with iridescent centres and contrasting tips and bases; this patch is the **speculum.**

36 **Primaries**
The outer primaries are sometimes widely spread in soaring birds, e.g. vultures.

37 **Tertials**
See, **35 secondaries.**

38 **Wing-tip**

39 **Leading-edge of wing**

40 **Trailing-edge of wing**

41 **Tarsus**
Often loosely referred to as the **leg.** Above it is the **thigh** or **shank,** the joint corresponding to our ankle.

42 **Webbed foot**
In some birds the webs are much reduced.

43 **Toe**
Most birds have four toes, which form the **foot.** Normally the first toe (**hallux**) points backwards, but swifts have all toes pointing forwards, cuckoos and parakeets have two pointing forwards and two backwards, and in some species the outer toe is reversible.

44 **Claw**

— **Under-wing**
The under wing-coverts are often called the **wing-lining.** There is a group of feathers, sometimes distinctively coloured, called the **axillaries,** which lie in the armpit or wing-pit between the wing-lining and the flank.

**The note-book**

Many observers, unconvinced of the value of a contemporary record of what they see and of the prevailing circumstances, lose precious months or years of hard-won records of the occurrence and behaviour of birds. It is a common mistake to assume that all is known about them; in Arabia the possibility of making observations new to the Peninsula and even to Science is very real, and it is well worth the trouble to jot down the details. It may only be later that the uniqueness of the observation is appreciated, but by then the details will not be fresh in the mind and even the date may have been forgotten.

What one enters in a note-book is a matter of personal preference, but it would be wise to enter more rather than less, so that at a later date the details can form the basis of a special report, of monthly reports to the central Oman record (c/o PO Box 246, Muscat), of a fuller diary or even of an article for publication.

A useful size of note-book is 100×180mm. Put a date at the top of the entry, with the initials of one's companions, and a note on the weather and viewing conditions. Put as sub-headings each place or section of the route and the times, and list under each sub-heading the species seen and the approximate numbers of each, noting whether this is a total of individual sightings or a flock. If it is impossible to count them all, try to estimate by counting perhaps in blocks of 10 or 50; or simply give an order of magnitude, e.g. the total is under 10, 100 or 1,000.

At this point any convenient shorthand can be developed, and this can be of great use if extended to include a rough outline sketch of any new bird seen (practise by tracing a bird in this volume), with marks and arrows to indicate the main characteristics of the bird under observation. But make the sketch only after a long look at the bird and its behaviour, as it may fly before another chance occurs to watch it. If possible, watch also for it to fly, when the diagnostic features of its flight, plumage and call should be noted. Compare it with other species present or known to you. The next step is to look in this volume to check any further field characters that need to be ascertained to help identification.Be sure to be honest and self-critical. Enter what was seen, and give reasons for any conjectures. Species unknown when observed may, with later experience, be identified from good notes.

This field note-book is a vital record and is worth retaining. A neater, indexed record under species headings, in the order shown in the Check List (Appendix 1) can be prepared from it later at home, and this, on a card-index or on separate lined sheets in a box-file, can build up into a valuable record.

**Photography**

The modern 35-mm single-lens reflex camera, and its sophisticated choice of lenses and films, permit very good photographs to be taken of some birds. However, much care, patience and thought is necessary to photograph most birds well. A quick snap may successfully complement the eye and the notebook in recording an unknown bird, but it must be said that as an aid to the identification of an unknown bird a snap-shot may prove to be disappointing; the bird may be too small, its plumage and behaviour cannot be captured fully, and more may be lost in trying to photograph it than in careful and continuous observation. Unless a firm support, such as a tripod or car door is available, the camera and lens must be capable of being carried and held steadily in the hand, with a fast enough shutter speed to stop any movement of the camera or bird, such as when photographing birds in flight. A shutter speed slower than $\frac{1}{250}$th second is rarely satisfactory and to stop the wing-tips of some birds $\frac{1}{1,000}$th or even $\frac{1}{2,000}$th will prove necessary.

In the tropics, extreme conditions of heat, humidity, dust and vibration are to be expected and must be guarded against. Cameras and film must be kept out of the heat of the sun. Containers, such as a small padded suitcase, insulated food box or cloth bags, will help protect some equipment.

The harsh light of summer, which gives extremes of light and shadow, can be avoided by photographing say before 10 a.m. and after 3 p.m. Always be ready for the chance shot, but by choosing the time and site with care, and by waiting still and partly concealed at a known or likely natural 'bird spot', such as a high-tide roost, a pool or marsh, it will be possible to obtain natural informative photographs of the birds and their behaviour. The birds may be feeding, flying or resting and all may require different techniques to photograph them satisfactorily without disturbance. Stalking on foot is a gamble, but may work if one approaches slowly and silently behind cover; otherwise a long and uncomfortable wait may be necessary before birds return within range. Flying birds are difficult to keep in focus, but the range changes less rapidly when they are soaring and when landing and taking off.

Photography at the nest requires special care to avoid disturbance of the bird, perhaps hundreds of birds if they are colonial. Not only does disturbance spoil the picture, but the young may be trampled upon by other birds and the eggs smashed, 'cooked' in the sun or stolen by predators. Photographs of nests, eggs and chicks without positive identification of the species at the time will be valueless. Photography of birds is often worth the effort, but visual observation remains the best way of studying birds.

---

These notes give some hints to those who wish to know more about the hobby of bird-watching, so that they may enjoy it all the more. It is a hobby which can provide at once a relaxation, an absorbing interest, and a greater awareness and appreciation of the beauty and variety of nature, and particularly of birds as living creatures.

The hobby also provides a subject of common interest, which is truly international in its appeal. Whether watching birds alone or with others, opportunities will arise when the results of one's experiences can be shared. Then, even more importantly, one's enthusiasm can be communicated to others, particularly the young, and a sympathetic interest kindled for the wild birds of Oman. If this volume helps to promote this enthusiasm and interest then it will have succeeded.

# GLOSSARY

(For other parts of a bird's body and plumage, the reader is referred to the sketches in Figure 3.)

| | |
|---|---|
| **Aquatic** | Living in or on water. |
| **Arboreal** | Living in trees. |
| **Bar** | (On plumage) a transverse mark. |
| **Bare Parts** | The un-feathered parts of a bird. |
| **Biogeography** | The study of the geographical distribution of animals and plants in the world. |
| **Brood-parasitic** | A species, such as the Cuckoo, which lays its eggs in the nests of another species which will care for them. |
| **Carrion** | Dead flesh. |
| **Carpal** | As in 'carpal joint', the 'wrist' or forward-pointing bend of the wing. |
| **Casque** | An enlargement on bill or head. |
| **Crepuscular** | Active in twilight or at dusk. |
| **Cryptic** | Concealing colours or pattern. |
| **Dispersal** | Movement after breeding; may be random or nomadic or prior to migration. |

| | |
|---|---|
| **Diurnal** | Active by day. |
| **Double-brooded** | When a second clutch of eggs is laid and hatched. |
| **Eclipse** | The dull plumage assumed by males of some colourful species for a short period after breeding (as in ducks). |
| **Endangered** | A species in danger of extinction in all or most of its range. |
| **Endemic** | Occurring naturally, in a particular area in which it remains. |
| **Eyass** | A nestling falcon. |
| **Eyrie** | The nest of a bird of prey. |
| *falaj* (pl. *aflaj*) | Channel for distributing fresh water. |
| **Feral** | Domesticated animal living wild. |
| **Filoplume** | A hair-like feather (as in nuptial plumage of cormorants). |
| **Flight-feathers** | The primaries and secondaries, (remiges). |
| **Frontal shield** | A hard plate from the base of the bill and over forehead (as in the Coot). |
| **Gape** | The mouth opening; the 'corner' of the mouth when closed. |

45

| | |
|---|---|
| **Guano** | The accumulated dried dung of sea-birds, sometimes used as a plant fertilizer. |
| **Gular** | Pertaining to the throat (as in the gular pouch of pelicans). |
| **Habitat** | An area containing suitable living conditions for a species. |
| **Hybrid** | An intermediate; an offspring resulting from a cross or inter-breeding between individuals of different species or sub-species. |
| **Immature** | Intermediate (e.g. in plumages) between juvenile and adult. |
| **Inshore** | Close to or within sight of shore, as in cormorants and gulls. |
| **Invertebrate** | Animals other than vertebrates, e.g. worms, snails, crabs, insects, spiders. |
| **Irruption** | Occasional and unpredictable migration of some species caused by an inadequate food supply. |
| **Isabelline** | A greyish-yellow colour. |
| *jabal* (pl. *jibal*) | Mountain. |
| *jazira(t)* (pl. *jaza'ir*) | Island. |
| **Juvenile** | Young bird, able to fly, in first set of true feathers. |
| *Kharif* | Summer (when the dates ripen); also used incorrectly to mean the SW monsoon or its cloud in Dhofar. |
| *Khawr* | A creek, sometimes temporarily sealed off from the sea as a lagoon. |
| **Lanceolate** | Like a spearhead (shape of feather). |
| **Lappet** | A fleshy wattle (as in Lappet-faced Vulture). |
| **Leg** | Used here to include the whole limb (excluding the toes if described separately). |
| **Lobe** | A round flat projection on the toes (not a web). |
| **Median** | In the middle. |
| **Migrant** | A species which migrates, i.e. is migratory (e.g. passage migrant or migrant breeder). |
| **Migration** | Regular cyclical movement between breeding-grounds and winter quarters; also local migration, altitudinal migration (see *partial migrant*). |
| **Mirror** | A white or translucent patch in the wings. |
| **Moult** | The periodic shedding and replacement of feathers. |
| **Nocturnal** | Active at night. |
| **Nomad** | A wanderer when not breeding, perhaps in a regular direction. |
| **Nominate race** | The race from which a species takes its name. |
| **Nuchal** | Pertaining to the nape. |
| **Offshore** | Further out than inshore, to the edge of the continental shelf. |
| **Orbit** | The eye-socket. |
| **Orbital** | Around the eye. |
| **Orographic** | Of rain caused when moist air is forced to rise over a mountain range. |
| **Partial Migrant** | A species or population some individuals of which migrate while others do not; often it is only the young which migrate. |

| | |
|---|---|
| **Passerine** | 'Song' or 'perching' birds of the Order Passeriformes (commencing in this volume with the larks). |
| **Pectoral** | Pertaining to the breast, as in 'pectoral band'. |
| **Pelagic** | Oceanic, capable of living for long periods away from land, e.g. petrels and shearwaters. |
| **Pellet** | Compacted undigested part of some birds' food, ejected through the mouth. |
| **Plankton** | Very small animals (zooplankton) and plants (phytoplankton) which float or drift mainly near the surface of seas and lakes; an important food for some fish and birds. Also 'aerial plankton', the food of swifts, etc. |
| **Pullus** | Nestling, chick or eyass, not yet flying. |
| **Race** | A sub-species. |
| **Raptor** | A bird of prey. |
| *ra's* (pl. *ru'us*) | Headland, cape. |
| **Relict** | A race or a species that has become geographically isolated in part of its former range. |
| **Rictal** | At the gape (as in *rictal* bristles). |
| **Rufous** | A reddish-brown colour. |
| *Sabkha* | Flat low ground or 'playa', hard when dry, quickly becoming mud or marsh during a rise of the water-table (as in high tides and rain-storms). |
| **Scrub** | Used here to describe miscellaneous desert plants, usually not exceeding 60cm in height, often well dispersed, not necessarily with trees. |
| **Sedentary** | Not migratory. |
| **Soar** | Glide in rising air (e.g. over sea-waves, cliffs or in thermals). |
| **Speculum** | A patch in the wing, of distinctive colour, often with a metallic sheen (as in ducks). |
| **Stoop** | A steep, fast, diving attack. |
| **Streak** | A longitudinal mark of the plumage (opposite of bar). |
| **Sub-song** | Quiet or whisper-song, often with bill closed, in or out of breeding season. |
| **Taxonomy** | The scientific classification of birds into Order, Family, sub-family, genus, species, race and cline. |
| **Terrestrial** | Living mainly on the ground. |
| **Thermal** | A column of warm rising air, of use to soaring birds. |
| **Tower** | To fly very steeply upwards. |
| **Vagrant** | Either an off-course migrant, stray or 'accidental', or a true wanderer. |
| **Vertebrate** | Animal with a skull, skeleton and backbone, e.g. fish, toad, lizard, snake, bird, mammal. |
| *wadi* | A valley or other water-course, often dry except after heavy rain. |
| **Wattle** | A bare fleshy appendage on the head or throat. |
| **Web** | A fleshy membrane between two toes; also the vane of a feather. |
| **Xerophytic** | The ability of a plant to survive prolonged drought. |
| **Zoogeography** | The study of the geographical distribution of the world's animals. |

# The Plates

## Systematic List and Index to Plates

(* = not illustrated)

47

# [OSTRICHES: Struthionidae

**Ostrich** *Struthio camelus syriacus* was a breeding resident in the interior of Oman, but it has been extinct there since at least 1930, and is probably extinct in Arabia.]


# GREBES: Podicipedidae

**World:** 20 species. **Oman:** 3 species (1 breeding). Duck-like, but body elongate or rotund, with rudimentary tail and small pointed bill. Legs set well back, trailed in flight; flattened tarsus and lobed toes aid propulsion in water. Wings very small, wing-beat and flight rapid. Plumage of sexes similar; in winter brown, grey or blackish above, silky-white below. Strictly aquatic, usually on still, fresh or brackish water with some vegetative cover, but coastal on passage, migrating by night. Dive readily to feed and to escape, riding low in the water when suspicious. Generally feed on fish and aquatic invertebrates. The nest is a floating pad of vegetation. Main points for identification are size, shape, bill and pattern of head and neck.


### Black-necked Grebe  *Podiceps nigricollis*

Black-necked Grebe

**World:** *P.n. nigricollis* breeds locally in Europe and central Asia, south to Iraq, Iran; also in parts of Far East; sedentary and migratory, northern birds reaching northern Africa, Arabia, N India, Far East. Other races in America, Africa.
**Oman:** Irregular winter visitor and passage migrant in very small numbers from late August to March.

33cm/13in. In *winter,* dark grey-brown with blackish cap extending to below the eyes, where it merges into white. The lower throat is mottled brown and white and there is a white patch in the trailing edge of the wing. The tip of the slender bill is slightly upturned (less obvious in *immatures*). Differs from the rather similar **Slavonian Grebe** *P. auritus* [33cm/13in, which has occurred as far south as Bandar Abbas, S Iran] in Black-necked's darker appearance, high fore-crown, upturned bill-tip of *adult,* cap to below the eyes and longer wing-patch.

*adult winter* E

On the coast and in creeks and pools, often without cover. Usually silent in winter.


### Great Crested Grebe  *Podiceps cristatus*

Great Crested Grebe

**World:** *P.c. cristatus* breeds in N Africa, Eurasia, south to parts of Iraq, Iran, NW India. Sedentary and migratory, reaching Egypt, Arabian Gulf, E Arabia, India, SE Asia. Other races in Africa, Australasia.
**Oman:** Very scarce and occasionally winter visitor (reported five times between November and April).

48cm/19in. The largest grebe, with the long slender white neck held upright except when retracted at rest. In *winter* the black and chestnut head-frills of summer are reduced or absent, and the cheeks are noticeably white, the back and flanks brownish-black, the under-parts white. In flight white in the dark secondaries is conspicuous, with white also on the under-wing and fore-wing.

*adult winter* D
*adult summer* C

On sheltered coastal waters and in creeks. Usually silent in winter.


### Little Grebe  *Tachybaptus ruficollis*

Little Grebe

**World:** *T.r. capensis* breeds in Africa, Arabia, central Asia, Iran, India, Burma; sedentary and migratory. Other races in Europe, N Africa, and elsewhere in Asia.
**Oman:** Fairly common breeding resident in coastal Dhofar; also a passage migrant and winter visitor, August–March, uncommon in the north.

23cm/9in. The smallest duck-like swimming and diving bird in Oman. The *adult (summer)* is dark brown, with chestnut cheeks and throat and a distinctive yellowish patch at the gape of the short bill; a white patch in the wing is noticeable in flight; the stern is rounded. In *winter* the chestnut is replaced by buff or white, the gape-patch is indistinct, and the under-parts are whiter. The *immature* is paler. The *juvenile* is striped black and brown with bold white streaks on the side of the head, and has a reddish-brown breast. Differs in *winter* from the Black-necked Grebe in smaller size and being browner above, duller below.

*adult summer* B

*adult winter* A

On fresh, occasionally brackish, lakes, creeks and marshes with some vegetation. Usually shy and skulking, partially submerging, diving quickly or pattering a short distance when alarmed. Rarely gregarious but often in pairs; territorial, with noisy mutual chasing at times. The nest, from about April, is a floating pad of vegetation. Eggs, 2–7, usually 3, smooth, whitish becoming stained pinkish; 2 or 3 broods. The young are sometimes carried on the adult's back. Call, a high-pitched whinnying trill; also *pee-eep* or *peep* and an alarm note *klik* or *whit.*

Plate 1

## PETRELS and SHEARWATERS: Procellariidae Plates 2–3

**World:** 55 species. **Oman:** 4 species. Nomadic, migratory and pelagic, coming ashore only to breed or when storm-driven. Nest colonially in crevices, burrows, rarely on open ground or in dense herbage, usually on small islands, but occasionally inland in hills; many species active at the nest site at night. Clues to nesting include: concentrations and display flights near suitable islands, coastal cliffs or inland slopes; individuals flying ashore at dusk and away at dawn; sighing calls ashore at night and a musky odour at the burrows. Lay one large white egg, rarely replaced; chick fed by regurgitation in the nest for a long period, then deserted. Wings long and narrow. Bill has a terminal hook and two tubular nostrils (hence 'tube-nose'). Toes webbed; legs set far back. Sexes may differ in size, but plumage is similar. Characteristic flight varies between species and with wind and sea conditions, but comprises gliding close to surface or wave contours ('shearwatering'), with an occasional series of wing-beats; occasionally swooping, banking or flapping upwards, to glide again. In calm weather take off with a pattering run. Feed on or below surface, often in association with terns, on plankton, fish, crustaceans, squid, offal, etc.

**Pale-footed Shearwater** (Flesh-footed Shearwater) *Puffinus carneipes*    Pale-footed Shearwater A

**World:** Breeds in SW Australia and New Zealand area in the southern summer, migrating north in the northern summer.
**Oman:** A common summer visitor to the cold waters off Dhofar, occasionally to Gulf of Oman, April–November, with most between June and mid-August; north-easterly passage has been observed in August.

51cm/20in. A large, dark sooty-brown or chocolate-black shearwater, paler on the fore-wing and on sides of head and neck. Distinguished from other species in Arabian waters by size, heavy build and long, heavy, pale bill with dark tip; and from Jouanin's Petrel and Wedge-tailed Shearwater also by short rounded tail. Legs yellowish-flesh. See Great Skua (plate 59).

Seen singly, in loose parties or in occasional large flocks, and not usually associating with other species. It settles, swims and dives freely. It appears large, dark and heavy, in direct flight flying upwards with a deliberate and steady wing-beat, swooping down to wave level and gliding there with occasional wing-beats until rising again.

**Audubon's Shearwater** (Dusky Shearwater) *Puffinus lherminieri*

**World:** *P.l. persicus,* the **Persian Shearwater** (named in 1872) is the N Indian Ocean race; breeding-    Persian Shearwater B
grounds not yet discovered, it occurs from Somali coast and S Red Sea across to Straits of Hormuz and NW India; resident with seasonal movements. (It is sometimes treated as a race of **Little Shearwater** *P. assimilis.)*
**Oman:** Locally common in Straits of Hormuz from October to early May, ranging widely for food; southward movement April–May; large concentrations off Dhofar June–August, then dispersing. Might breed in late winter in the north, or late summer in the south.

33cm/13in. A small, sturdy shearwater, the only black-and-white species in Oman waters. Brownish-black above (*immatures* paler); cheeks and under-parts white, under-wing dark with a varied white median streak. On the water the body looks dark and elongate, neck appears short and face white. Tail short and rounded, spread on landing and take-off. Bill slender, brown or grey. Legs pale.

It occurs singly, in parties or larger flocks. In calm weather it flies close to the surface with fairly rapid, shallow wing-beats, then glides low with wings tilted down, the tips nearly touching the water. It tends to flock over fish shoals and plankton, when it will circle, settle on the surface, immerse the head to observe and feed, and dive.

**Wedge-tailed Shearwater** *Puffinus pacificus*    Wedge-tailed Shearwater C

**World:** Breeds on islands in Indian and Pacific Oceans, dispersing widely; non-breeding birds reach Arabian Sea and Gulf of Aden throughout the year.
**Oman:** Reported at sea May–October, but status uncertain because of past confusion with the more common Jouanin's Petrel.

40cm/15½in. Medium-sized and slightly built. Usually dark brown, with blackish primaries and pointed wedge-shaped tail. (A pale phase, with paler upper-parts, white below and on under-wing and dark under tail-coverts, may occur rarely towards Arabia from S Pacific.) The bill is long, slender and grey (flesh-coloured in the pale phase), the legs flesh-coloured. Difficult to distinguish from Jouanin's Petrel except by longer, paler bill (which may appear dark), larger size and less rapid flight. Differs from Pale-footed Shearwater in smaller size, long wedge-shaped tail, slighter and darker bill, more graceful flight.

It has an easy, graceful flight, gliding low with shallow wing-beats, occasionally banking. It settles on the water, but dives infrequently and seems to prefer warm waters.

Plate 2

**Jouanin's Petrel**    *Bulweria fallax*

**World:** Ranges over N Indian Ocean and from Red Sea to Gulf of Oman; breeding-grounds not yet discovered. In winter, disperses more widely, reaching south into tropics; has strayed to central Pacific Ocean. (Until discovered in 1955 *B. fallax* was overlooked or confused with Wedge-tailed Shearwater and other species. *B. fallax* is the Indian Ocean representative of **Bulwer's Petrel** *B. bulwerii* of the Atlantic and Pacific, and is perhaps a race of it.)
**Oman:** In winter fairly common and widely dispersed in Arabian Sea; begins to assemble off SE coast and Masirah from March; very common near Kuria Muria Islands, May–August (breeding?); disperses after the summer monsoon (mid-September).

36cm/14in. Medium-sized and slightly built. Uniform brownish-black, sometimes with paler upper wing-coverts. The bill short, stout and blackish, the legs mainly pinkish. Tail wedge-shaped, appearing pointed. Difficult to distinguish from the larger Wedge-tailed Shearwater except by shorter and thicker black bill; smaller size and very fast swooping flight.

A little-known species. Pelagic, individually or in loose parties, rarely in flocks. Flight, five or six quick flaps, rising across wind, followed by a fast swoop and glide low over water. May be a nocturnal feeder.

## STORM-PETRELS: Hydrobatidae                                     Plates 3–4

**World:** 21 species. **Oman:** 3–5 species. Small or very small dark sea-birds, often with white on rump or under-parts. Pelagic, coming ashore only to breed (not in Oman) or when storm-driven. The sexes are similar. Bill short, dark with terminal hook and raised tubular nostrils forming a single orifice. Legs medium to long, toes webbed. When feeding, the toes often touch the surface singly or together as if the birds were walking, jumping or steadying themselves on the water ('pattering'). Feed on plankton, oily offal, etc., taken from the surface. Direct flight usually rapid and fluttery with short glides, varying with wind and sea conditions. Some species follow ships. They have twittering calls, sometimes heard at night.

**White-faced Storm-petrel** (Frigate Petrel)    *Pelagodroma marina*

**World:** Breeds in N and S Atlantic, S Australia, S Pacific.
**Oman:** A regular but uncommon summer visitor off Dhofar May–July, probably the S Australian race *P.m. dulciae*.

20cm/8in. Distinguished from other small petrels in Oman waters by pale upper-parts, conspicuous white forehead, face and supercilium, and white under-parts and under wing-coverts. The back is rather grey, the upper tail-coverts pale grey contrasting with blackish tail and primaries. The tail is almost square. The toes, with yellow-orange webs, project beyond the tail in normal flight.

Reported 80–160 km from the coast. The flight is erratic but, when foraging, the bird kicks at the surface and appears to bounce along with wings held horizontally. Does not usually follow ships.

**Black-bellied Storm-petrel**    *Fregetta tropica*

**World:** Breeds in Antarctica and sub-Antarctica in the southern summer, migrating northwards to central tropics in all oceans.
**Oman:** Though common in the central Arabian Sea in summer until about September, known in Oman waters only from sight records more than 50 km off the Dhofar coast, late May to July.

20cm/8in. Differs from Wilson's Petrel in its white abdomen, axillaries and middle of under-wing and in the diagnostic dark central streak down the belly (varied in extent and usually difficult to see). The tail is almost square. It differs from the rather similar White-bellied Storm-petrel in the dark belly-streak, and, in the hand, in the longer tarsus (over 39mm).

In normal flight somewhat similar to Wilson's Storm-petrel, but weaker, more fluttery and weaving. Foraging behaviour like that of White-faced Storm-petrel, but it occasionally follows ships.

**[White-bellied Storm-petrel**    *Fregetta grallaria*

**World:** Breeds on islands in sub-Antarctic and southern oceans in southern summer, migrating northwards towards central tropics.
**Oman:** Very occasionally reported in Arabian Sea in summer, but not near coasts.

19cm/7½in. Differs from Black-bellied in its lack of a dark belly-streak (but both species may be pure white or marked dusky below) and, in the hand, in the shorter tarsus (less than 39mm).

Behaviour is somewhat similar to that of the Black-bellied, fluttering and hopping; it also follows ships.]

Plate 3

**Wilson's Storm-petrel**    *Oceanites oceanicus*

**World:** Breeds in the Antarctic and sub-Antarctic in the southern summer, then migrates northwards, becoming widespread in all oceans in the northern summer.
**Oman:** Common and regular summer visitor, rare in winter. Arrives from April, becoming common June–August off the SE coast and abundant off Dhofar; most depart September–November but occasional birds are still present in December.

18cm/7in. A small, common and distinctive black storm-petrel with conspicuous white rump extending to a patch on each lower flank. The wing-coverts are pale brown, sometimes forming a slight diagonal bar; under-parts dark, very occasionally streaked whitish. The tail is square, rounded when spread. The long, black legs extend just beyond the tip of the tail when not dangling; part of the webs are yellow (difficult to observe at sea). Differs from Leach's and Swinhoe's in completely white upper tail-coverts, rounded fore-wing, longer legs and square tail; from Black-bellied Storm-petrel in all-dark under-parts, longer legs, and flight.

Though usually seen singly, it assembles in very large numbers in rich feeding areas. It often occurs near coasts, and frequently attends fishing-boats and ships, gliding for long periods in strong winds. The usual flight is low and rapid, with alternating glides, but when foraging it is more erratic, with sharp twists and occasional hovering and pattering as it pecks food from the surface. It occasionally drops on to the surface to secure food, and sometimes settles on the water, riding buoyantly like a phalarope.

**[Swinhoe's Storm-petrel**    *Oceanodroma monorhis*

**World:** Breeds in warm seas of SW Pacific Ocean. Nomadic, reaching Arabian and N Red Seas. (Sometimes regarded as a race of Leach's Storm-petrel.)
**Oman:** Non-breeding vagrant, recorded twice in the Arabian Sea near Oman waters, in May and August.

19cm/7½in. Both Leach's and Swinhoe's are similar to Wilson's Storm-petrel in size and general colour, but differ in their longer, more pointed and angled wings, slightly forked tails, shorter legs with black-webbed toes not extending beyond the tail in flight, and more erratic flight. The rump in Swinhoe's is dark; in Leach's it is usually white with an indistinct central grey streak, but it may be dark in birds from the Pacific.

Both species have a distinctive flight, fast, buoyant and erratic, leaping and swooping, but they will glide and patter when feeding. They settle infrequently and do not commonly follow ships.]

**[Leach's Storm-petrel**    *Oceanodroma leucorhoa*

**World:** *O.l. leucorhoa* breeds in N Atlantic and N Pacific Oceans, wintering to the tropics. Nomadic, it has occurred as a rare vagrant once in Arabian Gulf (June 1969) and once in Kenya (February 1969).
**Oman:** Not yet reported.]

## [FRIGATEBIRDS: Fregatidae

Two species breed on islands in tropical SW Indian Ocean, the **Great Frigatebird** *Fregata minor* and **Lesser Frigatebird** *F. ariel*. Though they rarely cross the Equator, some birds have wandered NW as far as 15°N in the Red Sea. No confirmed reports exist for NE Arabia (reports of two birds on Quoin island, Oman, 29 May 1972, and one off the Arabian Gulf coast of UAE in May 1955, are uncorroborated). Frigatebirds are large and distinctive, with long narrow wings (span about 180cm/72in), long forked tail and long hooked bill. Their soaring flight and piratical habits are also distinctive. Adult males are mostly black (with white flank-patches in *F. ariel*), females are larger with white breast; young birds are very varied, with much white and buff. See Skuas, plate 50.]

Great Frigatebird    *Fregata minor*

Plate 4

55

# TROPICBIRDS: Phaethontidae

**World:** 3 species. **Oman:** 1 species (breeding). These are robust white sea-birds with two extraordinarily elongate central tail-feathers, often called 'Bos'n birds', because of either this 'marlinspike' in the tail or their shrill call. The plumage of the sexes is similar. The wings are long and narrow, the tail wedge-shaped, the bill heavy and brightly coloured. The legs are short, with webbed toes, and set so far back that the birds shuffle when on the ground. The flight is powerful and agile, with rapid, shallow wing-beats. They range far out over the oceans, usually singly or in pairs. They feed on fish, squid, etc., taken by a twisting vertical plunge or off the surface, often at night. Near nest sites on islands and coastal cliffs they indulge in noisy screaming chases. The nest is a shallow scrape in a crevice, or under a rock or bush, preferably on a cliff or slope to aid take-off. One egg is laid.

### Red-billed Tropicbird    *Phaethon aethereus*

Red-billed Tropicbird

**World:** *P.a. indicus* breeds in Red Sea, Gulf of Suez, and from Somalia across to Arabian Gulf. Other races in Atlantic and Pacific Oceans.
**Oman:** Local breeding resident, in small numbers, dispersing far out to sea when not nesting; common off Dhofar during the SW monsoon.

51cm/20in (excl. white tail-streamers). Distinguished at a distance from gulls and terns by very white form, black bar at base of upper-wing and steady, rapid wing-beat and glides. The *adult* has a little black from bill to eye, fine black lines on the back, and black outer primaries. The bill is coral-red or orange. In the *juvenile* the crown and nape is spotted black, the back is more closely barred and there is more black on the primaries; the central tail-feathers are not long, and the bill is dull yellow or greenish. The **White-tailed** (or Yellow-billed) **Tropicbird** *P.l. lepturus* [45cm/18in, breeds in S Indian Ocean then wanders, unlikely to reach Oman] differs in its *adults'* unlined back and orange-yellow bill; but the *immature* is very similar to the *immature* Red-billed Tropicbird.

*adult* A

*juvenile* B

White-tailed Tropicbird
*adult* C

Pelagic, but when nesting comes to coastal cliffs and slopes, particularly on islands, where it is most often seen in morning or evening in aerial chases. The flight is rapid and parakeet-like, some birds gliding with wings raised in a V, calling a shrill *screeee-scree-scree-scree* and *screeee-kikikiki-scree*; occasionally a bird will swoop up to visit the nest scrape, in a crevice or under a boulder or other cover. It nests throughout the year, but dates of presence and peaks of laying differ between localities.

# PELICANS: Pelecanidae

**World:** 7 species. **Oman:** 1 species. Unmistakable, with a huge body and very large bill. In full adult plumage all but two species are white, with dark flight-feathers, but the confusing brown immature plumage is retained for at least a year. Plumage of sexes similar, females smaller. Tail and legs short; toes webbed. They waddle heavily on land, but fly and soar remarkably well on long broad wings with head and neck retracted; they also perch. Frequent shallow waters of inland lakes, creeks and coast, resting on shore for long periods. Gregarious, most species feed in flocks on the surface, mainly on fish. Food is retained briefly in the distensible gular pouch. Usually silent in winter quarters.

### White Pelican    *Pelecanus onocrotalus*

White Pelican

**World:** Breeds locally in Africa, SE Europe, W and SW Asia, NW India, south to Iran and formerly to head of Arabian Gulf. Migratory and nomadic.
**Oman:** Scarce irregular visitor between October and May.

140–178cm/55–70in. The *adult* in *winter* is creamy-white, with all-black flight-feathers when viewed from below, and black outer primaries when viewed from above. Eye red, legs flesh-pink. *Juvenile* is mottled brownish, paler below.

*adult* D

Two other species of pelican might occur in Oman: the **Dalmatian Pelican** *P. crispus* [173cm/68in, which breeds in SE Europe and SW Asia and winters commonly in Iraq and S Iran to the Arabian Gulf], and the **Pink-backed Pelican** *P. rufescens* [130cm/51in; a non-breeding summer visitor from Africa to Aden and N Yemen]. *Adult* Dalmatian differs from White in its generally greyer and shaggier plumage, whitish under-wings, yellow eye and grey legs. *Adult* Pink-backed differs from both in its smaller size, grey plumage, vinous-pink back and rump, and brownish flight-feathers. *Juveniles* of Dalmatian and Pink-backed are very similar to *juvenile* White, but the feathers at base of bill end in a concave border, not a point as in White.

Dalmatian Pelican

*adult* E

Capable of soaring and migrating at considerable height, but usually seen flying at sea-level and occasionally resting on the surface; also seen occasionally resting on the coast and banks of creeks and fishing in shallow waters, singly or in small parties.

56

Plate 5

# GANNETS and BOOBIES: Sulidae

**World:** 9 species. **Oman:** 2 species (1 breeding). The name 'booby' is generally applied to the six tropical and sub-tropical species because they allow close approach by humans. Large, goose-like sea-birds, with slim silhouette, long pointed wings and tail; long stout bill, and thick neck outstretched in flight. Plumage of sexes is similar; females are larger. The skin of the face and chin is bare and coloured. Adult plumage is attained in 2–4 years. The short legs, webbed feet and long wings make take-off from land difficult. Flight is fast, often close to the sea surface and direct like a cormorant; they also soar well. They plunge in clear water from heights of up to 30m for fish and squid, pursuing briefly underwater, when they may occasionally foul fish nets. Adults usually stay within a few hundred miles of their breeding-ground but immatures sometimes disperse great distances.

## Brown Booby        *Sula leucogaster*

Brown Booby

**World:** *S.l. plotus* breeds in the Pacific and Indian Oceans, also in the Gulf of Aden, Red Sea and Gulf of Suez, wandering outside the breeding season. Other races in Atlantic and Pacific Oceans.
**Oman:** Vagrant, (one, Kuria Muria Bay, 4 August 1963; one immature off Taqah, 22 February 1980; one off Salalah, April 1980); other reports suggest confusion with juvenile Masked Booby.

74cm/29in. Dark chocolate-brown above, reaching to the neck and upper breast; the primaries are blackish, the tail darker brown, the under-wing is brown with a distinct white median streak, the rest of the under-parts are white. The bill and feet are yellowish, and the facial skin turquoise. The *juvenile* is dark brown, with the pale belly usually contrasting with the dark upper breast. The *adult* differs from the rather similar *juvenile* Masked Booby in its brown upper breast and lack of white collar; from the brown-phase Red-footed Booby (see under Masked Booby) in dark tail-feathers; and from the smaller Sooty Gull in distant views in shape and behaviour. Its habits are rather similar to those of the Masked Booby.

*adult* C

*juvenile* D

## Masked Booby (Blue-faced Booby)        *Sula dactylatra*

Masked Booby

**World:** *S.d. melanops* breeds on islands off E Africa, S Red Sea, Socotra to E Arabia, and in SW Indian Ocean, and wanders outside the breeding season, the immature more widely than the adult. Other races in Atlantic and Pacific Oceans.
**Oman:** Resident and abundant breeding visitor on Kuria Muria Islands, occasional visitor off all coasts.

86cm/34in. The *adult* is white (hence 'White Booby'), except for the contrasting blackish on wings and tail. The bill is yellow, sometimes greenish, and the mask of bare skin on the face blue-black. The legs are blue-grey or greenish. The *young* bird is born naked and dark-skinned, becoming downy-white, and on fledging brown above except for a white collar and darker tail; the brown reaches the lower neck; the under-wing is whitish bordered with brown, the rest of the under-parts white; in the latter plumage it is easily confused with the adult Brown Booby, but it differs in the white collar, the white lower neck, and the fact that the white in the under-wing is not in a distinct median line. The *immature* becomes whiter with age. The *adult* differs from the white phase **Red-footed Booby** *S. sula rubripes* [41cm/26in, breeds on islands in S Indian Ocean and Pacific, wandering to Red Sea, Suez, Gulf of Aden, S Arabian Sea] in that species' smaller size, red feet and white tail and secondaries.

*adult* A

*immature* B

It is readily distinguishable at a distance as a booby by its large size, shape, colour, flight and height of plunge after fish, though it may also dive obliquely into shallows. Sometimes seen at sea perching on driftwood. It nests in thousands March–October, approximately annually, on a scrape on bare sand, gravel or rock decorated with gravel. 1–3 eggs, usually 2, but only one chick usually survives. At the breeding-ground the male's whistling *wheeoo* or *fweeoo* or *sweeoo* differs from the female's goose-like *ghaa* or *haa*.

Plate 6

# CORMORANTS: Phalacrocoracidae

**World:** 31 species. **Oman:** 2 species (1 breeding). Fairly large, mostly dark, aquatic birds, with long necks, elongate body and long, stiff, pointed tail; some minute white feathers (filoplumes) on head and body in early breeding plumage. The young are browner, with pale under-parts. Plumage of sexes is similar, males larger. Legs set far back, tarsus flattened and toes webbed. Bill long, straight with a terminal hook. Their food is mainly fish obtained by flopping on to the surface, then diving and pursuing under water. They swim low on the surface, bill up-tilted. They take off with a pattering run and fly strongly, with bowed wings, alternating with glides, and with long neck outstretched; usually in groups in V or echelon, when they are occasionally mistaken for geese or cranes. They stand upright on land or artifacts; some perch on trees. Sometimes they extend their wings at rest. Gregarious; most breed colonially; many species migrate. Some species (not in Oman) are called 'shags'.

## Socotra Cormorant    *Phalacrocorax nigrogularis*

Socotra Cormorant

**World:** Breeds in at least two populations, one on islands in Arabian Gulf in winter, others off SE Arabia in summer. Locally migratory, reaching W India and E Africa.
**Oman:** Common visitor locally in Musandam, mostly in spring and summer; common breeding resident locally off Dhofar, some reaching Masirah when not breeding.

76cm/30in. Smaller than Great Cormorant, with a shorter tail and more slender bill, the *breeding adult* is glossy black, the mantle-feathers dark bronze-green tipped black; before breeding it has white filoplumes on head, hind-neck and rump; the bill and facial skin are dark. The *nestling* is naked, becoming downy greyish-white. The *juvenile* has noticeably pale brown upper wing-coverts and is whitish below; the skin of the face is dull yellowish, the bill pale brown or greyish. The *immature* and *non-breeding adult* (to 3rd or 4th year) are browner. The *adult* differs from the Great Cormorant also in lack of yellow round the gape and lack of white in face and on thighs, and is often browner.

*adult breeding* E
*adult winter* F
*juvenile* G

In large and often immense roosts on coastal cliffs and rocky islets such as Hamar an Nafur; occasionally in huge flocks offshore. In large movements they fly in lines or echelon, usually close to the surface, with occasional undulations; large feeding movements can be mistaken for migration. When a suitable shoal of fish is seen the birds circle low, drop on to the water in a flock and dive, those surfacing at the rear of the flock flying to the front. Very shy, they avoid flying overland. Occasionally hold wings above body when at rest on water or land. They breed in dense colonies, nesting in bare scrapes on sand or gravel, on the level, on mounds or on hill slopes – on some islands, e.g. Kuria Muria, from late June to October. 2 or 3 eggs are laid, which are whitish, tinged with blue.

## Great Cormorant    *Phalacrocorax carbo*

Great Cormorant

**World:** *P.c. sinensis* breeds across Eurasia to Far East, incl. N Iran, India. *P.c. lucidus* (*=lugubris*) breeds in the southern half of Africa north to Ethiopia. Sedentary and migratory. Other races in N America, W Europe and Africa.
**Oman:** *P.c. sinensis* is a regular winter visitor locally in very small numbers October–March, occasionally in other months; occurs on passage in the desert interior in autumn, but rarely in spring. The status of *P.c. lucidus* is uncertain; possibly it is a regular visitor to Dhofar and a vagrant to N Oman (one obtained near Muscat, 19 December 1951).

*P.c. sinensis* 81cm/32in. A large, dark cormorant. The *adult* is blackish, with a metallic sheen and bronze centres on feathers of upper-parts; face and chin white; skin round eyes and gape bright yellow; *from January until early spring* it develops some white filoplumes on head and neck and a conspicuous white oval patch on each thigh. The *juvenile* is dull brown above, pale whitish below, with yellow skin round the eyes and gape. The *adult* differs from the Socotra Cormorant in its larger size, longer tail, darker plumage, white and yellow in face, white throat, white patch on thigh (not in *winter* or on *immature*) and in the hand in its chin-feathers' ending in a point.

*adult winter* B

*adult breeding* A
*juvenile* C

Frequents shallow coastal waters, fishing in flocks and perching upright on rocks, wrecks, trees, etc. Unlike the Socotra Cormorant it will fly overland, giving rise to reports of geese and cranes.

*P.c. lucidus (P.c. lugubris)* 79cm/31in. Similar to *P.c. sinensis,* but smaller, greener and usually with white from chin towards breast, but amount of white varies between individuals, and some are black as in *sinensis*.

*adult P.c. lugubris* D

60

Plate 7

# BITTERNS and HERONS: Ardeidae

Plates 8–12

**World:** 76 species. **Oman:** 14 species (2 or 3 breeding). **Herons** (Ardeinae) are slim wading birds, with a long kinked neck, long legs, toes and bill and long, broad wings, but a short tail. The neck is usually retracted at rest and in sustained flight, not extended as in cormorants, storks, ibises, spoonbills and flamingos. The feet extend beyond the tail in flight. Plumage of sexes is generally similar; some species in breeding condition have ornamental plumes on head, neck and scapulars, and the bare parts flushed brighter. Feed on fish, crustaceans, etc., by wading, stalking, chasing or waiting in or near edge of shallow water (Goliath Heron in deeper water and Cattle Egret more terrestrially), mostly in the open, often at dusk, some species nocturnally. Gregarious at roosts and in breeding season. Many are nocturnal migrants. **Bitterns** (Botaurinae) differ in their stouter build, shorter neck and legs, more solitary and crepuscular behaviour and cryptic colouration. Generally feed in dense vegetation, particularly reed beds in fresh or brackish water. They frequently perch on reeds, clutching the stems. When alarmed, typically adopt an erect 'freeze' posture.

## Night Heron (Black-crowned Night Heron)     *Nycticorax nycticorax*

Night Heron

**World:** *N.n. nycticorax* breeds locally in Africa, southern Eurasia, incl. Iraq, Iran, India, across to SE Asia; northern birds migrate, reaching Africa and SE Asia.
**Oman:** Passage migrant and winter visitor July–April, occasionally May–June, singly or in parties of 40 or more; at inland roosts in winter.

61cm/24in. A medium-sized heron, but hunched and short-legged. The *adult (breeding)* has a distinctive contrast of grey and white, with glossy black on crown, nape and back, and white plumes from the nape. *Immature* birds are dark brown above, the 1st-year bird covered in pale streaks and spots which are lost later; the under-parts are boldly streaked brown on a paler background. The *immature* differs from the Bittern in smaller size, pale (not black) spots, lack of dark crown and moustache. See Little Green Heron (plate 9).

*adult* E

*Immature* F

Roosts by day in thick bushes or trees, sometimes away from water. At dusk, flights singly or in succession to shallow fresh or salt water in marshes, creeks, streams or pools, where it feeds on small fish, toads and invertebrates. The call in flight is an occasional loud *kuwark* or *kwuk*.

## Bittern     *Botaurus stellaris*

Bittern A

**World:** *B.s. stellaris* breeds in NW Africa and across temperate Eurasia; sedentary and migratory, reaching Africa, Arabia, Iran, N India, SE Asia. Another race in southern Africa.
**Oman:** Very scarce passage migrant and winter visitor, September–February.

76cm/30in. The largest bittern, but seldom seen unless disturbed or watched for at dusk. Differs from immature Night Heron in larger size and heavier build, being golden brown with black mottling and barring, and having darkly barred wings in flight, black crown, nape and moustachial-streak. Below, it is pale buff, streaked tawny and black.

It is solitary and secretive, roosting off the ground in a bush or low tree near fresh or brackish water. At dusk it moves out, flying heavily on broad, round-tipped wings, sometimes calling with a deep *aark* or *awk,* to feed during a slow walk in or near dense reeds, mangroves, etc., on fish, reptiles, small mammals and invertebrates. It sometimes feeds by day.

## Little Bittern     *Ixobrychus minutus*

Little Bittern

**World:** *I.m. minutus* breeds in N Africa, W and central Eurasia, south to Near East, Iraq, Iran, NW India; migratory, most wintering in Africa.
**Oman:** Uncommon passage migrant August–October and March–May; some over summer, occasionally in winter; may breed.

36cm/14in. The smallest heron of Oman reed-beds, with distinctive wing-patches. The *adult male* is blackish above, except for the brown face and neck and the very pale wing-patch. In the *adult female* the black is replaced by dark brown and the wing-patch is rather indistinct. The *immature* is dark brown above, the feathers edged rufous; below, it is pale white and buff, streaked darker.

*adult male* B
*adult female* C
*immature* D

Stalks on and amongst dense reeds at creeks, pools and streams, where it is difficult to see when still. More active at dusk, and in the breeding season by day, flying rapidly then gliding into cover. The nest, from May(?), is a lined pad of plant stems in reeds above water. 4–10 white eggs are usually laid. When breeding the male utters a long series of single croaks at intervals of about a second.

Plate 8

**Little Green Heron** (Striated or Green-backed Heron)     *Butorides striatus*

**World:** Breeds in parts of America, Africa, Arabia, Arabian Gulf, Indian Ocean, India to Far East, Australasia, Pacific Ocean, in several races.

**Oman:** Fairly common breeding resident or partial resident; some passage occurs, particularly in autumn.

46cm/18in. A rather furtive heron, appearing very small, dark and often bittern-like. *Adult (summer)* has a greenish-black crown and pointed plume; a white line extends behind the eye, the rest of the upper-parts are dark grey tinged olive, the wing-coverts have pale fringes and the long scapulars cover the very short tail; below, buffish-white from chin to centre of breast, remainder grey, the belly and thighs sometimes buffish. When *breeding,* the legs and the naked skin before the eyes flush from grey, brown or green to orange-red, and the black and green bill becomes black. The *juvenile* is dark brown above, with buff streaks and spots; buffish-white below, boldly streaked dark brown. See Night Heron (plate 8).

Usually most active at dusk, but easily overlooked. It hunts in a crouched attitude, creeping, waiting, then lunging at fish and crabs in creeks, on coasts, rocks, harbour walls, etc.; usually in shade by day. The flight is low with slow wing-beats, the long bittern-like neck sometimes outstretched, the body looking plump, the feet protruding beyond the tail. It nests from March on a small platform of twigs, roots, etc., sparsely lined with feathers, chiefly under and amongst boulders, sometimes in mangrove trees. The 2–4 eggs, usually 2, are pale greenish-blue. The call is a loud, explosive *kyowk* or *chyowk,* sometimes repeated.


**Squacco Heron**     *Ardeola ralloides*

**World:** Breeds in S Europe across to W Asia, incl. Iraq and Iran, also southern Africa, Madagascar. Migratory, reaching S Africa.

**Oman:** Regular passage migrant, mostly in autumn, and winter visitor, between late August and April; some over summer in Dhofar.

46cm/18in. A small stocky heron, appearing mostly buff when at rest, but mostly white in flight. The head, neck, breast and mantle warm yellow-buff, the wings, rump and tail white. The *adult (summer)* has long head-plumes streaked black and white; in *winter* the plumes are shorter, the mantle brown, the neck streaked blackish. The *juvenile* lacks the head-plumes, and the mantle and scapulars are rusty brown. Distinction from the very similar Indian Pond Heron is often difficult, even in the hand, but *adults* differ in the black streaked plumes, the paler browns and the lack of grey on the head and neck.

Although more active at dusk it may be seen by day at fresh-water pools, reed-beds, marshes, in the open, and less often within mangroves, searching or waiting for insects, fish, toads and crustaceans.


**Indian Pond Heron**     *Ardeola grayii*

**World:** Breeds in SE Iran, India, Sri Lanka, Indian Ocean islands and Burma. Said to be mainly resident.

**Oman:** Regular passage migrant and winter visitor in small numbers, late August to May.

46cm/18in. The dark brown mantle at rest contrasts with white of wings, rump and tail in flight. The darker or greyer browns, the absence of black streaks in the bird's head-plumes and its preference for mangroves in winter help distinguish it from the adult Squacco Heron. The *adult (summer)* is distinctive, with cream head-plumes, deep maroon mantle and grey-brown head and neck. *Winter* and first *summer* birds lack the head-plumes, and have dark brown mantle and white upper-breast streaked brown. The older *immature* is very similar to the immature Squacco, but streaking on throat and breast is bolder dark brown on grey-buff, the back slightly darker. The bill of the *breeding adult* is greenish-yellow boldly tipped with black, much like the Squacco's.

In winter quarters it is generally rather shy, frequenting mangroves or reeds. It hunts at the water's edge, often retreating into cover if disturbed, or flying, with neck partly outstretched like the Little Green Heron. Its food is mainly crabs and other invertebrates, fish and toads.

Little Green Heron

*adult breeding* A
*adult non-breeding* B

*immature* C

Squacco Heron

*adult summer* D
*adult winter* E

Indian Pond Heron

*adult summer* G
*adult winter* F

64

Plate 9

## Western Reef Heron    *Egretta gularis*

**World:** *E.g. schistacea* breeds on coasts of Red Sea, Gulf of Aden, Arabia and Gulf, to India, Sri Lanka, Laccadives.
**Oman:** Partial resident, local and not numerous; common passage migrant and winter visitor, largest numbers September–October in N Oman and Masirah, fewer in Dhofar; a few non-breeding birds over summer.

61cm/24in. The common coastal heron in Oman. Two colour morphs, one all-white, the other grape-blue with white chin and throat; intermediates occur infrequently, usually white with dark marks, only rarely dark with white marks. Bill thick, dull greenish-yellow appearing dark in poor light; yellow to orange when *breeding*. Legs very varied, yellowish, greenish or blackish, with lower tarsi, toes and soles yellowish. White-phase differs from Great White Egret in smaller size, yellowish feet, and crown-plumes in *summer;* grey-phase differs from Grey Heron in smaller size, lack of black, lack of white on crown and under-parts. See Little Egret.

*white phase winter* A
*dark phase winter* B
*intermediate* C

Coasts, creeks and marshes, occasionally inland. Not gregarious except on passage and at roosts on shores, trees, boats, buoys. Fish, etc., are taken by stalking or dashing about with wings held out or flicked. Nests on islands and in some creeks, April–July, a platform of twigs on mangroves, scrub and cliff-faces, near or over water, colonially or in isolated pairs. 2–4 eggs, pale blue or greenish. Call, *krark* or *chrr.*

## Great White Egret    *Egretta alba*

**World:** Breeds locally from central Europe to Far East and Australasia (incl. SE Iran), Africa and Americas, in several races. Northern populations are migratory.
**Oman:** Regular winter visitor in small numbers, September–May, occasionally in summer. *E.a. alba* has been identified at Muscat; *E.a. modesta* (91cm/36in, Iran, India, E Asia, Australasia, once in UAE, Arabian Gulf) may also occur.

96cm/38in. A large all-white heron, almost the height of the Grey Heron. No head-plumes. Legs black, rarely partly yellow, toes black. Bill bright orange-yellow (black in *breeding* condition). Differs from Cattle Egret, Little Egret and white-phase Reef Heron in larger size, more pronounced slender kinked neck, and behaviour; from last two also in bill colour.

*adult winter* E

Usually at coastal pools, creeks and lagoons; occasionally on shores and at water inland. Usually singly, rarely 25 together. Pace, flight and feeding behaviour more leisurely and stately than smaller herons.

## Cattle Egret (Buff-backed Heron)    *Bubulcus ibis*

**World:** Breeds sporadically in Mediterranean basin, Africa, S Arabia, Iraq, Iran, India, Sri Lanka, Indian Ocean islands to Australasia, also Americas, in two races. Resident, migratory; movements complicated and erratic, sometimes irruptive.
**Oman:** Vagrant or irregular visitor; rarely in N Oman and Masirah; in Dhofar a few in most months, up to 10 over winter in some years.

51cm/20in. A medium-sized stocky white heron, more terrestrial than the others. Differs from other white herons in buff on crown (inconspicuous at a distance); in *summer* also buff on mantle and breast. Differs from Little Egret and white-phase Reef Heron in heavier build, protruding chin (jowl), more sturdy bill (yellow to orange), greenish legs (yellow to reddish in *breeding* condition). See Squacco and Indian Pond Herons (plate 9).

*adult winter* D

At creeks and marshes, but will also follow the plough, search vegetation, and walk amongst and perch on domestic animals for its main diet of insects. Normally gregarious and tree-roosting.

## Little Egret    *Egretta garzetta*

**World:** *E.g. garzetta* breeds in Africa, S Eurasia, incl. N Iraq, N Iran, India to SE Asia. Sedentary and migratory, reaching Africa, Arabia, SE Asia.
**Oman:** Passage migrant, winter visitor and some over summer, in small numbers except for a peak in September.

61cm/24in. Size and plumage as white-phase Reef Heron but differs in slender black bill, black legs, pure yellow toes and slighter build. *Adult* in *summer* has two head-plumes and numerous plumes on upper breast, mantle and scapulars which are reduced in *winter* and absent in *juveniles*. Differs from Great White Egret in yellow toes, small size, black bill in *winter* and head-plumes in *summer;* from Cattle Egret in more graceful form, black bill and legs.

*adult winter* F

Shallow fresh or brackish creeks, marshes and inland streams, occasionally coastal. Wades and searches grassy borders for small fish and invertebrates. Roosts and will fish in flocks, but is often scattered singly.

66

Plate 10

**Purple Heron**    *Ardea purpurea*

**World:** *A.p. purpurea* breeds in Africa and from W Europe to central Asia, south to Iraq, Iran and head of Arabian Gulf; sedentary and migratory, reaching Africa, Arabia. Other races in Madagascar, and from India to Far East.
**Oman:** Occurs in every month; common on autumn passage from July until peak in September, then small numbers until May; occasionally in June.

81cm/32in. Darker, smaller and more slender than Grey Heron, with head and neck chestnut and black, under-parts dark chestnut and black, under-wing appearing dark; differs from Grey Heron in flight in more pronounced bulge of folded neck, slender bill, much darker upper wing-coverts, and toes extending far beyond tip of tail, and from Goliath Heron in much smaller size, black crown in *adult,* brownish-yellow bill and legs. The *immature* is much paler rufous or cinnamon, the dark markings less obvious. Differs from Goliath Heron in much smaller size, black crown and legs in *adult,* paler uniform upper-parts in *immature*.

*adult* C

Shy and often solitary except on passage. Prefers fresh-water marshes, creeks, streams, preferably in or near deep vegetative cover. Roosts on the ground or in bushes. Call is like Grey Heron's, but less deep.

**Grey Heron**    *Ardea cinerea*

**World:** Breeds in most of Eurasia, incl. Red Sea (Dahlak Islands, April), Iraq, W and NW Iran, to India, Sri Lanka, Maldives and SE Asia, also Africa and Madagascar region, in several races. Northern birds migrate.
**Oman:** Regular passage migrant, most in autumn, common in winter, some over summer; *A.c. rectirostris* has been recorded.

96cm/38in. Large, grey and white, with black markings on fore-neck, shoulders, flanks; a black line from eye to nape forms a pendant plume (absent in *winter*). The *juvenile* is paler, the head and hind-neck grey; crown blackish. Differs from larger Goliath Heron and small Purple Heron in size and lack of rufous. Differs from grey-phase Reef Heron in larger size, paler head and under-parts, black flight-feathers on upper-wing in flight. Differs from Black-headed Heron (plate 12) in having head, neck and under-parts white, under-wing blue-grey, larger size, bill yellowish, legs brownish.

*adult* A
*juvenile* B

Marshes, coasts, margins of pools, creeks, streams. Usually solitary, but gathers loosely at roosts on ground, occasionally on trees. More active at dusk. Flies with slower beats than Purple Heron. Migration is mostly nocturnal in small parties. The call is a loud *frarnk,* higher-pitched in young.

**Goliath Heron**    *Ardea goliath*

**World:** Breeds in Africa, Madagascar, SE Iran (Clarence Straits). Wanders to S Arabian coasts, India, Sri Lanka.
**Oman:** Vagrant or very scarce winter visitor, between July and April or May.

142cm/60in. Like a huge Purple Heron and larger than Grey Heron, differing from both in size, ponderous flight, the *adult's* rich chestnut crown without black, huge dark bill and black legs and toes. The *immature* has a duller crown, the upper wing-coverts scaly with broad buff fringes to the feathers, the legs greenish.

*adult* D

The largest heron in the world, shy and usually solitary, frequenting creeks and marshes, standing on mangroves, sandbanks, mud-flats and shores. Roosts under cover of a bank or tall vegetation. The cry is said to be a deep-throated *aark,* like the hoarse bark of a dog (Heuglin).

Plate 11

**Black-headed Heron**    *Ardea melanocephala*

**World:** Breeds in Africa. Sedentary, migratory and nomadic.
**Oman:** Vagrant to Dhofar (one, August–December 1978).

*adult* A

97cm/38in. Somewhat resembles a small, dark slate-coloured Grey Heron, but crown and hind-neck black with contrasting white chin and upper fore-neck; under wing-coverts white (not grey), under-parts dark grey (not white). *Immatures* are dark grey-brown above, buff or brown on the neck, unmarked white below. Differs from dark-phase Reef Heron in greater size, in having more white on the neck and in behaviour.

A solitary bird of open, grassy plains and trees, also creeks, where it hunts large invertebrates and rodents, reptiles and fish. It calls with a loud nasal *kwark*.

**Abdim's Stork**    *Ciconia abdimii*        See family Ciconiidae, plate 14

**World:** Breeds from W to E Africa, S Red Sea (Dahlak), SW Arabia. Sedentary and migratory, mostly to southern Africa.
**Oman:** Vagrant or accidental to Dhofar (a potential breeding visitor?).

*adult* B

76cm/30in. The *adult* at rest has glossy black upper-parts; a black shaggy breast and white belly with a white line showing between shoulder and neck. In flight, shows white lower back, rump and upper tail-coverts; white below, except for the black breast, tail-feathers and most of wings. Bare skin around eyes and throat crimson, cheeks dull blue. Bill grey-green, tipped yellow or red. Legs olive with pink to crimson toes and joints. The *juvenile* is more sooty; bill blackish or dull reddish; legs pinkish-red. Differs from Black Stork – see under White Stork (plate 14) – in smaller size, white on back and dark bill and legs (not bright red).

Small, gregarious storks, these walk fearlessly through cultivation on creek margins and scrubland, searching for grasshoppers and other garden pests, small reptiles, fish, etc. They are fond of soaring very high up, and migrate by night. They roost and nest in trees, occasionally on bushes and buildings. The nest (from May, near Aden) is a large structure of sticks, lined with mud and grass; the eggs, 2–4, are buff or creamy-white.

# CRANES: Gruidae

**World:** 14 species. **Oman:** 2 species. Large, long-necked, long-legged, upright birds of marshy ground. Superficially like herons and storks, but the innermost secondaries extend noticeably over the short tail. Plumage of the sexes is similar, males slightly larger; they may pair for life. Northern species are strongly migratory, flying in flocks in echelon or V formation with neck and legs extended (unlike herons, but like cormorants, storks, etc). They are omnivorous and have sonorous calls. Some species have a ceremonial dance, seen in all seasons.

**Common Crane**    *Grus grus*

**World:** *G.g. grus* breeds from E Europe to W Asia. Migratory, reaching northern Africa, Arabia. Another race in E Asia, migrating SE.
**Oman:** Winter vagrant to Dhofar (3, 16 December 1978, one remaining until February 1979).

*adult* D

114cm/45in, height over 122cm/48in. Large, grey and heron-like, but with a prominent 'bustle' of elongate secondaries over the tail. Head and neck black with a conspicuous white line curving down sides of neck, skin of crown red, flight-feathers black. *Juvenile* has a smaller bustle, and brown head and neck. See Demoiselle Crane.

On shores of creeks and on open cultivation or scrub, in small shy parties. It feeds by day during a slow graceful walk, and congregates to roost on open ground, associating with other cranes in winter. Call, a strident clanging or metallic trumpeting, frequently uttered by migrating flocks.

**Demoiselle Crane**    *Anthropoides virgo*

**World:** Breeds in NW Africa, and from SE Europe to Manchuria. Migratory, reaching Africa, Arabia, India.
**Oman:** Vagrant (one reported seen near Salalah, 4 October 1978).

*adult* C

96cm/38in, height 76cm/30in. Often associates with Common Crane in winter, but differs in smaller size, long white tuft behind each eye, and the facts that the extensive black of the fore-neck falls as a black pointed plume over the breast and the plume formed by the black-tipped secondaries is less bushy, making the tail look longer. The *juvenile* is greyer on the head, and has shorter plumes.

As Common Crane. Feeds on vegetable matter and some invertebrates. On migration flies in V formation; distinguishable when with Common Crane by smaller size and higher-pitched trumpeting *kraw-kraw*.

Plate 12

## IBISES and SPOONBILLS: Threskiornithidae

**World:** 30 species. **Oman:** 3 species. Fairly large gregarious birds, mostly of marshes, lakes and mud-flats. They have long legs, neck and bill, and fly on long, broad wings by alternately flapping and gliding, usually with bill, neck and legs outstretched. They may feed by day or night; they roost on the ground or in trees. The sexes are rather similar, and in some species the face or head and neck of the adult is bare and the skin may be coloured. **Ibises** have long, slim, decurved bills for probing in mud, water and vegetation, where they feed on invertebrates and small vertebrate animals. In **spoonbills** (plate 14) the bill is long and flat, with a spatulate tip for sweeping in shallow muddy water.

### Glossy Ibis    *Plegadis falcinellus*

Glossy Ibis

**World:** Breeds in disjunct colonies in N America, Caribbean, Africa, Madagascar, S Eurasia (including Iraq, Iran, N India) to Far East, Australasia. Sedentary, migratory and nomadic, reaching Africa, Arabia, India.
**Oman:** Passage migrant and winter visitor, in N Oman August–December (under 10 a year); in Dhofar some every month, most in autumn (up to 30).

62cm/24in. Appears uniformly brownish-black, with longish neck and Curlew-shaped down-curved bill. Close views show deep chestnut upper-parts glossed with purple-green. *Adult (winter)* and paler *juvenile* have head and neck flecked whitish. See Bald Ibis.

*adult breeding* A
*adult non-breeding* C
*juvenile* B

Gathers in small flocks on grassy creek margins (occasionally in irrigated cultivation), in shallow water, probing deeply for insects, molluscs, worms and crustaceans. It is not shy in winter quarters. It flies with head and neck drooping slightly, legs extended beyond the tail. Periods of rapid wing-beats are punctuated by long glides, and flocks sometimes undulate, rather like cormorants.

### [Bald Ibis (Hermit Ibis, Waldrapp)    *Geronticus eremita*    (not illustrated)

**World:** Breeds in SE Turkey and Morocco, but declining; possibly also in Red Sea region of NE Africa, or SW Arabia. Migratory and dispersive, movements not well known; has reached Syria, Sudan, Ethiopia, occasionally S Arabia, Iraq. An endangered species.
**Oman:** Unconfirmed sightings at Batinah creeks in October 1962 and October 1967.

76cm/30in. Differs from Glossy Ibis in larger size, heavier red bill, shorter neck, shorter red legs (not reaching end of tail in flight), dull crimson skin of bare head and throat, dark, ragged ruff and a copper-tinted patch on upper-wing. The *young* bird has a dark head and short pale bill and legs.

May be found on cultivated, grassy and scrub ground, near or away from water.]

### Sacred Ibis    *Threskiornis aethiopicus*

Sacred Ibis

**World:** Breeds in Africa, Madagascar, Aldabra, S Iraq. Sedentary, partial migrant and nomadic. Regular in SW Iran, has occurred rarely in Sinai (formerly), S Arabia, Kuwait, Black and Caspian Seas. Formerly resident in Egypt where revered during Dynastic times.
**Oman:** Vagrant; 1 to 4 occasionally visit coastal Dhofar July–November, but might occur in any month.

66cm/26in. Fairly large and distinctively white with contrasting black of the decurved bill and bare head and neck, and the blackish (violet-blue) ornamental 'bustle' of scapular plumes over the lower back; the black tips of the flight-feathers can be seen in flight; some bare skin on the sides of the breast and on the under-wing is grey or dark red. The *juvenile* has the head and neck covered in white and black feathers, less developed scapulars, broader dark tips to the flight-feathers, and paler bare parts.

*adult* D

It feeds in marshes, creeks, cultivation and shore pools on locusts, other invertebrates, reptiles, fish, etc. Gregarious when breeding and roosting (in trees if available) otherwise singly or in small groups. It flies in formation with rapid wing-beats and intermittent glides.

Plate 13

**Spoonbill**   *Platalea leucorodia*

**World:** *P.l. leucorodia* breeds locally off W Africa and across Eurasia, south to Iraq, Iran, India, Sri Lanka; migratory, reaching Africa, Arabia, SE Asia. Another race in Red Sea.
**Oman:** Irregular and uncommon passage migrant and visitor, found singly and in small groups very locally in each month.

86cm/34in. A fairly bulky white bird, with a flat, spoon-shaped tip to the long black bill (hence 'father of the spoon'); it flies with this and the longish neck outstretched. The *adult (summer)* has a buffish patch on the fore-neck and a pendant buff-tinged crest (both lost in *winter*). The *immature* has black tips to the primaries and secondaries, no yellow on the throat, and dull yellowish bill and legs.

Stands for long periods on margins of creeks and mud-flats in compact flocks. It is more active at dusk or at night, walking or running in shallow muddy water, sweeping the bill from side to side, snapping up crustaceans, molluscs and other invertebrates. It flies in line or echelon, with intermittent glides.

## STORKS: Ciconiidae                     Plates 12 and 14

**World:** 17 species. **Oman:** 2 species. Medium-sized to large; heavily built, with long neck, bill and legs. Sexes similar. Gregarious. Most fly with neck, bill and feet extended, and soar well on long, broad wings. Tail rather short. Bill long and sturdy. Perch readily in trees.

**White Stork**   *Ciconia ciconia*

**World:** *C.c. ciconia* breeds in N Africa, Iberia, central Europe to Turkey, Iraq, Iran. Migratory, reaching Africa, Arabia, India. Other races from Turkestan to Far East.
**Oman:** Regular autumn passage migrant across interior and Dhofar in hundreds, August–October, peak September, some pause and occasionally over-winter.

102cm/40in. Large and white except for black flight-feathers, scapulars and greater coverts, and red legs and long sturdy bill. Differs from pelicans and Egyptian Vulture, in distant flight, in having neck and legs extended. **Black Stork** *C. nigra* [97cm/38in, breeds in Eurasia and S Africa; migratory and has occurred in SW Arabia and Arabian Gulf], could also occur in Oman; it differs from White Stork in being completely black except for white lower breast, belly, axillaries and under tail-coverts.

Occurs on cultivation, scrub and marshes, where it walks sedately, searching for locusts, etc., also taken in flight. Flight strong with frequent soaring in loose silent flocks, often at high altitude on passage. Venerated in parts of Middle East for nesting and settling on mosques; once thought to fly to Mecca.

## FLAMINGOS: Phoenicopteridae

**World:** 5 species. **Oman:** 1 species. Large, with very long neck and legs, front toes webbed. The bill is curiously bent to permit filter-feeding in an upside-down position whilst the bird stands or swims. Feed on small crustaceans, molluscs, algae and diatoms restricted to saline or alkaline waters, but may also need fresh water. Sexes similar. Adult plumages white, with some red and black. Flight is fast with neck and legs extended; they run to take off and land. Very gregarious.

**Greater Flamingo**   *Phoenicopterus ruber*

**World:** *P.r. roseus* breeds locally and irregularly in Africa, S Europe, east to Iraq, Kuwait, Iran, Afghanistan, NW India. Disperses widely, reaching Africa, Arabia, Sri Lanka.
**Oman:** Passage migrant and winter visitor in irregular numbers from July, in small and large flocks, some non-breeding birds present throughout the year.

135cm/53in. A tall, mainly white, distinctive wading bird, with very long legs and neck, a thick down-bent pinkish bill, tipped black, and contrasting scarlet and black in wings. The *immature* is smaller; the *youngest and smallest* are dark grey-brown, *older* birds greyish-white with traces of pale pink and dark in wings; bill and legs dull greyish, becoming pink; mature in 3–4 years. Occasionally misidentified as **Lesser Flamingo** *P. minor* [84cm/33in, breeds in Africa, NW India, dispersing and has reached Aden and Mekran], which is much smaller, with shorter, thicker and more goose-like neck, smaller bill appearing uniformly very dark red, shorter and darker red legs, and in *adult* plumage deeper pinks and reds.

Highly gregarious, gathering in some creeks and mud-flats. Call, a goose-like gabble and honking.

Spoonbill

*adult summer* B
*immature* C

White Stork

*adult* A

Greater Flamingo

*adult* D
*immature* E

Lesser Flamingo

*adult* F

Plate 14

# SWANS, GEESE and DUCKS: Anatidae

Plates 15–20

**World:** 142 species. **Oman:** 18 species. A large and very varied family, mostly gregarious and migratory. Aquatic, with short legs, webbed toes, longish necks and broad, flat, round-tipped bills edged with fine lamellae. Wings rather small, usually pointed. Fly with neck extended and rarely glide.

**Swans** are very scarce vagrants in Oman. Large, long-necked, and all-white, immatures with grey-browns to 3rd year. Short legs not extended in flight. Herbivorous. Male is 'cob', female 'pen'.

**Geese** are occasional winter visitors to Oman. Large, heavy, with long necks. Flight is direct and fast. Bill and leg colours help identify the rather similar 'grey geese', which fly in Vs or lines, and have typical flight-calls as well as gabbling notes. Herbivorous.

**Ducks** are migrants to and through Oman, often near coasts in mixed parties. Many cross the desert interior in autumn and winter, commonly in coastal Dhofar. Generally smaller than geese and swans, with shorter legs and neck. Male is 'drake', female 'duck' or 'hen'. When plumage of sexes differs, male has eclipse plumage (moulting late summer), resembling female and immature except for bill colour. Most have a coloured speculum on secondaries, appearing as a bar in flight. Dabbling ducks feed on the surface, or by up-ending in shallow water, rarely diving; they take flight by leaping from the surface. Diving ducks habitually dive and swim under the surface on inland waters feeding on vegetable matter, or at sea on fish, etc.; they patter along the surface to take flight (compare grebes, cormorants, etc.).

## Greylag Goose    *Anser anser*

Greylag Goose

**World:** Breeds from Iceland across Eurasia, south to Iraq, Iran, NW India, in two races. Mainly migratory, reaching N Africa, Iraq, Iran, occasionally Arabian Gulf, Arabia, India, Far East.
**Oman:** Vagrant, or scarce and irregular winter visitor, in very small numbers, from November in some years.

76–89cm/30–35in. A large grey-brown goose. It differs from other likely grey geese in its pale grey fore-wing in flight and not noticeably dark head; bill thick and pink in the eastern race *A.a. rubriros-tris* (orange in the western race *A.a. anser*) without black, nail white; the legs pink, greyish in *immatures*.

*eastern race* C
*western race* B

Marshes, mud-flats, grass, open cultivation. Its flight-call is a resonant *harnk-ung-ung*.

## White-fronted Goose    *Anser albifrons*

White-fronted Goose A

**World:** *A.a. albifrons* breeds in extreme N Eurasia; migratory, reaching Egypt, Iraq, Iran, head of Arabian Gulf, E Arabia, northern India, Far East. Other races, Siberia to Canada, Greenland.
**Oman:** Vagrant or scarce winter visitor (three reports since 1901, in November and December).

66–76cm/26–30in. Darker and smaller than the Greylag; the wings are narrower, the fore-wing brownish; a diagnostic bold white border surrounds the base of the shorter pink bill, and there are heavy irregular dark bars on the lower breast and flanks, both features absent in *juveniles*. Legs orange-yellow. Differs from **Lesser White-fronted Goose** *A. erythropus* [53–66cm/21–26in, breeds in extreme N Eurasia; migratory, reaching Iraq, Iran, head of Arabian Gulf] in that species' smaller size, darker brown colouration, having more white at the base of the smaller bill, extending up the forehead to a point above the eye (absent in *juveniles*), yellow eye-ring, shriller call and quicker rate of feeding.

Marshes, mud-flats, grassland, open cultivation and at fresh water. In flight it can be very agile, and the call is a laughing, high-pitched *kow-kow*.

Plate 15

**Bewick's Swan** *Cygnus columbianus*

**World:** *C. columbianus bewickii* breeds in arctic Eurasia; migratory, reaching Europe, Iran (Caspian), straggling further in cold weather e.g. to E Arabia, Baluchistan and NW India. Another race, the **Whistling Swan** *C.c. columbianus,* in N America.
**Oman:** Vagrant (a party of 10 near Salalah in January and February 1978, one lingering until late July).

122cm/48in. An all-white swan, with rounded head and black-and-yellow bill. The yellow ends behind the nostril, but is variable in extent; in greyish *juveniles* the area is pinkish or white and extends to below or beyond the nostril as in the Whooper Swan. The *adult* differs from the Whooper in its shorter neck, rounder head, and the fact that the yellow of the bill does not extend in a wedge below or beyond the nostril; from the Mute Swan in that species' larger size and the *adult's* red bill.

On creeks, lakes, coastal waters. It feeds on aquatic vegetation by dabbling and up-ending, and it grazes grass and cultivation. Calls a quiet *whoo-woo,* sometimes stronger, also a louder honking. It bobs the head when considering flight.

[The **Mute Swan** *C. olor,* with red bill, and **Whooper Swan** *C. cygnus,* with black-and-yellow bill, are both larger, averaging 150cm/59in, and occur in winter in Iran, straggling rarely to the Arabian Gulf and NW India. There is a record of several unidentified swans near Sohar in early 1960, and of 8 'small swans' there in August 1961.]

**Ruddy Shelduck** *Tadorna ferruginea*

**World:** Breeds in NW Africa, S Spain, SE Europe to E Asia, south to Palestine, Iraq, Iran, Afghanistan. Partial migrant, reaching Egypt, Arabia, India, Far East.
**Oman:** Scarce and irregular passage migrant and winter visitor in very small numbers in some years, between late September and April.

64cm/25in. Large, goose-like and a distinctive orange-chestnut, except for the paler head, black collar of the *breeding male,* black glossed-green tail and flight-feathers, white wing-patch (coverts) and wing-linings (conspicuous in flight). The bill is small and black.

Creeks, marshes and at fresh water, where it feeds on vegetation, grain, carrion, fish, crustaceans, etc. The flight is strong but laboured. Call, a noisy, nasal, goose-like trumpeting.

**Shelduck** *Tadorna tadorna*

**World:** Breeds in W and S Europe, W and central Asia to China, south to Iran, Afghanistan. Sedentary and migratory, reaching N Africa, Arabia, NW India, Far East.
**Oman:** Scarce and irregular passage migrant and winter visitor in very small numbers between October and February in some years.

61cm/24in. Large, appearing black-and-white at a distance. The *adult* is distinctive: white except for the dark green head and upper neck, broad chestnut band round breast and 'shoulders', and black central belly streak, scapulars, flight-feathers and tip of tail. Duller and whiter in eclipse. Bill red, *male* with knob *(breeding)*; legs pink.

Coasts, tidal mud-flats, salt and brackish creeks and marshes, where it digs in mud and dabbles for molluscs, crustaceans, fish and vegetable matter. Its flight is strong, fast and goose-like. Generally rather silent outside the breeding season.

**Mallard** *Anas platyrhynchos*

**World:** *A.p. platyrhynchos* breeds in N America, Iceland, NW Africa, Eurasia, south to Palestine, Iran, Afghanistan; sedentary and migratory, reaching N Africa, Arabia, India to Far East. Other races in Greenland, America and Pacific Ocean.
**Oman:** Regular passage migrant and winter visitor September–April, main passage October–December, in small numbers.

58cm/23in. The largest dabbling duck. The *adult male* is distinctive in full plumage, with green head, white collar, chestnut breast, grey body, black-and-white tail with two black feathers curled up; in eclipse it may be identified by the yellow bill and purple-blue speculum with parallel white borders. The *female* is brown, with a pale supercilium and large speculum; it differs from female Pintail in more bulky form, shorter neck, and white on both sides of speculum; from Gadwall in larger size and speculum colour; from female Shoveler in larger size, longer neck and smaller bill.

On creeks, marshes and locally along the coast, where it finds its mainly vegetarian diet by dabbling and up-ending.

Plate 16

**Wigeon** (European Wigeon)    *Anas penelope*

**World:** Breeds in Iceland and northern Eurasia. Migratory, reaching Africa, Arabia, India, Sri Lanka, Far East.
**Oman:** Regular passage migrant and winter visitor, October–May, in small numbers except in Dhofar where fairly common.

46cm/18in. A medium-sized dabbling duck. The *male* is distinctive, with the chestnut head marked by a pale buff forehead and crown, pinkish-brown breast, grey body and black stern; the white fore-wing at rest shows as a line dividing the grey of the back from the flanks and in flight contrasts with the dark green and black speculum. The *female* is unstreaked rufous brown, but differs from the Mallard in smaller size, small bill, steep forehead, white belly, pointed tail and duller green and black speculum. The grey bill often looks very pale. See Gadwall (plate 18).

*male* A

*female* B

Fresh or brackish creeks, lakes, marshes; also coastal mud-flats. Feeds on vegetation, taken from the surface and by grazing. The male has a characteristic high whistling *wee-oo* or *wip-wee-oo*.


**Garganey**    *Anas querquedula*

**World:** Breeds across Eurasia, including NW Iran. Migratory, reaching Africa, Arabia, India, Indian Ocean islands and Far East.
**Oman:** Common early passage migrant and fairly common winter visitor, with considerable annual variations, August–May, occasionally June, fewer on spring passage.

38cm/15in. A small dabbling duck, larger than Teal, with shorter neck, flat crown and straighter bill. The *adult male* has a distinctive broad white stripe over the eye curving down towards the nape, and brown of breast contrasts with white of abdomen. The blue-grey fore-wing is diagnostic in flight (*female* has grey, Shoveler has bright blue), the speculum is dull green between parallel white bars. The *female* is brown, with a white belly; the head-pattern of dark crown, pale supercilium, dark eye-stripe and pale patch over base of bill distinguishes it from the Teal.

*male* E

*female* F

On shallow creeks, lakes, pools and streams with cover, frequently inland. Invertebrates, small vertebrates and vegetation are taken by dabbling and occasionally up-ending. Flight is very fast, but less erratic than Teal. The male has a rattling call in spring.


**Shoveler** (Northern Shoveler)    *Anas clypeata*

**World:** Breeds in N America, Iceland, across N Eurasia. Chiefly migratory, reaching Africa, Arabia, Maldives, India to Pacific Ocean.
**Oman:** Regular passage migrant and winter visitor, late August to April, in small numbers, varying annually; sometimes common in Dhofar, occasionally to June.

48cm/19in. Another distinctive dabbling duck; thick-set, hunched, with large spoon-tipped bill. The *male's* dark green head often looks black and contrasts with the pale eye; the neck, breast, scapulars and under-wing are white, and the flanks and belly chestnut. Both sexes have a blue fore-wing, divided from the green speculum by a white bar. The mottled-brown *female* differs from the Mallard in its massive bill, green speculum, blue fore-wing (female Garganey has grey) and whitish tail.

*male* G

*female* H

On fresh and brackish creeks, lakes, pools and marshes. It feeds on small crustaceans, molluscs and other invertebrates, etc., by dabbling, by sweeping the bill from side to side in the water and by up-ending.


**Pintail**    *Anas acuta*

**World:** *A.a. acuta* breeds in N America, Iceland, N Africa, across N and central Eurasia incl. Turkey. Migratory, reaching Africa, Arabia, India, Pacific Ocean. Other races in S Indian Ocean.
**Oman:** Regular passage migrant and winter visitor September–March, occasionally August–May, in small numbers except at Dhofar where fairly common.

60cm/24in. A fairly large dabbling duck with slender graceful neck and bill and a long pointed tail. The *male* is distinguished by the white stripe (just visible in eclipse) up the side of the neck from the white breast and belly; the speculum is green to black, bordered buff in front and with a white trailing-edge. The *female* is pale mottled brown with a whitish belly, and differs from the female Wigeon, Mallard and Gadwall in shape, long slender neck, pointed tail and white trailing edge of its speculum.

*male* C

*female* D

Frequents creeks, marshes, pools and coasts, and feeds by dabbling in floating vegetation and up-ending.

Plate 17

**Gadwall**  *Anas strepera*

Gadwall

**World:** Breeds in N America, Iceland, Eurasia, south to Turkey and Iran. Mostly migratory, reaching Africa, Arabia, India, Far East.

**Oman:** Irregular passage migrant and winter visitor between November and early April, scarce or in very small numbers.

51cm/20in. Dull and rather uniform in most plumages. The greyish *male* has a white belly, black tail-coverts (visible at rest), chestnut wing-coverts and a black-and-white speculum. The *female* is like a small Mallard except for the more steeply sloping forehead, white belly, speculum, and orange sides to the dark bill; it differs from the Pintail also in shorter tail and neck. The *immature* resembles the *female* but is spotted below.

*male* A
*female* B

At fresh and brackish reedy marshes, creeks and shallow pools with shore cover. It feeds on vegetation whilst swimming with head under water. The flight is rapid, rather like the Wigeon's, but its general behaviour is more like that of the Mallard.

**[Baikal Teal**  *Anas formosa*

Baikal Teal

**World:** Breeds in NE Siberia south to Lake Baikal. Migratory, wintering south to Far East, wandering to N India, Alaska, etc. Recorded on Abu Dhabi island September–November 1972 ('very tame'); it is popular in captivity in some countries and has escaped often. Not yet confirmed in Oman. (A bird trapped on Masirah Island in October 1976 and initially reported as this species is now thought to have been a Garganey.)

41cm/16in. Larger and more thick-set than Teal. The *adult male* has a distinctive head pattern, drooping scapulars and a vertical white border at each end of the grey flanks. The *female* is like a large female Teal, but with a round white spot at the base of the bill near the gape, and a dark line behind the eye with a broken pale supercilium above it. The *immature* resembles the *female,* but lacks the white spot near the bill. Legs long and grey. (*Formosa* is Latin for beautiful.)

*male* C
*female* D

Mainly on fresh water in marshes, creeks, rivers. It feeds on vegetable matter, especially seeds, sometimes obtained at night, and is gregarious. The flight is like that of Teal, but less swift.]

**Teal**  *Anas crecca*

Teal

**World:** *A.c. crecca* breeds in N America, Iceland, across N and central Eurasia to Japan; mostly migratory, reaching Africa, Arabia, India, Far East.

**Oman:** Regular passage migrant and winter visitor September–April, widespread and fairly common.

36cm/14in. The smallest common duck in Oman. The *male's* dark chestnut head, with a large curving dark green eye-patch bordered with buff, contrasts with the spotted buff breast, grey upper-parts and flanks, white belly and black and buff tail. A horizontal white stripe shows on the grey scapulars. In flight the speculum is green and black between buffish bars fore and aft. The *female* is brown, marked darker above, with whitish belly; it differs from Mallard in small size, whitish belly, speculum; from Garganey in dark fore-wing (not grey), dark neck and larger speculum.

*male* E

*female* F

Prefers fresh-water creeks, marshes, very shallow muddy pools and streams; frequently at water inland; often hidden in low, wet vegetation, from which it jumps into very fast, erratic flight (see Garganey). Like some other species, has been known to dive into water from flight to escape a predator. Feeds mainly on vegetable matter.

**Marbled Teal**  *Marmoretta angustirostris*

Marbled Teal

**World:** Breeds irregularly in NW Africa, S Iberia, Near East, S Turkey, Iraq, Iran to SW Russia and NW India. Sedentary and partial migrant, occasionally reaching Sahara, N and E Arabia, India.

**Oman:** Vagrant (one photographed near Muscat, 19 September 1977).

41cm/16in. A small grey-brown dabbling duck with pale spots on the upper-parts and flanks, and a large, slightly crested head with a dark eye-patch; there is no speculum but the secondaries are paler than the rest of the wing. Sexes similar. The *juvenile* is less heavily spotted.

*male* G

On fresh or brackish pools with fringe cover, feeding in shallow water. Usually very shy, flying for short distances if disturbed.

Plate 18

83

**Pochard**  *Aythya ferina*

**World:** Breeds in Iceland, NW Africa, W Europe to central Asia, south to NW Iran. Chiefly migratory, reaching Africa, Arabia, India to Far East.
**Oman:** Irregular passage migrant and winter visitor between late September and April, in very small numbers, sometimes fairly common over winter in Dhofar.

46cm/18in. A tubby diving duck. The *male* differs from the Red-crested Pochard in its darker chestnut head, grey back and flanks, mostly grey bill with black tip, and pale grey wing-stripe (not white). The *female* has a similar bill and wing pattern, but is rather uniform grey-brown with a pale patch around the base of the bill. See Tufted Duck (plate 20).

Fresh-water creeks, lagoons, lakes, pools. It swims low in the water; dives freely, rarely dabbles and up-ends, and feeds on vegetation, invertebrates and small vertebrates.

**Ferruginous Duck** (White-eyed Pochard)  *Aythya nyroca*

**World:** Breeds locally and erratically in Europe and SW Asia, south to NW Africa, Turkey and Iran. Chiefly migratory, reaching Africa, Arabia, India and Burma.
**Oman:** A late passage migrant and occasional winter visitor between late October and March, in small numbers, mostly in Dhofar.

41cm/16in. A smallish brown diving duck. The *male* has a rich chestnut-brown head and breast, dark brown back and wings and bold white under tail-coverts in flight; its belly and conspicuous wing-bar are white, contrasting with the dark remainder. *Male's* eye is white. *Female* is duller brown and differs from female Tufted Duck in having a more chestnut crown and whiter under tail-coverts.

Creeks, lagoons, pools, marshes, with cover nearby. Rather shy, and it may skulk in dense vegetation. It rides high in the water, usually apart from other species. It feeds on vegetation, some insects and small vertebrates, taken by dabbling, up-ending and diving.

**Red-crested Pochard**  *Netta rufina*

**World:** Breeds from Europe to central Asia, perhaps NW Africa, locally in Iran. Chiefly migratory, reaching N Africa, Iraq, Iran, India, Burma, rarely to Arabia.
**Oman:** Vagrant. (Report of a total of 10 birds on the N Batinah, between 18 November and 15 December 1964.)

56cm/22in. The *male* is distinctive, with bright orange-red, slightly crested head and coral-red bill. In flight it shows white oval flank-patches on the black body and two long wing-bars formed by the white leading edge and white flight-feathers; see Pochard. The *female's* head pattern is also distinctive, and the flight-feathers are almost as conspicuously white as the *male's*. See Common Scoter, (plate 20).

Though a diving duck, it is usually on fresh or brackish creeks, and lagoons, swimming high in the water, and feeding on vegetation by up-ending, dabbling and occasionally diving, and by grazing on land.

Pochard

*male* C

*female* D

Ferruginous Duck

*male* E

*female* F

Red-crested Pochard

*male* A

*female* B

84

Plate 19

[**Common Scoter** (Black Scoter) *Melanitta nigra*

**World:** Breeds in N America, Iceland, extreme N Eurasia, in two races. Migratory, reaching coasts of N Atlantic and Pacific Oceans, straggling to Mediterranean, Black Sea, Caspian Sea. Unconfirmed records in Arabian Gulf in November 1970 and 1971.
**Oman:** Two reports of two black ducks off N Batinah, November 1962 and January 1963, but identity not confirmed.

48cm/19in. A largish diving sea-duck. The *male* is all-black except for a patch of yellow-orange on the bill. The *female* is browner, with a pale patch on the face and upper neck; under-parts mottled paler; differs from female Red-crested Pochard (not a sea-duck) in darker plumage, lack of wing-bar. Differs from Coot (plate 39) in larger size, lack of white in forehead and bill; in flight, in lack of whitish tips to secondaries (but flight-feathers appear paler than coverts); pointed tail might be confused with extended legs of Coot.

Marine, usually on the open sea, off-shore or in creeks. It swims buoyantly with pointed tail raised, but floats lower when alarmed. Gregarious, it forms tight flocks on open water. Food is mostly molluscs, also other invertebrates and small vertebrates, obtained by diving.]

**Tufted Duck** *Aythya fuligula*

**World:** Breeds in Iceland and N Eurasia. Mostly migratory, reaching Africa, Arabia, India and Far East.
**Oman:** Passage migrant and winter visitor between late September and April in very small numbers.

41cm/16in. A smallish diving duck. The *male* is mainly black, with conspicuous white flanks and a pendant crest; in flight the white of abdomen, under-wing and long wing-bar contrasts with the black remainder. The *female* is dark brown to black, sometimes paler on flanks and under-tail (but not as white as the Ferruginous Duck); the short crest is diagnostic when visible; it occasionally has a ring of white feathers round the base of the grey bill. The eye of both sexes is yellow.

On creeks, lagoons, pools, marshes. Usually gregarious and very much like Pochard (plate 19) in habits. It feeds on vegetation, etc., by a jump-dive, rarely up-ending and dabbling.

**Cotton Teal** (Indian Pygmy Goose) *Nettapus coromandelianus*

**World:** *N.c. coromandelianus* breeds in India, Sri Lanka, Burma to East Indies. Partial migrant and vagrant, has strayed once to Iraq and Iran.
**Oman:** Uncommon winter visitor November–May in most years, some occasionally linger into summer; most in Dhofar.

33cm/13in. The smallest duck in Oman, appearing white and black. The very small white head, with a dark crown and a small goose-like black bill, is distinctive. The *male* is white except for a black collar (lost in *autumn*) and dark blackish-brown back, wings, under-wing and under-tail; the upper-parts have a metallic gloss (partially lost in *autumn*). In flight a long sub-terminal white wing-bar adds to the contrast. The *female* is duller, with no collar, a less prominent wing-bar and a dark line through the eye.

On creeks, lagoons, and ponds, usually in rather shy groups, sometimes with other species. It feeds on the surface on vegetable matter and invertebrates, but can dive well. It is clumsy on land, but can perch in trees. The flight is strong, fast and low over the water, sometimes with agile twists and turns.

[Other ducks have been reported in winter south to the Arabian Gulf, some of them doubtfully. The following have occurred and may reach Oman rarely:

**Smew** *Mergus albellus* breeds in N Eurasia; an irregular migrant, reaching SE Iraq, NW and SW Iran, NW India, once to Riyadh (December 1973). 41cm/16in. A diving duck; *male* mostly white, with black eye-patch and two black lines on side of the breast; *female* greyer, with chestnut crown and nape; cheeks and throat white; both sexes with conspicuous white wing-patches in flight; on ponds and coast.

**Red-breasted Merganser** *Mergus serrator* breeds in N America, N Eurasia; migratory, reaching Arabian Gulf, SE Iran, NW India. 58cm/23in. A diving duck with slim red bill; *male* has dark green shaggy head, white collar, dark chestnut breast-band, dark back, grey flanks; *female* has chestnut head and crest, white fore-neck and grey-brown body; both sexes have conspicuous white wing-patches in flight; creeks and coasts.]

Common Scoter

*male* F
*female* G

Tufted Duck

*male* D

*female* E

Cotton Teal

*adult male* A

*adult female* C
*immature male* B

86

Plate 20

## OSPREY: Pandionidae

**World:** 1 species. **Oman:** 1 species (breeding).

### Osprey    *Pandion haliaetus*

Osprey

**World:** *P.h. haliaetus* breeds across Eurasia, south to the Mediterranean basin, Africa, Arabia, and N India; sedentary and migratory, reaching S Africa, Arabia, India, SW Pacific.
**Oman:** A breeding resident, fairly common around Musandam, thinly distributed elsewhere; also a regular and fairly common passage migrant and winter visitor, September–May, some in other months.

56cm/22in. Eagle-like, with long, angled wings and usually seen near water, plunging for fish. Dark brown above, except for white head with broad dark patch through and behind eye to nape; white below except for dusky breast-band, black patches at the carpal joints, black wing-tips and a dark diagonal bar across under-wing. Over land it might be confused with the Short-toed Eagle, but this is larger, with broader paler wings, not angled; Bonelli's Eagle is larger (plate 31).

*adult* A
*immature* B

Perches on cliffs, poles or on the ground, etc., near shallow coastal water and creeks, also at water in desert interior on passage. Flies with deliberate wing-beats, and glides with wings arched above the body like a gull. Feeds only on fish; it dives head-first with feet outstretched forward, then carries prey in its feet to an eating-place. The nest, a large structure of twigs, seaweed, etc., is usually placed high in an isolated position among rocks of coast and islands, but can be on a beach, tree or artifact, used (with alternatives) repeatedly. Pairs return to the nest sites by August and the 2-3 large eggs are laid between October and January. The call is a repeated, high, short *cheeep* or *wew,* also a scream resembling the call of the Red-billed Tropicbird.

## SEA EAGLES, KITES, VULTURES, HARRIERS, HAWKS, BUZZARDS, EAGLES: Accipitridae          Plates 21–31

**World:** 205 species. **Oman:** 31 species. A large, diverse family of diurnal birds of prey. All have hooked bills, powerful feet and claws. Most hunt live prey, but some eagles and all vultures scavenge and take carrion. The broad wings permit fast flight and majestic soaring in some. Plumage varied within species, young of larger species reaching adult plumage after four to six annual moults. Plumage of sexes similar, females usually larger.

### FISH and SEA EAGLES: *Haliaeetus*
This genus includes some of the largest birds of prey, usually near water.

### [Pallas' Fish Eagle    *Haliaeetus leucoryphus*

Pallas' Fish Eagle

Breeds from N Caspian Sea east to Mongolia, south to N India, Burma. Sedentary and migratory, reaching Iraq, Iran (to Arabian Gulf coast now very rarely), also India, SE Asia, not to Oman.

81cm/32in. A huge dark eagle, wing-span 183cm/72in, smaller than the White-tailed Eagle. The *adult* is blackish-brown except for pale head and upper back and breast, and has a broad white band across the centre of its dark, rounded tail; bill dark. The *immature* is brown, feathers fringed paler; tail uniformly dark – very similar to immature White-tailed, but longer, more rounded and with mottling, if present, confined to the base.

*adult* C

Inland marshes, lakes, broad rivers, rarely coasts. Feeds on carrion, fishes, birds, reptiles, small mammals; fish are snatched from surface, some food is obtained by piracy.]

### [White-tailed (Sea) Eagle (Grey Sea Eagle)    *Haliaeetus albicilla*

White-tailed Eagle

**World:** Breeds in Greenland, Iceland, Eurasia, south to Turkey, Iraq, N Iran. Resident and migratory, reaching N Africa (rarely), Arabian Gulf (mostly on coast of Iran), coastal Baluchistan in NW India (rare), Japan, etc.
**Oman:** Possible scarce winter vagrant in the north.

89cm/35in. A massive, dark eagle with huge wings. The *adult* is dark brown except for pale head, neck, upper breast and upper wing-coverts, and has a short wedge-shaped white tail and heavy yellow bill. The *immature* is blackish-brown, with irregular white streaking below and some white in axillaries and wing-linings; the short wedge-shaped tail is dark, with white mottling which increases with age. *Adult* differs from adult Pallas' Fish Eagle in white tail, yellow bill, larger size; *immature* differs in darker colouration and shorter, mottled tail. Differs from vultures in fact that head protrudes further in flight. See Black Vulture (plate 24).

*adult* D
*immature* E

Sea-coasts, inland lakes, large rivers. In flight it is heavy and clumsy; it soars with wings flat like a vulture or heron, but with the head projecting. It feeds on fish taken from the surface, rarely plunging; also on sea-birds, other animals, carrion and items obtained by piracy.]

Plate 21

## KITES: *Elanus* and *Milvus*

*Elanus* are small, grey-and-white hawks with black shoulders, mostly sub-tropical; they hawk and hover for rodents, etc., and nest in trees. *Milvus* are buzzard-sized scavengers with long wings and long forked tails.

### [Black-winged Kite    *Elanus caeruleus*

**World:** *E.c. caeruleus* breeds in Iberia, Africa, Madagascar, S Arabia (formerly), India to SE Asia; sedentary and irregularly migratory.
**Oman:** Birds claimed to be of this species were reported on Masirah in 1944–45 (*Ibis,* 1949, 91: 459–464). Between 18 March and 1 April 1945, five nests were visited; each contained only one chick. Another five nesting pairs were located. It was thought that the unusual behaviour of scavenging on beaches for fish, circling slowly, perching on crags, nesting on ledges without a true nest and laying only one egg were adaptations to the desert environment. However, these habits are those of the Egyptian Vulture (plate 23), which is resident with up to 12 pairs now, but was not reported then. Furthermore, a photograph of a nestling, accompanying the report, is not of that species, but of a larger raptor. The Egyptian Vulture is the most obvious alternative (*Ibis,* 1974, 116: 94). There have been no other reports of the species in Oman; it has therefore been deleted from the list.

33cm/13in. A little larger than the Kestrel, very pale, with black marks, owl-like head and dainty flight. The *adult* is blue-grey above except for white forehead, black fore-wing in flight, appearing as a conspicuous shoulder-mark at rest, and short, whitish tail; below, it is white except for black wing-tips. The *juvenile* is brownish-grey above, the black fore-wing flecked white, breast chestnut. At a distance the colouration could cause confusion with the larger grey harriers.

Open country near trees. It soars, glides and hovers like a Kestrel or harrier, and preys upon rodents, reptiles, small birds, crabs and other invertebrates, taken from a perch, in a hovering descent or stoop, or in falcon-like pursuit. It will quit an area if food fails, and may not return. Nest, in spring, a flimsy twig platform in a tree. Eggs, 2–3, dull white. The call is a high-pitched whistle and chatter.]

### Black Kite    *Milvus migrans*

**World:** Breeds in Africa, Madagascar, Eurasia to Australasia, incl. Near East, Aden, Iran, India, in several races and intermediates. Sedentary and migratory.
**Oman:** Passage migrant and winter visitor in very small numbers; scarce and irregular in N Oman, but regular in Dhofar, with a few seen in all months, and one report of a nest and fledged young, near Salalah, 21 July.

56cm/22in. Distinctive in slow, floppy or swinging flight, with long angular wings usually arched, the long forked tail 'twisted' from time to time and appearing almost straight-tipped when spread. Predominantly brownish, the head paler and streaked, the under-parts more rufous, streaked blackish. The under-wing is usually brown or rufous with a pale patch at the base of the primaries (white in the Indian race *lineatus*). The legs and cere are yellow; the bill small and black (yellow in *M.m. aegyptius* adult). The *immature* is paler and brighter, feathers with pale tips giving a streaked effect; *young* birds may have rufous tails and can be confused with Red Kite, but differ in duller, less reddish plumage, less deeply forked tail and smaller, pale under wing-patch (but consider *lineatus*). See Marsh Harrier (plate 25).

A sociable scavenger, attending habitation, stables, refuse, creeks and occasionally coasts. It feeds on carrion, refuse, live or dead fish, small, sick birds, etc., snatched in the feet from the ground or water surface and eaten in flight or at rest. It roosts in trees. The cry is a distinctive whinnying *kweee-errr,* also other whistles and *ke-ke-ke-ke.*

### [Red Kite    *Milvus milvus*

**World:** *M.m. milvus* breeds in Canary Islands, NW Africa, Europe to SW Caspian; sedentary and migratory, wintering in the Mediterranean basin and rarely to S Caspian and NW India.
**Oman:** Once reported (on Batinah, 28 March 1978), but confirmation of occurrence is desirable.

61cm/24in. The rufous plumage, distinct whitish patch on the under-wing and long deeply forked tail, the fork clearly visible even when the tail is fully spread, should distinguish it from the Black Kite, but see under that species.

Its habits are broadly similar to those of the Black Kite, but its flight is more buoyant and harrier-like, it soars like a buzzard and it takes live prey more regularly.]

Black-winged Kite

*adult* A

*juvenile* B

Black Kite

*M.m.migrans* C

*M.m.aegyptius* D
*M.m.lineatus* E

Red Kite F

90

Plate 22

Medium-sized to huge beneficial scavengers. Mostly dark, the plumage of both sexes is similar, but that of immatures often inadequately known; males are larger. The wings are large and usually very broad; the tail is medium to short. The head is bare, partly bare or downy. They can soar at great height, with the neck retracted into a ruff. They collect at carrion, on which the larger species are dependent. The larger species have a long breeding season, probably not annual. The tree-nesting species are very vulnerable to human disturbance. The genera in Oman include *Neophron*, one species, small and wedge-tailed; *Gyps*, one species, large and brown; and *Torgos*, and *Aegypius*, one species each, both very large and mostly blackish (plate 24).

**Egyptian Vulture**   *Neophron percnopterus*                                               Egyptian Vulture

**World:** *N.p. percnopterus* breeds from S Europe to Turkestan, south to the Atlantic islands, Africa, Arabia, Iraq, Iran to NW India; sedentary and migratory. Another race in India.
**Oman:** Seen throughout the year, numbers fluctuating seasonally. A breeding resident, widespread but not very common, some flocking from July. Also a common passage migrant and winter visitor, with a peak in October and November in N Oman, mainly November at Salalah; lesser numbers over-winter and decrease from February during spring passage, most leaving Salalah by April.

66cm/26in. The smallest vulture in Oman. The *adult* is distinctive, black-and-white in flight, the white       *adult* A
tinged with buff; the head small, face bare yellow to orange-red; bill long, slender, yellow with
blackish tip, giving a pointed flight silhouette. The *immature* (to 6th year) is blackish-brown, becom-       *immature* B
ing paler at each moult; face and bill greyish. The *nestling* is white. The *adult's* black-and-white
pattern can cause momentary confusion with pale-phase Booted Eagle and White Stork. In reflected
light from desert the white may appear as brown as in the much larger Griffon Vulture. Dark
*immatures* can cause confusion with superficially similar dark raptors, but differ in the pointed
wedge-shaped tail, rather pointed wings and pointed head; tail shape may lead to reports of the larger
*immature* **Lammergeyer** (Bearded Vulture) *Gypaetus barbatus* [109cm/43in, resident of high mountains from S Europe across to N India and Mongolia, also Africa and SW Arabia, not in Oman].

In mountains, semi-desert, near habitation and refuse. Not very sociable, but it congregates at food
and roosts. It struts like a domestic fowl (hence 'Pharaoh's Chicken'). The flight is fairly fast, and it
glides and soars well on flat wings with a notable habit of making 'skid turns'. It flies before sunrise to
feed on carrion, offal, manure, etc., and it comes to water regularly if available. The nest, from
February or March, is of sticks and rubbish on a cliff ledge or in a shallow cave or crevice, or, rarely,
on a tree or building, in hills and mountains inland and on coasts and islands; nest sites are re-used and
become stained white. The eggs, 1 or 2, are large, reddish-brown with darker mottles, or buff or dirty
white; incubation period is 42 days and the young fledge in about three months.

**Griffon Vulture**   *Gyps fulvus*                                                          Griffon Vulture C

**World:** *G.f. fulvus* breeds in S Europe, N Africa, Near East, Arabia, Asia Minor to NW India and
central Asia; sedentary and migratory, reaching Africa, Arabia, India. Another race in N India.
**Oman:** Irregular and uncommon passage migrant and winter visitor July–March, occasionally to May.

97–104cm/38–41in. Very large, with distinctive contrasting pale tawny and dark brown plumage. The
wings are broad, about 244cm/96in in span, with bulging trailing edges; the tail is short, rather square
or rounded. The *adult's* white head and neck may be stained darker after feeding; the ruff is creamy-
white. The *immature* (to 4th year) is darker red-brown, the ruff with brown lanceolate feathers.

Mountains and plains, roosting gregariously on cliffs, crags, or trees, or on the ground after feeding. It
soars for long periods high over plains, searching for and descending to feed on carcases of large
mammals. The nest (not confirmed in Oman) is of sticks, etc., on a cliff ledge, colonially. It grunts and
hisses when with others at food.

**[Rüppell's Vulture**   *Gyps rueppellii*                                                   Rüppell's Vulture D

*G.r.erlangeri* breeds in Ethiopia and Somalia; resident and vagrant, reaching S Arabia, reported but
not confirmed in Oman. 95–107cm/37–42in. The size of Griffon, but the *adult* is blackish-brown
above with diagnostic pale spots (fringes to feathers); brown below, with the feathers tipped buff,
forming irregular wing-bars; a dark brown crop-patch is visible in flight. The *immature* has brown
down on the head, a more uniform and darker mantle without spots, and pale streaks below. Habits
like Griffon; see Black Vulture (plate 24).]

Plate 23

**Lappet-faced Vulture** (Nubian Vulture)　*Torgos tracheliotus*　

**World:** Breeds in Africa and Near East. Resident and wanders.
**Oman:** Status uncertain due to confusion with Black Vulture; an uncommon visitor, but possible scarce breeding resident in Dhofar.

96–102cm/38–40in. The second-largest vulture in Oman. The *adult* is very dark brown above, except for the bare head and neck with pinkish-red skin forming lappets; below, the wing is dark except for a whitish streak along the coverts; the body is downy-white, the breast spotted brown, the belly partly concealed by long dark-centred lanceolate feathers (diagnostic) giving a variegated effect, the thighs downy-white and the feet blue-grey. The bill is massive, with nostrils which are vertical slits. The *immature* is like the *adult,* but the skin of head and neck is brownish, flecked with white down; it is darker below, with brown thighs. See Black Vulture.

Open, dry plains and mountains; capable of soaring very high up for long periods. It feeds on carrion, but will also kill birds and invertebrates. Usually in pairs, but it collects at food. It roosts and nests in trees, very occasionally on ledges. The nest, commenced in winter, is a huge structure of branches and sticks, lined with finer material. It lays one egg, probably not annually, dull white, spotted brown; incubation and fledging periods probably similar to those of Black Vulture.

**Black Vulture** (Cinereous Vulture)　*Aegypius monachus*　

**World:** Breeds in parts of Mediterranean basin to Asia Minor, Syria, Iran to N India, Mongolia. Chiefly sedentary, but also a partial migrant, reaching N Red Sea, Arabia, India to Far East.
**Oman:** Uncommon passage migrant and winter visitor, probably regular; in N Oman also a scarce breeding resident.

99–107cm/39–42in. The largest vulture in Eurasia, its wing-span nearly 274cm/108in. The *adult* is brownish-black above; the head is very broad with a huge pale bill, the crown and face black, whitish above eyes and on nape, the neck naked blue-grey, appearing whitish from a distance in some birds; below, it is either similarly dark, or the under wing-coverts, body and thighs are brown, with irregular whitish feathers forming mottling or patches, sometimes with a slight streak near the fore-wing (see Lappet-faced Vulture); the flight-feathers and short, rounded or slightly wedge-shaped tail are blackish. The *immature* is similar to the *adult,* but darker. The feet are always very pale, contrasting with the black tail in flight. The nostrils are almost square. It differs from the Lappet-faced Vulture in darker plumage and in lack of pinkish facial skin, of lappets and of white on thighs; from the Griffon (plate 23) in lack of paler contrasting browns on the wings; from the adult Rüppell's in lack of heavy spotting. Differs from adult White-tailed Eagle (plate 21) in lack of white in tail, and less protruding head in flight, but care is required to distinguish it from immature *Haliaeetus* species (plate 21). See Spotted Eagle (plate 29) and adult Imperial Eagle (plate 30).

Mountains, foothills and plains, also on coasts in winter. It soars and glides for long periods on flat parallel-sided wings, descending to water and to feed on carrion and small animals. Usually in pairs, singly, or in groups at food. On Jabal Akhdar it is said to drop stones (pellets of indigestible remains?). The nest is an enormous structure of branches and sticks on a tree or cliff ledge, lined with smaller material. It lays one egg, probably not annually, white or creamy-buff with rich red-brown marks, incubated for over 50 days; young fledges in three or four months, stays near nest one to two months more. Silent, except for hisses, croaks and yelps at food.

**Verreaux's Eagle**　*Aquila verreauxii*　　　See *Aquila* eagles, plate 29　

**World:** Breeds from Near East to S Africa and S Arabia.
**Oman:** Uncommon resident in Dhofar.

79–97cm/31–38in. A large black eagle with bold white marks and distinctive wing-shape. The *adult* is black above with much white on the upper tail-coverts and in a V up the back (varied in extent), in flight also a large white patch on the upper-wing; black below with a large whitish patch at base of primaries. The inner secondaries of the long wing are short, making the wing remarkably broad-ended. The *juvenile* is pale rufous-brown above, except for a black cheek-patch, the wing-coverts mottled, the rump and lower back white streaked with brown, and the tail and flight-feathers blackish; it is pale brown below, except for black on the breast and a conspicuous white patch at the bend of the under-wing; it becomes blacker in successive moults and differs from the Steppe Eagle (plate 30) also in larger size and heavier bill and feet.

Dry mountains, ranging widely over a large territory, searching for hyrax, hares, birds, reptiles. The flight is powerful and very graceful, often soaring along cliff-edges. At the onset of the breeding season, in October, the male makes spectacular silent aerobatic display flights, sometimes joined by the larger female. The nest, a huge pile of branches and sticks on a cliff ledge or tree, is added to annually; the bird may have alternative nests to use. 1 or 2 eggs, but the second chick has never been known to survive. Call, a shrill *cheep* or whistle, a cluck and a savage alarm-call, *chyow*.

Plate 24

## HARRIERS: *Circus*

Medium-sized raptors, with long wings, tail and legs, small bill, and facial disc bordered by a ruff. All except Marsh Harrier are slender, with narrow wings and buoyant flight, the males grey with black wing-tips, the females and immatures ('ring-tails') brown with narrow white rump. The latter are distinguished only with difficulty in the field, thus limiting most certain evidence of status to males. Flight is leisurely, flapping between long searching glides with head turned down and wings raised in a shallow V, and wavering, checking and pouncing. Roost communally on migration in 'forms' on the ground. Immatures acquire adult plumage in about two years.

### Marsh Harrier    *Circus aeruginosus*

**World:** *C.a. aeruginosus* breeds across W and central Eurasia, south to NW Africa, Palestine, Iraq, Iran; sedentary and migratory, reaching Africa, Arabia, Sri Lanka, Far East.
**Oman:** Passage migrant and winter visitor in small numbers September–April; rarely in May.

48–56cm/19–22in. The largest harrier in Oman, heavier in build and with broader, more rounded, buzzard-like wings than the others, but with similarly long legs and tail. Sexes rather similar in size. The *adult male* is dark reddish-brown, with secondaries and some coverts ash-grey showing as an oblique band in flight, and contrasting with the black primaries; the tail is also ash-grey. It is pale rufous from nape to breast, and the under-wings are pale. The *adult female* is dark chocolate-brown above and dark chestnut-brown below, with varying amounts of pale buff on the cap, throat and fore-wing; some, however, are all dark, and may be confused with Black Kite, dark Buzzard, etc., except for silhouette and behaviour. The *immature* is similar to the *female* but generally darker, with a browner crown.

Usually seen hunting low over reeds, marshes and mud-flats, sometimes over scrub and cultivation, in long wavering glides with wings raised in a shallow V, occasionally flapping, checking and dropping on to birds, reptiles, fish and rodents, which it eats on the ground; it has been seen to devour eggs from a dove's nest on a mangrove bush. It roosts on the ground, not gregariously. The sexes migrate in separate groups.

### Montagu's Harrier    *Circus pygargus*

**World:** Breeds in NW Africa, across temperate Europe to central Asia and NW Iran. Migratory, reaching Africa, Arabia, Sri Lanka.
**Oman:** Scarce passage migrant and winter visitor September–April (based on specimens and male records).

39–46cm/15½–18in. Requires care to distinguish from Hen and Pallid Harriers (plate 26). The *adult male* has a grey head and mantle, the wings broadly tipped black, and a blackish bar across the centre of the secondaries above and below; the rump is pale grey, rarely whitish, and the tail is greyish with lightly barred outer-feathers; it is whitish below, with rufous streaks or flecks on flanks, thighs and under-wing. The *female* has dark brown upper-parts with some rufous feather-edges, a white face contrasting with dark ear-coverts, a narrow white rump, brown tail strongly barred blackish; buff or pale rufous below with brown streaks, the under-wing conspicuously barred, the secondaries either barred or uniformly dark and contrasting with the rest of the under-wing. The *immature* is similar to the *female*, but is darker, with bolder rufous marks above; deep uniform rufous under-parts except for a whitish chin. Both sexes differ from the Hen Harrier in being slightly smaller and slimmer, with longer wings and tail. The *male* is darker than either Hen or Pallid, and has a diagnostic black bar across the secondaries and rufous streaks on the flanks. The *female* is very similar to female Hen and Pallid; best distinguished from Hen by dark ear-coverts and usually narrower white rump, and from Pallid by absence of whitish collar. *Immatures* separable from immature Pallid (which also has unstreaked rufous under-parts) by less prominent eye-stripe and lack of white collar.

Open grassland, scrub, cultivation, etc., in graceful buoyant and typical harrier flight, occasionally hovering. Preys upon reptiles, birds and eggs, grasshoppers and small mammals on the ground. Rests on a mound, post, tree, etc., but roosts in long vegetation, the males often separately.

Marsh Harrier

*adult male* A
*adult female* B

*immature* C

Montagu's Harrier

*adult male* D

*adult female* E

*immature* F

Plate 25

## Hen Harrier    *Circus cyaneus*

Hen Harrier

**World:** *C.cyaneus cyaneus* breeds in NW Africa and across northern temperate Eurasia; sedentary and migratory, reaching S Europe, Iran, N India, SE Asia, rarely to N Africa, Arabia. Other races in N and S America.
**Oman:** Very scarce passage migrant and winter visitor between October and May (based on male sight records only).

43–51cm/17–20in. Requires care to distinguish from Montagu's Harrier (plate 25) and Pallid Harrier. The *adult male* is uniform grey above with black primaries, faint black trailing-edge to wing visible from above and below, and clear white rump; the throat and upper breast are grey, contrasting with white lower breast and belly. Readily distinguishable, even at a distance, from male Pallid by much more extensive black in the wing-tip. The *adult female* is similar to female Montagu's and Pallid but larger and heavier, with broader wings, usually more conspicuous white rump, more conspicuous, almost owl-like facial ruff, and rather uniform face lacking the conspicuous dark ear-coverts of Montagu's and Pallid and the whitish collar of Pallid. The under-wings, including the secondaries, are always heavily barred (secondaries often uniformly dark in Montagu's and Pallid). The *immature* is almost identical to the *adult female,* with buff under-parts heavily streaked brown (uniform rufous-brown in immature Montagu's and Pallid).

*adult male* A

*adult female* B

Open grassland, marshes, coasts, flying high on passage, but mostly seen quartering the ground in search of birds, reptiles, insects, small mammals, etc., like Montagu's though less buoyant in flight. It will occasionally pursue birds, even over water; and will take dead fish from the water or shore. It perches on stumps, posts, etc., and roosts on the ground.

## Pallid Harrier    *Circus macrourus*

Pallid Harrier

**World:** Breeds from E Europe to central Asia, south to NE Iran(?). Migratory, reaching Africa, Arabia, Sri Lanka.
**Oman:** Uncommon passage migrant, occasionally in winter, September–May (based on specimens and male records).

43–48cm/17–19in. The *adult male* is strikingly pale, with white forehead, supercilium and face, pale grey mantle and wings, a narrow wedge of black in the wing-tip, pale grey rump, grey tail with white outer feathers faintly barred grey; white under-parts. *Adult female* and *immature* are very similar to female and immature Montagu's Harrier, and difficult to distinguish in the field. More lightly built and graceful than Hen Harrier, with more pointed wings, and usually with a narrower white rump-patch; the under-side of the secondaries may be barred, or uniformly dark as in Montagu's (always barred in Hen). The *immature* is uniformly chestnut-buff below like immature Montagu's, but frequently appears somewhat paler. Only safely distinguished from Montagu's by facial pattern; both *adult female* and *immature* have a more prominent white supercilium, dark line through the eye, whitish cheek, and a whitish collar behind the black crescent on the ear-coverts.

*adult male* C

*adult female* D

Open grassland and desert scrub, with behaviour similar to Montagu's and Hen Harriers. In autumn passage the males appear after the females and young birds; in spring they may display and pair *en route.*

Plate 26

99

# HAWKS: *Accipiter*

*Accipiter* and near relatives specialise in hunting birds and other animals amongst trees in dextrous flight on short rounded wings and long tail. Small to buzzard-sized, the female usually much larger than the male, the legs usually long and slender.

## Goshawk    *Accipiter gentilis*

Goshawk

**World:** Breeds in N America, Eurasia, south to NW Africa, N Iran (?), NW India, in several races. Sedentary and migratory, reaching Egypt, E Arabia, S Iran, N India, N Burma.
**Oman:** Vagrant or scarce winter visitor to N Oman (reported once in December), but status requires confirmation.

48–61cm/19–24in. Resembles a female Sparrowhawk (male about the same size, but female the size    *adult female* C
of Honey Buzzard, plate 28) with short broad wings and long barred tail, but legs and tail comparatively shorter. *Adult* is dark brown above, with a white supercilium and dark ear-coverts; the underparts are whitish, finely barred with black-brown, the under tail-coverts white. The tail is dark brown,    *immature* D
strongly barred, with rounded tip (not straight as in Sparrowhawk). The *immature* is paler rufous-brown above, and buff below with bold brown drop-marks or streaks (not bars). It differs from other birds of prey (except the Sparrowhawk) in more uniform under-parts, short, broad, blunt wings (which may appear pointed in fast flight) and (except kites, harriers, Honey Buzzard) in longer tail.

Though usually hunting amongst trees in fiercely agile Sparrowhawk manner with frequent long glides, it appears heavier, with slower, falcon-like wing-beats. It occasionally circles and soars with some wing-beats and the tail spread. Unlike the Sparrowhawk it sometimes stands on an exposed post or branch awaiting prey, which is any bird or animal up to its own size or larger.

## Sparrowhawk    *Accipiter nisus*

Sparrowhawk

**World:** *A.n. nisus* breeds from Europe to central Asia, south to NW Iran; sedentary and migratory, reaching NE Africa, Arabia; most spring migration is over W Arabia in April. Other races in Atlantic islands, NW Africa, Mediterranean, E Asia.
**Oman:** Regular passage migrant and winter visitor October–April in small numbers.

28–38cm/11–15in. A lightly-built bird-hawk, with short broad wings, long, dark-barred, straight-tipped tail, long yellow legs, and yellow to orange eyes. *Adult male* is uniform dark grey above, usually    *adult male* B
with a small white nape-patch, and rufous ear-coverts; it is closely barred pale rufous below, with whitish chin and under tail-coverts. *Female* is larger, near size of male Goshawk, browner above; paler    *adult female* A
below, with strong brown bars. *Immatures* are usually brown above, with broader bars and drop-marks below; the iris is greenish, becoming yellow.

In or near thick trees and cultivation on plains and in wadis. As with other predators of birds its presence may be indicated by noisy mobbing by other birds. The hunting flight is low and fast, with frequent glides, weaving between trees, pouncing on birds, mammals and insects, then swooping up into a tree. Soars with occasional wing-beats and may then be confused with Kestrel. (See Levant Sparrowhawk.)

## [Levant Sparrowhawk    *Accipiter brevipes*    (not illustrated)

Breeds from SE Europe to Volga R and Iran. Migratory, but movements little-known; has occurred in E Africa, Near East, Arabia incl. Bahrain. In Oman probably overlooked on passage or in winter. 33–38cm/13–15in. Both sexes paler than Sparrowhawk, with more pointed wings, whitish under-wing with black tips, and red-brown iris. *Adult male* is distinctive, pale blue-grey above, with grey ear-coverts; whitish suffused with pinkish-buff below, unbarred central tail-feathers. *Immature* more heavily spotted and barred below, with dark throat-streaks. Habits as Sparrowhawk; flight said to resemble that of Collared Dove (plate 70).]

## [Dark Chanting Goshawk    *Melierax metabates*

Dark Chanting Goshawk

*M. metabates ignoscens* breeds in SW Arabia east to Shabwah, S Yemen, a partial resident; reports from Dhofar need confirmation. 38–50cm/15–20in. A large grey goshawk with long orange legs. *Adult* dark grey above except for black primaries, secondaries and upper tail-coverts speckled white    *adult* E
and dark grey, appearing pale in flight; throat and breast grey, belly and flanks closely and finely barred dark grey and white; central tail-feathers dark grey, rest banded black-and-white, broadly tipped white; cere orange. *Immature* is browner. Stands upright on exposed perch in scrub country with    *immature* F
tall trees, awaiting reptiles, birds, etc., or chasing them like Sparrowhawk. Nests in a fork of a thick tree in spring. Call, a prolonged musical fluting note.]

100

Plate 27

101

## BUZZARDS: *Pernis* and *Buteo*

*Pernis,* a buzzard-like genus with the lores densely feathered as protection from the stings of bees and wasps; a small head and longish, unusually barred tail. *Buteo,* true buzzards, have small heads, broad wings and rounded tails, varied brown plumage and more soaring flight.

### Honey Buzzard    *Pernis apivorus*

Honey Buzzard  A

**World:** Breeds across Europe to central Asia, south to Asia Minor, N Iran. Winters in tropical and southern Africa.
**Oman:** Vagrant or very scarce autumn passage migrant (five reports between September and December in N Oman).

51–58cm/20–23in. Rather like the Steppe Buzzard, but with a different silhouette caused by the smaller head protruding on a longer neck, the wings longer and comparatively narrower, the tail longer with double dark bar near the base and a dark tip. The *adult* above is usually dark to greyish-brown, sometimes flecked white; individuals vary below from a typical white ground strongly barred and blotched blackish, with dark wing-tips, trailing edges and carpal patches, to very pale or very dark brown with pale primaries; the iris is orange-yellow. *Immatures* are usually dark brown above, but some have the head and rump very pale, and whitish tips to feathers of the mantle; below, either dark, pale or intermediate, all have dark carpal patches, the tail showing more bars than the *adult;* the iris is dark.

Prefers trees and open ground near them. Flies with deep wing-beats, and soars on flat wings. It feeds on the larvae of honey-bees and wasps, also on other invertebrates and small vertebrates, usually on the ground.

### Buzzard    *Buteo buteo*

Steppe Buzzard  B

**World: Steppe Buzzard** *B.b. vulpinus* breeds from NE Europe to central Asia; strongly migratory, reaching southern Africa, Arabia (mostly in west), India. Other races in W Europe, Asia Minor, N Iran, Socotra, E Asia to Japan.
**Oman:** Scarce passage migrant September–October and March–April, occasionally over winter; confusion is possible with the more common Long-legged Buzzard.

51–56cm/20–22in. Plumage very similar to that of Long-legged Buzzard, with a variety of colour-phases, mostly rufous (more so than in larger W European race *buteo*), but a little smaller, slighter build, with shorter wings and shallower wing-beats. The *adult* is usually dark grey-brown above with some rufous, but some have pale heads; below, the streaks and blotches vary from pale rufous to brown, sometimes with dark upper breast or thighs, the under-wing rather similar to Long-legged but usually duller, the carpal patch not so obvious; the tail is rather pale and usually faintly barred near the tip, unlike adult Long-legged. The *immature* is indistinguishable in the field from Long-legged immature, except by its build.

Amongst trees or open areas near them. It preys on small mammals, reptiles, etc., taken by pouncing from a perch or in flight, when it sometimes hovers. Like other raptors it migrates by soaring high in thermals, gliding to the next up-current, also along mountain ridges and cliff-faces.

### Long-legged Buzzard    *Buteo rufinus*

Long-legged Buzzard

**World:** *B.r. rufinus* breeds from Greece eastwards to Asia Minor, N Iraq, Iran, Arabia, NW India, central Asia (i.e. arid country south of Steppe Buzzard); sedentary and migratory, northern birds reaching Africa, Arabia, India. Another race in N Africa.
**Oman:** Rather uncommon and local breeding resident; also a regular passage migrant and winter visitor September–April in small numbers.

*pale phase*  C

*dark phase*  D

61cm/24in. Very similar in plumage to the less common Steppe Buzzard, but larger and more bulky, with longer legs, longer, broader wings (span about 122cm/48in) and more buoyant flight. It has a variety of colour-phases, mostly pale or rufous, but a dark phase occurs rarely. The *adult's* head is pale or rufous; the under-parts are varied, but it often shows a dark belly and vent (leading to confusion with **Rough-legged Buzzard** *B. lagopus,* which has not occurred south of Iran), and occasionally a dark breast-patch; the under wing-linings may be dark or pale but always end in a black carpal patch contrasting with the white primaries and pale secondaries; the wing-tips and trailing-edge are black as in Honey and Steppe Buzzards; the tail is pale or bright rufous, unbarred in most *adults* but faintly barred in *immatures.* See the larger Bonelli's Eagle (plate 31).

Near trees in open semi-desert and in or near mountains. It perches on the ground, rocks or trees, and obtains rodents, hares, reptiles, etc., by dropping on to them from a perch, or by gliding, soaring, hovering and pouncing; but it is often a carrion-feeder. The nest, with 2 eggs from February, is a bulky structure usually in the fork of a small tree, more rarely on a rock ledge. Rather silent, but it has a short, sharp mew.

Plate 28

# EAGLES: *Aquila*

Plates 24, 29–30

Larger than buzzards, with larger, prominent heads and bills, and usually more aggressive, though shy. They live in open country, soaring well on long, broad wings. The plumage is brown, often confusing, particularly in immatures, but silhouette is important in recognition; plumage of sexes similar.

## Spotted Eagle    *Aquila clanga*

Spotted Eagle

**World:** Breeds from E Europe in a narrow belt across to China, perhaps south to N India. Sedentary and migratory, reaching NE Africa, Arabia, India, SE Asia.
**Oman:** Regular passage migrant and winter visitor October–April in small numbers.

62–74cm/24–28in. A very dark medium-sized eagle, with small head, broad wings, and rather short, square or wedge-shaped tail giving a compact vulturine appearance when soaring. The *adult* is dark brown tinged with plum-purple above, rump usually with some white, tail blackish; duller below, with a little contrast between the blackish wing-linings and paler flight-feathers. *Immatures* are very dark brown, the *youngest* birds heavily 'spotted' whitish on the back and in rows across the upper wing, have a whitish U at the base of the tail, and are sometimes streaked paler on the under-wing, belly and under tail-coverts; the whitish marks gradually disappear with age (to 4th year). The nostrils are rounded or square. *Adults* differ from Lesser Spotted in slightly larger size, darker colouration, broader wings, shorter, often wedge-shaped tail, and the fact that flight-feathers are paler than wing-linings; the *immature* is usually darker and more heavily spotted above.

*adult* D

*juvenile* E

Usually in trees near water, but often seen at refuse and in marshes. Its flight is heavy, but it soars well. Frequently comes to carrion, but it also preys on small animals.

## Lesser Spotted Eagle    *Aquila pomarina*

Lesser Spotted Eagle

**World:** *A.p. pomarina* breeds in central and E Europe, Turkey to Caucasus and N Iran. Resident and migratory, reaching southern Africa, Arabia. Another race in India.
**Oman:** Scarce vagrant, reported between October and March.

54–69cm/21–27in. Difficult to distinguish from the rather similar but slightly larger and more common Spotted Eagle. The *adult* is grey-brown, paler than Spotted, with the flight-feathers always darker than the wing-linings; the tail is ample and rounded. The *immature* (to 3rd or 5th year) is darker than the *adult;* the primary wing-coverts and secondaries have small pale tips forming indistinct bars on the wing, and there is a pale patch at the base of the primaries visible in the upper-wing, an irregular pale U at the base of the tail, and in some birds a buff nape. The nostrils are rounded.

*adult* A
*juvenile* B
*immature* C

Prefers trees, occasionally near water. It feeds on small animals (mammals, birds, reptiles, etc.), mostly taken on the ground.

Plate 29

**Imperial Eagle**    *Aquila heliaca*

**World:** *A.h. heliaca* breeds from SE Europe and Turkey to central Asia, south to N Iran and N India. Sedentary and migratory, reaching E Africa, Arabia, India to Far East. Another race in Iberia.
**Oman:** Passage migrant and winter visitor October–March in small numbers, return passage from February.

81–90cm/32–35in. Large, near the size of Golden Eagle and often confused with it and with Steppe Eagle. The *adult* is blackish-brown with pale tawny on the forehead, crown and nape (not restricted to the nape as in Steppe Eagle), a white patch on the shoulders (tips of upper scapulars), blackish flight-feathers and a long rounded or square tail which is greyish with a broad blackish tip. The *immature* differs from the Steppe Eagle in its paler sandy-buff colouration, with dark mottling above and black streaks on the breast; it lacks the conspicuous double white wing-bars on the under-wing. The nostrils are longitudinal.

Plains with some trees, rarely in mountains. It comes to rubbish-tips and carrion, and preys on small animals.

**Golden Eagle**    *Aquila chrysaetos*

**World:** Breeds in N America, Eurasia, south to N Africa, Sinai, Arabia, Iran, N India. Sedentary, but a few adults and many young wander or winter southwards.
**Oman:** Scarce winter visitor.

75–88cm/30–35in. A very large, dark eagle, with powerful bill, broad wings, long square-ended tail and strong majestic flight. The *adult* is rich dark or rufous brown, sometimes with golden or rusty from crown to hind-neck, dark tail with dark greyish bars, and the under-parts sometimes flecked with gold. The *nestling* is downy-white. The *juvenile* is very dark brown, with gold-flecked nape, a white wing-bar (base of inner primaries and secondaries), white 'trousers' and the basal two-thirds of the tail white with a contrasting broad dark terminal band. During successive annual moults the *immature* becomes more like the *adult*, less dark, the wing-bar reduced to a patch, the white base and dark tip of the tail both reduced; it differs from the adult White-tailed Eagle (plate 21) in longer square-ended tail and less rectangular wings. See other *Aquila* eagles.

In mountains and on desert plains with trees. It stands more upright than Steppe Eagle, and is more buoyant in flight. It hunts actively, soaring, searching, then stooping upon hares and other small animals, including birds as large as Brown-necked Raven taken on the ground or in flight; it also visits carrion. The nest, from January, is a bulky lined structure of sticks and scrub on a desert tree (or cliff ledge). 1 to 2 eggs, white or spotted brown.

**Steppe and Tawny Eagles**    *Aquila rapax*

**World:** Breeds in Africa, SE Europe across to Mongolia, SE Iran to India and Burma, in several races. (Steppe Eagle *A.r. orientalis* and *A.r. nipalensis* is sometimes treated as a distinct species *A. nipalensis*.)
**Oman:** Passage migrant and winter visitor September–March, fairly common, very rarely in summer. *A.r. orientalis* is the usual race, but a specimen in 1895 was identified as *nipalensis*.

**Steppe Eagle** *A.r. orientalis* 76–80cm/30–32in. A fairly large eagle. The *adult* is dark brown without white, and in some the nape is rusty. The *immature* is dark or pale brown, with a pale patch at the base of the dark primaries and two white wing-bars (pale tips to coverts and secondaries above and below); the tail is dark, with a whitish U at the base and a pale tip. *A.r. nipalensis* is larger and darker. The *adult* differs from the very similar Imperial Eagle in having the head protruding more in flight, and the lack of streaks and pale shoulder-marks; the *immature* differs in its usually darker colouration and two conspicuous white wing-bars. All differ from Spotted and Lesser Spotted (plate 29) in larger size, longer wings and tail, and long, oval nostrils.

Widespread in open semi-desert, foothills, etc. Usually singly and timid, but it congregates in winter at refuse-tips and carrion. It also preys upon small animals and comes to water regularly if available.

Plate 30

## SNAKE EAGLES: *Circaetus*

Live principally on snakes; the bare tarsi are protected by scales and the toes and soles adapted to holding the prey; soar and hover well.

### Short-toed Eagle    *Circaetus gallicus*

Short-toed Eagle    A

**World:** *C.g. gallicus* breeds in S and central Europe east to Mongolia, south to N Africa, Near East, Iraq, Iran, India, Burma. Sedentary and migratory, reaching Africa, Arabia, India, Far East. Other races in Africa.
**Oman:** Fairly common passage migrant, occasional winter visitor and probably a local breeding resident.

63–69cm/25–27in. Larger than Osprey, mostly white below, with long, broad wings, owl-like head and large golden-yellow eyes. The *adult* is grey to brown above, the primaries blackish, the tail rather long and dark, with three broad, indistinct darker bars; mostly white below but often dark from chin to upper breast, and with lines of spots across the under-wing. The *immature* is browner; the *nestling* is downy-white. It differs from the Osprey (plate 21) in broader, flatter wings with no black bar or carpal patch on the under-wing.

In open country from desert to mountains and edges of cultivation, where it preys on snakes and other small animals. Its flight is slow and powerful, but it often soars and frequently hovers whilst hunting. The nest, in winter or spring, is a pad of slender sticks, usually hidden in a tree-top, occasionally on a cliff-edge. Only one white egg is laid. Silent except for whistles and fluting calls when pairing.

## HAWK EAGLES: *Hieraaetus*

Rather similar to *Aquila,* but small to medium-sized, often with striking light and dark in plumage, long, rather pointed wings and fairly long tail.

### Booted Eagle    *Hieraaetus pennatus*

Booted Eagle

**World:** Breeds in N Africa and extreme S Africa and from S and E Europe, Asia Minor, Iraq, N Iran to NW India, also central Asia. Migratory, reaching Africa, Arabia, India, Sri Lanka, SE Asia.
**Oman:** Uncommon passage migrant, occasionally in winter, September–April.

46–53cm/18–21in. A little smaller than the Steppe Buzzard and Bonelli's Eagle, more slender and longer-tailed; it has a pale phase and a less common and perhaps overlooked dark phase. The *adult* of both phases appears dark above, with a broad pale band on the wing-coverts, a narrow pale rump and small white shoulder-patches; from below, the pale phase has distinctive dark flight-feathers contrasting with whitish body, wing-coverts and tail; the dark phase is uniform dark brown below. The long legs are feathered to the toes. *Immature* resembles adult, but is more rufous. The pale phase differs from the Egyptian Vulture (plate 23) in that species' larger size and wedge-shaped tail; the dark phase differs from the Black Kite (plate 22) in wing- and tail-shape, and from the Marsh Harrier (plate 25) in having level, not raised, wings when soaring.

*adult pale phase* B
*adult dark phase,*
*from below* C

Forests, wooded ravines and mountain slopes, also semi-desert near trees. The flight is swift and agile, often at treetop height, but it frequently soars, singly or in pairs. It preys upon small mammals and birds, reptiles, etc., taken from the ground by a rapid stoop from a tree or the air. The call is a high double whistle, *ki-keeee.*

### Bonelli's Eagle    *Hieraaetus fasciatus*

Bonelli's Eagle

**World:** *H.f. fasciatus* breeds in the Mediterranean region, Asia Minor, Iraq, Iran, Arabia, N India to China; sedentary and migratory, reaching Arabia, Sri Lanka. Other races in Africa, Indonesia.
**Oman:** Uncommon breeding resident and passage migrant; some over winter.

66–74cm/26–29in. A fairly large but slender, small-headed hawk-eagle with a distinctive flight silhouette with protruding head, long tail, long rounded wings. *Adult* is dark brown above, usually with a large white patch on the upper back; below, the chin, body and thighs are white, the under-wing is dark (or whitish with a contrasting dark diagonal bar), the tail is grey with a dark sub-terminal bar. The *immature* is grey-brown above, buff to dark brown below, becoming whiter on the body and darker on the under wing-coverts with age. Differs from buzzards in more slender form and silhouette; from pale phase Booted Eagle in larger size.

*adult female* D
*adult female, from above* E

Among mountains and foothills, preferably with trees, often in pairs. Soars near cliff-faces. The flight is very agile and it pounces on birds, mammals, reptiles, etc. The nest, from February, is of large sticks with annual additions, on a cliff ledge or tree. 1–2 eggs, but the second chick rarely survives. Usually silent, but has a mellow, fluting *klee-klee-klee* or chattering *ki-ki-ki.*

Plate 31

# FALCONS: Falconidae

Plates 32–35

**World:** 58 species. **Oman:** 10 species (2 breeding). Rather small diurnal birds of prey with long, pointed wings and rapid flight. Include the large and varied genus *Falco*, the real falcons, with dark iris and tooth and notch in the stout bill. Many kill their prey whilst in flight, knocking them down in a high-speed stoop or seizing them in their talons; this and their amazing eyesight has made them favourites with falconers, a fact which has contributed to the decline of some populations. Females are larger than males.

## Kestrel    *Falco tinnunculus*                                                  Kestrel

**World:** Breeds over most of Eurasia, Africa, India to Sri Lanka, in several races. Northern birds are migratory.
**Oman:** Fairly common breeding resident, and passage migrant and winter visitor September–April.

34cm/13½in. A small falcon with long, pointed wings and long tail, habitually hovering with tail outspread. *Adult male* differs from the smaller male Lesser Kestrel in its black-spotted mantle, black moustachial-streak, lack of grey in the upper-wing, and more heavily marked under-parts and under-wing. *Female* and *immature* are very similar to Lesser Kestrel but the tail is more round and under-wings more heavily barred. Claws are black. Differs from Sparrowhawk in that species' shorter, more rounded wings, and in its habits.

   *adult male* C
   *adult female* D

Open plains, semi-desert, mountains, occasionally in trees, singly, in pairs or family parties. In loose parties on passage, sometimes with Lesser Kestrel. It preys upon small rodents, birds, reptiles, invertebrates, etc., after a searching flight, glide, hover and pounce; some insects are taken in flight. It perches on trees, posts, wires, etc. The nest, from January, is unlined in a crevice, cave, old building or hollow tree. Eggs, 3–5, are heavily speckled with red-brown. Call, a shrill *keee-keee-keee* and a chattering *kik-kik-kik*.

## Manchurian Red-footed Falcon    *Falco amurensis*                      Manchurian Red-footed Falcon

**World:** Breeds in E Asia (SE of Lake Baikal, Manchuria, N Korea, N China). Migratory, crossing India and Indian Ocean, occasionally S and E Arabia, to winter in Africa. (Sometimes treated as a race of **Red-footed Falcon** *F. vespertinus*.)
**Oman:** Very uncommon passage migrant, July–November, March–May (seven reports since 1901).

30cm/12in. A small dark Hobby-like falcon. The *adult male* is slate-grey, darker on the head and back; paler grey below, with deep chestnut thighs, lower belly and under tail-coverts; the under wing-coverts and axillaries are white; the eye-ring, bill, cere and legs are orange. The *adult female* is dark grey above with faint black bars on the back and tail, and a white collar; it is rusty-white below, heavily streaked and barred black, the thighs, etc., are buffish, the under wing-coverts white mottled with black; the bare parts are paler orange. *F. vespertinus* [breeds from E Europe to Siberia, wintering in Africa, not identified in Oman] differs in the *male's* all-dark under-wings (though some have white in the primaries), and in the chestnut on the *female's* head, under-parts, under wing-coverts and axillaries, with finer dark streaks. The *immatures* of both species are similar to *F. vespertinus female*, but paler. See Hobby and Sooty Falcon (plate 33).

   *adult male* E
   *adult female* F

   *immature* G

Open plains, coast, trees. Usually very gregarious, sometimes migrates in mixed parties with Lesser Kestrel, etc. Hovers like Kestrel, pouncing on invertebrates and small rodents, or catching insects in the air.

## Lesser Kestrel    *Falco naumanni*                                          Lesser Kestrel

**World:** Breeds in NW Africa, S and SE Europe across to central and E Asia, south to Iran. Migratory, reaching Arabia, India.
**Oman:** A rather uncommon passage migrant March–May, October–November, a few over winter.

30cm/12in. A small slender falcon superficially similar to the Kestrel, but the *adult male* is distinguished by its generally brighter colouration, unspotted mantle; it has pale pinkish-buff under-parts, whitish under-wing with black tips and a blue-grey patch on the upper wing-coverts; the central pair of tail-feathers are slightly elongate, often giving a slightly wedge-shaped appearance; claws white (not black). The *female* and *immature* are very similar to the Kestrel, except for paler under-parts.

   *adult male* A

   *adult female* B

More fearless and gregarious than the Kestrel, roosting communally and migrating high up in loose parties, occasionally with the Kestrel. It hovers less often, hawking insects from the air, also dropping on these and other small animals on the ground. When eating on the wing one foot is used to carry prey to the bill. The call is a more varied, noisy *kikik* and *che-che-che*.

Plate 32

**Hobby**    *Falco subbuteo*

**World:** *F.s. subbuteo* breeds in NW Africa and Eurasia; highly migratory, reaching Africa, Arabia, India and Japan. Another race in SE China.
**Oman:** Scarce but regular passage migrant, September–December, March–May, occasionally in summer.

30–36cm/12–14in. Like a small, dashing Peregrine or Barbary Falcon, but more Swift-like, with longer wings and shorter tail. The *adult male* is dark above with a slight rufous collar and distinct moustachial mark; whitish below, boldly streaked blackish from upper breast to belly, and with deep rufous vent, thighs and under tail-coverts. The *female* and *immature* are similar but browner, the rufous paler. It differs from Peregrine and Barbary in under-parts streaked (not barred) and rufous thighs; from Red-footed female in shorter tail, face-pattern, streaked under-parts and unbarred upper tail. See Sooty Falcon.

Open country, scrubland amongst trees. Follows, chases and stoops upon migrants such as swifts and swallows, but also catches and eats aerial insects and occasionally bats. Often active at dusk and at bird-roosts. It has a rapid wing-beat interrupted by glides, and tends to be gregarious on passage.

**[Merlin**    *Falco columbarius*

**World:** *F.c. pallidus* breeds in central Asia. Migratory, reaching Iraq, Arabian Gulf (scarce except at Kuwait), and India. Several other races in N America, N Eurasia.
**Oman:** Possibly a scarce winter visitor in the north.

27–33cm/10–13in. A very small, dashing falcon; *F.c. pallidus*, is the palest race. The *male* is blue-grey above, with a rufous collar and a blackish sub-terminal tail-band; below, it is pale rufous with dark streaks. The *female* and *immature* are dark brownish-grey above; pale and heavily streaked brown below, the under-wing heavily streaked and barred and the tail evenly barred; rather similar to the Kestrel, but darker, more stocky and swift-flying. See Hobby, Kestrel (plate 32), Sparrowhawk (plate 27).

Open country, scrub and cultivation, in low, fast and often erratic flight, hunting and pouncing upon small birds, etc., and taking some insects in flight. It perches on trees and on the ground.]

**Sooty Falcon**    *Falco concolor*

**World:** Breeds in isolated places in N and E Africa, Near East, coasts and islands of Red Sea and Arabia. Migratory, wintering off E Africa and Madagascar. The southern representative of **Eleonora's Falcon** *F. eleonorae* of the Mediterranean.
**Oman:** Regular breeding visitor and passage migrant April–November, occasionally in other months.

32–36cm/13–14in. An all-grey falcon. The *adult male* is grey, the head and tail darker, the primaries blackish. The *female* is darker and slightly larger. The eye-ring and cere are bright yellow to orange, the legs orange-yellow to reddish. The *juvenile* is blackish above, the feathers fringed rufous, and has a pale rufous collar, and cheeks with a dark moustachial patch, causing confusion with Barbary Falcon (plate 35); below, the chin is pale, the body pale pinkish-rufous blotched with black; the eye-ring and cere blue-grey at first, the legs yellow. The *nestling* is downy-white.

Coastal and island cliffs (if free from ground predators), also feeding inland occasionally. It perches prominently on crags, but also on shady ledges, and it soars in the up-draught above the cliff-faces. The nest, from July, is an unlined scrape in dust or gravel under a ledge on a slope, cliff or rocky outcrop, singly or semi-colonially. The eggs, usually 3, rarely 4, are brownish or white. It hunts at dawn and dusk, sometimes during the day, the male climbing high with rapid wing-beats, chasing and seizing migrant birds in its feet and bringing them to the female near the nest. They also feed on insects and bats, often over marshes or cultivation some way from the coast, and eat these on the wing. Calls, near the nest, include a rapid *kikiri-kikiri-kiriri* and a slower *keea-keea-keea*.

Hobby

*adult* A

Merlin

*adult male* B

*adult female* C
*immature* D

Sooty Falcon

*adult* E

*juvenile* F

Plate 33

## Lanner    *Falco biarmicus*

**World:** Breeds in Africa, S Arabia(?), Near East to S Iraq, SE Europe, Turkey, Armenia, in several races. Resident, not truly migratory, but some wander or move seasonally.
**Oman:** Status uncertain; unexpected, except as a visitor; reports (infrequent, in most months) may include escapes and misidentified Saker.

43cm/17in. The size of the Peregrine (plate 35), but with looser plumage, longer and slightly narrower wings and longer tail. The *adult* has a buff or chestnut crown and nape, whitish forehead, narrow moustachial-streak and grey-brown upper-parts; it is whitish or pale buffish-pink below, sparsely spotted black on lower breast and belly (not streaked or barred like Peregrine). The *immature* is more heavily streaked with dark brown on the crown and under-parts.

Open country and desert, soaring over hills and perching on crags and trees. It actively hunts birds and bats by stooping and chasing, but it also takes small mammals, reptiles, etc., from the ground. Used by falconers, but it lacks the strength of the Saker and the speed of the Peregrine. Thought to be resident in S Arabia, but nesting has not yet been proved; the usual nest is a pile of sticks on a cliff ledge or tree.

## Saker    *Falco cherrug*

**World:** *F.c. cherrug* breeds from central Europe to central Asia, south to Iran; resident and migratory, reaching Africa, Arabia, NW India. Other races in E Asia.
**Oman:** Passage migrant and winter visitor September–April, not common but probably regular; occasionally in summer.

46cm/18in. A large and robust falcon. Difficult to distinguish from the slightly smaller Lanner (which may occur rarely), but the *adult* is generally paler, with very pale, often whitish crown and nape, streaked brown, an inconspicuous moustachial-streak, and brown (not grey-brown) upper-parts, and the tail appears more spotted than barred; below, it is lightly streaked (rather than spotted), and often shows a dark band along the centre of the under-wing (dark tips to coverts). The *immature* is heavily streaked below and very similar to immature Lanner, though generally paler above, with a pale crown, and contrasting dark flight-feathers. The plumage is looser than that of the Peregrine (plate 35).

Open country and semi-desert plains, occasionally in foothills nearby, resting on the ground, crags or trees. It is bold and aggressive, and is said to be stronger and to have a keener intelligence and eyesight than Peregrines and occasionally to take prey from them. It is captured and trained for falconry in some countries, and will then pursue the Houbara, hare and even gazelle. It normally hunts small mammals, lizards, large insects and birds in low flight, occasionally hovering; it sometimes stoops upon flying birds. The wing-beat is slower than that of the Peregrine. The name derives from the Arabic *saqr*.

Plate 34

115

**Peregrine**   *Falco peregrinus*

**World:** *F.p. calidus* breeds across northern Eurasia; highly migratory, reaching Africa, Arabia, India to New Guinea. Other races almost world-wide.

**Oman:** Seen occasionally in all months; passage migrants and winter visitors occur regularly in small numbers; the status of others is uncertain (but one was seen nesting with an apparent Barbary Falcon on Jabal Akhdar in May 1978 and may be resident, and others may be non-breeding birds).

38–50cm/15–20in. A medium-sized falcon of classic proportions; robust, with pointed wings, fairly short tail and compact plumage. The *adult male* is dark to pale slate-blue above, the black moustachial-stripe is conspicuous on the distinct white cheek-patch, the crown is black and the hind-neck occasionally buffish; it is buffish-white below, flecked and narrowly barred black. The *female* is larger, darker and more heavily marked below. The *immature* is sooty-brown above, with paler fringes to the feathers; the under-parts are broadly streaked brown on buffish-white. The adults of all races differ from the adult Lanner and Saker (plate 34) by the much more conspicuous moustachial-stripe and greyer upper-parts; the rufous on the head, when present, is darker. *Immatures* may be confused with young Sooty Falcons (plate 33).

*adult male* A

*adult female* B
*immature* C

Mostly seen along coasts, but pairs would occur at inland as well as coastal cliffs when breeding. It perches erect on isolated rocks, crags, ledges and bare branches. Most active at dawn and from late afternoon to dusk, it rests in shade in the hottest hours except when feeding young. Much has been written of the species' noble and fearless character and its superb mastery of flight. It hunts singly, and stoops headlong, with wings partly closed, striking down birds such as small passerines and waders, up to the size of Rock Dove, sandgrouse and larger. It will also seize prey in flight, and on occasions will quarter the ground like a harrier for birds and other prey. Large prey is taken to a 'plucking post', but bats and insects are usually eaten on the wing. Level flight is a series of rapid, shallow, pigeon-like wing-beats with occasional glides. It is much prized by falconers, whose birds are taken from the nest (eyrie) as eyasses, or captured from the wild, increasing the pressure upon a declining species. Birds released after the hunting season may be disorientated and remain locally to feed and breed. The nest, from February to May, is a scrape on a bare ledge, in a shallow cave or occasionally an old tree nest, used repeatedly. 2–3 eggs, buffish with rusty speckles. It cries with a loud shrill *hě-hě-hě-hě* or *keek-keek-keek-keek,* also *ka-yak,* particularly near the nest. The male is a 'tiercel', the female is a 'falcon'. Arabic is *shahīn.*

**Barbary Falcon**   *Falco pelegrinoides*

**World:** Breeds in the Canaries, northern Africa, S Arabia, Near East, Iraq, Iran(?), NW India, and from Transcaspia to Mongolia, in two races. Sedentary and partly migratory. (Often treated as races of Peregrine.)

**Oman:** Some breed; but there are several reports of Barbary on passage, some of which suggest confusion with other species such as immature Sooty Falcons (plate 33).

*F.p. pelegrinoides* 35–45cm/14–18in. A small, pale, desert version of the Peregrine. The *adult male* is pale blue-grey above, the forehead to hind-neck shading to rufous, the crown appearing dark; only lightly spotted below on pinkish-buff. The *female* is darker buff below and narrowly barred. The *immature* has more buff on the head and is blackish above, and heavily streaked brown below. *F.p. babylonicus* is paler and the head is more rufous. The *immatures* differ from Lanner (plate 34) in the more rufous colouring above and less heavy streaking below.

*adult male* D

*adult female* E
*immature* F

Habits are similar to those of the Peregrine.

Plate 35

117

# PARTRIDGES, FRANCOLINS, QUAILS: Phasianidae         Plates 36–37

**World:** 165 species. **Oman:** 5 species (4 resident, breeding). Terrestrial, but many roost in trees. Heavy, with short, rounded wings, short to very long tail, strong legs adapted for running and scratching. Flight fast but not always sustained. In some species the male is brilliantly coloured; most are dull, sexes somewhat similar, and difficult to observe. Dull species are generally monogamous. Most have loud, simple calls. All but Old World quails are said to be sedentary, moving to feed, water and roost; the quails are highly migratory. In Oman some are netted and domesticated and some eggs are collected for hatching by village hens. In Oman *Alectoris* (two species) are the largest, greyish and sometimes misidentified as guinea-fowl; *Ammoperdix* (one) is the smallest hill partridge; *Francolinus* (one) of coast and cultivation in N Oman is intermediate in size: if originally introduced to Oman and sedentary, the francolins have shown an astonishing ability to spread.

### Arabian Red-legged Partridge    *Alectoris melanocephala*

Arabian Red-legged Partridge

**World:** Breeds only in Arabia, from Mecca south to Aden, east to S and N Oman. A pale race occurs in northern Hadhramaut. Resident, sometimes kept and bred in captivity.
**Oman:** Fairly common breeding resident in the mountains of Jabal Akhdar and Dhofar.

*adult* B

38cm/15in. A fairly large partridge, pale blue-grey above with a striking head-pattern, consisting of a blackish stripe from forehead to nape, a broad white band above each red-rimmed eye, and a blackish line running through each eye and downwards to meet on the lower neck; the throat is white and the rest of the under-parts pale blue-grey and buff, the flanks narrowly barred black, white and grey and often partly concealed by the wings at rest. The bill is bright red, the feet dull or pale red. Sexes are similar, but the *female* is a little smaller. The *juvenile* is as illustrated.

*juvenile* C

Mountains, wadis and upland plains with vegetation, also raiding cultivation particularly at harvest time. It feeds on vegetable matter, seeds and invertebrates, and visits water in the morning and evening. Usually heard more often than seen, it occurs in family groups and small coveys, creeping amongst rocks or through vegetation. In flight it appears large and dark, giving rise to reports of other species. The nest, from March, is a small scrape under cover of a rock or bush, usually above 600m. The eggs, 5–8, are sometimes taken for hatching in villages. The call comprises a few preliminary *cucks,* increasing in tempo and loudness – *cuck, cuck, cuck, owk-owk-owk* or *crowk, crowk, crowk*; also a softer oft-repeated contact or rally call *cook, cookcookcookcook*; the alarm flight-call is *kerkow-kerkow-kerkow*; it also has various soft conversational clucks, punctuated by a high-pitched mew.

### Chukar    *Alectoris chukar*

Chukar A

**World:** Breeds in SE Europe, Asia Minor, Near East, Arabia, Iran to NW India, and from the Caspian to China, in several races. Resident, often kept in captivity.
**Oman:** Resident in mountains of Musandam in small numbers.

38cm/15in. It differs from the Arabian Red-legged Partridge principally in its range, its grey (not black) crown and nape, the bars on its flanks being broader and edged with rufous, and in its different facial pattern.

Rocky hills and plateaux with some vegetation. It visits cultivation, often in family groups or larger coveys to feed on vegetable matter and seeds, invertebrates and occasionally small lizards. It visits water daily. When flushed, parties disperse, flying downhill or following the contours. The nest, from March, is a small scrape, sometimes lined with vegetation, under cover of a rock or bush. Eight or more eggs in a clutch; a second clutch may be incubated by the male. The call is a high-pitched, cackling *chuk-chuk-chukar,* and *cacaba-cacaba* or *kak-kak-kak-kawak-kak,* higher-pitched than in the Arabian Red-legged; flight-call *scree-scree-scree* and *churra-churra.*

### [Helmeted Guineafowl    *Numida meleagris* (Family: *Numididae*)         (Not illustrated)

Mainly African, but also a breeding resident of SW Arabia from Asir to S Yemen; has been reported once from Jabal Qara, Dhofar, but not confirmed. 45cm/22in. It is large and robust; the plumage is blackish, profusely spotted with white, with bare head and neck, a brown casque on the crown and red lappets below the eye. Family parties or flocks roost in trees and have a distinctive rasping cackle, *kek, kek, kek.*]

Plate 36

**Sand Partridge**   *Ammoperdix heyi*

**World:** *A.h. intermedia* breeds in W, S and E Arabia; sedentary. Other races in NW Arabia, Egypt, Sudan.
**Oman:** Common breeding resident in Musandam, south through N Oman and Dhofar.

29cm/9in. A small, brown partridge of the hills. The *adult male* has a buff streak on the ear-coverts, the crown and mantle are maroon, the wings, rump and tail greyer with brown vermiculations; below, the deep chestnut chin shades into maroon on the throat and breast, then chestnut; the flanks and belly are darkly streaked rufous and black with some white. The *male* has no spur. The *adult female* and *immature* are browner, barred and vermiculated.

Boulder-strewn wadis and rocky slopes from sea-level to over 2000m. It is often unwilling to fly, running nimbly uphill; but when surprised it flies with a sudden metallic whirr, to glide and swerve behind the next hill-crest. Often in small coveys when not breeding. It feeds on vegetable matter such as leaves, seeds and berries and also on some invertebrates. It comes to water each evening, usually just before dusk. The nest, from March or April, is a scrape under a boulder or bush where 4–6 glossy buffish eggs are laid. The female has an injury distraction display. The call when breeding is a prolonged series of sharp notes *kwip, kwip, kwip* (about two in three seconds); at other times it is repeated faster ringing, *tew, tew, tew,* or *teeyuk, teeyuk, teeyuk*; there is also a soft contact-call.

**Grey Francolin** (Indian Grey Partridge)   *Francolinus pondicerianus*

**World:** *F.p. mecranensis* breeds in SE Iran, Baluchistan, S Afghanistan, NW India, N Oman; sedentary. Other races in India and Sri Lanka.
**Oman:** Common breeding resident in N Oman along Batinah and in some wadis in foothills on both sides of Hajar mountains, reaching Al Awaifi and southwards on both sides of the Wahiba Sands.

33cm/13in. A sturdy grey-brown game bird of the plains. The sexes are alike, but the *male* is a little larger and has a single or double spur. It is mottled, barred and vermiculated above and below; the forehead is chestnut and there is a buff streak from the lores to behind the eye (not as prominent as in the male Sand Partridge); the throat is yellowish and enclosed in a black fringe. The tail has chestnut sides, visible in flight. The *juvenile* is similar, but has less chestnut on the forehead and less black surrounding the paler throat. It differs from the Sand Partridge in habitat, mottled plumage and distinctive call.

Amongst bushes and trees, in which it roosts, and particularly near cultivation, in which it can be a pest. Usually in pairs, family parties or small coveys. It walks, pecking and digging at fallow ground but also taking young shoots, grain, and other vegetable matter, as well as dung, invertebrates, etc. When disturbed it will run faster than a man, or fly, a party splitting up in different directions with rapid wing-beats and a glide, running again on landing. It does not apparently need to drink regularly. The nest, from January, is a lined scrape on the ground under cover of a bush to give protection from foxes. The 4–8 eggs are pale buff or creamy. The voice is distinctive, starting with a few clucks or *cheekada-cheekada* and increasing to a loud, ringing *chakeeta chakeeta chakeeta*; the female calls *see see see* or *keela keela keela,* and duets with males to form *see-ka-kow, see-ka-kakow* or *kateela* or *kikichew,* etc.

**Common Quail**   *Coturnix coturnix*

**World:** *C.c. coturnix* breeds across Eurasia to Mongolia, south to Near East, Iran, N India, perhaps SW Arabia; migratory over long distances, reaching Africa, Arabia, India. Bred commercially in the Middle East. Other races on Atlantic islands, in southern Africa, Madagascar, Mauritius.
**Oman:** Regular passage migrant September–November, a few in December; spring passage, February–March, is noted only occasionally.

20cm/8in. Like a very small partridge, but rarely seen. The *adult male* is dark brown with black barring above, and with conspicuous pale buff streaks on the back and wings and contrasting buff streaks in the centre of the crown and over each eye, curving down to the nape; the black or chestnut of the chin extends downwards, then up at the sides (as an 'anchor', often indistinct), a pale buff 'cut-throat' band separates it from the cinnamon-buff breast, pale belly and streaked flanks. The *female* has no chin 'anchor', the throat and upper breast are spotted darker and the flanks are streaked. It differs from the Corncrake (plate 39) in having no chestnut in the wing and in not dangling the legs in flight.

Usually hides in crops or other vegetation, or takes shelter under a desert bush or rock. When flushed it jumps up and skims low in whirring flight for a short distance, until dropping down, unwilling to rise again. It migrates in parties by night, but is found in cover by day. It feeds on seeds, invertebrates, etc. The contact-note is *cruc-cruc* or *kik-kik*; a soft whistling *krwee* is sometimes given on rising; it may also call on passage, a loud whistling *quic, quic-ic.*

Plate 37

# RAILS, CRAKES, MOORHENS, COOTS: Rallidae Plates 38–39

**World:** 129 species. **Oman:** Eight species (one breeding). The rails and crakes are small, with narrow bodies for passage through dense vegetation at the margins of fresh water, where their dark plumage and very shy, skulking habits make observation difficult; however, they will appear in the open briefly, usually at dusk, if they think they are not observed. The Corncrake prefers drier ground. The Moorhen and Coot are larger, less secretive, and have an ornamental frontal shield. The wings are short and rounded, the tail short and often flirted. The legs and toes are long, lobed in the Coot. Their short flight with dangling legs may appear weak, but all can fly strongly.

### Water Rail  *Rallus aquaticus*

Water Rail  A

**World:** Breeds in several disjunct populations in N Africa and across temperate Eurasia, south to Near East, Iraq, Iran, N India, in several races. Sedentary and migratory, reaching N Africa, Arabian Gulf, occasionally Arabia.
**Oman:** Scarce passage migrant, occasionally over winter; reported between August and April or May, mostly in N Oman.

28cm/11in. A fairly small, dark, skulking bird, the largest of the rails and crakes in Oman and sometimes resembling a small, thin, brown Moorhen. It is distinguished by its long red bill and black-and-white barred flanks. The *adult* is olive-brown above with black streaks; the sides of the head, throat and breast are grey, the belly buff, and the under tail-coverts greyish-white. The *juvenile* is mottled below.

Creeks and marshes, where it walks in water through vegetation with lowered bobbing head. The tail is held horizontally, cocked or jerked when walking with high-stepping gait or swimming. Call, *chik-chik,* and weird grunts, groans and squeals, mostly at night; rather silent in winter.

### Baillon's Crake  *Porzana pusilla*

Baillon's Crake  E

**World:** Breeds locally from SW Europe across to Far East, incl. Iran, N India; also in Africa, Madagascar, Australasia, in several races. The Palaearctic races are migratory, reaching Africa, Arabia, India, Far East.
**Oman:** Autumn passage migrant and winter visitor August–December, rarely seen or identified with certainty.

18cm/7in. The smallest crake. Sexes are similar and difficult to distinguish in the field from male Little Crake, but they are more rufous above, with the back and wing-coverts flecked with white, the belly, flanks and under tail-coverts more distinctly barred black-brown and white, the bill short and green (no red base), and the legs dull flesh to brownish (not green). The chin is white in *winter,* grey in *summer.* The *juvenile* is greyer, with the breast and flanks more heavily barred than those of the Little Crake.

Its habits are similar to those of the other crakes.

### Little Crake  *Porzana parva*

Little Crake

**World:** Breeds from E and S Europe to central Asia. Migratory, reaching Africa, Arabia, N India.
**Oman:** Passage migrant and winter visitor August–April, but rarely seen.

19cm/7½in. A very small, dark crake, rather similar to Baillon's and like a tiny, short-billed Water Rail. The *adult male* is dark olive-brown above with black marks and some white flecks on the back (not on the wing-coverts); it is grey below, the flanks and under tail-coverts only faintly barred white. The *female* has a white throat and is pale buff below. The bill is green, with red at the gape, and the legs and toes are green. The *juvenile* is not grey and its under-parts are slightly barred.

*male*  C

*female*  D

Like Baillon's and Spotted Crakes, in wet vegetation and on floating plants; extremely secretive.

### Spotted Crake  *Porzana porzana*

Spotted Crake  B

**World:** Breeds from W Europe to central Asia, incl. Iran. Migratory, reaching Africa, Arabia, India, Burma.
**Oman:** Autumn passage migrant and winter visitor September–December in small numbers.

23cm/9in. Sexes alike, dark olive-brown and black above, spotted and streaked with white, the short wings also spotted on dark brown, not chestnut as in the paler Corncrake (plate 39), with some white on the outer edge as in Baillon's Crake. The breast is olive-grey with indistinct pale spots, the flanks barred brown and white, and the under tail-coverts conspicuously pale buff. Differs from Little and Baillon's Crakes in those species' much smaller size and barred under tail-coverts; from Water Rail in smaller size and short bill.

Thick vegetation on borders of creeks, marshes and in ditches, venturing into the open if not disturbed, but readily bolting or dropping into cover after a short flight. It occasionally swims.

Plate 38

**Corncrake**   *Crex crex*

**World:** Breeds from W Europe to E Asia, south to Turkey, and possibly N Iran. Migratory, most to Africa, a few to India.
**Oman:** Autumn passage migrant, September–October, scarce or infrequently seen.

27cm/10½in. Usually seen when flushed from cover, when it resembles a small partridge or quail, but differs in the conspicuous chestnut wings and in dangling the legs in short flight. It differs from other crakes in its larger size, browner colouration and preference for drier ground.

Grassland, cultivation, scrub, in which it skulks unless disturbed. A solitary nocturnal migrant, flying low, some colliding with overhead wires, etc. Silent on migration.


**White-breasted Waterhen**   *Amaurornis phoenicurus*

**World:** Breeds in India, Burma, Sri Lanka, the Maldives, Andaman and Nicobar Islands, and Far East, in several races. Said to be resident.
**Oman:** Vagrant (one near Salalah, 29 November 1977).

32cm/12½in. A large rail, the size of a Moorhen. It is dark slaty-grey above; white below, with rufous-cinnamon on the lower flanks, vent and under tail-coverts. The *juvenile* is olive-brown, the face marked with grey and the cinnamon paler.

Undergrowth in cultivation and at the margins of fresh water, skulking but climbing occasionally into view, the tail frequently jerked up, displaying cinnamon.


**Moorhen**   *Gallinula chloropus*

**World:** *G.c. chloropus* (incl. *indica*) breeds across Eurasia to Far East, south to N Africa, Arabia, India, Sri Lanka; northern birds are migratory, reaching northern Africa, Arabia, India.
**Oman:** Very local breeding resident; passage migrant and winter visitor July–April, most in autumn, in small numbers except near Salalah where it is common; few reported on spring passage.

32cm/12½in. A dark brown water-bird which jerks the tail. The *adult* differs from the larger, blacker Coot in its red frontal shield and red bill with yellow tip, white streaks on the flanks, white under tail-coverts with black in the centre, and in the lack of a white wing-bar in flight; it is greyer below, and the toes are not lobed. The *juvenile* has the white under tail-coverts of the *adult*, but is paler brown above, the chin and under-parts almost white, and the bill and shield greenish. The *chick* is black, with a red bill.

At any fresh water with marginal cover and aquatic vegetation, including creeks, wadis and even ditches. Shy on passage and in poor localities, but when at ease it swims on open water, jerking the head with each pace, cocking and flirting the tail spasmodically, and walks amongst vegetation and on to grassy banks. The food is mainly vegetable matter, also invertebrates and fish. The nest, February–September, is a bulky mass of dead vegetation amongst cover on the ground, over water or floating. Two or three clutches of 5–12 eggs may be laid; the chicks swim soon after hatching. Call, a loud liquid *prrruk* or *kuruk* or harsher *kikikik* or *kikik*; chicks have a shrill *keep* or *kee-ip*.


**Coot**   *Fulica atra*

**World:** *F.a. atra* breeds from Iceland across temperate Eurasia to Japan, south to N Africa, Palestine, Iraq, Iran, India; sedentary, northern birds migratory, reaching northern Africa, Arabia, SE Asia. Other races in Australasia.
**Oman:** Irregular passage migrant and winter visitor, more arriving in midwinter, between October and April or May, in small numbers except near Salalah where often common over winter and occasional in summer.

38cm/15in. A bulky, black water-bird, differing from the smaller, browner Moorhen in its white bill and frontal shield, the lack of white on its flanks and under tail-coverts, the narrow white wing-bar on the trailing edge of its secondaries showing in flight, and the lobed toes. It differs from swimming ducks in its small head and rounded back. The *juvenile* is dark grey, with throat and upper breast whiter and bill paler than the juvenile Moorhen.

Creeks and pools, sometimes coastal. Singly and in small parties on passage, congregating in large numbers in suitable places, often with ducks. It may be seen shyly walking and feeding amongst vegetation near the water's edge, but more often it swims and jump-dives for aquatic vegetation, fish and invertebrates, which it eats on the surface. Direct flight is strong, the legs projecting beyond the tail: see Common Scoter (plate 20). Rather silent in winter, but it has a loud barking *tewk* or *kow-kow-kow* or *kik-kowk*.

Plate 39

# BUSTARDS: Otididae

**World:** 22 species. **Oman:** 2 species (1 breeding). Medium-sized to large diurnal terrestrial birds of semi-desert and grassland. The legs are strong and fairly long; the three short front toes, the lack of hind toe and the broad sole give a distinctive footprint. Shy and cryptically coloured above, they are difficult to see on the ground, when they walk, run or crouch rather than fly, the long, thickish neck and large, flattened head stretched forward. In flight they are distinctive, the wings large and broad, often with large white patches, the neck extended. They are sedentary and migratory, usually gregarious in winter, and omnivorous. World populations of some species have been dangerously reduced by disturbance, egg-collecting, shooting and falconry; the species found in Oman deserve and have been granted total protection.

### Little Bustard    *Tetrax tetrax*

Little Bustard

**World:** Breeds from S Europe to central Asia, south to NW Africa, NW Turkey, NE Iran. Sedentary and migratory, reaching Iraq, Iran, NW India.
**Oman:** Vagrant (one record, Batinah, December 1964).

43cm/17in. Much smaller than the adult Houbara. It is mottled sandy-brown above, but in flight the wings appear mostly white with black tips. The winter plumage of the sexes is similar, but in *summer* the *male's* face is blue-grey, the neck conspicuously black with a white V and a white bar below.

*male* A
*female* B

Rough grassland and crops, singly or in parties. Shy and wary, crouching in cover if approached, but when pressed will fly with fast partridge-like wing-beats, the wings of the male making a distinctive sibilant whistling.

### Houbara (Macqueen's Bustard)    *Chlamydotis undulata*

Houbara C

**World:** *C.u. macqueenii* breeds in central Asia, south to Near East, Arabia, Iran, NW India; migratory and nomadic, reaching Arabia, NW India. Other races in northern Africa and Canary Islands.
**Oman:** Breeding resident; also a passage migrant and winter visitor August–March in small, irregular numbers.

64cm/25in. The size of a large goose. The *adult (breeding)* is vermiculated rufous-brown above, with vertical black-and-white erectile plumes on the neck; the crown is black, with long narrow white central feathers with black tips, the five outer primaries are white with black tips and there is a black diagonal band across the upper-wing – together giving a noticeable pattern in flight; the tail has three dark bars; the throat and belly are white. The *chick* differs from the sandgrouse in its long neck and long, thick legs with no hind toe; it is golden-buff with black marks, whitish above and below the eye and down the sides of the neck to the belly. The *adult* differs from the **Arabian Bustard** *Ardeotis arabs* [*male* 90cm/35in, *female* 74cm/29in; breeds or formerly bred from SW Saudi Arabia to S Yemen, Somalia, Ethiopia] in that species' huge size and grey neck. It differs from the Little Bustard in its larger size, in its slower wing-beat and in having less white on the wing. See stone curlews (plate 42).

Sandy to stony desert plains with a covering of grasses and scrub, often with some bushes and trees, also on firm dunes and in hollows between mobile dunes. Usually seen singly, in pairs or in loose parties which move locally by day but usually migrate by night. It may be overlooked on the ground because of its cryptic colouration, even when striding away, the head and neck inclined forward; but it is immediately obvious when it springs into flight, the black and white noticeable in the wings, the wing-beat slow and owl-like. It is the preferred prey of falconers, but it will fight falcons on the ground and eject a sticky anal fluid. It is also favoured for its meat and eggs and is thus liable to disturbance even when nesting. The nest, from February in some years, is an unlined scrape. The eggs, 1–4, usually 3, are glossy olive-brown with brown streaks. Incubation and rearing is by the female, which may sit tight or give a distraction display. It feeds primarily on desert vegetation, but also on grasshoppers and other small animals; it does not need water regularly, but will come to it if available, usually at night. It is generally silent, but chicks have a shrill peeping call, and juveniles have a soft ventriloquial whistle.

Plate 40

## JACANAS (LILY-TROTTERS): Jacanidae

**World:** 7 species. **Oman:** 1 species. From the Brazilian word *jaçaná*. Plumage is striking; only the Oman species has a distinct breeding plumage and long tail. Rail-like, but not secretive. Legs long, bare, with toes and hind-claw very elongate for walking on floating vegetation.

### Pheasant-tailed Jacana  *Hydrophasianus chirurgus*

Pheasant-tailed Jacana

**World:** Breeds in India, east to S China, SW Pacific. Sedentary and migratory.
**Oman:** Regular winter visitor in very small numbers October–April, occasionally over summer, mostly seen in Dhofar.

31cm/12in (56cm/22in with tail). The *adult (summer)* is distinctive, with its long, down-curved, blackish tail; it is dark chocolate-brown except for the white face, fore-neck and wings, and golden hind-neck bordered black. In *winter* it has a much shorter tail, brown crown, hind-neck and back, a trace of yellow and black on the sides of the neck, and white under-parts with a black breast-band. The *juvenile* is similar but paler brown above, with black-tipped wings and incomplete breast-band.

*summer* A

*winter* B

Marshes and creeks. Not shy, often in pairs, said to be gregarious. Walks on floating vegetation in the open, feeding on invertebrates and vegetable matter, occasionally immersing the head or fluttering the wings. In short flight the slow wing-beat resembles a lapwing's.

## STILTS and AVOCETS: Recurvirostridae

**World:** 7 species. **Oman:** 2 species. Medium-sized waders, with long bill and legs, longish neck and small head; most are black-and-white.

### Black-winged Stilt  *Himantopus himantopus*  See also plate 58

Black-winged Stilt D

**World:** *H.h. himantopus* breeds from S Europe to China, south to Africa, Near East, Arabia, Iraq, to SE Asia; the northern birds are migratory but erratic.
**Oman:** Irregular passage migrant and winter visitor, some in summer; in small numbers, except in Dhofar where it is fairly common.

38cm/15in. An unmistakable black-and-white marsh bird with very long, thin, pink legs and a fine straight bill. In flight the pointed wings show black below, and the legs extend far beyond the tail. The crown and nape vary: in the *breeding male* usually black, but white in *winter*; in the *female* mottled brownish-grey; the *juvenile's* crown and back are brown.

Shallow pools, creeks and marshes with mud and vegetation. Singly or in parties. Walks and wades deeply with long, high-stepping strides, and feeds on invertebrates and some seeds. Call, *kik-kik-kik*.

### Avocet  *Recurvirostra avosetta*  See also plate 58

Avocet E

**World:** Breeds locally from Europe to China, south to Africa, Iraq, Iran, NW India. The northern birds are migratory but erratic.
**Oman:** Irregular passage migrant and visitor in small numbers, September–March in N Oman, rarely to Masirah, in any month in Dhofar.

43cm/17in. Fairly large, strikingly black-and-white, with a long, fine up-curved bill and bluish legs. The *adult female* has a brown-black head. The *juvenile* is tinged buff. See Crab Plover (plate 42).

Mud-flats, salt or fresh creeks, marshes and pools with vegetation. Singly or in small parties. It feeds in shallow water by sweeping the bill from side to side and by pecking; it will also swim and up-end. It flies with the neck partly retracted, the legs extended beyond the tail.

## OYSTERCATCHERS: Haematopodidae

**World:** 6 species. **Oman:** 1 species.

### Oystercatcher (Old World Oystercatcher)  *Haematopus ostralegus*

Oystercatcher

**World:** Breeds on coasts of Americas, Europe, E Asia, S Africa, Australasia, and inland central Eurasia, in several races. Sedentary and migratory, reaching northern Africa, Arabia, India, Far East.
**Oman:** Small numbers present in all months; regular common passage migrant in N Oman to Masirah area, where locally very common.

43cm/17in. A distinctive, robust, black-and-white wader with long, stout, reddish bill, rather short reddish legs, and conspicuous white rump and wing-bar visible in flight. *Young* and *winter adults* have a white 'cut-throat' band and darker end to the bill (not always featured together).

*summer* C

Shores and mud-flats in small, wary parties or large to very large flocks. It feeds on molluscs, and flies low and direct with rapid, shallow wing-beats. Call, a loud, whistling *klee-eep*.

128

Plate 41

## STONE CURLEWS: Burhinidae

**World:** 9 species. **Oman:** 2 species (1 breeding?). Large, plover-like birds, with large head ('dikkop'), large, yellow eyes, strong bustard-like legs with thick tibiotarsal joint ('thick-knee'). Mainly nocturnal. They crouch in cover by day, but are wary, running with head lowered, or flying with rapid wing-beats, legs outstretched. They feed mainly on invertebrates.

**Stone Curlew** *Burhinus oedicnemus* See also plate 58 Stone Curlew B

**World:** Breeds from Europe to central Asia, and in the south in northern Africa, Arabia(?), Iraq, Iran, India to SE Asia, in several races. Sedentary and migratory, reaching Africa, Arabia.
**Oman:** Scarce, irregular passage migrant and winter visitor, September–April, most in October. *B.o. saharae* has been identified.

41cm/16in. Care is required to distinguish this species from the Spotted Thick-knee; it differs in larger size, streaky appearance, white bar on closed wings and double white bar in flight.

Open semi-desert, some coasts on passage. Calls, at night, a plaintive *curl-wee* or *coo-lee*.

**Spotted Thick-knee** (Dikkop) *Burhinus capensis* See also plate 58 Spotted Thick-knee C

**World:** *B.c. dodsoni* breeds in coastal E Africa and Red Sea, W Saudi Arabia, S Yemen, Oman(?); sedentary and locally migratory.
**Oman:** Reported very occasionally between February and October; status uncertain, but may breed.

36cm/14in. Differs from Stone Curlew in smaller size, lack of wing-bars, and boldly spotted upperparts. The *juvenile* is similar, but has broader pale marks.

Semi-desert with trees or bushes, often in pairs near cover. Nest and eggs undescribed, probably as African races, from March or April, a shallow unlined depression on the ground, with 2 eggs, buff, blotched with brown. Calls, at night, a plaintive *tui tui tui* or *tche-uuu,* gradually dying away.

## CRAB PLOVER: Dromadidae

**World:** 1 species. **Oman:** 1 species (breeding).

**Crab Plover** *Dromas ardeola* See also plate 58 Crab Plover A

**World:** Breeds irregularly on some islands off E Africa, E Arabia, and in Arabian Gulf. Migratory to Indian Ocean coasts and islands.
**Oman:** Irregular migrant and visitor, breeding irregularly near Masirah where common in winter.

41cm/16in. A large wader, white with black flight-feathers and black mantle, stout black bill and long, blue legs. The *juvenile* is white with a broad, grey mantle and tail, and black in wings.

Coasts. Gregarious. Often accompanied by begging young in autumn. Feeds chiefly on crabs, often nocturnally. Flies with neck and legs extended. Nest, from April, an unlined chamber in a long burrow dug in sand by the bird in a colonial warren. 1 large, white egg. Calls, shrill *ki-ki-kew-ki*, barking *crow-ow-ow*, musical *prooit.*

## COURSERS and PRATINCOLES: Glareolidae Plates 42 and 43

### COURSERS: Cursoriinae

**World:** 9 species. **Oman:** 1 species (breeding?). Resemble slim plovers, but with longer legs and slender bill. Mostly sandy-brown, matching their desert environment.

**Cream-coloured Courser** *Cursorius cursor* Cream-coloured Courser D

**World:** Breeds from northern Africa, Near East, Arabia, Iraq, Iran to Baluchistan, in several races. Sedentary and migratory, reaching northern Africa, Arabia, NW India.
**Oman:** Irregular passage migrant and visitor July–May, in varied small numbers; may breed (one unconfirmed report on the Batinah).

23cm/9in. Sandy-brown above, with bold black-and-white eyestripes meeting in a V on the grey nape; black primaries and under-wings, slightly curved black bill and pale legs. The *juvenile* has dark wavy marks above and lacks the black border to its buff eye-stripe. See Sociable Lapwing (plate 47).

Open desert and edges of cultivation, occasionally coasts, in inconspicuous parties. Stands upright and runs fast in spurts after insects and lizards, taken by dipping forward with legs bent. The flight is jerky and fast, revealing the black in the wings. The nest, from April(?), is an unlined depression in dry ground. The 2 eggs are sandy, with dense spots or scribbles. The call in flight is a hoarse double *hark*.

Plate 42

## PRATINCOLES: Glareolinae

**World:** 7 species. **Oman:** 3 species. Smaller than coursers and more aerial. Plumage of sexes similar, dull brown with white rump, and black-and-white in the long, forked tail. Wings long and pointed; legs short; bill slight but broad-gaped. Flight, often at dusk in pursuit of insects, resembles that of a large swallow. Best watched for near water at dusk.

**Pratincole** (Collared Pratincole)  *Glareola pratincola*                                            Pratincole A

**World:** *G.p. pratincola* breeds from the Mediterranean region to central Asia, south to Iraq, Iran, NW India; sedentary and migratory to northern tropical Africa. Other races in Africa.
**Oman:** Passage migrant, June–November and March–May, main passage August–October, generally in small numbers, but larger numbers occur in some years; occasionally in winter.

25cm/10in. Olive-brown, with black primaries, white trailing-edge to the secondaries, deeply-forked black tail with white base and white rump; it is buff below, with a creamy throat faintly bordered black (indistinct in *winter);* the wing-linings are chestnut but often appear blackish in flight and are best seen when the wings are raised at rest.

Mud-flats, marshes, rubbish-tips near water. Singly or in small parties. Often crepuscular, and may be overlooked until it runs or flies. Its flight is tern- or swallow-like, swift and buoyant, and it feeds on flying insects. It sometimes gives a rippling call, *kikki-kirrik* or *kikikiki.*

**Black-winged Pratincole**  *Glareola nordmanni*                                     Black-winged Pratincole B

**World:** Breeds from E Europe to central Asia, south to Turkey (irregularly). Migratory to southern Africa. (Sometimes treated as a race of *G. pratincola* because intermediates occur.)
**Oman:** Vagrant or very scarce passage migrant, reported very occasionally, August–October (five reports between 1969 and 1977).

25cm/10in. Very difficult to distinguish from the Pratincole in the field, but it differs in the black wing-linings and lack of a white trailing-edge to the secondaries.

Habits are similar to those of the Pratincole and mixed flocks may occur, as in Africa. Call, *keerlik.*

**Little Pratincole**  *Glareola lactea*                                                      Little Pratincole C

**World:** Breeds from E Afghanistan through India to Sri Lanka and Burma. Sedentary, local migrant and nomadic; occasionally to Arabian Gulf and Oman.
**Oman:** Vagrant or scarce passage migrant and winter visitor November–February, probably overlooked.

17cm/6½in. A small pratincole, distinguished by its slightly forked white tail with black tip, white wing-bar (base of the secondaries) and black wing-linings. It is sandy-grey above, browner on the forehead, with a black line through the eye; it is white below except for the rufous-brown upper breast. The *juvenile* is 'scaly' above (pale feather-edges), and the throat and fore-neck are spotted blackish. See Little Swift (plate 77).

Marshes, creeks, streams and pools over which it hawks for flying insects in fast, erratic flight reminiscent of a bat. Usually crepuscular and gregarious, mixing with feeding swifts and bats.

Plate 43

# PLOVERS and LAPWINGS: Charadriidae    Plates 44–47

**World:** 63 species. **Oman:** 15 species (3 breeding). Small to medium-sized birds, usually near water. Unlike the Scolopacidae (plate 48) the bills are fairly short, and they feed on open ground by running with head held up, sometimes turned to one side, stopping, then tilting to take food. Most have a dark breast-pattern, a few species have seasonal changes. The plumage of the sexes is very similar. Chicks run soon after hatching. Includes sand plovers, golden plovers and lapwings.

## SAND PLOVERS: *Charadrius*    Plates 44–45

Small and compact, with short necks, brownish upper-parts and white under-parts, with distinct patterns on head and breast.

### Ringed Plover    *Charadrius hiaticula*    See also plate 56

Ringed Plover

**World:** Breeds in northern N America and Eurasia, in several races. Migratory.
**Oman:** Passage migrant and winter visitor in small numbers, September–May, some in summer.

19cm/7½in. Rather small and plump, with a rounded breast and belly. Similar to the Little Ringed Plover, but slightly larger, with a white wing-bar conspicuous in flight; bill more stubby, yellow tipped with black (darker in *winter female* and *immatures*); legs orange-yellow; eye-ring indistinct; also differs in call and habitat. The *juvenile* is 'scaly' above, with the black of the plumage replaced by brown, and a broken breast-band, blackish bill and yellowish legs; it differs from the Kentish Plover in having yellowish (not black) legs, and the breast-band more complete.

*adult* A

*juvenile* B

Seashore, marshes, creeks and inland pools. Scattered whilst feeding; resting and migrating in flocks, often with other species. The call is a loud, tuneful *too-ee, too-lee* or *pee-eep*.

### Little Ringed Plover    *Charadrius dubius*    See also plate 56

Little Ringed Plover

**World:** *C.d. curonicus* breeds across Eurasia, south to N Africa, Near East, Arabia, Iraq, Iran, NW India; sedentary and migratory to the tropics.
**Oman:** Widespread passage migrant and winter visitor in small numbers; main passages February–March and October–November; it also breeds in N Oman, possibly Dhofar, then disperses.

15cm/6in. A small bird, usually found near fresh water. It is brown above and white below, with a distinctive head-pattern. It differs from the rather similar Ringed Plover in the yellow eye-ring, lack of white wing-bar in flight, smaller size and different call and habitat; also in the dark bill and pale mud-coloured legs. The *juvenile* is drab, the black replaced by brown, and the breast-band is broken; it differs from the Kentish Plover in yellowish legs (not black) and lack of a wing-bar. The *chick* is white, mottled with brown on crown and back, and has darker legs.

*adult* C

*juvenile* D

At any fresh-water streams, marshes, pools and sullage, including desert interior and coastal creeks. Not very gregarious and can be overlooked. It nests from March to June in a small scrape, sometimes decorated, on pebbles, sand or dried mud near water. The eggs, 3 or 4, are buffish, tinged green and speckled brown; probably double-brooded. Adults have an injury-feigning distraction display. Call, a high-pitched *peee-u* or *phee-oo*, also a rapid *zip-rip-rip-rip;* during breeding, *peee-u* followed by a trill, uttered on the ground or in butterfly-like display flight.

### Kentish Plover    *Charadrius alexandrinus*    See also plate 56

Kentish Plover

**World:** *C.a. alexandrinus* breeds in coastal Europe, and from Black Sea across to W China, south to NW Africa, Near East, Somalia, Arabia, Iraq, Iran, NW India; sedentary and migratory.
**Oman:** Common passage migrant and winter visitor; breeding visitor to Masirah and Dhofar, perhaps to N Oman; some over summer.

16cm/6¼in. Smaller and slimmer than the ringed plovers, with blackish bill and legs. The *adult male* has a rufous crown in summer (brown in *winter),* a white supercilium, a white collar without black, black marks on the sides of the breast (reduced or brown in *winter),* a white wing-bar and white sides to the tail. The *adult female* is paler, with brown instead of black marks. The *juvenile* is similar to the *female,* but the upper-parts are 'scaly' (pale edges to feathers). *Chicks* are mottled on head and back, with relatively long legs. It can be confused with the slightly stouter Lesser Sand Plover (plate 45).

*adult male* E

*adult female* F
*juvenile* G

Seashore, creeks and mud-flats and pools inland. Very small numbers nest from March, a round scrape, usually sparsely lined or rimmed with fragments, on open ground not far from water, usually amongst scattered scrub (similar to the site of Saunders' Little Tern, plate 66). The eggs, 1–3 and normally 3, point downward, and are sometimes partly covered with sand by the adult. Parents have a distraction display. The call is a pleasant *wit-wit-wit, poo-eet* or *prrr-ip*, the alarm *kittup*, and there is a trill during butterfly-like display flight.

134

Plate 44

**Lesser Sand Plover** (Mongolian Sand Plover)  *Charadrius mongolus*  See also plate 56

**World:** Breeds in S Russia, N India to W China and in NE Asia, in two groups. Migratory.
**Oman:** A regular and fairly common passage migrant and winter visitor, locally abundant on Masirah over winter, less common in Dhofar, a few occasionally over summer; *C.m. atrifrons* is the usual race.

*C.m. atrifrons* 20cm/8in. A small robust shore-bird, about the size of the Ringed Plover. The *adult male (summer)* has a distinctive broad black mask from forehead to bill and ear-coverts, with a narrow stripe of white above and below the forehead, and rufous-cinnamon on the crown, hind-neck and broad breast-band across the white under-parts; in the *female* the black is replaced by brown. In *winter* difficult to distinguish from Greater Sand Plover, except by smaller size, shorter stubbier bill, possibly shorter and darker legs; differs from Kentish Plover in the more bulky form and lack of a white collar. In *summer, males* differ from Greater Sand Plover in the black mask and broader breast-band; and from Caspian Plover in the paler breast-band in summer without a blackish lower border.

*summer A*

*winter B*

On mud-flats in loose flocks; roosting on dry ground. Calls include a *short chidik* and *twik-twik-twik*.

**Caspian Plover**  *Charadrius asiaticus*  See also plate 56

**World:** Breeds in central Asia (Caspian eastwards to Lake Balkhash). Migratory, reaching Africa, W India.
**Oman:** Scarce autumn passage migrant August–October.

19cm/7½in. Although near the size of Lesser Sand Plover it is noticeably longer-legged, more upright and elegant; in flight the legs project beyond the tail as in Greater Sand Plover. *Adult (winter)* similar to Lesser and Greater Sand Plovers, but differs in bold pale supercilium, upper-parts with pale fringes to feathers, grey-brown neck and breast, rather more upright posture, slender bill and habitat preference. *Adult (summer)* has a white face and supercilium and a bold chestnut breast-band with blackish lower border. The *juvenile* has distinct paler fringes on the sandy-brown upper-parts; the white under-parts are tinged buff. The legs are dull greenish or yellowish.

*winter D*

*summer C*

Prefers grassy plains and semi-desert, and should be looked for behind beaches and inland, like Lesser Golden Plover. Usually in small flocks but sometimes singly in Oman. The call is *ku-wit*.

**Greater Sand Plover** (Geoffrey's Sand Plover) *Charadrius leschenaultii*  See also plate 56

**World:** Breeds from Turkey east to Manchuria. Migratory, reaching coasts of E Africa, Arabia, India, SE Asia, Australasia.
**Oman:** Regular and fairly common passage migrant and winter visitor, locally abundant on Masirah over winter, less common in Dhofar, a few over summer.

23cm/9in. Difficult to distinguish from Lesser Sand Plover in *winter* and *juvenile* plumages except when direct comparison shows its larger size and longer, bulbous-tipped bill. The *adult male (summer)* has a white forehead, a narrow dark streak through eye to ear-coverts, and cinnamon-rufous on crown, hind-neck, collar and narrow breast-band. The *female* lacks the black on the forehead and face, and the breast-band is less bright. In flight the dark flight-feathers contrast with a narrow white wing-bar (more extensive than in the Lesser). The *juveniles* of both species have pale fringes to the feathers of the upper-parts.

*winter F*
*summer E*

On mud-flats in loose parties, roosting on dry ground. The call is a rippling *tiriri-tiriri-tiriri*, also a gentle *pririt*.

**Dotterel**  *Charadrius morinellus*  See also plate 56

**World:** Breeds in widely separated populations across Eurasia to Alaska. Migratory, reaching Mediterranean, Sudan, Arabian Gulf.
**Oman:** Vagrant (two reported on a ship 50 miles east of Masirah, 6 April 1960).

22cm/8½in. *Adult (winter)* is dark brown above, the crown darkest, the feathers with rusty fringes, the broad dingy white supercilium meeting as a V at the nape, tail fringed white with dark band near tip; below, smoky from throat to lower breast, with a faint whitish band on the breast, belly white. *Adult (summer)* has black crown, mantle-feathers fringed rufous, the chin, face and supercilium white; below, the upper breast grey-brown with dark streaks, the lower breast chestnut, the belly black. Legs fairly short, brownish-yellow. *Juvenile* is similar to *winter adult*, but looks more spotted, with paler fringes on upper-parts, supercilium buff. No wing-bar in flight. See Lesser Golden Plover (plate 46).

*winter H*

*summer G*

Usually inland on grass or cultivation, sometimes near water, rarely on seashore. Often quite tame.

Plate 45

## GOLDEN PLOVERS: *Pluvialis*

Medium-sized and upright; speckled above, and mostly black below in summer.

**Lesser Golden Plover**   *Pluvialis dominica*                    See also plate 57

**World: Asiatic Golden Plover** *P.d. fulva* breeds in Arctic Siberia and W Alaska; migrant and vagrant, reaching Arabia, India, SE Asia, Indo-Pacific Oceans, etc. Another race in N America.
**Oman:** Passage migrant and winter visitor in small numbers July–April, most in October and November, occasionally in May and June.

24cm/9½in. Very similar to the Golden Plover, but differs in smaller size, comparatively longer legs, duller colours in *winter*, and having the under-wing and axillaries smoky-grey (not pure white). *Adult (winter)* is uniform dark brown with golden and black speckles above, including rump and tail (which look dark), and has only a faint wing-bar; below, whitish, except for mottled golden-buff on throat and breast. The *juvenile* is similar but more buff. *Adult (summer)* is black from face to under tail-coverts, with a contrasting white streak from forehead to flanks. Young Grey Plover also have golden-yellow speckles above, but have black axillaries, white wing-bar and rump. See Dotterel (plate 45).

*winter* B

*summer* A

Open grass and cultivation, on seashore on passage. Gregarious, scattering to feed on invertebrates and seeds. Call, a far-carrying whistle, *tee, lu-eee* or *tl-ee-ee*, somewhat like the Greenshank.

**Golden Plover**   *Pluvialis apricaria*                    See also plate 57

**World:** Breeds from Iceland to Siberia, in two races. Migratory, reaching the Mediterranean, N Iran, W India; casually to Arabia, etc.
**Oman:** Vagrant or scarce passage migrant and winter visitor to N Oman, between July and May; other reports suggest confusion with Lesser Golden.

28cm/11in. Care is required to avoid confusion with the more common Lesser Golden Plover, from which the Golden differs in its larger size, white axillaries and under-wing, and bolder white wing-bar. In *summer* plumage the ventral region is white (not black).

*winter* D

*summer* C

Habits are similar to those of the Lesser Golden, and the call is a rather similar *tloo-ee* or *tloo-ee-ee*.

**Grey Plover**   *Pluvialis squatarola*                    See also plate 57

**World:** Breeds in Arctic Asia and N America. Migratory, almost world-wide.
**Oman:** Passage migrant and winter visitor July–May in small numbers, most during autumn in N Oman and Masirah, few in summer.

28cm/11in. A thick-set plover of the sea-shore, stouter than the Golden, larger than the Lesser Golden and distinguished from both in flight by distinct black axillaries (appearing as an oval spot contrasting with the white under-wing), bold white rump and base of tail, and white wing-bar. The *adult (winter)* is brownish-grey above, mottled with white; white below, with brown mottling on throat and upper breast. The *adult (summer)* is strikingly black-and-white below, and dark with bold silver-grey speckles above. The *juvenile* is similar to the *winter adult*, but the mottling above is tinged with pale gold or cream, which may cause confusion with the Lesser Golden or Golden until it flies.

*winter* F
*summer* E

Shores, mud-flats and creeks, rarely inland. Usually more solitary than the Lesser Golden or Golden, except in roosts. The flight is strong, often over the sea. The call is *tlee-oo-ee* or *tloo-wee*, rather plaintive and high-pitched.

## LAPWINGS                                                        Plates 46-47

Fairly large, with long legs, long, broad and conspicuously black-and-white wings, and a white tail usually tipped black. Some have crests or facial wattles.

**Spur-winged Lapwing**   *Hoplopterus spinosus*                    See also plate 57

**World:** Breeds from W to E Africa, north to SE Europe and Near East, has wandered to Odessa, Iraq, Iran, Arabian Gulf, Arabia.
**Oman:** Vagrant (one near Salalah, 19 October 1977).

28cm/11in. A black-and-white lapwing with greyish-brown mantle and wing-coverts. The crown and short crest over the nape are glossy black, and the cheeks and neck are white except for the diagnostic black streak leading down the chin to the black breast and flanks. The belly, under-wing, rump and base of tail are white, and there is a conspicuous white patch in the wing-coverts. The flight-feathers, most of the tail and the legs are black. The *juvenile* has buff fringes to the feathers of the brown upper-parts, and the black of the under-parts is sooty and broken.

Usually on short vegetation near water. Rather silent in winter.

Plate 46                                                                        139

**Red-wattled Lapwing**   *Hoplopterus indicus*                    See also plate 57

**World:** *H.i. aigneri* breeds in Transcaspia, Iraq, S Iran, UAE, N Oman, Afghanistan and NW India; sedentary and migratory. Other races in India, Sri Lanka and SE Asia.
**Oman:** Breeding resident and partial migrant in N Oman; a scarce visitor in Masirah and Dhofar.

33cm/13in. The largest lapwing in Oman, with long yellow legs and distinctive crimson eye-rim, small wattle in front of each eye, and bill with black tip. The combination of black crown, broad white neck-streak, bronze mantle, black bib and white belly is also distinctive. In flight it shows a striking combination of black primaries, white secondaries, brown coverts, and white tail with a broad black terminal bar. The *juvenile* is recognisably similar, but has a paler crown, a white face and chin, a buff tip to the tail and pinkish legs. The *chick* is sandy-brown, with black speckles, a black line round the nape, white from eye to collar, and a faint black bib.

Near fresh or brackish water of creeks, pools, wadis, irrigated cultivation and date-groves, coastal and inland. It feeds on invertebrates and vegetable matter. Usually singly or in pairs, but in groups in spring. The nest, March–July, is a natural depression or scrape, occasionally decorated, amongst stones or on sand in the open near water and vegetation. The eggs, 3–4, are buff or greenish, with heavy dark blotches. The noisy cries of nesting birds, often heard at night, include a loud *Did 'e do it?* or *Did, did, did 'e do it?*, also *krik-krik*, etc.


**White-tailed Lapwing**   *Chettusia leucura*                    See also plate 57

**World:** Breeds in SW Russia, south to Iraq and Iran. Sedentary and migratory, reaching NE Africa, Arabian Gulf, NW India, Burma, and has wandered elsewhere.
**Oman:** Rather scarce sporadic passage migrant and winter visitor August–April.

26.5cm/10in. A long-legged, pale brown-and-white bird, smaller than the Sociable Lapwing, and not always reminiscent of a lapwing until it flies and shows black primaries, a broad white bar on the wings and an all-white tail and rump. The *adult's* head and mantle are vinous or bronze, the forehead and supercilium whitish; the chin is whitish, the neck pale brown, the breast grey (paler grey in *female*), the belly rosy-buff and the under tail-coverts white. The bill is black, and the long legs are pale yellow. The *juvenile* is lightly streaked with dark brown, the feathers fringed buff.

Margins of creeks and marshes, wadis with water, and irrigated cultivation. It has a slow, stately walk, pecking deep into mud for invertebrate food. Usually silent in winter, but the call is *kit-kit*.


**Sociable Lapwing**   *Chettusia gregaria*                    See also plate 57

**World:** Breeds in central Asia. Migratory, reaching NE Africa, Iraq, NW India, wandering further to Arabia, Sri Lanka, etc.
**Oman:** Vagrant (one certain record on Masirah, 1 December 1974).

33cm/13in. A drab ash-grey lapwing when at rest in *winter*, with a dark crown without crest, a dark stripe through the eye, broad buff supercilia from the forehead meeting on the hind-neck – see Cream-coloured Courser (plate 42) – dusky-white under-parts except for the breast mottled with grey-brown. In flight the black primaries, white secondaries, white rump and white tail with a partial sub-terminal black bar are obvious. The *juvenile* is similar but has rufous fringes to feathers, and more buff below, with dark V-shaped flecks on the breast. *Adult (summer)* has the crown and eye-stripe brown-black, supercilium white, throat and breast grey, lower breast black and belly rufous-chestnut.

On grassland and sub-desert, also near water.


**Lapwing**   *Vanellus vanellus*                    See also plate 57

**World:** Breeds across temperate Eurasia, south to NW Africa, Turkey, N Iran. Sedentary and migratory, reaching N Africa, Palestine, Arabian Gulf, N India, Far East, wandering further.
**Oman:** Scarce winter visitor to N Oman in some years, to Dhofar rarely, between November and March.

30cm/12in. Fairly large, appearing black-and-white at a distance, with broad rounded blackish wings with white tips, and black-tipped tail (viewed from above in flight). *Adult (summer)* is unmistakable, with curved crest, glossy black head and mantle, black breast, white belly, white patch on the under-wing and rufous under tail-coverts. The *adult (winter)* has a brown crown, the *female* with a shorter crest and whitish chin; the *juvenile* is similar but less glossy, with buff fringes.

Edges of cultivation, wadis, creeks, occasionally into date-groves. Gregarious, but in ones and twos in Oman. The flight is a rather slow flapping. Usually silent in winter.

Plate 47

# SANDPIPERS, SNIPE, GODWITS, etc: Scolopacidae    Plates 48–55

**World:** 82 species. **Oman:** 28 species. A varied family of small to medium-sized marsh, shore and tundra birds. Plumage dull or cryptic; patterns on wing, tail and rump important for identification; some have brighter summer plumage, occasionally seen in Oman; many in juvenile plumage occur in autumn; sexes similar. Bill long in most species, slender, often curved, for probing for mainly animal food. Most breed in high latitudes and migrate in flocks over long distances on long pointed wings. Includes small sandpipers and Ruff (sub-family Calidridinae), snipe (Gallinagininae), woodcock (Scolopacinae), godwits, etc. (Tringinae), turnstones (Arenariinae), and phalaropes (Phalaropodinae).

## SANDPIPERS: Calidridinae    Plates 48–49 and 51

Small sandpipers are 'peeps' in USA, the smallest are 'stints' in UK.

### Dunlin    *Calidris alpina*    See also plate 56

Dunlin

**World:** *C.a. alpina* breeds from N Norway to NW Asia; migratory, reaching W and E Africa, Arabia, NW India. Other races in N America, Iceland, W Europe, NE Siberia.
**Oman:** Regular passage migrant and winter visitor, July–April, only locally common, abundant near Masirah over winter, some May–June.

19cm/7½in. *Adult (summer)* has a diagnostic large black belly-patch, and the upper-parts appear marbled (dark brown with chestnut feather-fringes). *Juvenile* rather similar above; white below, the breast streaked buff, the flanks spotted black. *Adult (winter)* resembles winter Curlew Sandpiper, but rump is black with white sides, bill usually shorter, straighter and broader; it differs from the winter Sanderling in darker mantle, greyish breast and lack of black shoulder.

*summer A*

*winter B*

Mud-flats, sand, creeks, muddy pools, etc. Gregarious, feeding with rapid 'stitching' probes in a hunched manner, often with other species. Flight-call a harsh nasal *tree* or *twee*.

### Curlew Sandpiper    *Calidris ferruginea*    See also plate 56

Curlew Sandpiper

**World:** Breeds in Siberia. Migratory, reaching Africa, Arabia, Indian Ocean, India, etc.
**Oman:** Regular passage migrant and winter visitor; fairly common July–November, some over winter, slight spring passage April–May, a few in June.

19cm/7½in. *Adult (winter)* resembles winter Dunlin except for the conspicuous white rump, more prominent white supercilium, more upright stance and distinctive call. *Adult (summer)* is rich chestnut, with pale fringes to feathers of upper-parts, and whitish around bill. *Juvenile* is grey-brown above, with pale feather-fringes; white tinged buff below, with some streaks on upper breast..

*winter D*
*summer C*

Mud-flats, sand, creeks, muddy pools, etc., sometimes with Dunlin. Its habits are similar but its stance is noticeably more graceful and less hunched. Call, a distinctive *chirrip* or *chirririp*.

### Broad-billed Sandpiper    *Limicola falcinellus*    See also plate 56

Broad-billed Sandpiper

**World:** *L.f. falcinellus* breeds from Scandinavia to NE Asia; migratory, reaching E Africa, Arabia, India. Another race in E Asia.
**Oman:** Passage migrant and winter visitor in very small numbers, July–December, rarely January.

16.5cm/6½in. Like a large Little Stint or small Dunlin, noticeably hunched, short-legged, and with the long, broad-based bill bent at the tip. *Adult (winter)* resembles Dunlin but the white supercilium forks behind the eye into double snipe-like crown streaks. *Adult (summer)* is dark brown above, with a bold snipe-like pattern. The legs are grey-green (not black).

*winter E*

Wet mud and sand. It walks slower than the Little Stint and Dunlin, pecking occasionally, stopping to drill or probe deeply for worms, which it drags out, washes and swallows. Less gregarious than other small sandpipers, except on passage. Call, *tchiprit* or *chrreek*.

### Sanderling    *Calidris alba*    See also plate 56

Sanderling

**World:** Breeds locally in Arctic from N America eastwards to Siberian islands. Migratory, almost cosmopolitan in winter.
**Oman:** Fairly common passage migrant and winter visitor, August–May with peak passage April and May; some present in June and July.

20cm/8in. A squat, fast-running bird of sandy beaches, slightly larger than the Dunlin, with a more conspicuous white wing-bar. *Adult (winter)* is pale grey above, with a dark patch on the bend of the wings, and pure white below. *Adult (summer)* is rufous, with fine blackish marks above and on the breast; the belly is white. *Juvenile* is chequered black-and-white above and lacks the dark wing-patch.

*winter G*
*summer F*

Sandy beaches in small groups, pecking food from sand at the edge of waves, running in, out, then on. It rarely 'stitches' like the Dunlin. The flight note is a liquid *twick twick*.

Plate 48

# STINTS

The smallest wader species in Oman. The Little Stint is common but in very varied plumage. Temminck's and Long-toed Stints have diagnostic features. Great care is required with the Red-necked Stint.

**Temminck's Stint**    *Calidris temminckii*        See also plate 56      Temminck's Stint

**World:** Breeds across N Eurasia. Migratory, reaching Africa, Arabia, India, etc.
**Oman:** A regular passage migrant and winter visitor in small numbers from late July to early May.

15cm/6in. Very small. The *adult (winter)* is rather similar to other stints, but differs in more dull uniform greyish upper-parts and breast; the pale wing-bar is indistinct, and the outer tail-feathers are white (not grey), contrasting with dark centrals and rump, best seen from behind. The legs are yellowish, brownish or greenish. In *summer* it appears mostly dull greyish, despite additions of darker and rufous marks. The *juvenile* is brownish-grey above, the feathers with dark centres and narrow buff fringes.

Muddy margins of fresh or brackish water near but rarely on coast, preferably with cover; also inland. It is less gregarious than the Little Stint. On flushing it tends to tower singly, rising fast and high like the Long-toed Stint. Call, a distinctive high-pitched rapid trilling *trrrt* or *trr-it-it*.

*winter* B

*summer* A

**Little Stint**    *Calidris minuta*        See also plate 56      Little Stint

**World:** Breeds in N Eurasia. Migratory, reaching Africa, Indian Ocean, India.
**Oman:** Common passage migrant and winter visitor July–May, most in autumn, some in June.

15cm/6in. The most common stint in Oman. Like a very small winter Dunlin, but with a short fine straight bill, whiter breast, and no black belly in *summer*. The *adult (summer)* is rufous above, mottled black, with a clear, narrow white wing-bar; the sides of the head are more or less rufous, leading to misidentification as Red-necked Stint; the rump and centre of the tail are dark, with white sides to the rump and grey outer tail-feathers. It is white below, except for a rufous breast-band with dark brown mottles at the sides. The legs are black. In *winter* sometimes confusing, greyish above, the feathers with darker centres; white below, with grey marks at the sides of the breast. *Juveniles* in *autumn* are like varied pale *summer adults*, but the nape and face are pale, the outer tail-feathers are greyish and there is a distinct creamy V on the back.

Open mud-flats and muddy margins to coastal creeks and pools, not so often inland as Temminck's and Long-toed Stints. Very active, rapidly walking and pecking, often in small parties. Call, *tit-tit-tit*.

*summer* C

*winter* D

**[Red-necked Stint** (Rufous-necked Sandpiper)    *Calidris ruficollis*      Red-necked Stint

**World:** Breeds from NE Siberia to E Alaska. Migratory, reaching SE Asia, Australasia; also reported from Durban and Seychelles.
**Oman:** Vagrant? (Reported in August and May, but confirmation necessary.)

16cm/4½in. Requires greatest care to distinguish from Little Stint, but bill is more stubby, and it may appear slightly larger and longer at rest because of longer wings and tail. The *adult (summer)* has chestnut-red throat, cheeks and upper breast, and some dark spotting on sides of lower breast. In *winter* probably indistinguishable in the field from Little Stint, and best identified in the hand by wing–tarsus ratio. *Juvenile* is similar to Little Stint, but lacks the V mark on the mantle.

On coasts, with habits similar to those of Little Stint. Often noisy, calling a high-pitched *chit-chit-chit*.]

*summer* E

**Long-toed Stint**    *Calidris subminuta*        Long-toed Stint

**World:** Breeds in Siberia. Migratory, reaching Indian Ocean, India, Sri Lanka, SE Asia and casually to E Africa, Seychelles, Australia.
**Oman:** Scarce passage migrant and winter visitor, reported singly between September and May.

15cm/6in. The darkest stint, with finer bill than Little Stint, upright stance, long neck, legs and toes, legs pale like Temminck's Stint, and with a distinctive call. The *adult (summer)* has blackish mantle-feathers fringed with bright ochre (not chestnut), crown, cheeks and neck tinged rufous and a breast-band of dark streaks. The tail is dark with grey sides, like the Little Stint. The legs are yellowish, brownish or greenish; the centre toe is 2–5mm longer than in other stints. In *winter* it is dark brown above with black feather-centres, giving a bold scaly, streaky or mottled appearance; the grey streaks on the breast are usually distinct. The *juvenile* has a dark nape, bright chestnut fringes and a slight pale V on the mantle.

Marshy margins to fresh water, and other damp vegetation, sometimes coastal on passage. It towers like Temminck's Stint, sometimes jinking. Call, a quiet *churrup,* or purred *trerp,* or *trrr-trrr*.

*summer* F

*winter* G

Plate 49

## SNIPE: Gallinagininae, WOODCOCK: Scolopacinae

Sturdy-bodied waders with long straight bills, short necks, short legs and cryptic plumage.

### Jack Snipe    *Lymnocryptes minimus*

Jack Snipe A

**World:** Breeds from Scandinavia to NE Siberia. Migratory, reaching tropical Africa, Arabia, India, SE Asia.
**Oman:** Passage migrant and winter visitor in very small numbers October–March.

19cm/7½in. Like a small Common Snipe; difficult to observe on the ground but can be distinguished by different flight and much shorter bill. It lacks the central buff stripe on the crown, which is black with a double buff stripe over each eye; the tail is wedge-shaped, without white, and the buffish-white flanks are mottled or streaked instead of barred.

Habitat similar to that of Common Snipe, but it is flushed less easily; it rises silently and flies more slowly and directly, turning less abruptly and not usually towering, more often dropping back into cover after a short distance. It feeds on invertebrates and vegetable matter on the surface, and by probing. Usually silent.

### Common Snipe    *Gallinago gallinago*

Common Snipe B

**World:** *G.g. gallinago* breeds across Eurasia mainly north of 40°N. Sedentary, northern birds migratory, reaching tropical Africa, Arabia, India, SE Asia. Other races in Americas, NW Europe.
**Oman:** Passage migrant and winter visitor August–April, regular and locally common; few in summer.

27cm/19½in. A shy marsh bird with a characteristic towering flight, harsh call, very long straight bill and cryptic plumage. The crown is black with a central buff streak and streaks above and below each eye, the mantle is black and rich rufous with bold creamy streaks, the tail (14 feathers) shows a little white at the sides; mostly white below, with some barring on the flanks. In flight it shows a narrow white bar on the trailing-edge of the secondaries. It differs from the Great Snipe in slightly smaller size, less white on tail, more extensive white on belly, a white trailing-edge to the wing, and lack of white spotting on the wing-coverts; from **Woodcock** *Scolopax rusticola* [34cm/13½in, breeds across Eurasia, wintering southwards but only occasionally reaching Arabia, Sri Lanka] in much smaller size, pointed wings, and lateral crown-stripe instead of transverse bars.

Marshes, pools and streams, etc. with damp vegetation. Usually first seen as it springs up, zig-zags, then towers in rapid flight, calling a harsh rasping *scǎǎp* or *krǎtch*. Partly crepuscular. Searches with rapid drilling movements, sometimes wading, mostly for worms and other invertebrates. Not gregarious, but numbers may occur in the same area; migration is in tight 'wisps'.

### Great Snipe    *Gallinago media*

Great Snipe D

**World:** Breeds from NE Europe to central Asia. Migratory, wintering mainly in Africa, has occurred in Arabian Gulf, E Arabia, India.
**Oman:** Vagrant or very scarce autumn passage migrant September–November.

28cm/11in. Slightly larger, darker and bulkier than the Common Snipe, with heavier flight and, in *adults*, more white on the outer tail-feathers. *Adults* are difficult to distinguish on the ground from Common Snipe, but wing-coverts are boldly spotted white, the tips forming at least one bar, the tips of all 16 tail-feathers except the central pair are unbarred white, visible when spread, the white trailing-edge of the secondaries is narrower and there is more distinct barring on breast and flanks, extending on to the belly; the bill is comparatively stouter and shorter. The *juvenile* lacks the white in the tail.

Marshes, etc., often in drier situations than other snipes and usually singly. When flushed it flies slower, more directly and generally not as high nor as far as the Common Snipe; usually silent.

### Pintail Snipe    *Gallinago stenura*

Pintail Snipe C

**World:** Breeds in northern central and E Asia. Migratory, reaching India and islands, SE Asia, but has occurred in Africa, Socotra, E Arabia.
**Oman:** Vagrant or very scarce passage migrant and winter visitor September–April, probably overlooked.

27cm/10½in. Differs from Common Snipe in flight in the lack of a white trailing-edge to secondaries, under-wing and flanks dark with dense barring, blunter wing-tips, less contrasting upper-parts and paler brown upper-wing; in the hand by the diagnostic very narrow outer tail-feathers.

Occasionally with Common Snipe, but often on drier grass near water; it probes less, takes more insects; it is less shy; rises in slower, heavier, more direct flight; and is usually silent.

Plate 50

**Ruff** *Philomachus pugnax* (sub-family Calidridinae, plates 48–49)   See also plate 57

**World:** Breeds from W Europe to NE Siberia, occasionally further south. Migratory, reaching Africa, Arabia, India, SE Asia.

**Oman:** Regular and fairly common passage migrant and winter visitor between July–April, most September–October, fewer on spring passage, some in May and June.

23–30cm/9–12in. The *male* (Ruff) in *summer* plumage, with coloured ruff and head-tufts, is distinctive but rarely seen in Oman. In *winter* the *male* resembles the much smaller *female* (Reeve). Both differ from the Redshank (plate 53) in their erect posture, fairly short, almost straight bill, varied scaly pattern on the upper-parts, conspicuous white oval patches on each side of the dark tail (often joined), narrow wing-bar and orange-yellow to brownish legs. The *juvenile* is smaller, its crown more rufous, its back more boldly marked with darker feathers and buff fringes; its breast is tinged buff and its legs are greenish.

Margins of marshes, creeks, streams and pools, and on damp vegetation; coastal and inland. Usually in groups which coalesce into large gatherings, especially in autumn. The food is mostly invertebrate, but grain is taken when available. Migration is at night, the males first. Usually silent.

## GODWITS, CURLEWS and LARGE SANDPIPERS: Tringinae    Plates 51–54

Includes the largest long-billed waders.

**Bar-tailed Godwit**    *Limosa lapponica*                    See also plate 58

**World:** *L. lapponica lapponica* breeds from N Scandinavia to Taimyr (110°E). Migratory, reaching coasts of Europe, Africa, Arabia, Indian Ocean, NW India. Another race from eastern Siberia to Alaska.

**Oman:** Passage migrant and winter visitor on coasts July–May; fairly common in N Oman July–October; locally abundant in thousands in the Masirah area; only in small numbers in Dhofar.

38cm/15in. A large wader with a reddish *summer* plumage, but more commonly seen in pale mottled greyish-brown *winter* plumage; the slightly (and variably) upturned bill and shorter legs distinguish it from curlews; from the Whimbrel it also differs in lack of crown-stripes, and from the Black-tailed Godwit in flight also in its less distinct wing-bar and pale tail without the black terminal bar; the feet project very little beyond the tail. The *adult (winter)* is ash-brown above, some feathers with darker centres and paler fringes; the lower back, rump and tail are white, with the tail-feathers irregularly mottled and barred brown; whitish below, with some slight brown streaks. The *juvenile* is browner above, the feathers with buff fringes, the tail strongly barred and the breast tinged buff. *Adult male (summer)* has head, neck and all under-parts chestnut; the *female* is duller, pale pink-chestnut, with grey on the breast and almost white belly and vent.

Mud-flats, sandy beaches and creeks. When not resting in compact or mixed flocks it walks, often wading deeply, and searches for worms, crabs, molluscs, etc., with deep skewering probes, also occasionally taking prey from the surface. In its quite rapid flight the neck is retracted, the bill pointed forward. Over mud-flats flocks will occasionally rise and glide down slowly. Mostly silent in winter, but it has a soft flight-call, *kirruk*.

**Black-tailed Godwit**    *Limosa limosa*                    See also plate 58

**World:** *L.l. limosa* breeds from W Europe to central Asia. Migratory, reaching tropical Africa, Arabia, N and W India. Other races in Iceland, NE Asia.

**Oman:** Passage migrant and winter visitor between late July and April, only occasional in N Oman and Masirah, more regularly in small numbers in Dhofar; a few in May and June.

41cm/16in. A large, tall, long-billed wader, differing in winter from the Bar-tailed Godwit, Whimbrel and curlews in its long straight bill, and in flight in its conspicuous white wing-bar, black-and-white tail and long legs extending well beyond the tail; also in its more fresh-water habitat. *Adult (winter)* is almost uniform brownish-grey above, darker than Bar-tailed; whitish below, with a grey wash particularly on the breast. The *juvenile* is dark brown above, the feathers with reddish fringes, the neck and breast are tinged reddish-buff, and the belly is white or creamy. *Adult (summer)* is dark brown above, with chestnut fringes; the cheeks, neck and breast are dull chestnut, and the belly to under tail-coverts white with some brown barring on the flanks. (See Bar-tailed female.)

Prefers mud of marshes, creeks and pools, particularly in fresh water, though rarely far inland in Oman. It feeds like the Bar-tailed Godwit, but more gracefully and often in deeper water; it tends to be rather shy and silent in winter.

Plate 51

**Whimbrel**  *Numenius phaeopus*                         See also plate 58     Whimbrel A

**World:** *N.p. phaeopus* breeds from Iceland, N Europe to NW Asia; migratory, reaching Africa, Arabia, Indian Ocean, W India. Other races in N America, NE Siberia.
**Oman:** Passage migrant and visitor; first arrivals May or June, becoming fairly common from August to November with large flocks very locally from September especially in the Masirah area; very few over winter; return passage February–April.

41cm/16in. Like a small Curlew, from which it differs in call, diagnostic crown-stripes (one narrow pale buff between two broad and dark), and relatively shorter bill; it is also generally darker above at all seasons. The *juvenile* is darker brown, spotted buff. It differs from the Slender-billed Curlew in head-pattern, less contrasting wing-pattern and call.

Habitat is similar to that of Curlew, but it wanders behind beaches more frequently. In winter it feeds more often on rocky shores, where it is rather more noisy. It flies with quicker wing-beats and has a loud distinctive tittering call.

**Slender-billed Curlew**  *Numenius tenuirostris*          See also plate 58     Slender-billed Curlew B

**World:** Breeds in central Asia (W Siberia) where it is now much reduced in numbers; a rare and endangered species. Migrates south-westward, reaching Arabia, Mediterranean, NW Africa, occasionally W Europe.
**Oman:** Very scarce vagrant (one reported in N Oman, April–May 1976).

41cm/16in. Like a small Curlew, and the size of a Whimbrel. It differs in the lack of the buff crown-stripe of the Whimbrel (but it has dark streaks above the pale supercilium), blackish heart-shaped spots on lower breast and flanks (diagnostic, but absent in the brown-flanked *juveniles*), much paler upper-parts with bolder white fringes (though some Curlews are as pale), more white on the back; the white tail (not buff) with dark barring, and the paler secondaries, give a flight-pattern like that of the Bar-tailed Godwit (plate 51). The bill is rather thick at the base but slender near the tip.

Usual Curlew habitat, but also inland at areas of temporary flooding. The flight is swifter and more erratic and it mixes with other species on passage. The call is like that of the Curlew, but shorter and higher-pitched.

**Curlew** (Eurasian Curlew)  *Numenius arquata*            See also plate 58     Curlew C

**World:** Breeds from W Europe to central Manchuria, in two races. Migratory, reaching Africa, Arabia, Indian Ocean, India, SE Asia.
**Oman:** Passage migrant and winter visitor July–April, a few over summer, most in autumn when very common in Masirah area, quite common locally elsewhere; smaller numbers in winter and spring. *N.a. orientalis* occurs.

53–58cm/21–23in. The largest wader, with a long down-curved bill, but it is variable in size and colouration. The *adult* is browny-buff above, closely streaked from head to breast, the mantle heavily mottled, the lower back and rump white, the tail heavily barred dark brown; buffish-white below with some bars on the flanks, the under-wing and axillaries white with some brown marks. The *juvenile* is more buff. The eastern race *orientalis* is generally paler and larger than the western race, and more buff in *summer*. It differs from the Whimbrel in the lack of crown stripes, larger size, and call; from the Slender-billed Curlew in longer, thicker bill, larger size and darker secondaries.

Coasts, creeks and mud-flats, singly or in groups. It walks and wades, probing deeply for invertebrate food, occasionally probing sideways under rocks and picking from the surface. The call is a ringing *croo-ee*, or *cur-lee* or *cor-wee*, etc., occasionally a titter rather like that of a Whimbrel.

Plate 52

**Spotted Redshank**    *Tringa erythropus*                    See also plate 57                    Spotted Redshank

**World:** Breeds in extreme N of Eurasia. Migratory, reaching Mediterranean, tropical Africa, Arabia, India, SE Asia.
**Oman:** Scarce and irregular passage migrant and winter visitor, July–April; reports suggest some confusion with Redshank.

30cm/12in. Like a slightly larger and more elegant Redshank, but distinguished in *winter* by lack of a    *winter* A
distinct white wing-bar, plainer ash-grey upper-parts, longer, thinner bill, longer orange-red to dark
reddish legs, and distinctive call. *Juvenile* is similar, but darker above, with pale spots; below, it is
barred and tinged grey-brown on white. *Adult (summer)* is distinctive, mostly black, with pale
feather-fringes above. In *winter* the *adult* differs from the Greenshank in bill, call and leg-colour.

Borders of coastal creeks and marshes, also at fresh or brackish pools inland. Shy, mostly single,
sometimes with other species. The call is *to-wee* or *tchoo-eet*, also a *tuk-tuk-tuk* alarm.

**Redshank**    *Tringa totanus*                    See also plate 57                    Redshank

**World:** Breeds from Iceland across Eurasia to central or NE China, south to E Turkey, Iran, Kashmir,
in several races. Migratory, reaching tropical Africa, Arabia, India, SE Asia.
**Oman:** Common passage migrant and winter visitor, some over summer, main passages July–
September, February–April.

28cm/11in. A medium-sized, grey-brown wader, conspicuous by its loud call and broad white wing-    *winter* B
bar (tips of secondaries); its lower back and rump are white, and the tail is also white but closely
barred blackish. The legs are orange-red, bright in *summer,* yellowish in *juvenile.* In *summer* the
upper-parts are warmer brown with much black streaking, and the breast is darker. *Juvenile* also warm
brown above, the feathers fringed with buff. Differs from the Spotted Redshank in smaller size,
wing-bar, shorter bill and legs; from Terek Sandpiper (plate 54) in larger size, straight bill and longer
legs; from Ruff (plate 51) in wing-bar, white rump and longer bill.

Creeks, mud-flats, marshes, inland water. Shy, it bobs its head and flies up at the slightest pretext,
giving the alarm-call *teyook-teyook-teyook*; the usual call is a single musical *teeew* or *tew-hew-hew.* It
feeds off the surface and by probing, sometimes wading and swimming.

**Greenshank**    *Tringa nebularia*                    See also plate 57                    Greenshank

**World:** Breeds across northern Eurasia. Migratory, reaching Africa, Arabia, India to Australasia.
**Oman:** Passage migrant and winter visitor, in small numbers July–April, a few May and June.

33cm/13in. Somewhat like a large Redshank, but distinguished by its streaky grey upper-parts, thicker    *winter* C
upturned bill, longer green legs, lack of white in the upper-wing, dark under-wing and the fact that the
white reaches further up the back; it is white below, except for fine streaks on the breast. In *summer*
the upper-parts are dark grey to dark brown, marked with black, the upper breast boldly streaked and
spotted blackish. The *juvenile* is also dark above, with pale feather-fringes, but is more darkly
streaked below, and the legs are yellowish. It differs from the smaller Marsh Sandpiper in its much
stouter, slightly upturned bill, shorter legs and less graceful appearance, but care is needed in distingu-
ishing them at long distances.

Borders of creeks, marshes, pools and streams, at coastal roosts often on rocks. Not gregarious except
at roosts and on migration. It feeds on animal matter obtained by probing, by pecking off the surface,
by side-to-side sweeps in water like an Avocet and by running in water with the bill open like a
Spoonbill. Call, a loud *tew-tew-tew*, lower-pitched than that of the Redshank, also a repeated *chip* of
unease.

**Marsh Sandpiper**    *Tringa stagnatilis*                    See also plate 57                    Marsh Sandpiper

**World:** Breeds from SE Europe to central Asia and China. Migratory, reaching Africa, Arabia, India
to Australasia.
**Oman:** Passage migrant and winter visitor in very small numbers August–April, a few in summer.

23cm/9in. Resembles Greenshank in *winter* plumage and general flight-pattern; in distant view some-    *winter* D
times difficult to distinguish unless both species are together. It differs in being smaller, slighter and
more graceful; the long needle-fine bill is not upturned, and the spindly legs appear longer and project
further beyond the tail in flight. In *summer* it becomes buff, mottled blackish above; white below, the
chin to breast spotted, and some bars on the flanks and under tail-coverts.

Prefers fresh-water marshes, pools, etc., but occurs with Greenshank in creeks. Its feeding habits are
similar, but more active and graceful. Typical flight-call, a feeble *tew*, unlike that of the Greenshank.

152

Plate 53

153

**Common Sandpiper**   *Actitis hypoleucos*                     See also plate 56     Common Sandpiper A

**World:** Breeds across Eurasia, south to Mediterranean, E Africa, Iran, N India. Migratory, reaching Africa, Arabia, India and islands, SE Asia, Australasia.
**Oman:** Common and widespread passage migrant and winter visitor July–May, most July–October, some over summer.

20cm/7¾in. Like a small *Tringa* sandpiper, but with distinctive flight and behaviour. The *adult (winter)* has an indistinct supercilium and is olive-brown above, finely barred on the wing-coverts; there is a clear white wing-bar (tips of coverts), the rump is brown, and the tail brown edged with white; the sides of the breast are olive-brown, the rest of the under-parts white. The *juvenile* is similar, but the brown feathers have extensive buffish tips. *Adult (summer)* is darker, with darker marking reaching the upper breast. Differs from Green and Wood Sandpipers in smaller size and lack of white rump.

Margins of creeks, marshes, streams, coastal and inland. Often quite tame, walking or running in spurts along the water-edge, with frequent bobbing up and down of the end-part of the body, reminiscent of a wagtail (Wood and Green Sandpipers also bob). Food is pecked from the surface. If disturbed it flies low for a short distance with distinctive short flickering wing-beats, and glides on down-curved wings. The call is a shrill, whistling *twee-wee-wee-wee*, particularly noisy at dusk.


**Green Sandpiper**   *Tringa ochropus*                          See also plate 56     Green Sandpiper

**World:** Breeds from N Europe across Eurasia. Migratory, reaching tropical Africa, Arabia, India, SE Asia.
**Oman:** Fairly common passage migrant and winter visitor July–April, very few May–June.

23cm/9in. Larger than Wood Sandpiper, with more contrasting black-and-white plumage, especially    *winter* B
in flight, when black under-wing, whiter rump and different call are noticeable; the legs darker olive-green, and the supercilium not reaching behind the eye. *Adult (winter)* is blackish-brown above, with indistinct pale flecks sometimes making it confusable with the Wood Sandpiper; rump and upper tail-coverts white, tail whiter than that of Wood Sandpiper; below, as Wood Sandpiper except for black under-wing. *Juvenile* olive-brown above with buff spots. *Adult (summer)* more heavily spotted with buffish-white above.

Margins of marshes, pools, streams, with cover, occasionally with Wood Sandpiper and frequently inland, more often singly or in pairs in wadis over winter. Flies up with a noisy *tweet weet-weet*.


**Wood Sandpiper**   *Tringa glareola*                           See also plate 56     Wood Sandpiper

**World:** Breeds from N Europe across Eurasia. Migratory, reaching Africa, Arabia, India, SE Asia, Australasia.
**Oman:** Passage migrant and winter visitor July–May, widespread, not numerous, few in winter.

20cm/8in. Larger than Common Sandpiper, a little smaller than Green Sandpiper, differing from    *winter* C
Common in white rump, lack of wing-bar, and longer legs; from Green in grey-brown under-wing (not black), in being generally paler especially in flight, in the supercilium extending behind the eye, in the smaller rump-patch, and in the longer pale green to yellowish legs. *Adult (winter)* is dark brown above, with pale spotting (tips and edges of feathers), the upper tail-coverts are white with brown marks, and the tail is barred white and brown; white below, except for a brown wash from cheeks to breast. The *juvenile* is similar, but spotted buff. *Adult (summer)* is more contrasting, with bolder spots on the upper-parts and streaking on the breast.

Margins of marshes, pools, streams, preferably fresh with cover, often inland where it is outnumbered by the Green Sandpiper in winter. When flushed, calls a loud *chiff-chiff-chiff*, less shrill than Green.


**Terek Sandpiper**   *Xenus cinereus*                           See also plate 56     Terek Sandpiper

**World:** Breeds from Finland across N Eurasia. Migratory, reaching eastern Africa, Arabia, India to Australasia.
**Oman:** Passage migrant and winter visitor, fairly common from late July to November, some over winter, slight passage March–May, a few over summer.

23cm/9in. A greyish shore-bird with distinctive feeding behaviour. Short orange legs (rarely pale) and    *winter* D
white wing-bar may make it resemble a small, short-legged Redshank (plate 53), but the upturned bill is diagnostic, and its rump and tail are grey, not white. In *summer*, there are black centres to the mantle-feathers, and the sides of the breast are streaked darker. The *juvenile* is rather similar, dark above with reddish-buff fringes.

Shores, mud-flats and creeks, feeding singly or in large scattered groups which roost together. Very active, usually running with head low in a distinctive crouched posture, faster than the Common Sandpiper, catching insects and small crabs. Not shy. The usual calls include *pee-pee-pee-peep*.


154

Plate 54                                                                                           155

## TURNSTONES: Arenariinae
Boldly patterned shore-birds; sometimes placed in the family Charadriidae.

**Turnstone** (Ruddy Turnstone)     *Arenaria interpres*     See also plate 56     Turnstone

**World:** *A.i. interpres* breeds on arctic coasts of N America, Eurasia, and some islands, south to Scandinavia; highly migratory, reaching islands and coasts of Atlantic, Indian, Pacific Oceans. Another race in N America.
**Oman:** Common passage migrant and winter visitor, peak August–October, lesser peak March–May, a few over summer.

23cm/9in. A squat shore-bird with a distinctive black-and-white pattern in flight and short upturned bill. In *summer* it is unmistakable; the head is black, brown and white, the mantle bright 'tortoise-shell' (white, black, brown and chestnut), the back, rump and tail are patterned black-and-white; white below, except for a broad black breast-band. The short legs are bright orange. In *winter* it is much duller, but the bill, breast-band and variegated flight-pattern are still distinctive. The *juvenile* is like the *winter adult*, but with pale fringes to the feathers of the breast and upper-parts.

*summer* A

*winter* B

Rock, gravel and sand beaches, often roosting on rock. It walks rapidly in small parties, searching for small invertebrates, turning over seaweed, pebbles and objects with a heave of its sturdy bill. When disturbed it usually flies in low, wavering flight, calling with a harsh rattling *kitititit* or *tuk-a-tuk.*

## PHALAROPES: Phalaropodinae
Small, graceful, pelagic, swimming 'sandpipers' with dense plumage and partially webbed and lobed toes. The females are larger and brighter-coloured than the males in summer. Sometimes placed separately in the family Phalaropodidae.

**Red-necked Phalarope** (Northern Phalarope)     *Phalaropus lobatus*     See also plate 56     Red-necked Phalarope

**World:** Breeds across the northern fringe of Eurasia and N America, in Greenland, Iceland, etc. Migratory, wintering at sea, chiefly in the tropics, wherever plankton is sufficient.
**Oman:** Common passage migrant and winter visitor. Southward passage over land and sea from July, becoming abundant off Dhofar August–September, flocks wandering locally during winter; return movement March–April, lesser numbers in May, very few in June.

18cm/7in. A small dainty pelagic wader, usually seen in *winter* or *juvenile* plumage, when very difficult to distinguish at sea from winter Grey Phalarope; differences include smaller size, all-dark needle-fine bill, and less uniform darker grey upper-parts with white feather-edges. The *juvenile* is similar but has a browner crown, darker mantle with buff fringes and streaks, and a buff or vinous tinge on the white breast. *Adult (summer)* is unmistakable, but the *male* is much duller and browner than the *female.*

*winter* D

*summer* C

Individually or in small flocks at sea, occasionally storm-driven on coasts, sometimes on inland pools or running on the beach like the Sanderling. It swims buoyantly, pecking at surface plankton in a random manner, and in pools paddling and spinning to bring prey to the surface, occasionally up-ending. Shy at sea, but very tame inland. The short flights are erratic but swift, the calls include *twit* and *tirric-tirric.*

**Grey Phalarope**     *Phalaropus fulicarius*     See also plate 56     Grey Phalarope

**World:** Breeds along Arctic coasts of Greenland, Iceland, Siberia, N America. Migratory, wintering at sea chiefly off western S America and W Africa wherever plankton is sufficient, and further south than Red-necked Phalarope. Observed on passage in Caspian Sea, at Riyadh and in Straits of Hormuz.
**Oman:** Reported occasionally between autumn and spring; probably a scarce passage migrant and winter visitor, but more information on its status is needed.

20.5cm/8in. Very difficult to distinguish with certainty at sea in *winter* or *juvenile* plumage from the very similar winter Red-necked Phalarope, but it differs in larger size, short stout bill (usually with some yellow at the base), plainer grey upper-parts and more conspicuous white wing-bar; it differs from the winter Sanderling in the dark eye-patch, more elongate appearance and swimming habits. *Adult (summer)* is unmistakable; the *female* (as illustrated) brighter than the *male.* The *juvenile* with upper-parts like the summer male, except for white forehead, dark eye-patch and white under-parts tinged buff or vinous.

*winter* F

*summer* E

Its behaviour is similar to that of the Red-necked Phalarope, and it has a similar twittering call.

157

# SMALL WADERS IN FLIGHT:

Adults in winter plumage, from above.

**Caspian Plover**     *Charadrius asiaticus*                                     Plate 45            Caspian Plover A
Uniform brown upper-parts with ill-defined wing-bar and very little white in tail; white face and supercilium.

**Ringed Plover**     *Charadrius hiaticula*                                      Plate 44            Ringed Plover B
Conspicuous white wing-bar, broad white border to dark tail, well-defined head-pattern.

**Little Ringed Plover**     *Charadrius dubius*                                  Plate 44            Little Ringed Plover C
Differs from Ringed Plover in lack of wing-bar and in distinctive call; often inland near fresh water.

**Kentish Plover**     *Charadrius alexandrinus*                                 Plate 44            Kentish Plover D
Pale upper-parts with white collar, white wing-bar and conspicuous white sides to tail.

**Turnstone**     *Arenaria interpres*                                           Plate 55            Turnstone E
Distinctive black-and-white pattern on wings, back and tail.

**Greater Sand Plover**     *Charadrius leschenaultii*                           Plate 45            Great Sand Plover F
Large; sandy upper-parts with no white collar; white wing-bar, white sides to tail, and relatively long bill.

**Lesser Sand Plover**     *Charadrius mongolus*                                 Plate 45            Lesser Sand Plover G
Smaller than Greater Sand Plover, with less white on wings and tail; stubbier bill.

**Dotterel**     *Charadrius morinellus*                                         Plate 45            Dotterel H
Uniform dark brown upper-parts, tail has a dark sub-terminal band and white tips; conspicuous white supercilium and narrow whitish breast-band. (Scarce.)

**Sanderling**     *Calidris alba*                                               Plate 48            Sanderling I
Very pale grey upper-parts with conspicuous wing-bar, black at bend of wing and white sides to rump.

**Curlew Sandpiper**     *Calidris ferruginea*                                   Plate 48            Curlew Sandpiper J
White rump, narrow white wing-bar, rather long decurved bill; *chirrip* call.

**Dunlin**     *Calidris alpina*                                                 Plate 48            Dunlin K
Differs from Curlew Sandpiper in dark rump with white sides, shorter, heavier bill, harsher call.

**Broad-billed Sandpiper**     *Limicola falcinellus*                            Plate 48            Broad-billed Sandpiper L
Like a small Dunlin, but darker, with indistinct wing-bar and broader bill.

**Terek Sandpiper**     *Xenus cinereus*                                         Plate 54            Terek Sandpiper M
Rather grey, with a bold white trailing-edge to wing, greyish rump and upturned bill.

**Grey Phalarope**     *Phalaropus fulicarius*                                   Plate 55            Grey Phalarope N
Very similar to Red-necked Phalarope, but slightly larger, plainer grey on mantle and wing-coverts, and with a shorter, thicker bill. Usually indistinguishable at sea. (Scarce.)

**Red-necked Phalarope**     *Phalaropus lobatus*                                Plate 55            Red-necked Phalarope O
Small and dainty, with dark grey upper-parts, white wing-bar and sides of rump, black patch through eye, and needle-fine bill. Usually seen at sea.

**Temminck's Stint**     *Calidris temminckii*                                   Plate 49            Temminck's Stint P
Very small, with uniform greyish upper-parts, indistinct pale wing-bar, pure white sides to tail and rapid trilling flight-call.

**Little Stint**     *Calidris minuta*                                           Plate 49            Little Stint Q
Similar to Temminck's, but darker and mottled above, greyish sides to tail and tittering flight-call.

**Wood Sandpiper**     *Tringa glareola*                                         Plate 54            Wood Sandpiper R
Dark brown above, with white rump and pale barred tail; under-wings pale grey-brown.

**Green Sandpiper**     *Tringa ochropus*                                        Plate 54            Green Sandpiper S
Slightly larger than Wood Sandpiper, with blackish upper-parts, more white on rump and tail, black under-wings and shriller call.

**Common Sandpiper**     *Actitis hypoleucos*                                    Plate 54            Common Sandpiper T
Greyish-brown above and on sides of breast, a clear white wing-bar and white border to tail. Distinctive flight, with rapid shallow wing-beats and a glide on down-curved wings.

Plate 56

## MEDIUM-SIZED WADERS IN FLIGHT:

Adults in winter plumage, from above.

**Golden Plover**   *Pluvialis apricaria*                                   Plate 46         Golden Plover  A
Dark golden-brown upper-parts with indistinct pale wing-bar and dark tail; axillaries and under-wing white. (Scarce.)

**Lesser Golden Plover**   *Pluvialis dominica*                             Plate 46    Lesser Golden Plover  B
Slightly smaller and more buff than Golden Plover, with grey axillaries and under-wing.

**Grey Plover**   *Pluvialis squatarola*                                    Plate 46           Grey Plover  C
Larger than Golden Plover, with white rump, whitish barred tail, white wing-bar and black axillaries.

**Lapwing**   *Vanellus vanellus*                                           Plate 47              Lapwing  D
Large, with broad, rounded wings; blackish above, with pale nape, white wing-tips and white tail with broad black terminal band.

**Red-wattled Lapwing**   *Hoplopterus indicus*                            Plate 47    Red-wattled Lapwing  E
Large, with black crown, olive-brown mantle, black primaries, white secondaries, and white tail with black terminal band; long yellow legs; often very noisy.

**White-tailed Lapwing**   *Chettusia leucura*                             Plate 47   White-tailed Lapwing  F
Pale brown with black primaries, white secondaries, all-white rump and tail, and long pale yellow legs protruding well beyond tail.

**Greenshank**   *Tringa nebularia*                                         Plate 53           Greenshank  G
Uniform dark wings and grey mantle contrasting with white back and rump; rather heavy, slightly upturned bill and long green legs.

**Spur-winged Lapwing**   *Hoplopterus spinosus*                           Plate 46    Spur-winged Lapwing  H
Pattern of upper-parts similar to that of Red-wattled Lapwing, but with less white on secondaries; under-parts largely black, legs black. (Scarce.)

**Sociable Lapwing**   *Chettusia gregaria*                                 Plate 47       Sociable Lapwing  I
Rather similar to White-tailed Lapwing, but with a partial black band on tail, conspicuous white supercilia, and black legs. (Scarce.)

**Redshank**   *Tringa totanus*                                             Plate 53             Redshank  J
Distinctive broad white wing-bar, white lower back and rump and red legs. See Terek Sandpiper (plate 56).

**Spotted Redshank**   *Tringa erythropus*                                  Plate 53      Spotted Redshank  K
Differs from Redshank in lack of distinct wing-bar, paler and greyer upper-parts, longer, darker legs and finer bill.

**Marsh Sandpiper**   *Tringa stagnatilis*                                  Plate 53       Marsh Sandpiper  L
Like a small, slender Greenshank, with longer, fine, straight bill, and longer legs protruding further beyond tail.

**Ruff**   *Philomachus pugnax*                                             Plate 51                 Ruff  M
Dark, scaly upper-parts with indistinct wing-bar, and white oval patches at sides of tail, often almost uniting to form white horse-shoe; rather short, almost straight bill.

160

Plate 57

## LARGE WADERS IN FLIGHT:

Adults in winter plumage, from above.

**Oystercatcher**   *Haematopus ostralegus*                                    Plate 41                    Oystercatcher  A
Black-and-white, with bold white wing-bar and rump and large red bill.

**Avocet**   *Recurvirostra avosetta*                                    Plate 41                    Avocet  B
Black-and-white, with long upturned black bill and long bluish legs.

**Black-winged Stilt**   *Himantopus himantopus*                    Plate 41             Black-winged Stilt  C
White, with black back and wings (above and below); very long pinkish legs extend far beyond the tail; long thin black bill.

**Crab Plover**   *Dromas ardeola*                                    Plate 42                    Crab Plover  D
White, with black mantle and flight-feathers, very heavy black bill and long blue-grey legs; juveniles are brown above.

**Stone Curlew**   *Burhinus oedicnemus*                                    Plate 42                    Stone Curlew  E
Brown, streaked with black, with double white wing-bar bordered with black, white-tipped wedge-shaped tail, short stout bill and large yellow eyes.

**Spotted Thick-knee**   *Burhinus capensis*                    Plate 42             Spotted Thick-knee  F
Differs from Stone Curlew in spotted (not streaked) upper-parts, and lack of wing-bars.

**Bar-tailed Godwit**   *Limosa lapponica*                    Plate 51             Bar-tailed Godwit  G
Grey-brown above, with no distinct wing-bar; white rump, white tail barred brown, and long, slightly upturned bill; legs barely project beyond tail.

**Black-tailed Godwit**   *Limosa limosa*                    Plate 51             Black-tailed Godwit  I
Larger than Bar-tailed Godwit, with conspicuous white wing-bar, white tail with black terminal band, longer, straight bill and longer legs.

**Whimbrel**   *Numenius phaeopus*                                    Plate 52                    Whimbrel  H
Differs from Curlew in smaller size, darker plumage, shorter, straighter bill and tittering call; crown-stripes visible at close range.

**Slender-billed Curlew**   *Numenius tenuirostris*                    Plate 52             Slender-billed Curlew  J
Size of Whimbrel, but paler, with more white on rump and tail, and pale secondaries contrasting with darker coverts and primaries. Clearer white under-parts, with black spots on flanks visible at close range.

**Curlew**   *Numenius arquata*                                    Plate 52                    Curlew  K
Very large; brown, with white lower back and rump, and very long decurved bill.

Plate 58

# SKUAS, JAEGERS: Stercorariidae

**World:** 5 species. **Oman:** 4 species. Resemble immature gulls, the smaller species long-winged like falcons. Sexes similar, dark brown above with a pale wing-flash, central tail-feathers elongate in adults. Agile, predatory and piratical, pursuing other sea-birds until they disgorge food. Also take animals, carrion, fish, insects, etc. Long, complex migrations over sea and land.

## Arctic Skua    *Stercorarius parasiticus*

**World:** Breeds in northern N America, Greenland, N Eurasia. Migratory through all oceans and Arabian Gulf, to 30–50°S.
**Oman:** Fairly common passage migrant, peak July–October; some in winter.

43–51cm/17–20in. Very similar to Pomarine in dark, pale and intermediate forms, but usually smaller and slighter, with two central tail-feathers elongated to fine points in *adults'* fresh plumage (see Long-tailed Skua). Dark phase *adult* dark brown, with neck tinged yellowish. Pale phase *adult* grey-brown above, with blackish cap, pale collar and belly, dusky under tail-coverts and sometimes a dusky breast-band. *Immatures* (to 3rd year) very similar to young Pomarine Skua.

At sea, mainly coastal, chasing gulls and terns or foraging for surface fish and ships' offal. Agile, buoyant and graceful flight with regular wing-beats and hawk-like glides. Occasionally settles on sea. The main passage off Oman coincides with an abundance of terns.

## Pomarine Skua    *Stercorarius pomarinus*

**World:** Breeds in Arctic N America, Greenland, Siberia. Migratory through all oceans and Arabian Gulf to tropics.
**Oman:** Passage migrant in small numbers, a few immatures over summer, occasional in winter.

53–56cm/21–22in. Smaller than Great and McCormick's Skuas, larger and heavier than others. Like the Arctic Skua it has dark, pale and intermediate forms making distinction difficult, but the *adult's* long central tail-feathers with rounded, twisted tips are diagnostic when present. Palest *adults (summer)* as Arctic Skua but with a yellowish collar, usually a dusky breast-band, and barred flanks.

Similar to Arctic Skua but less agile, with heavier flight. Rests on shore with migrating terns, etc.

## Great Skua    *Stercorarius skua*

**World:** Northern Skua (Bonxie) breeds on islands north of Scotland and Iceland; migratory to N Atlantic and Mediterranean. Four other races (incl. Brown and Southern Great) breed in Antarctica; migrate northwards in northern summer.
**Oman:** Uncommon summer visitor, occasionally in winter; likely to be a southern race.

53–61cm/21–24in. Large, heavy build, resembling immature Herring Gull but more uniform dark brown, with a prominent white patch at base of primaries, shorter, stouter bill and shorter tail. Differs from smaller skuas also in broader, less pointed wings. *Juvenile* has less white in wing. See Pale-footed Shearwater (plate 2).

Ordinary flight is heavy and gull-like. It obtains food by fiercely harrying boobies, tropicbirds, etc., also by following ships. Settles on the sea freely.

## [McCormick's Skua (South Polar Skua)    *Stercorarius maccormicki*

**World:** Breeds in Antarctica. Migrates northwards in southern winter  has reached W India in August.(Previously considered a race of Great Skua)
**Oman:** A possible summer visitor.

53cm/21in. Similar to Great Skua, but slightly smaller, paler brown above, pale brown or buff below, the neck with narrow buff or whitish streaks forming a collar, the white wing-patch larger.]

## Long-tailed Skua    *Stercorarius longicaudus*

**World:** Breeds in northern N America, Greenland, Scandinavia to Siberia. Migrates southwards in Pacific and Atlantic to 10–50°S, casually elsewhere.
**Oman:** Accidental (four seen on the Batinah, 10 May 1977).

53–58cm/21–23in incl. tail. Resembles pale Arctic Skua, but is smaller and more slender, with very long, flexible central tail-feathers (except in *young* or when moulted), dusky lower belly and under tail-coverts, unmarked breast, complete white collar and paler greyish back. There is a very rare dark phase. *Juvenile* almost indistinguishable from Arctic Skua, but greyer brown above, and greyer below.

Like Arctic Skua, but less piratical, and with a more graceful tern-like flight, occasionally hovering.

Arctic Skua

*dark phase* B

*pale phase* A

*immature* C

Pomarine Skua D

*immature* E

Great Skua F

McCormick's Skua G

Long-tailed Skua H

164

Plate 59

# GULLS: Laridae

Plates 60–62

**World:** 45 species. **Oman:** 8 species (1 breeding). Familiar medium-sized to large birds of coasts, oceans and some inland waters, differing from terns (Sternidae) in sturdier bodies and bills and mostly square-tipped tails. Sexes are similar, males larger. Immatures of some pale gulls are brown for 2–4 years. The long pointed wings permit strong, graceful flight, gliding and soaring. Social, in loose flocks. Most species are omnivorous; they feed mostly by day in shallow plunges for fish, by catching small vertebrates and invertebrates, by scavenging and sometimes by piracy. They spend much time resting on beaches, etc., sometimes on the sea, swimming well with webbed feet. Long movements between feeding and roosting may be mistaken for migration.

## Slender-billed Gull    *Larus genei*

Slender-billed Gull

**World:** Breeds off W Africa, in Mediterranean region, Black Sea to central Asia, south to Iraq, S Iran, NW India. Sedentary and migratory, reaching S Red Sea, S Arabia, occasionally E Africa.
**Oman:** Common to very common passage migrant and winter visitor, August–March; small numbers locally over summer.

41–47cm/16–18in. Rather similar to Black-headed Gull in winter (plate 61), but more graceful in form and habits, the head and neck more slender, the neck often up-stretched when swimming, the forehead more sloping to the longer, unicoloured bill, the eye set further from the gape, and the wings, tail and legs slightly longer. *Adult (summer)* has an all-white head, and under-parts flushed pink in fresh plumage; dark red bill appearing blackish, deep coral-red legs and pale iris. In *winter* often with a dark smudge on the ear-coverts, and bright red or orange bill and legs. *Juvenile* is like the *winter adult*, but with brownish marks on wing-coverts and secondaries (never as pronounced as in Black-headed ) and dark tip to tail, pale orange-yellow bill and legs, brown iris.

*summer* A
*winter* B

A graceful gull of inshore waters and creeks, sometimes with Black-headed Gull. Feeds on small fish and plankton picked from or near the surface, and by repeated shallow plunges of head and neck with wings raised, often in a flock over a shoal. Feeding flocks utter a pleasant babble; occasionally calls a grating *krerk,* otherwise silent when not breeding.

## Sooty Gull (Hemprich's Gull)    *Larus hemprichii*

Sooty Gull

**World:** Breeds in summer on islands of S Red Sea, E Africa, S and E Arabia, E Arabian Gulf, Mekran. Sedentary and migratory.
**Oman:** Common breeding resident, summer visitor and passage migrant, March–October, wintering in small numbers, most commonly at Masirah.

43–48cm/17–19in. The familiar gull of Oman's coastal waters, with distinctive brown-and-white plumage. *Adult (breeding)* has a dark brown hood, brown lower neck, breast, back, wings and flanks; white half-collar (reaching up sides of neck), trailing-edge to wings, rump and tail, and rest of under-parts. A white crescentic mark above the eye (occasionally repeated below as in White-eyed Gull); dark brown iris and red eye-rim; yellow or greenish-yellow bill with black, red and yellow at the tip, and yellow to green legs. In *winter* similar, but duller brown and the collar indistinct. *Immature* (to 3rd year) is paler mottled brown above, with a dark sub-terminal tail-bar and no white collar; pale iris and grey bill with a black-and-red tip.

*adult* C

*immature* D

A common scavenger on beaches, around fishermen and ships, in harbours and on rubbish-tips, but it will also catch fish from the sea surface in flight or whilst swimming. It is piratical and raids colonies of sea-birds for eggs and chicks. It nests on islands from April to October, in a bare scrape, occasionally decorated, usually singly but sometimes in large loose colonies, on sand-flats, stony slopes and prom-ontories, often overlooking tern colonies. It lays 2–3 large eggs, dark buff with heavy brown marks. It is single-brooded, but will lay again if a nest fails. Noisy calls whilst breeding include a loud mournful *keee-yaow,* also a repeated shorter *keeow* with head bent backwards (courtship) and a rapid *kekk-kekek* (alarm).

## White-eyed Gull    *Larus leucophthalmus*

White-eyed Gull

**World:** Breeds in summer in Red Sea, Gulf of Suez and Gulf of Aden. Resident or partial migrant.
**Oman:** Vagrant (three single records on Masirah in April, September, October–November).

41–43cm/16–17in. Smaller, more handsome and of slighter build than the superficially similar Sooty Gull. The *adult (breeding)* is unmistakable, with black hood, conspicuous white crescentic mark above and below the eye; the brown parts are more greyish-brown than in the Sooty Gull and the primaries are blacker. The iris is pale; the bill is long, slender and very dark red, with a darker tip which is not always noticeable. The *adult (winter)* and *immature* are similar to the Sooty Gull, but best disting-uished by build, the slender red bill with a black tip, and greyer breast.

*adult* E

*immature* F

Habits are similar to those of Sooty Gull, but less piratical.

166

Plate 60

167

## Great Black-headed Gull  *Larus ichthyaetus*

**World:** Breeds from Crimea and Caspian, eastwards to central Asia. Migratory, reaching E Africa, Arabia, India, SE Asia.
**Oman:** A regular passage migrant and winter visitor in very small numbers September–April, most from January; rarely in summer.

69cm/27in. A very large gull with a heavy bill; it is striking in *breeding* dress, but otherwise requires care to distinguish from large Herring Gulls when at rest. *Adult (summer)* is distinctive, with a jet-black hood, a small white crescentic mark above and below the red eye-rim, a white neck, a very pale grey mantle and distinctive white primaries with black spots near the tip. This elegant plumage is complemented by a bright orange-yellow bill with a black sub-terminal band and red tip, and yellow legs. In *winter* the head becomes white, with varied dusky marks around the eyes, crown and nape, and the bill is duller yellow, still with a black band. The *immature* has a whitish head with dark smudges through and behind the eyes, the grey mantle mottled with dark brown, black primaries, brown secondaries with contrasting pale tips, and the white tail with a sharply defined dark terminal band, reducing with age; the bill is often dark, but in older birds there is a black sub-terminal band and orange tip.

Usually seen roosting on beaches near or with other birds, or floating with the white neck up-stretched, or flying or soaring (when the wing-pattern should be noted). Not very gregarious, though groups do occur. It is omnivorous, and feeds by fishing, seizing food from other birds, etc.

## Black-headed Gull  *Larus ridibundus*

**World:** Breeds across Eurasia between 66°N and 40°N. Sedentary and migratory, reaching Africa, Arabia, India, SE Asia.
**Oman:** Common passage migrant and winter visitor September–March, numbers vary annually and in some years it is abundant in N Oman; a few remain over summer.

38–43cm/15–17in. In *winter* it is very similar to the Slender-billed Gull (plate 60), with a conspicuous white leading-edge to the wing in flight, but it is less slim and graceful, with shorter neck, more rounded head with a more distinct ear-spot, and shorter bill, dull reddish with a black tip. The *immature* (to 2nd winter) differs from the Slender-bill immature also in more extensive brown marks on the upper-wing and a blacker tail-band. The *adult (summer)* has a dark brown hood (sometimes developed in January) with a narrow white eye-rim, dark red bill and legs. Differs from **Brown-headed Gull** *L. brunnicephalus* [41–43cm/16–17in, breeds in southern central Asia to N India and winters inland and inshore in Pakistan, India, Burma, SE Asia] in that species' larger size and different wing-pattern; the *adult* has black primaries with a large white patch at the base and a small white spot near the tip of the outer two; the *immature* lacks these spots.

Scavenges round ships, harbours, habitation and rubbish-tips well inland, drinking and bathing at any 'fresh' water before flighting in flocks (of thousands in some years) to roost in creeks, near pools, etc. In peak years a hazard to low-flying aircraft. Coastal flocks often include some Slender-billed. Very gregarious and, unlike winter Slender-billed, often noisy, calling a high-pitched *kwăǎ*.

## [Little Gull  *Larus minutus*  (Not illustrated)

Breeds sporadically across Eurasia in three groups; migratory to the west, occasionally south to N Red Sea, Arabian Gulf (Kuwait to UAE, S Iran), N India, not confirmed in Oman. 25–31cm/10–12in. Much smaller and with more tern-like flight than Black-headed Gull; *adult (winter)* has a short blackish bill, pale grey upper-wings with white tips, and blackish under-wings; the *immature* has browner upper-parts with a bold blackish zig-zag pattern on the upper-wing and a slightly cleft black-tipped tail.]

Great Black-headed
Gull

*summer* F

*winter* E
*immature* D

Black-headed Gull

*winter* C

*immature* A
*summer* B
*juvenile* G

168

Plate 61

**Common Gull** (Mew Gull)     *Larus canus*

**World:** Breeds across Eurasia to NW America. Sedentary and migratory, reaching N Africa, Iraq, N Arabian Gulf, Caspian, Far East, occasionally further south.
**Oman:** Vagrant or scarce winter visitor.

46cm/18in. A medium-sized gull, smaller, more elegant and with slighter bill than the Herring and Lesser Black-backed Gulls, but often difficult to distinguish in the field, especially when *immature*. The *adult (breeding)* has the head, neck, under-parts, rump and tail white, the mantle and wings pale grey, the wing-tips black with large white spots at the tip; the bill and legs are yellowish-green, with no red spot on the bill. The *adult (winter)* is similar but streaked grey on the head. The *immature* (1st winter) has varied dark mottling on the white parts, greyish mantle, brown wings, coverts heavily mottled (pale edges to dark-centred feathers) and a broad, dark sub-terminal tail-band; the bill is blackish, becoming pale with a black tip or sub-terminal band. The iris is usually brown.

*adult winter* C
*immature* D

It scavenges along the shore and inshore waters in winter and will rob smaller gulls of food.


**Herring Gull**     *Larus argentatus*

**World:** Breeds in N America, Europe to NE Siberia, also from W Africa, Mediterranean to NW Manchuria, incl. NW Iran, in many races. Sedentary and migratory, reaching Gulf of Aden, India, SE Asia.
**Oman:** A common passage migrant and winter visitor; some over summer.

51–56cm/22–24in. The most common large gull in Oman. Sizes and colours of mantle and legs vary, making distinction from Lesser Black-backed Gull sometimes difficult or impossible in the field; confusion is also possible with Common Gull. The *adult (breeding)* has white head, neck, under-parts, rump and tail, and pale or dark grey mantle and upper-wing (some as dark as pale Lesser Black-backed); the wing-tips are black with white spots; the bill is yellow with a red spot on the gonys, and the legs are pink to yellow (never the yellowish-green of the Common Gull). The *adult (winter)* has dark streaks on the head. The *immature* is heavily streaked and mottled brown like Lesser Black-backed immatures, with dark brown flight-feathers and a mottled tail with an irregular dark terminal-band; the bill is dark, becoming greyish with a black tip or black sub-terminal mark – see Great Black-headed Gull (plate 61) and Common Gull. All have a yellowish iris.

*adult winter* A
*immature* E

Coastal and in creeks and harbours. It is omnivorous and feeds by fishing and scavenging at sea and at rubbish-tips. Migration is by day in steady flight, not close to the surface, singly and in parties. It rests for long periods at the water's edge, often with other species.


**Lesser Black-backed Gull**     *Larus fuscus*

**World:** Breeds from Iceland to NW Russia in several races. Migratory, reaching tropical Africa, Arabia, India.
**Oman:** Passage migrant and winter visitor in small numbers; a few in summer.

51–61cm/20–24in. A large gull, not as common as the Herring Gull, but some overlap in plumage colouration makes some identifications uncertain. The *adult (summer* and *winter)* is like the Herring Gull, but the mantle and upper-wing are black to dark slate-grey and the legs are usually yellow. The *immature* is very similar to the immature Herring Gull, but is usually darker by the 2nd year. Very large Lesser Black-backed may be misidentified as **Great Black-backed Gull** *Larus marinus* [69–76cm/27–30in, breeds on Atlantic coasts and in Scandinavia, sedentary and migratory, reaching Mediterranean, wandering to S Russia and Caspian, and unlikely to reach Oman].

*adult winter* B

Habits are like those of Herring Gull, but more pelagic outside the breeding season.


# SKIMMERS: Rynchopidae

**World:** 3 species. **Oman:** 1 species. Sociable tern-like birds of warm coastal and inland waters with unique bill-shape and feeding method. Lower mandible longer, tip laterally compressed to blade-thinness. Fish by skimming tip in calm water, mouth open, body tilted down, wings held up in graceful flight. Plumage of sexes similar, young duller; dark above, white below; bill colour and head-pattern diagnostic. Tail short and forked; legs short; iris cat-like.


**Indian Skimmer**     *Rynchops albicollis*

**World:** Breeds in N India, Burma, SE Asia. Resident, nomadic.
**Oman:** Vagrant (3 Muscat, 13–15 August 1979).

40cm/16½in. At rest, like a large dark tern, with a very heavy-looking red and yellow bill and very short reddish legs. Blackish-brown on crown, nape, mantle, most of the wings and central tail-feathers; white forehead, face, collar, trailing-edge of wings, tail and under-parts.

Plate 62

171

# TERNS: Sternidae

Plates 63–66

**World:** 36 species. **Oman:** 17 species (6 breeding). More slender and graceful than gulls, with long narrow wings and buoyant flight, particularly in courtship. The tail is often deeply forked (hence 'sea swallow'). Grey or white, most with a black cap when breeding; two noddy terns are dark with pale crowns. The long pointed bill is held downwards during searches for food, which is seized in plunges and from the surface. Gregarious and migratory. Nesting birds are frequently disturbed and robbed of their eggs.

### Caspian Tern    *Sterna caspia*    See also plate 67

Caspian Tern

**World:** Breeds locally in N America, Africa, Baltic, Black Sea and Caspian, eastwards to China, south to SW Iran, Arabian Gulf, NW India, Sri Lanka. Sedentary and migratory, reaching Africa, Arabia, India.

**Oman:** Passage migrant and winter visitor, but not very common; some over summer.

48–56cm/19–22in. The largest tern in Oman, distinctive by its size and huge red bill, though this sometimes has a dusky tip and is more orange in *immatures*. The *adult* has a black cap, which becomes white streaked with black in *winter;* the upper-wing is pale grey with dusky tips, the under-wing whitish with blackish primaries, and the rump and slightly forked tail are white. The *immature's* crown is brownish streaked with white, the mantle and wings mottled brown, the tail with a dark tip.

*adult summer* A

*immature* B

Usually coastal or in creeks. It usually hunts and plunges for fish singly, but it is more gregarious in roosts. It very occasionally calls a deep *kraa* or *ayowk.*

### Crested Tern (Swift Tern)    *Sterna bergii*    See also plate 67

Crested Tern

**World:** *S.b. velox* breeds in Red Sea, Gulf of Aden, E Arabia, Arabian Gulf, India, Sri Lanka, Bay of Bengal; sedentary and migratory.

**Oman:** Resident, summer visitor, passage migrant and winter visitor.

46–48cm/18–19in. The second-largest tern in Oman, rather similar to the smaller, paler Lesser Crested Tern, but the *adult (breeding)* has white between the bill and the black forehead, uniform dark grey mantle and wings, and yellow bill (not orange as Lesser Crested). The *adult (winter)* has a varied amount of white on the crown and wings, and dull or greenish-yellow bill. The *immature* is darker, with mottled brown wing-coverts, black outer primaries and three dark wing-bars in flight.

*adult breeding* C
*adult winter* D

At sea and on coasts. Gregarious, particularly on passage and when breeding. By early summer, courting birds assemble in large noisy groups. The nests, from July, are unlined scrapes on open ground in close-packed colonies, or in small numbers near other nesting terns. The eggs, usually 1, occasionally 2, are very variable, pale or buff with red-brown marks. Feathered chicks form crèches which run or attempt to swim from danger. Calls, a loud grating *kur-ik* and *kraa(rk).* The young give a high-pitched *skree-ee.*

### Gull-billed Tern    *Gelochelidon nilotica*    See also plate 67

Gull-billed Tern

**World:** *G.n. nilotica* breeds locally across central and S Eurasia, south to Iraq, Iran (to Arabian Gulf), NW India; migratory, reaching Africa, Arabia, India.

**Oman:** Passage migrant and winter visitor July–May, rather scarce in N Oman, small numbers further south; a few in summer.

38–41cm/15–16in. Rather gull-like, and differing from Sandwich Tern (plate 64) in habits and in having shorter, stouter black bill without pale tip, less deeply forked tail, broader wings and heavier body, and standing higher on longer legs. The *adult (breeding)* is uniform grey above except for a black cap, which in *winter* is reduced to a distinctive black patch before and behind the eye and on to the nape. The *immature* is similar to the *winter adult,* but mottled brown and buff above.

*adult breeding* F
*adult winter* E

Unlike the Sandwich Tern it searches more over land, with slower wing-beats, swooping to take small crabs from mud-flats, insects from the air, other animals from the ground and fish from streams and pools (see Whiskered Tern, plate 66). Call, a rasping *ker-vik* or *kay-wak;* immatures call *pee-eep.*

### Lesser Crested Tern    *Sterna bengalensis*    See also plate 67

Lesser Crested Tern

**World:** Breeds in N Africa, Red Sea, Gulf of Aden, Arabian Gulf, India to Australasia. Migratory.
**Oman:** Fairly common passage migrant, some present in summer and winter.

39–41cm/15–16in. Like a small Crested Tern, but the bill is more orange at all ages, the upper-parts and particularly the flight-feathers are paler grey, and in breeding plumage the black of the cap reaches the base of the bill. The *immature* is like the *winter adult,* but the wing-coverts are distinctly barred and mottled, and the outer tail-feathers are dark.

*adult summer* G
*adult winter* H

Its habits are generally similar to those of the more common Crested Tern.

172

Plate 63

**Sandwich Tern**    *Sterna sandvicensis*                        See also plate 67

**World:** *S.s. sandvicensis* breeds in W Europe, Mediterranean, Black Sea, Caspian; migratory, reaching S Africa, Arabia, NW India. Other races in Americas.
**Oman:** Abundant on passage, common over summer, very local in winter.

41–46cm/16–18in. A very pale medium-sized tern with a long, black, yellow-tipped bill. It differs from the Gull-billed Tern (plate 63) in bill, longer narrow wings with dusky outer primaries, short forked tail giving a chunky appearance, and behaviour and call. The *adult (breeding)* has a black cap with shaggy crest, reduced when not breeding. The *immature* is similar to the *non-breeding adult* but may lack the pale tip to its bill.

*adult winter* A
*adult breeding* B

Coastal. It feeds in scattered groups, circling, hovering and plunge-diving. It roosts commonly on shores, often with other species and migrates in small flocks. It calls whilst feeding, with a noisy metallic *krrk, kreek* or *skeetch*.

**Common Tern**    *Sterna hirundo*                        See also plate 67

**World:** *S.h. hirundo* breeds in N America, Eurasia except in the east, south to Iraq, Iran (head of Gulf); migratory, reaching S Africa, Arabia, NW India. Other races in E Asia, N India.
**Oman:** Fairly common passage migrant, non-breeding birds present locally over summer in small numbers; fewer in winter.

35.5cm/14in. Rather similar to the slightly smaller Roseate and White-cheeked Terns, almost indistinguishable in *non-breeding* and *immature* plumages. *Adult (breeding)* is pale blue-grey above, with distinct white rump and tail, the outer feathers dark and not extending beyond wing-tips at rest; under-parts tinged pale vinous-grey (some White-cheeked may appear as pale). *Adult (non-breeding)* like White-cheeked but usually paler. *Immature* doubtfully separable from White-cheeked in the field.

*adult breeding* D
*adult winter* C
*immature* E

Coasts and creeks. It fishes by occasionally hovering, splashing on to or just below the surface, or swooping on prey as it emerges. Call, *kik-kik-kik* and *kree-err*, rather similar to that of White-cheeked Tern.

**Roseate Tern**    *Sterna dougallii*                        See also plate 67

**World:** Breeds locally in America, W Europe, Indian Ocean, SE Asia, Australasia, in several races. Migratory, movements little known.
**Oman:** Breeding summer visitor March–October in small numbers.

38cm/15in. A slender, graceful and distinctly whitish tern. The *adult's* long, slender, pale outer tail-feathers project beyond the folded wing-tips when at rest. At the outset of breeding the bill is blackish, but it soon becomes red at the base, and by the end of July is completely red. The legs are bright red in breeding birds, and dusky in others. *Immature* similar to White-cheeked Tern but paler above.

*adult summer* F
*adult winter* G

Pelagic, very occasionally on coasts, plunge-diving from buoyant flight with shallow wing-beats. Shy. It nests on some islands in small compact colonies, also in small groups amongst White-cheeked Terns, from May, in unlined scrapes on rocky or sandy ground. 1–2 eggs, pale buff or grey, flecked or blotched brown. Calls when nesting, a distinctive high-pitched *skreek, eek* and *zerk*.

**White-cheeked Tern**    *Sterna repressa*                        See also plate 67

**World:** Breeds in Red Sea, Gulf of Aden, E Africa, Arabian Sea, Arabian Gulf, W India. Migratory to E Africa, W India and islands.
**Oman:** Common passage migrant and breeding summer visitor March–November; a few overwintering on Masirah.

35cm/13½in. Slightly smaller than Common Tern. *Adult (breeding)* usually distinct with white sides to head contrasting with black cap and nape, dark grey upper-parts and dark to pale vinous-grey under-parts. In *winter* with white forehead and under-parts. *Immature* similar to *winter adult*, but some are paler grey above with dark primaries, pale rump and tail, very similar to Common Tern.

*adult breeding* J
*adult winter* H

Coasts, islands and harbours, fishing in shallow waters by hovering low and splashing briefly on to the surface with wings raised. It nests on islands in small compact colonies from April or May, on rocky headlands or sand, the nest scrape decorated during occupation. The eggs, 1–2, become encrusted with salt from adults' wettened belly-feathers. Breeding calls include a complaining nasal *skwee-err, skip-skip-skwee-rr, skee-ip,* shrill *keek-keek-keek* and purring *krrr*.

Plate 64

**Lesser Noddy** (Black Noddy)   *Anous tenuirostris*   See also plate 67

**World:** Breeds on islands in Indo-Pacific, occasionally wandering north to W India, E Africa, Arabia.

**Oman:** Irregular summer visitor in small numbers, Masirah June–September, usually with Common Noddy.

33cm/13in. Very similar to Common Noddy in distant views, but it is smaller and somewhat darker, the bill is comparatively longer and more slender, the white of the crown extends to the lores and the tail is shorter. The *immature* is similar to the *adult,* but is paler brown, with less extensive white on crown and nape.

Habits are generally similar to those of Common Noddy, but it flies more buoyantly, with more rapid wing-beats, and feeds closer inshore in more fluttering flight. It roosts on bushes and rocks.

**Common Noddy** (Brown Noddy)   *Anous stolidus*   See also plate 67

**World:** Breeds locally on islands in tropical and sub-tropical seas, incl. off E Africa, Gulf of Aden, Oman, in several races.

**Oman:** Uncommon local breeding summer visitor; small numbers irregularly at other times.

41cm/16in. A chocolate-brown tern with a pale lavender-grey crown, a whitish forehead and black lores; the wings and tail are blackish, the throat and under-wing paler brown; the longish tail is graduated and rounded with a slight notch at the tip. The *immature* has a greyish crown, paler forehead and supercilium and pale bars along the upper wing-coverts, the marks being accentuated when moulting. It differs from dark shearwaters in its characteristic flight and pale crown.

Usually seen near coasts, occasionally gregariously in 'rafts'. The normal flight is rather leisurely, low over the surface, but never gliding like shearwaters. It feeds by day and on bright nights on small fish snatched in a skilful hover and swoop as the prey jumps, also by pecking from the surface during low quartering flights with fairly rapid wing-beats. It nests colonially or in scattered pairs, from July, on isolated rock stacks, sometimes upon collected coral, shell and stick fragments. The one white egg is flecked brown. Fledged young accompany parents for over 100 days. Call, a harsh *kyaar.*

**Sooty Tern**   *Sterna fuscata*   See also plate 67

**World:** Breeds in tropical and sub-tropical seas, incl. Indian Ocean to Gulf of Aden, in several races.

**Oman:** Vagrant, usually tired birds (e.g. two near Salalah, 2 May 1980); some other reports suggest confusion with Bridled Tern.

43cm/17in. Very similar to and confused with Bridled Tern, but the broad white of the forehead does not extend behind the eye; it lacks the pale collar of the Bridled Tern, and the mantle and wings are deep sooty-black. The *juvenile* is very different from young Bridled, being completely dark brown except for small white flecks and a pale belly and under-wing.

More pelagic than Bridled Tern. It nests colonially on islands in the open, not under cover. The distinctive call is a loud *ker-wacky-wak* uttered by day and night when breeding (hence 'wide-awake tern').

**Bridled Tern** (Brown-winged Tern)   *Sterna anaethetus*   See also plate 67

**World:** Breeds on islands from the Red Sea to Arabian Sea and Arabian Gulf, Indian Ocean, SE Asia, Australasia, Pacific and Atlantic, in several races. Migratory.

**Oman:** Common passage migrant and breeding summer visitor March–November, less common off Dhofar; a few over winter.

36–38cm/14–15in. A fairly large, long-winged pelagic tern with a long, deeply forked tail, differing from all other terns except Sooty by appearing almost black above and white below. The *adult* has white forehead, supercilium reaching behind the eye, collar, leading-edge to wing, outer web of tail-feathers, and under-parts; it has a black crown, nape and stripe through the eye, and dark greyish-brown mantle and wing (not sooty-black). The *juvenile* is similar to the *adult,* but has a buff collar and buff fringes to the brown mantle and crown.

Ranges over the warm oceans, concentrating over shoals of fish, which are obtained in shallow plunges or from the surface. It perches commonly on net floats. It comes inshore to nest colonially on some islands May–October. The nest is a shallow unlined scrape in sand or on rock, under cover of low vegetation, boulders and ledges and in crevices, but occasionally more exposed and decorated. 1 and occasionally 2 eggs, pale creamy with brownish speckles. The calls in breeding colonies by day and night include a deep barking *crowk* or *cruk-cruk,* and a nasal *kraaa* or *krerr-krerr-krerr* changing to a rapid *kiririri* when with chick; some birds call *kewick,* resembling Sooty Tern.

Plate 65

177

**Little Tern**   *Sterna albifrons*                              See also plate 67                    Little Tern

**World:** *S.a. albifrons* breeds from Europe to central Asia, south to Mediterranean, Iraq, Iran, NW India; migratory, reaching S Africa, India. Several other races in America, Africa, Far East to Australia.
**Oman:** Probably a regular passage migrant, but rarely recorded and probably overlooked.

24cm/9½in. Very similar to Saunders' Little Tern, but differs in having lighter outer primaries, in the fact that in *summer* the border of the black fore-crown points towards the bill, and in having mantle and wings slightly darker blue-grey, contrasting with the whiter rump and tail; feet are brighter yellow to orange-yellow.                                                                                  *adult summer*  A

Coasts and inland waters; habits otherwise similar to those of Saunders' Little Tern. Call, a chattering *kikikiki*.


**Saunders' Little Tern**   *Sterna saundersi*                   See also plate 67                Saunders' Little Tern

**World:** Breeds along Red Sea to E Africa, Arabian Sea to Arabian Gulf, NW India. Migratory to Africa, Indian Ocean, India. (Sometimes considered a race of Little Tern, and is confusable with it.)
**Oman:** Common passage migrant, and uncommon breeding summer visitor, March–November; a few over winter.

24cm/9½in. It differs from other sea terns, except for the very similar Little Tern, in very small size and rapid wing-beats. *Adult (breeding)* has the black of the crown meeting the white forehead in a        *adult breeding*  B
straight line (not a point), black on the outer three primaries, the rump and tail pale grey as the mantle (rarely white); the bill bright yellow, usually tipped black; legs brownish-yellow. In winter the black recedes to the nape. The *juvenile* has ginger-buff forehead and crown, dark patches behind each eye           *juvenile*  C
sometimes meeting on the nape, the mantle mottled pale buff, blackish along the leading-edge and bend of the wing and on the outer primaries; the bill is blackish, becoming yellow.

Coasts and creeks. Searches in fluttering flight over surf and shallow water for small fish, obtained by shallow plunges, occasionally from surface. Nests well spaced out, singly or semi-colonially, in natural depressions in sand near coasts. 2 eggs, very pale olive with dark specks. Call, very similar to that of Little Tern.


**Black Tern**   *Chlidonias niger*                             See also plate 67                    Black Tern

**World:** *C.n. niger* breeds from W Europe to central Asia; migratory to tropical Africa. Another race in N America.
**Oman:** Vagrant (one reported seen in breeding plumage near Muscat, 24 March 1976).

24cm/9½in. One of 3 marsh terns, difficult to separate in varied *winter* and *immature* plumage. *Adult (breeding)* differs from White-winged Black Tern in slate-grey back, wings and tail and pale under-      *adult breeding*  E
wings. *Adult (winter)* and *immature* best identified by grey smudge down sides of breast in front of          *adult winter*  D
wing (sometimes present in moulting White-winged), uniform mantle and rump.


**White-winged Black Tern**   *Chlidonias leucopterus*          See also plate 67   White-winged Black Tern

**World:** Breeds from E Europe to Far East, south to Iraq. Migratory, reaching Africa, Arabia, India to Australasia.
**Oman:** Regular passage migrant and winter visitor in small numbers, a few over summer.

23cm/9in. Distinctive in breeding dress, but otherwise difficult to distinguish from Black and Whisk-ered Terns. *Adult (breeding)* black, including wing-linings, except for white shoulders, rump, tail and        *adult breeding*  G
under tail-coverts; bill short, black tinged with red. In *winter* grey above with black nape, white collar          *adult winter*  F
and pale rump; white below; bill black. *Immature* as *winter adult*, but the mantle is darker, mottled with brown, and the rump whitish, giving a saddled appearance.

Marshes, creeks, crops, coastal on passage, usually in small or scattered flocks. Like the others, has a slow, searching, hovering flight, dipping to peck insects from surface, rarely immersing.


**Whiskered Tern**   *Chlidonias hybrida*                        See also plate 67                  Whiskered Tern

**World:** *C.h. hybrida* breeds locally in Mediterranean basin, SE Europe, SW Russia, south to Iraq, Iran; migratory, reaching tropical Africa, Arabia.
**Oman:** Uncommon on passage, a few at other times, mostly in Dhofar.

25.5cm/10in. The largest of the three marsh terns, with the heaviest bill. *Adult (breeding)* is dis-            *adult breeding*  H
tinctive, with a white streak ('whiskers') separating the black cap from dark grey under-parts and silver-grey upper-parts; under wing-coverts and under tail-coverts white, tail grey; bill and legs dark red. see White-cheeked Tern (plate 64). In *winter* has less black on crown than the White-winged Black Tern and is more uniform grey above; differs from Black Tern in absence of breast patches.                    *immature*  J
*Immature* as *winter adult*, but mantle barred dark and buff, contrasting with grey wings.


178

Plate 66

179

# TERNS IN FLIGHT:

Adults in winter plumage (non-breeding), from above.

**White-cheeked Tern**   *Sterna repressa*                                   Plate 64          White-cheeked Tern   A
Grey mantle and wings, pale grey rump and tail, black nape and blackish bill.

**Common Tern**   *Sterna hirundo*                                           Plate 64          Common Tern   B
Very similar to White-cheeked, but larger, paler on wings and mantle, and with whitish rump and tail.

**Roseate Tern**   *Sterna dougallii*                                        Plate 64          Roseate Tern   C
Distinctly paler above than White-cheeked and Common Terns, usually with longer tail-streamers and more contrast between blackish outer primaries and rest of wing.

**Whiskered Tern**   *Chlidonias hybrida*                                    Plate 66          Whiskered Tern   D
Slightly larger than Black and White-winged Black Terns, with less black on crown, heavier bill and uniformly grey upper-parts; lacks smudge on sides of breast. Shallow forked tail and different habits separate it from White-cheeked. Pecks from surface.

**Sandwich Tern**   *Sterna sandvicensis*                                    Plate 64          Sandwich Tern   E
Thickset, mostly white, with long narrow wings, short white tail with shallow fork and long black bill tipped with yellow. Coasts and offshore, plunge-diving.

**Gull-billed Tern**   *Gelochelidon nilotica*                              Plate 63          Gull-billed Tern   F
Differs from Sandwich in more gull-like form, shorter, stouter, all-black bill, less deeply forked tail, black patch through eye and longer legs. Over muddy shores and marshes, swooping on crabs, insects, etc.

**Bridled Tern**   *Sterna anaethetus*                                       Plate 65          Bridled Tern   G
Brownish-black above, with long white supercilium, white collar, white leading edge to wing and white outer edge to long forked tail; bill black. Pelagic.

**Sooty Tern**   *Sterna fuscata*                                           Plate 65          Sooty Tern   H
Similar to Bridled, but sooty-black above, shorter white supercilium, and no white collar. Scarce.

**Lesser Crested Tern**   *Sterna bengalensis*                              Plate 63          Lesser Crested Tern   J
Pearl-grey above, with pale grey rump and tail; smaller and paler than Great Crested, with orange-yellow bill.

**Caspian Tern**   *Sterna caspia*                                          Plate 63          Caspian Tern   K
Very large and gull-like; huge red or orange-red bill, blackish nape, pale grey upper-parts, blackish under wing-tips, and white tail with shallow fork.

**Crested Tern**   *Sterna bergii*                                          Plate 63          Crested Tern   L
Large; dark grey above, with black nape, long, pale, forked tail (often closed and appearing pointed), and large dull yellow or greenish-yellow bill.

**Lesser Noddy**   *Anous tenuirostris*                                     Plate 65          Lesser Noddy   M
Smaller and darker than Common Noddy, with more slender bill, shorter tail and white crown and lores. Usually feeds closer to shore, with more fluttering flight.

**Common Noddy**   *Anous stolidus*                                         Plate 65          Common Noddy   N
Chocolate-brown, with pale crown and long graduated tail. Flies low to snatch food from surface.

**Little Tern**   *Sterna albifrons*                                        Plate 66          Little Tern   O
Differs from Saunders' Little Tern in having less black in outer primaries; grey mantle and wings contrast with whitish rump and tail. Shallow splash dives, also in fresh water.

**Saunders' Little Tern**   *Sterna saundersi*                              Plate 66          Saunders' Little Tern   P
Small, active, with very rapid wing-beats; outer primaries appear largely black; pearly-grey mantle, wings, rump and tail (tail rarely white); bill usually yellow with black tip (may be all yellow or all black). Shallow plunge-dives.

**White-winged Black Tern**   *Chlidonias leucopterus*                      Plate 66          White-winged
Similar to Whiskered Tern, but smaller; black nape, white collar, and grey mantle and wings contrast-          Black Tern   Q
ing with whitish rump; usually lacks dark smudge on side of breast. Pecks from surface.

**Black Tern**   *Chlidonias niger*                                         Plate 66          Black Tern   R
Similar to Whiskered Tern, but has grey smudge on side of breast, and usually more black on crown. Pecks from surface.

180

Plate 67

181

# SANDGROUSE: Pteroclididae

**World:** 16 species. **Oman:** 4 species (breeding). Pigeon-like terrestrial seed-eaters, nomadic for food, some partially migratory. Small head, short bill, robust body, long, pointed, black-tipped wings; tail long, some with very long central feathers, like parakeets in fast flight. Walk or waddle on short legs. Plumage dense, pale with cryptic marks; pattern of male's head, breast or belly diagnostic, female less distinctly marked. Calls are diagnostic. Fly long distances in small flocks to drink at favourite fresh-water places, occasionally saline, at regular times, some species in large gatherings by day, one species in Oman in darkness. Drink with few rapid 'sip and swallow' motions like domestic fowl. Water is carried to the nest in deliberately soaked uniquely modified feathers of breast and belly. Breed solitarily, the nest a small unlined depression on open ground. 2–3 eggs, glossy, round at both ends. Some parents give distraction display. Chicks run soon after hatching.

## Coronetted Sandgrouse (Crowned Sandgrouse)    *Pterocles coronatus*

Coronetted Sandgrouse

**World:** Breeds in Africa, Sinai, Arabia, Palestine to NW India, in several races. Sedentary, nomadic and irregular.
**Oman:** Fairly common widespread breeding resident.

28cm/11in. The tail is only slightly elongate and the belly is pale. The *male* has a rufous-brown crown, grey and buff collar and white forehead encircled by a black line extending to the chin. The *female* is sandy with dark vermiculations, and has yellow on sides of neck. The under-wing is dark except for whitish coverts. Bill black.

*male* A
*female* B

Stony desert, and foothills. It drinks in the morning. Nests from March/April. Calls, *chee-wuk chewukeroo* or *gatut-gadidada* or *chiruk-chirugaga*.

## Lichtenstein's Sandgrouse    *Pterocles lichtensteinii*

Lichtenstein's Sandgrouse

**World:** *P.l. lichtensteinii* breeds in N and NE Africa, Socotra, Arabia, SE Iran to NW India; sedentary and nomadic. Other races in Africa, Hadhramaut. (Sometimes treated as conspecific with **Painted** or **Close-barred Sandgrouse** *P. indicus* of India.)
**Oman:** Common breeding resident, not on Masirah.

27cm/10½in. It is closely barred and speckled blackish on buff, with a square tail. The *male's* forehead is barred black-and-white, with orange-yellow bill and orbital skin, and a double buff and black breast-band. The *female* is vermiculated without other marks.

*male* C
*female* D

Mountains, wadi beds, stony areas with some scrub. By day feeds in small loose parties. Comes to water after sunset and before dawn. Nests May–September, also in captivity. 2 eggs, rarely 3. Call, a liquid musical whistle, *wee-up* or *kwee-oo*, occasionally a shorter *kwit* or *kiti*; when flushed, a guttural *krerwerwerwer*.

## Chestnut-bellied Sandgrouse    *Pterocles exustus*

Chestnut-bellied Sandgrouse

**World:** *P. exustus erlangeri* breeds in S and E Arabia; resident. Other races in Africa, SE Iran to India.
**Oman:** Common and widespread resident.

28cm/12½in incl. long central tail-feathers. The whole belly appears dark chestnut. The *male* is plain yellowish from head to breast, the sandy-buff wing-coverts are tipped dark brown, and there is a narrow black bar across the breast. The *female* is heavily vermiculated and streaked except for yellowish throat and sides of head, buff breast-band, and dark belly with paler bars. The under-wing is blackish, the inner primaries tipped white.

*male* E
*female* F

Gravel plains, less frequently on sand. Drinks during the day. Usually nests from March, but from January in some years. Call, a deeper note than other Oman species, *kurra-kurra* or *gata-gata*.

## Spotted Sandgrouse    *Pterocles senegallus*

Spotted Sandgrouse

**World:** Breeds in Africa, Arabia, Near East, Iraq to NW India. Sedentary and migratory.
**Oman:** Locally common breeding resident, not Batinah or Masirah; less common in summer.

36cm/14in, incl. long central tail-feathers. It is pale with a diagnostic black patch on centre of belly. The *male* differs from the Coronetted Sandgrouse in its yellow throat and lack of black-and-white forehead. The *female* is darkly spotted on a pale base, except on the throat, lower breast and belly.

*male* G
*female* H

Open sandy and stony desert. Waters during the day after feeding. Nest not yet found in Oman, probably from February. Call, a loud *wittow-wittoo* or *crakow-crakow*, and a musical gabbling in flocks.

Plate 68

# PIGEONS and DOVES: Columbidae

Plates 69–71

**World:** 255 species. **Oman:** 10 species (5 breeding). Almost world-wide, mostly arboreal, a few species cliff-dwelling or terrestrial. The largest are called pigeons. The head is small, the body plump, the bill small with a soft naked cere, the legs usually short and the plumage dense. Usually gregarious, feeding on fruit, seeds, other vegetable matter and some invertebrates. They drink by sucking. The young are fed with crop-milk. The flight is usually strong, sometimes with wing-claps, especially in display flights. The nest is a pad of twigs. Usually 2 eggs, in 2 or 3 broods. The calls are diagnostic.

## Yellow-bellied Green Pigeon (Bruce's Green Pigeon) *Treron waalia*

Yellow-bellied Green Pigeon

*male* A
*female* B

**World:** Breeds from Senegal across Africa to Sudan, E Africa, Socotra, SW Arabia.
**Oman:** Found in the Dhofar mountains between April and October in small numbers; status uncertain, may breed.

32cm/12½in. Despite its size and distinctive colourful plumage it is liable to be overlooked in well-foliaged trees. The upper-parts are green, except for the paler olive-green head and neck, a bold mauve shoulder-patch (coverts), yellow-edged greater-coverts and secondaries, and dark primaries and tail; the breast and belly are bright yellow, and there are some chestnut flecks on the paler under tail-coverts. The bill is pale with a lavender-red base, and the legs are orange. The iris is blue with an outer ring of red or yellow.

In thick-foliaged trees. It climbs about like a parrot, searching for fruit, especially figs, *Zizyphus* berries, etc.; when alarmed it will often stand motionless and silent. It has a fast, furtive, rattling flight, swooping upwards into cover. Gregarious, in pairs or parties, often near water. The nest (from March in SW Arabia), is a flimsy twig platform 3–5m up, often at the end of a branch. It does not coo, but has a 'rippling note', a 'crooning whistle' and a 'chatter'.

## Rock Dove *Columba livia*

Rock Dove C

**World:** *C.l. palestinae* breeds in S Palestine, Sinai, Arabia. Other races in Eurasia, northern Africa, India, Sri Lanka; sedentary.
**Oman:** Fairly common breeding resident.

33cm/13in. Very similar to some domestic pigeons (which are descendants of the Rock Dove and may escape to the wild). Blue-grey, darkest on the head, neck, breast (which is glossed green-mauve) and tail, and palest on the wings, back and upper rump; there is a double black bar across the secondaries, the tail has a black terminal-band and pale outer edges, and the under-wing is white. See Stock Dove (plate 70).

In and near mountains, foothills, sea cliffs and some islands. Gregarious, particularly in winter, wandering far for food and water. The flight is rapid, in a swerving rush, following cliff contours in compact flocks, suddenly and silently alighting; in display it claps the wings in level flight and glides with wings raised. The nest, from March, is unlined, on a ledge or the floor of a cave, in a crevice in a cliff or old building, or down a well, rarely in trees. It calls like a domestic pigeon, *oh-roo-coo* (song), *co-roo-cootcoo* (display) (Goodwin), and a quieter guttural *gurr-oo* or *kurrk-roo*.

## Woodpigeon *Columba palumbus*

Woodpigeon D

**World:** Breeds in Azores, NW Africa, Europe to SW Russia, south to Iran, N India, in several races. Sedentary and migratory.
**Oman:** Breeding resident locally in mountains of N Oman, wandering in winter; the Oman birds resemble *C.p. casiotis* of SW Russia, SE Iran, N India.

43cm/17in. Oman's largest pigeon. Dark grey, darkest on flight-feathers and tail-tip, with a diagnostic white wing-bar in flight, a buff patch on each side of the neck surrounded by green-purple gloss, a mauve breast and a white band across the middle of the under tail-feathers. The *immature* is paler vinous-grey, with a vinous breast, no neck-patch, and some black on the coverts, but the same diagnostic wing- and tail-pattern as the *adult*.

Mountain gullies with trees, some descending to interior plains and the Batinah in winter. Singly, in pairs and parties, and in winter sometimes in flocks of over 50. Very shy, flying off with a clatter, swerving between trees and jinking behind hill crests. In display flight it towers, then wing-claps and glides on level wings. The tail is often raised and lowered after alighting. It feeds on fruit, seeds, leaves, buds and invertebrates, taken on trees and on the ground. The nest, from March, is a pad of twigs in a tree or on a rock ledge between the altitudes of about 1500 and 2500m. Calls, *(coo) crow-coo coo-coo (cuck)*, with variations.

Plate 69

**Turtle Dove**    *Streptopelia turtur*

**World:** *S.t. arenicola* breeds in NW Africa, Palestine, SE Arabia, Iraq, Iran to Mongolia. Other races in N Africa and from Europe to central Asia. Migratory, reaching Africa, Arabia, India.
**Oman:** Common passage migrant, also a local breeding summer visitor (in N Oman), March–November.

28cm/11in. Larger than the Palm Dove but smaller than the others on this plate, and smaller and paler than the northern race (which might occur rarely on passage). It is sandy-rufous above, with a chequered patch (black feathers with grey to white tips) on each side of the neck, the mantle is mottled rufous and black (black centres to rufous-edged feathers), and the flight-feathers are dark grey; the neck and breast are mauve, the belly and under tail-coverts white; the outer tail-feathers are tipped white above (as with the Palm Dove), the under-tail tipped white (but narrower than on the Collared Dove). The *juvenile* is pale brown, with many feathers edged rufous or buff, and with no neck-patch.

Small trees, perching in open positions and feeding on the ground, singly or in pairs, and in parties on passage. Its flight and behaviour resemble those of a large, heavy Palm Dove. It nests in small trees on the Batinah from April. Song, a soft purring *toorrr-toorrr*; display, *croor(wa)* (Goodwin).


**Rufous Turtle Dove** (Eastern Turtle Dove)    *Streptopelia orientalis*

**World:** Breeds in central, E and SE Asia, in several races. Resident and migratory, reaching SE Arabia, SE Iran, India, SE Asia.
**Oman:** Passage migrant in very small numbers, September–December, February–May.

33cm/13in. Very similar to the Turtle Dove, particularly the European race, but most differ in larger size, more stocky build and having the black feathers of the neck-patch tipped pale blue-grey (not white), the upper-parts duller and less distinctly marked, the under tail-coverts pale grey and the tail edged pale grey and tipped blue-grey (not white). The west Indian race *erythrocephala* is the smallest and is rich pink and rufous. The *juvenile* is similar to the juvenile Turtle Dove, but is dull grey-brown with conspicuous rufous or buff fringes to the feathers of the mantle and breast.

Singly or in small parties, often amongst other doves.


**Collared Dove**    *Streptopelia decaocto*

**World:** *S.d. decaocto* breeds from Europe to Palestine, E Arabia, Iraq, Iran, India, across to Japan; sedentary and migratory. Other races in Burma, China.
**Oman:** Passage migrant and winter visitor, widespread and very common on the Batinah only in some years; also a breeding resident on N Batinah and near Salalah, locally common.

32cm/12½in. A large pale dove, almost uniform grey-brown. The *adult* has a pinkish-grey head, black half-collar with white border (absent in *juveniles*) and dark flight-feathers contrasting with very pale under wing-coverts (dark grey in Turtle and Rufous Turtle Doves); from above the tail is grey-brown with whitish tips to the outer feathers, and from below black tipped with white. It differs from the Turtle and Rufous Turtle Doves also in its longer tail, half-collar and lack of mottling on the back; from the Palm Dove (plate 71) in larger size, more uniform colouration, black-and-white half-collar and pale under-wing. See female Red Turtle Dove (plate 71).

Amongst trees, perching in the open, feeding on the ground. Gregarious after nesting. It habitually flies higher than the Palm Dove; in display it towers, sometimes with wing-claps, and glides with wings and tail outspread. Comes to water in the morning and evening. Nests in trees, from February. Song, a trisyllabic *coo-coo-co*; display *coo-coo(cuck)*, excitement-call in flight a long nasal moan *few*, *froo* or *whaow*.


**Stock Dove**    *Columba oenas*                                                        (Not illustrated)

**World:** Breeds from W Europe to C Asia, south to NW Africa, N Iran, Turkestan. Sedentary and migratory, reaching N Africa, Sinai, SW Iran, Afghanistan.
**Oman:** Vagrant (one shot, Batinah, 28 October 1965).

33cm/13in. A dull uniform-grey pigeon, with two or three short black bars across the folded wing, black wing-tips and trailing-edges, grey tail with a dark terminal-band, and a green neck-patch. It differs from Rock and most feral pigeons in the darker back, greyer under-wing with contrasting black tips (not grey), less distinct black wing-bars; from Wood Pigeon (plate 69) in its smaller more compact form, lack of white on wings and neck.

Trees, cliffs and old buildings. It will mingle with other species and flock with its own. The flight is faster than Wood, but not so rapid as Rock Dove.

Plate 70

**Namaqua Dove** (Long-tailed or Masked Dove)    *Oena capensis*

Namaqua Dove

**World:** Breeds in most of Africa, Madagascar, Socotra, S and central Arabia east to Hadhramaut and Riyadh.

**Oman:** Vagrant to Dhofar, one or two reported on five occasions between May and October since 1975, and a possible future breeder.

28cm/11in, incl. tail. A very small lark-sized dove, with a disproportionately long graduated tail which is black with a dark grey base to the central feathers and some white in the outers. The *adult male* has a distinctive black mask and bib, contrasting with the white lower breast and belly; the pale blue-grey of the crown merges into the pale brown of the mantle, the sides of the head and the shoulder-patch are paler grey and the primaries are brown and deep rufous or chestnut (which is noticeable in flight); there are two rows of dark metallic-coloured spots across the back; the bill is red, sometimes tipped yellow. The *adult female* differs in its pale face, lack of black and darker bill. The *immature* is lightly barred or speckled black and buff.

*male* B

*female* A

Remarkable for its sudden appearances and disappearances. Usually on dry open ground, feeding normally or with very rapid rat-like movements, on very small seeds, rarely amongst crops. Singly, in family parties, infrequently in flocks. The flight is very fast and direct, showing chestnut in the pointed wings; the tail is sometimes raised and fanned after alighting. It perches low down, and is said to drink in the heat of the day. The nest (March–September, near Aden), is a very flimsy platform of stems, usually very low and often exposed, in *Tamarix*, etc., or low vegetation, or even on a mound. The eggs are pinkish-cream, rarely white like other doves. The call is a deep, mournful, booming and ventriloquial *ho, ho-ho-ho* or *hu-hoo.*

**Red Turtle Dove**    *Streptopelia tranquebarica*

Red Turtle Dove

**World:** *S.t. tranquebarica* breeds in India, except NE; sedentary and locally migratory. Another race in SE Asia.

**Oman:** Vagrant (two on Masirah, October 1975).

23cm/9in. A small plump dove, between the sizes of the Palm and Namaqua Doves, the *male* brightly coloured. The *adult male* has a dark grey head, black half-collar round the hind-neck, reddish body, grey coverts to the blackish flight-feathers, pale grey under wing-coverts and dark blue-grey lower-back, rump and shortish tail; the outer tail-feathers are broadly tipped white. The *adult female* is very different, being much duller and browner, and resembling a small Collared Dove (plate 70) except for the somewhat darker under wing-coverts.

*male* C

*female* D

It will associate with other doves, feeding on the ground with them. It is very shy and if disturbed it may fly swiftly for some distance before re-alighting.

**Palm Dove** (Laughing Dove)    *Streptopelia senegalensis*

Palm Dove E

**World:** *S. senegalensis senegalensis* breeds in Africa, Near East, Arabia except in east; *cambayensis* breeds in E Arabia, Iran, India. Other races in N Africa, Socotra, SW Russia. Sedentary and partially migratory.

**Oman:** Common breeding resident, *senegalensis* in Dhofar, *cambayensis* elsewhere; some regularly on passage, mostly in autumn.

27cm/10½in. The commonest dove in Oman, small, slim and pinkish-brown; some birds (particularly *females*) are pale, while others are dark or brightly coloured. The *adult's* head is lilac-pink (often bright), the neck and upper breast is mauve with black bases to the feathers appearing as spots, the under-parts are whitish; the mantle is dull brown or reddish-brown, and the outer wing-coverts are blue-grey; in flight the wing shows contrasting brown and blue-grey patches and dark flight-feathers, the outer tail-feathers are tipped white above and visible when fanned to land, and the tail is broadly tipped white below. The *juvenile* is paler grey-brown with pale feather-fringes. It differs from the rather similar adult Turtle Dove (plate 70) in its smaller size, uniform back and lack of the black-and-white neck-patch. It differs from the Collared Dove (plate 70) in smaller size, lack of collar, lower flight, more blue on the wing, dark under-wing and call.

Widespread, particularly near cultivation (less so on Salalah plain, where it is scarce), singly or in pairs, although larger parties gather at food, water and roosts and on passage. The flight can be fast, and is usually low, with a whistle of feathers; in display it towers, occasionally giving wing-claps, and then gliding with wings bowed and tail fanned. It is shy, except locally. The nest, from January or February, is on a tree, bush or building. The song, from January, is varied but distinctive, ending in a rapid descending bubble or 'laugh', *cu-coo-coo-cucuk, pu-poopoo-pupupooo* or *poo, poo, poopidoo.*

Plate 71

189

# PARROTS: Psittacidae

**World:** 330 species. **Oman:** 1 species (breeding). Arboreal; widespread across the tropics. Varied in size, all with the bill short, hooked and very powerful, with a soft cere; neck and body compact; wings short, rounded; tail long in parakeets. Legs short, two toes directed forward, two backward, permitting the typical clamber, aided by the bill, in search of fruit and seeds, which most can hold up to eat. Mostly gregarious, all are noisy and most nest in holes. The flight is strong and rapid. Some wander seasonally to ripening fruit and seeds.

**Rose-ringed Parakeet** (Ring-necked Parakeet)    *Psittacula krameri*    Rose-ringed Parakeet

**World:** *P.k. borealis* breeds in N India, Burma, SE China, and has been introduced into Iraq, Iran, Arabian Gulf, N Oman, Aden, E Africa, UK, etc. Resident with some seasonal movements. Other races across central Africa, Mauritius, S India.
**Oman:** Resident on the Batinah; vagrant to Masirah.

42cm/16½in, incl. tail. A medium-sized parrot, bright green tinged with yellow and blue, with a red bill and a very long pointed tail. The *adult male* has a thin black line from bill to eye, a half-collar of black on the chin (acquired at seven months) and another of rose-pink on the hind-neck (after two years). The *female* has the half-collars replaced by an indistinct emerald-green ring. The *juvenile* is more yellowish.    *male* A<br>*female* B

Trees in and at the edge of cultivation. It occurs individually and in small parties, and roosts communally, often away from the feeding area. The flight is swift and level with rapid wing-beats, the long tail distinct, and the birds often calling. It swerves down to feed on seed-pods, dates, other fruit, grain and especially sunflower seeds. Despite the bright plumage it is difficult to see in trees, and its presence is often noted first by a noisy screaming *kee-ak*. It is often kept captive. It nests, from January or February, in a hole or crevice in a tree, old building or rock face, excavated or enlarged by the bird. The eggs, 3–6, usually 3 or 4, are small and white.

[Other ex-captive parrots occur occasionally in Oman, such as the **Budgerigar** *Melopsittacus undulatus* and the **Large Indian Parakeet** *Psittacula eupatria* 51cm/20in, but there is no evidence of their naturalisation.]

# CUCKOOS: Cuculidae    Plates 72–73

**World:** 127 species. **Oman:** 3 species (1 breeding). Mainly arboreal and solitary, ranging in size from that of sparrow to that of raven. Plumage of sexes often differs; a few are crested, some have an eye-ring. Tail medium to long. Bill stout, slightly decurved, heavy in some species. Legs, except terrestrial species, short, the outer hind-toe reversible. Males have loud calls. Most are insectivorous, but fruit, invertebrates and small vertebrates may be taken. The sub-family Cuculinae is broodparasitic, laying eggs in the nest of certain other species, to be hatched and the young reared by the foster-parents. The sub-family Centropodinae, the coucals, are large, clumsy birds of the ground, bushes, or tree-tops, with short wings, long tails and heavy hooked bills [represented in SW Arabia, not Dhofar, by the **White-browed Coucal** *Centropus superciliosus* 38cm/15in].

**Cuckoo**    *Cuculus canorus*    Cuckoo

**World:** Breeds across Eurasia, south to NW Africa, Asia Minor, Iran, N India, in several races. Migratory.
**Oman:** Regular passage migrant, August–November, occasionally from late July, and April–May, in small numbers, most in autumn.

33cm/13in. In flight or on an open perch it can be mistaken for a Sparrowhawk (plate 27), but it differs in the graduated spotted tail, pointed wings and bill-shape. The *adult male* is dark blue-grey above, with the blackish tail spotted and tipped white; the ear-coverts, throat and upper breast are pale grey, the lower breast and belly white strongly barred with dark brown and the under tail-coverts white with faint barring. The *adult female* is similar, but has the back and breast tinged brown. A hepatic (rufous-brown) form of the *female,* resembling a female Kestrel (plate 32), also occurs.    *male* D<br>*female, hepatic form* C

It perches on bushes, trees and posts, dropping down heavily on insects, etc., and walking or hopping clumsily on its short legs. The flight is direct and fast, with a long glide before settling. Numbers gather at good feeding-places, such as coastal Dhofar in autumn. It migrates by day or night.

Plate 72

**Koel** *Eudynamys scolopacea*

**World:** *E.s. scolopacea* breeds in India; sedentary, locally migratory and nomadic. Other races from NE India to Australasia.
**Oman:** Vagrant, November–December to Masirah.

43cm/17in. About the size of a House Crow (plate 112), but more slender, with a longer graduated tail. The *male* is black with a metallic gloss. The *female* and *immature* are dark brown above, glossed olive and spotted and barred with white; white below, heavily spotted and barred sooty-brown. The iris is bright crimson, the bill dull green and the legs blue-grey.

*male* A
*female* B

Trees, bushes and other cover. It is furtive and rarely seen except in flight or where there is no cover, thus it may be overlooked. It feeds in cover on fruit, invertebrates, small vertebrates and birds' eggs. In India it is brood-parasitic on House Crows, laying one or more eggs in the nests of that species; it has not been heard or seen amongst House Crows on the Batinah. It is noisy when breeding, the principal calls being at dawn, a prolonged shrill *uruk-keook-keook-keook*, and in song, a repeated di-syllabic *ko-el* or *ku-oo* ascending and increasing in excitement.

**Didric Cuckoo** *Chrysococcyx caprius*

Didric Cuckoo C

**World:** Breeds in Africa south of the Sahara, and S and SE Arabia. Migratory.
**Oman:** Breeding summer visitor to Dhofar May–October.

19cm/7½in. A little larger than a bulbul, and more often heard than seen. The *adult male* is metallic green above, with a bronze gloss, white streaks above and through eye, dark wings with white spots, and greenish-black tail also spotted white; it is white below, with a green moustachial streak, and the flanks and under tail-coverts are barred dark bronze-green. The *adult female* is duller, more bronze or chestnut above, with no white above the eye, the under-parts tinged buff to rufous and the flanks more extensively barred. The *immature* resembles the *adult female*, but the throat to breast is streaked and blotched green. The bill is blue-black, red in fledglings. It differs from **Klaas' Cuckoo** *C. klaas* [18cm/7in, range and habits broadly similar but not known east of Aden] in its song and the presence of white spots and marks on the wing; the young bird is streaked below (not barred as in Klaas').

Amongst trees, bushes and creepers on hill slopes and in wadis. It rests lengthwise on a branch like a nightjar. It feeds on invertebrates obtained by searching trees and bushes slowly and methodically, clinging to stems like a woodpecker. It calls frequently when breeding. It is brood-parasitic upon Rüppell's Weaver (plate 115), possibly also on sunbirds (plate 109). The territory is small, and occasionally may be limited to one weaver colony. In display flight the male flaps, then glides with wings, head and tail raised. The female skulks and is infrequently seen. The eggs, from June (at least 4 each season in Africa), are laid singly in hosts' nests. The chick evicts other eggs and also the hosts' chicks if these are younger than itself. The parent cuckoos assist in feeding the fledgling. The song is a high-pitched whistling *too-tee-tee-tititit* and *(dee) dee-dee-deedarik*, the last notes raised, uttered in flight and at rest; the female calls *deea-deea-deea*; calls by juveniles resemble those of their host species; some young call like adults before migrating (which is possibly after the adults).

**Jacobin Cuckoo** (Pied Crested Cuckoo)　*Clamator jacobinus*

Jacobin Cuckoo D

**World:** *C.j. serratus* breeds in Africa south of Sahara, India north of 18°N, Burma; migratory, Indian birds arrive in late May to June, depart September–October, presumably crossing the ocean to winter in Africa. Other races in S India, Sri Lanka.
**Oman:** Vagrant or scarce passage migrant (single birds on 14 June 1977, 28 October 1977 and 16 November 1978).

33cm/13in. A slender-bodied, crested bird, black above, glossed green, with a white patch in the browner wings and conspicuous white tips to the outer feathers of the long, graduated tail; it is white below, sometimes greyish. The plumage of the sexes is similar. The *immature* is more brownish above and below, with a shorter crest. The iris is red-brown, the bill black, the legs blue-grey.

In trees and bushes, and less secretive than some cuckoos. It repeatedly flirts the tail. It feeds mainly on invertebrates, in cover, on the ground and in aerial sorties. In its breeding quarters it is brood-parasitic upon babblers, and is then noisy, calling with a shrill metallic *pliu* or *piu . . . piu . . . pee-pee-piu*.

192

Plate 73

# OWLS: Tytonidae and Strigidae

Plates 74–75

**World:** 131 species. **Oman:** At least 9 species (6 breeding). Soft-plumaged, round-winged, silent-flying birds of prey, mostly nocturnal. Vision and hearing excellent, large eyes set in flattened facial disc facing forward. Head large and round on short neck, giving distinctive silhouette. Tail short; bill powerful, partly concealed. Small food swallowed whole, indigestible material regurgitated as pellets. Most are arboreal and sedentary, but some live in marsh or desert and several are migratory. Considered birds of ill omen, yet beneficial to man. Calls generally diagnostic. Tytonidae differ from Strigidae in long legs, unified facial disc, black eyes and lack of head-tufts.

## Barn Owl  *Tyto alba*

Barn Owl  B

**World:** *T.a. erlangeri* breeds in Near East, Arabia, Iraq, Iran.
**Oman:** Widespread breeding resident.

33cm/13in. A medium-sized very pale owl, with a white heart-shaped facial disc. It is golden-buff and grey above, flecked black and white; white below. The legs are long and down-covered.

Roosts in caves, old buildings, holes in trees, wells, etc., often in pairs. It hunts low over scrub desert and fields, preying on small rodents, birds, bats, etc. The nest, from April, is on debris in similar places to roosts. 3–4 eggs. Call, a screech; also squeaks, chirrups, snores, purrs, chatters and tongue-clicks.

## Little Owl  *Athene noctua*

Little Owl  A

**World:** *A.n. saharae* breeds in N Africa to Egypt, Arabia; sedentary. Other races in Near East, Eurasia south to Iraq, Iran, India.
**Oman:** Fairly common and widespread breeding resident (not on Masirah).

22cm/8½in. Small, with a large, rounded, flat-topped head, broad rounded wings and short tail. Pale greyish or brownish, profusely spotted white above with a pale collar; some dark streaks below.

Low rocky hills, buildings, trees in semi-desert. Partly diurnal, more often seen than other small owls. Sits upright in the open, morning and evening, bobbing the head, and bolting down a hole if alarmed. Calls and hunts mostly from sunset, and feeds on beetles, small vertebrates, etc. The nest, from February, is in an unlined hole in a cliff, tree, or under rocks. 3–5 eggs. Call, a mournful *m-wew* repeated at intervals, also a long series of sharp yelping *kyew*.

## Scops Owl  *Otus scops*

Scops Owl  C

**World:** *O.s. turanicus* breeds in Transcaspia, Iraq, Iran to NW India; migratory, reaching NE Africa, Arabia. Other races in Africa, Eurasia, India to Far East.
**Oman:** Common passage migrant; some reports suggest confusion with Bruce's Scops.

19cm/7½in. Small, grey-brown, with head-tufts. Finely streaked and spotted with brown, black and white above, with a V of white spots on the scapulars; belly whitish. Toes unfeathered.

Roosts in trees; hunts and migrates by night. Mainly insectivorous, but will take small birds, etc.

## Bruce's Scops Owl (Striated Scops Owl)  *Otus brucei*

Bruce's Scops Owl  D

**World:** *O.b. exiguus* breeds from Palestine to Iran, E Arabia, NW India; sedentary and migratory. Other races in central and E Asia. (Sometimes regarded as a race of *O. scops* or *O. sunia*.)
**Oman:** Fairly common but local breeding visitor to N Oman; some reports suggest confusion with Scops Owl.

21cm/8¼in. Very similar to Scops Owl, but larger, paler, greyer, and usually without ochreous tinge. In the hand, the feathering of the tarsus can be seen to extend slightly on to the toes (not in Scops).

Scattered trees in mountains, semi-desert plains and cultivation. It feeds on insects and small vertebrates. It nests, from February or April, in a crevice in a tree or on old bird-nests. 2–5 eggs. Song, a long sequence of short notes at 1–3-second intervals, *bup . . . bup . . . bup*; also mews and bill-clicks.

## Oriental Scops Owl  *Otus sunia*

Oriental Scops Owl  E

**World:** *O.s. pamelae* breeds from SW Arabia to Dhofar; resident. Other races on Socotra, in N and central India. (Sometimes regarded as a race of *O. scops* or *O. senegalensis*.)
**Oman:** Breeding resident in the Dhofar mountains.

21cm/8¼in. Very similar to Scops Owl, but more uniform and less variegated above, the scapular spots greyish to dull ochre (not white); toes unfeathered.

Trees on hill slopes. Habits unrecorded, but probably similar to other *Otus* species. Call, a series of loud notes *prrok, wokk, kyar* or *kwar*, heard most of the year, more often in spring.

194

Plate 74

**Short-eared Owl**   *Asio flammeus*

**World:** *A.f. flammeus* breeds in N America, Iceland, N Eurasia; sedentary, migratory and nomadic, reaching N Africa, Arabia, S Asia.
**Oman:** Passage migrant in small numbers, November–December, February–March.

38cm/15in. The most likely medium-sized owl to be seen by day. Pale buff to dark brown above, boldly blotched and streaked darker; the head-tufts are short and visible only at close range; it is pale buff below, streaked with dark brown particularly on the breast; there is a black patch on the long narrow wing near the carpal joint, visible from above and below. The yellow eyes are surrounded by dark feathers in a pale facial disc.

Open dunes, plains and marshes by day and at dusk, singly or in loose parties. It settles on the ground or on a stump, etc., less upright than most owls. The slow and regular wing-beat in direct flight is reminiscent of the Houbara (plate 40), but the Short-eared Owl is much smaller and lacks white in the upper-wing. It hunts in low, wavering owl-flight or flaps and glides like a blunt-headed harrier. It feeds on small rodents, also larger mammals and birds, invertebrates, reptiles, bats.

**Long-eared Owl**   *Asio otus*

**World:** *A.o. otus* breeds across Eurasia, south to Azores, NW Africa, Near East across to N Iran, NW India (rarely); sedentary, migratory to latitude of Iraq, vagrant further south.
**Oman:** Vagrant (one, N Oman, 1 March 1975).

36cm/14in. A slim medium-sized owl with long head-tufts. Mottled and streaked grey-brown and buff above; boldly streaked and blotched dark on buff below. Differs from the Short-eared Owl in nocturnal habits, broader wings, slimmer form, longer tufts and bright orange (not yellow) eyes.

Thick trees near open country. Crepuscular and nocturnal. Singly, or in parties on migration and in winter. Roosts very upright, close to tree-trunk or rarely on the ground against a tussock. Hunts in silent wavering flight to feed on small rodents, hares, birds up to partridge size, invertebrates.

**Spotted Eagle Owl**   *Bubo africanus*

**World:** *B.a. milesi* occurs in S and E Arabia from Mecca to Muscat. Other races in Africa.
**Oman:** Breeding resident in Dhofar; a few old records from 'Muscat' between September and December, where status is uncertain.

43cm/17in. A large dark brown owl with conspicuous head-tufts and dark facial discs. Tinged rufous and vermiculated above, the tail and flight feathers more boldly barred, a pale fawn patch on the outer primaries; chin and throat-patch white, breast rufous with dark spots, belly finely barred dark and white.

Cliffs and rocky slopes with trees and caves, roosting by day, hunting at dusk over roads (where it is often killed), other open areas and near cultivation and habitation. Feeds on rodents, large grasshoppers, beetles, etc., occasionally birds and reptiles. Nest not yet found in Arabia (African races nest March–May, on the ground under a ledge, boulder or tree, occasionally in a cave or on a tree nest of another species; 2–3 eggs). Call, a soft *hoo-hoo-hoo* and a deep, fluty, nasal *wheeoo*.

**Eagle Owl**   *Bubo bubo*

**World:** Desert Eagle Owl *B.b. ascalaphus* (or *desertorum*) breeds from N Africa across Near East to Sinai, Arabia, Iraq; mainly sedentary. Other races across Eurasia, south to India.
**Oman:** Widespread resident.

50cm/19½in. The largest owl in Oman, though smaller and paler than other races of Eagle Owl. Pale golden with dark and pale bars, spots and vermiculations; conspicuous head-tufts, white facial discs and large orange-yellow eyes.

Occupies caves or crevices in large outcrops of rock or cliffs at the desert border of foothills and in open desert. Nocturnal, but occasionally seen exposed in evening sunlight. Hunts mainly at dawn and dusk for desert rodents, but will also take hares, birds, and reptiles. It nests, from February or March, on the unlined floor or ledge of a cave. 2–4 eggs, usually 2. Call, a distinctive deep barking *whu* or *boo-boo* or *ooo-hu*.

**[Hume's Tawny Owl**   *Strix butleri*                                        (Not illustrated)

Breeds in Near East, Arabia, possibly S Iran, Baluchistan, Dhofar. 33cm/13in. A medium-sized gold-and-white owl with orange-yellow eyes. Of desolate cliffs, gorges, rocks or trees nearby. Call, one long followed by two double notes *hooo hu-hu hu-hu*.]

Plate 75 197

# NIGHTJARS: Caprimulgidae

**World:** 70 species. **Oman:** 3 species. Most species are crepuscular or nocturnal, not commonly seen and thus inadequately known. They rest by day perched along a branch or on the ground near cover, where the cryptic colours and patterns make them difficult to find unless flushed. They feed mainly on insects, which are caught in the air either during slow, silent, agile hunting flight or hawking from the ground or from a perch like a flycatcher; some hover and peck from vegetation, some feed on the ground. The gape is huge, usually bordered by strong bristles. The large dark eyes are partly closed in daylight. The plumage is very soft, and the sexes are often dissimilar, the males often with white patches on the long wings and tail. Named after the churring song of the Nightjar. They lay 1–2 eggs on the ground.

## Nubian Nightjar  *Caprimulgus nubicus*

Nubian Nightjar

**World:** *C.n. tamaracis* breeds from Palestine to central and SW Arabia; migratory. Other races in E Africa, Socotra.
**Oman:** Recorded on passage near Salalah, Dhofar, in October; status uncertain.

22cm/8½in. A small greyish nightjar with a small white patch on either side of the throat, puffed out and conspicuous when it calls; and a rufous-buff collar on the hind-neck. In flight it shows a rufous patch on the upper-wing, which appears as 2–3 rows of rufous spots when the wing is closed. The *male* has conspicuous white in the wing and tail (patch on the middle of the outer blackish primaries and terminal third of outer two tail-feathers). The *female* is similar, or with the white replaced by buff.

*male  A*

On the ground in open places where it feeds, especially in wadis with scrub, bushes and trees; occasionally in trees. Nests (in SW Arabia) from April. Call, a hollow resonant *koww koww*, 2–3 notes at 1–4-second intervals (King), or *kroo-kroo*.

## Egyptian Nightjar  *Caprimulgus aegyptius*

Egyptian Nightjar  B

**World:** Breeds in N Africa, Egypt, Iraq, Iran, central Asia, in several races. Migratory, reaching NE Africa.
**Oman:** Regular passage migrant in small numbers, some in winter, September–May.

25cm/10in. A sandy-buff to pale grey desert nightjar, with faint dark vermiculations above and a conspicuous white throat-patch. It differs from the Nightjar in smaller size, pallid colour, lack of black streaks on head and back, having white in the *male's* wing limited to the inner webs of the primaries and having the outer tail-feathers tipped buff, not white.

Semi-desert with scrub, feeding also in vegetated areas on passage. One of the many land species frequently recorded at sea on autumn passage.

## Nightjar  *Caprimulgus europaeus*

Nightjar

**World:** Breeds in W and central Eurasia, south to NW Africa, Turkey, Iran to N India in several races. Highly migratory, mostly to Africa.
**Oman:** Regular passage migrant, mostly September–November and April–May, some in winter; *C.e. unwini* is usual.

*C.e. unwini* 25cm/10in. It is smaller and paler than the other races of Nightjar, and is grey-brown, with rufous and black vermiculations, spots and streaks. The *adult male* has white coverts, a large white spot on the first three primaries, broad white tips to the outer tail-feathers and a narrow white patch on the lower throat. The *female* has smaller buffish spots in the primaries instead of white, and buff spots on the tail. It differs from the immature Cuckoo (plate 72) in the lack of barring on the under-parts.

*male  C*

Widespread, and usually seen in ones and twos, but up to 50 occasionally occur on Masirah in autumn. It flies actively from dusk, when it feeds and migrates. Usually silent on passage, but has a flight-call *choo-ik*, and an alarm note, a chuckling *kuik-kuik-kuik*; when alarmed it will also gape and hiss.

## [Plain Nightjar  *Caprimulgus inornatus*  (Not illustrated)

Breeds from W to E Africa and has occurred east to the Hadhramaut, but not yet in Oman; migratory. 23cm/9in. Rather uniform sandy, grey, dark or rufous brown, with some dark streaks, no collar or white neck-patch, primaries rufous-brown with a white patch in the *male*, the two outer tail-feathers broadly tipped white in the *male*, buff in *female*, rictal bristles extend beyond tip of bill; call, a prolonged *churr*.]

Plate 76

# SWIFTS: Apodidae

**World:** 75–80 species. **Oman:** 4 species (1 breeding). Fast-flying birds, very aerial, usually gregarious, resembling swallows (plate 84) but with longer, narrow, curved wings. True swifts catch insects, small spiders, etc., in the air in the large gape, sometimes at high altitudes, descending to drink, bathe, nest and occasionally perch on cliffs and trees, rarely on flat ground. The legs are very short, and the toes adapted for clinging; species without a spiny tip to the tail have the hind-toe reversible. Most nest in holes or burrows, some in caves, in trees or cliffs; some colonially. The nest material is glued together with saliva; the eggs are white. The plumage of the sexes is similar, usually plain black or brown, with or without white.

### Alpine Swift *Apus melba*

Alpine Swift A

**World:** *A.m. tuneti* breeds in N Africa, Near East, Sinai, SW Asia, south to Iran, NW India, possibly SW Arabia; migratory, probably to Africa. Other races from S Europe to N Iran, Africa, Madagascar, India, Sri Lanka.

**Oman:** Occasional passage migrant in March and October, one seen on Batinah, 16 March 1976, 2 October 1979; three, Dhofar, 7–20 October 1977.

22cm/8½in. A large pale brown swift with distinctive white chin and belly, brown breast-band and brown under tail-coverts; wing-span 53cm/21in.

Hills and mountains. Its flight is like that of a Swift, with which it sometimes flies, but its greater size and frequent gliding may give a momentary impression of a falcon. It roosts on cliffs. It is silent on passage, but utters short screams and a trilling falcon-like whistle when breeding.

### Pallid Swift *Apus pallidus*

Pallid Swift B

**World:** *A.p. pallidus* breeds in N Africa, Near East, Arabia, Iraq, S Iran, Baluchistan; sedentary and migratory, reaching E Africa. Other races in S Europe, Madeira, etc., NW and E Africa.
**Oman:** Common breeding visitor and passage migrant January–October, some over winter.

16.5cm/6½in. Very similar to Swift *A.a. pekinensis*, but paler brown, with pale tips to many of the body-feathers and wing-coverts, more extensive white on the throat and more contrast between the paler secondaries and the rest of the wing; the head is broader and the wings often appear more bulbous in outline.

Cliffs on islands, coastal mainland and mountains. Feeds and flies like Swift. Visits water if available, usually at dusk, and roosts on cliff-face. Nest, from January/February, a pad of hair, feathers, etc., in crevices in caves and cliff-faces, colonially. 2 eggs; probably 2 broods. Calls in loud thin screams near nests and during chases, *seeeyrr* and shorter *pseek-pseek*.

### Swift *Apus apus*

Swift C

**World:** Breeds across Eurasia, south to NW Africa, Palestine to Iran, NW India, Mongolia, in two races. Migratory, reaching S Africa.
**Oman:** Passage migrant, August–October and March–April; it may occur over winter but reports show confusion with Pallid Swift; it has been found in Dhofar in July, when status is uncertain; *A.a. pekinensis* is usual.

*A.a. pekinensis* 16.5cm/6½in. Paler and a little smaller than the western race *apus* (which might also occur); generally difficult to distinguish from the Pallid Swift, but slightly darker. Dark brown except for the paler forehead, whitish chin and throat contrasting with the dark belly.

Mostly aerial in very fast wheeling flight. When feeding on insects, high up or close to ground, it glides and twists with an occasional flicker of the wings. Nest similar to that of Pallid Swift, but not yet found in E Arabia. Calls in long harsh screams, rarely heard in Oman.

### Little Swift (House Swift) *Apus affinis*

Little Swift D

**World:** Breeds locally in Africa, SW Arabia, Near East, Iraq, Iran, India, Far East. Sedentary, migratory and a vagrant.
**Oman:** Vagrant (recorded singly in N Oman in March and October).

14cm/5½in. A small tubby swift, black except for the conspicuous white rump, pale forehead, brown crown and whitish chin and throat; the short tail is square or slightly forked, but can appear rounded. Differs from House Martin (plate 85) in black, not white, under-parts.

Reported only near coasts in Oman. Normally gregarious in parties like the Swift, flying with fluttering wing-beats, glides and agile twisting. It roosts before sunset. In India it is normally found near habitation, where it builds globular nests in colonies. It calls (in India) in musical twittering screams, and trills and churrs in roosts.

Plate 77

# HOOPOE: Upupidae

**World:** 1 species. **Oman:** 1 species (breeding).

### Hoopoe    *Upupa epops*

Hoopoe    A

**World:** *U.e. epops* breeds from Europe to central Asia, south to NW Africa, Near East, Arabia to NW India; sedentary and migratory.
**Oman:** Regular passage migrant in small numbers from February, most from August, occasional in all months; breeds on N Batinah, where some may be resident.

26–30cm/10½–12in. Pinkish cinnamon with a conspicuous erectile crest, bold black-and-white pattern on rounded wings and square tail. The bill is long, slender and decurved.

Open ground at edges of cultivation. Fairly tame. Flight undulating, wings closed regularly. Erects crest on landing and when excited. Roosts in trees. Feeds on invertebrates and small vertebrates, mainly taken on the ground. The nest, from March, is in a hole or crevice in a tree, old building, rocks, etc., foul-smelling. 4–6 eggs, blue to olive. Song, a rapid soft ventriloquial *hup-hup-hup* (hence 'Hoopoe' and Arabic *hudhud*).

# KINGFISHERS: Alcedinidae

**World:** 87 species. **Oman:** 3 species (2 breeding). Small to medium-sized, colourful or well marked. Large head, and short neck, tail and legs. Perch upright, fly rapidly and sometimes hover. Most nest in burrows. Fishing kingfishers (sub-family Alcedininae) have long pointed bills and dive for fish, etc. Woodland kingfishers (Daceloninae) have heavier bills and feed on invertebrates and small vertebrates, often far from water.

### Grey-headed Kingfisher    *Halcyon leucocephala*

Grey-headed Kingfisher    B

**World:** *H.l. semicerulea* breeds from Mecca to Dhofar; migratory. Other races in Africa.
**Oman:** Common breeding summer visitor to Dhofar April–November.

20cm/8in. A colourful, noisy land kingfisher. In the *adult*, the blues of flight-feathers, rump and tail contrast with the black mantle, grey-brown head and hind-neck; the chin to upper breast is whitish, the lower breast to under-tail and under-wing chestnut. In flight it shows a white wing-patch. The bill and feet are coral-red. The *juvenile* is darker on the head, and has the mantle sooty or mottled, blackish marks on neck and breast, the chestnut paler and restricted, legs pinkish and bill blackish.

Amongst trees in mountain valleys and cultivation. It feeds on invertebrates, small vertebrates, usually taken on the ground by a swoop from a perch, occasionally fish, etc., from the surface of a pool or in a shallow splash. Nest, from April/May, an unlined chamber in a burrow in a cliff or bank. 3–5 eggs, white. Calls, noisy and varied, *sisisi* intensifying to a loud, hard *chak-chak-chak*, also *djik, djik, djik* and *kwikwikwikwik*.

### White-collared Kingfisher    *Halcyon chloris*

White-collared
Kingfisher    C

**World:** One race breeds in N Oman and eastern UAE; resident with local movements. Other races from Eritrea, India to Far East, Australasia.
**Oman:** Uncommon and very local breeding resident in N Oman.

24cm/9½in. Dark green except for a broad white collar, short white supercilium, blue wings, rump and tail and white under-parts. The bill is black with a pale lower mandible. The *immature* is flecked with black on the neck and has a pale forehead.

Thick mangroves in tidal creeks, wandering occasionally to scrub. Its flight is weak. It nests near water in a hole in a tree or bank. 3–4 eggs, white. Call, a noisy whinny and *kee-kee-kee*.

### Kingfisher    *Alcedo atthis*

Kingfisher    D

**World:** *A. atthis atthis* breeds from Mediterranean to Siberia, south to NW Africa, Near East, Iraq, Iran, Arabian Gulf, NW India; sedentary and migratory, reaching Sudan, Arabia, N India.
**Oman:** Fairly common and regular passage migrant and winter visitor, August–May.

16.5cm/6½in. Small, with a brilliant blue-green back, darker blue head, wings and tail, chestnut and white patches on the side of the head, white throat and chestnut under-parts. Bill all-black in *males*, the lower mandible reddish in *females*.

At water in creeks, on sea coast, in wadis, pools, where it is usually solitary and most active at dusk. It calls with a thin distinctive whistle, *chee, see* or *chikee*.

Plate 78

# BEE-EATERS: Meropidae

**World:** 24 species. **Oman:** 3 species (breeding). Brightly coloured insectivorous birds, feeding primarily on bees and wasps caught in the air in circling, gliding flight or by pursuing from a conspicuous perch; the stings are removed. Some will dive or splash into water. The plumage of the sexes is similar and all have a black eye-stripe. The wings are fairly long and pointed. The bill is long, slender, decurved and pointed. The legs and feet are small. The tail is long, often with the central pair of feathers elongate. Mostly gregarious, usually not very shy. Some species are migratory. The nest is an unlined chamber at the end of a long burrow, excavated by the birds, in flat ground or banks, usually in colonies. The 2–6 eggs are white and spherical. The species occurring in Oman belong to the genus *Merops*.

**Blue-cheeked Bee-eater**   *Merops superciliosus*              Blue-cheeked Bee-eater A

**World:** *M.s. persicus* breeds in Transcaspia south to Near East, Iraq, Iran, E Arabia, NW India; migratory to Africa. Other races in Africa, Madagascar.
**Oman:** Very common passage migrant, March–May, August–November, rarely in June; breeds on N Batinah, dispersing from July, numbers varying annually.

30cm/12in. Similar in size to the Bee-eater, but with longer central tail-feathers. Mainly green with a distinctive chestnut throat below the yellow chin, no black gorget, a little pale blue-green and white across the forehead and bordering the black eye-stripe (barely sufficient blue to justify its name), and green wings with the coverts tinged blue.

Open areas, usually with trees, near cultivation. Gregarious, migrating by day and night in parties, usually quite high, sometimes with Bee-eaters, pausing to feed in loose aerial groups, and roosting amongst trees, on cliffs, etc. Less gregarious when nesting, from March/April. 4–6 eggs. Call, similar to that of Bee-eater but deeper and less musical.

**Bee-eater**   *Merops apiaster*                                    Bee-eater C

**World:** Breeds in S and SE Europe, SW Asia, south to NW Africa, Palestine, Iraq, Iran, E Arabia, NW India. Migratory to Africa.
**Oman:** Not very common passage migrant, March–May, August–November, most in N Oman, where small numbers remain to breed on the Batinah with Blue-cheeked Bee-eater; numbers vary annually.

28cm/11in. Its plumage is multicoloured, with distinctive chestnut shading into yellow from the head to mantle; yellow chin and throat with black gorget, bluish breast and belly, copper wing-linings and a dark trailing-edge to the wings conspicuous in flight.

Open areas with sandy banks and trees near cultivation. Its habits are rather similar to those of the Blue-cheeked Bee-eater. The nests, from April, are outnumbered by those of Blue-cheeked. 4–6 eggs. Call, a liquid far-carrying *krook-krook* and *treeb,* usually heard before the birds are seen.

**Little Green Bee-eater**   *Merops orientalis*                     Little Green Bee-eater D

**World:** Breeds from W to NE Africa, Arabia, S Iran, India to SE Asia, in several races. Resident and partial migrant.
**Oman:** Common but local breeding resident with some seasonal movements; *M.o. cyanophrys* (incl. *M.o. muscatensis)* occurs.

*M.o. cyanophrys* 23cm/9in. A small green bee-eater with golden crown and nape, blue supercilium, chin and throat and a narrow black gorget; the flight-feathers and under-wing are copper with a dark trailing-edge, and the central tail-feathers are slightly elongate in fresh plumage; bill blackish. The *immature* is paler, with whitish-green throat and shorter, reddish bill. It differs from the Bee-eater and Blue-cheeked Bee-eater in smaller size, lack of yellow or chestnut on throat, and call. It differs from the **White-throated Bee-eater** *M. albicollis* [30cm/12in, an occasional summer breeding visitor from       White-throated Bee-eater B
Africa to S Arabia and Hadhramaut, not yet confirmed in Oman], in that species' larger size, paler colours, white forehead, supercilium and throat, and black crown, eye-stripe and gorget.

Semi-desert, edges of cultivation, usually with some trees. Usually in pairs or family parties, but in larger groups when roosting or on passage. Some disperse in winter, reaching the mountains. It hawks insects from a perch. It nests from January to August, in the ground, on a bank or in an old building. 3–5 eggs. It calls with a far-carrying *tree-tree-tree*, also *krrrew, krreeuk* and *trititit.*

Plate 79

# ROLLERS: Coraciidae

**World:** 16 species. **Oman:** 3 species (1 breeding). Typical rollers (Coraciinae) are medium-sized and stocky, with large head, short neck and legs, strong, slightly hooked bill and broad wings; some species have long tail-feathers. Plumage is colourful, always with blue; sexes similar. Perch conspicuously, swoop on to large insects, etc., taken on the ground, in the air, occasionally in water. Noisy when breeding and named after their acrobatic tumbling displays.

**Roller**    *Coracias garrulus*    Roller A

**World:** *C.g. semenowi* breeds from Iraq to NW India, north to Transcaspia, Turkestan; migratory to Africa, India.
**Oman:** Regular passage migrant, locally common, end March to May, end July to November, occasionally in winter.

31cm/12in. A distinctive bird, mostly pale greenish-blue with chestnut mantle, purple rump, dark green central tail-feathers, and deep blue and black in the wings visible in flight; the pointed outer tail-feathers are tipped pale and black. The *juvenile* is duller with a brownish throat.

It occurs singly and in scattered groups on passage, and nests commonly by day on trees, etc.

**[Abyssinian Roller**    *Coracias abyssinicus*    Abyssinian Roller B

Breeds from W to E Africa and SW Arabia; partly migratory, once reported at Salalah, but not confirmed. 46cm/18in. Differs from Roller in larger size, brighter colours, brown mantle, rich purple primaries (not black) and black terminal half of the long outer tail-feathers. *Immature* lacks the tail streamers and has a whiter forehead.]

**Indian Roller**    *Coracias benghalensis*    Indian Roller C

**World:** *C.b. benghalensis* breeds in N Oman, S Iraq to N India. Sedentary and migratory·
**Oman:** Widespread breeding resident in N Oman on coast and foothills south to Sur, some seasonal movements; more on passage and in winter, occasionally reaching Masirah between October and February.

31cm/12in. The common roller of northern Oman, appearing squat, heavy and dull brownish whilst perched, but flashing vivid dark and pale blues in wings and tail in flight. It differs from the Roller in vinous colouration from face to breast, duller back, and deeper blue bars in wings and tail.

Trees and cultivation, old buildings, hillsides at low altitude. It perches in exposed positions, depressing the tail frequently, gliding down upon large insects, reptiles, rodents, toads, occasionally fish, or pursuing insects in the air. The nest, from January/February, is on debris in a natural hole in a tree, old building or hillside. The eggs, 3, rarely 4 or 5, are white. Calls, a loud *kak*, like two stones knocked together, a loud *chyak-chyak-chyak* in display, also *shrark*, *tseeek*, a plaintive *kew*, etc.

# WOODPECKERS: Picidae

**World:** 210 species. **Oman:** 1 species. Includes wrynecks (sub-family Jynginae, 2 species) and true stiff-tailed woodpeckers (Picinae). Mostly arboreal. Plumage of sexes almost similar, often crested, spotted, barred or streaked. Wings rounded; tail usually wedge-shaped. Legs short, feet strong, one toe reversible. Head usually large, neck slender. Bill long and straight in Picinae, weaker in the rest; tongue very long and sticky. Feed on insects, sap, fruit. Flight usually undulating. Nest in holes.

**Wryneck**    *Jynx torquilla*    Wryneck D

**World:** Breeds in NW Africa, across Eurasia south to N Turkey, NW Iran(?), NW Himalayas, in several races. Mostly migratory, reaching Africa, Arabia, India.
**Oman:** Regular passage migrant in small numbers, September–November, occasionally over winter until April; *J.t. torquila* occurs.

16.5cm/6½in. Smaller than a bulbul, slim with an unusually mobile neck and slight crest. Nightjar-patterned, grey above, with black and brown streaks and vermiculations; buffish and whitish below, finely mottled and barred black. The tail has conspicuous dark bars.

Trees and bushes, often near cultivation or on the ground nearby, moving in short hops with the tail raised. It feeds on ants, insects, berries taken on trees or ground or in aerial flutters. It clings to trunks like a woodpecker, but perches like a passerine. It is inconspicuous and shy. The flight is slow, a little undulating, suggestive of a large sparrow.

Plate 80

207

# LARKS: Alaudidae

Plates 81–83

**World:** 75 species. **Oman:** 11 species (7 breeding). Terrestrial birds of open country. Plumage mostly drab, streaky and cryptic, some species closely matching local ground colour. Frequently hang wings down to cool. Bill-shape varies from long and pointed of insect-eaters to conical and heavy of some seed-eaters, but most take both foods. Most have a distinctive song and song-flight. All nest on or very near the ground. See pipits (plates 86–87).

**Singing Bush Lark**    *Mirafra cantillans*    Singing Bush Lark A

**World:** *M.c. simplex* breeds in S Arabia, east to Dhofar. Other races in Africa. (Sometimes treated as conspecific with **Eastern Bush Lark** *M. javanica*, India to SE Asia.)
**Oman:** Common local breeding visitor to Dhofar from April, some may over-winter.

13cm/5in. A small, un-crested, broad-winged, sandy-brown lark, with dark streaks, a pale buff supercilium, the wing-feathers fringed rufous and the tail dark with buffish-white outer feathers; it is buffish-white below, the upper breast tinged and streaked brownish (see Lesser Short-toed Lark) and the under-wing rufous. The *immature* has pale buff fringes above, and darker breast-marks.

Grassy ground, from sea-level to hilltops. Conspicuous when singing from the ground or small trees, and occasionally in low, fluttery, hovering, weaving and jerking song-flight with wings held low. The song is remarkable for its intensity, variety and mimicry, e.g. *tew-tew-tew-zitzitzitzit*, sometimes preceded or ended with a quiet *see* or *tew*, e.g. *see-trrptrrptrrp*, *tissip-tissip-zitzitzit sew*. At other times shy and inconspicuous. The nest, from April, is a grassy cup, sometimes partly domed by living stems. 2–4 eggs, pinkish-brown, densely speckled brown.

**Bar-tailed Desert Lark**    *Ammomanes cincturus*    Bar-tailed Desert Lark B

**World:** *A.c. arenicolor* breeds in NW Africa, Near East, Iraq, Arabia. Other races in Cape Verde, Iran, NW India.
**Oman:** In Dhofar interior a breeding resident with local movements; reported occasionally in N Oman in spring, but status uncertain.

13cm/5in. A small un-crested desert lark, pale sandy-buff or pinkish above and whitish below, with a blackish bar at the end of the central tail-feathers, partly obscured by the upper tail-coverts and best seen from behind, when the tail is spread; whitish below. In flight the upper-parts look pale ginger. It differs from Dunn's Lark in smaller size, paler colours, black-tipped primaries and having little black under the tail; from Desert Lark in smaller size, more slender form and paler colouration.

In sandy desert with grass and scrub. In winter in mixed flocks with Dunn's and Desert Larks. The nest, from February, is a small lined hollow protected by a tuft or stone. 2 or 3 eggs, dull white with freckling. The song is a prolonged fluty whistle, from a low perch or song-flight.

**Dunn's Lark**    *Eremalauda dunni*    Dunn's Lark C

**World:** *E.d. eremodites* breeds in SW Arabia east to Riyadh. Another race in N Africa.
**Oman:** In Dhofar interior, a breeding resident with local movements.

14cm/5½in. Very similar to Bar-tailed, but larger, the tail mostly black and appearing black from below, the bill larger and stouter, some brown streaks on the upper parts.

Sandy and gravel desert with some grass and scrub, and very active. The nest is undescribed. The call-note is a rather nasal, oft-repeated *pee-ooo-peep*, the song a rather creaky twittering.

**Black-crowned Finch Lark**    *Eremopterix nigriceps*    Black-crowned Finch Lark

**World:** *E.n. melanauchen* breeds in E Africa, Socotra, Arabia, S Iraq, SE Iran to NW India ('*affinis*').
**Oman:** Breeding 'resident', but nomadic, not uncommon locally; also passage migrant and winter visitor.

13cm/5in. A very small desert lark, showing a black under-wing in flight. The *male* is distinguished by its black-and-white head-pattern and black under-parts. The *female* is sandy-brown above, and pale below except for the under-wing. The *juvenile male* shows traces of the head-pattern.    *male* D
*female* E

On dry sand and gravel with grasses or scrub. It crouches and runs erratically when feeding, and usually occurs in scattered parties. The flight is slowly undulating and erratic, soon pitching again. The nest, from February/April, in sandy areas, is a lined cup, usually with others nearby. 2–3 eggs, whitish with grey-brown speckles. Call, in undulating song-flight, a plaintive far-carrying *trip-treeee*.

208

Plate 81

**Bimaculated Lark** (Eastern Calandra Lark)   *Melanocorypha bimaculata*

**World:** Breeds from Asia Minor, Lebanon, Iraq, Iran, Afghanistan, north to central Asia, in several races. Sedentary and migratory, reaching Sudan, Arabia, NW India.
**Oman:** Uncommon irregular passage migrant and winter visitor, September–February, usually singly, rarely in groups on Masirah.

16.5cm/6½in. A stocky un-crested brown lark with a distinctive small black patch on each side of the breast, a thick bill and a short tail. Differs from the **Calandra Lark** *M. calandra* [19cm/7½in, Mediterranean region to Iran, central Asia, only partly migratory, not to the Arabian peninsula], in smaller size, having less black on the sides of the neck, and a conspicuous white supercilium, white spots at the tips of the tail-feathers (not sides) and lack of white bar on the trailing-edge of the wing.

On dry ground with scrub, etc., edge of cultivation and water. Said to have a warbling chatter.


**Crested Lark**   *Galerida cristata*

**World:** Breeds from W Europe across S Asia, south to Africa, Arabia, N India, in several races. Sedentary and migratory.
**Oman:** Breeding resident, locally common, with some seasonal movement.

17cm/6¾in. A common broad-shouldered lark with a distinctive long erectile crest. Sandy-brown above, some populations darker; the rump is buff, the tail darker brown with buff outer feathers; pale below with dark blotches on the breast, the orange-buff under-wing visible in flight. The *immature* is spotted with bold buff feather-tips on the upper-parts, and has a shorter crest. The bill is robust and slightly curved.

Dry, fairly level sub-desert, often near cultivation, habitation, and roadsides, in pairs or groups and some flocks after breeding. Feeds mainly on invertebrates and vegetable matter, often digging fiercely with the bill. Courting begins in winter. The nest, from February, is a lined cup in the ground, with one edge built into the north side of a bush. Eggs, 3–5, are whitish, finely speckled; it is probably double-brooded. Call, a sad whistling *wee-tee-tso* and *kwee-tee,* occasionally mimics other birds; the song, from a perch or in flight, is a series of warbled phrases.


**Desert Lark**   *Ammomanes deserti*

**World:** Breeds in N Africa, Near East, Arabia, Iraq to NW India, Transcaspia, in several races.
**Oman:** Common and widespread breeding resident.

16cm/6½in. A robust round-headed lark with a pale eye-ring and a robust yellowish bill. The upper-parts are unstreaked, and populations vary in colour from pale sand to dark grey, matching the local ground; the tail has no white, but most have dark markings which might cause confusion with the smaller, paler Bar-tailed Desert Lark (plate 81). The under-parts are pale with a rufous tinge and sometimes with obscure streaking on the breast.

Broken rocks and gravel, especially near wadis, where it comes frequently to water if available; occasionally in or at edge of sandy desert. In loose tame parties, feeding mainly on seeds. In flight rather slow on broad wings. The nest, from January/March, is a grassy cup set in the ground, usually under cover of a boulder or bush. 2–4 eggs, usually 3, pinkish-white with lilac marks. Call, a pleasant soft *wew* or *tew,* varied when with others to a louder *swee-shirrup* or *chewee, chee-wew,* etc.; song, a louder series of these notes, some rather similar to those of Long-billed Pipit (plate 86).


**Hoopoe Lark** (Bifasciated Lark)   *Alaemon alaudipes*

**World:** *A.a. doriae* breeds in Iraq, E Arabia, SE Iran to NW India. Other races across N Africa, Near East, NW Arabia.
**Oman:** Thinly distributed and rather local breeding resident with undefined seasonal movements.

19cm/7½in. A large and distinctive lark, upright and slim, with long legs and long slightly curved bill, reminiscent of a courser (plate 42). When flushed it is immediately made obvious by the black and white bars across the wings (hence its names) and the black tail with white sides. The *immature* is paler grey with indistinct facial pattern and wing-bars.

Open sandy desert plains, *sabkha,* and small dunes with scrub bushes. Not gregarious, nor very shy. It prefers to run, bill up-tilted, but will fly low for short distances. It feeds on seeds, invertebrates and small reptiles, some obtained by fierce probing, by clambering on low scrub and in pursuit flight. Nest, from February, a lined cup of fibres set amongst a looser mass of thicker twigs in the centre of a low scrub bush, rarely on the ground, occasionally overwhelmed by drifting sand. 2–4 eggs, usually 3, white with heavy brown marks. Call, a thin tremulous whistle; in display, flies steeply up, then swoops down, calling *troop-troop-troop-trrreeee,* lands and runs.

Plate 82

**Skylark**   *Alauda arvensis*

**World:** Breeds across Eurasia, south to NW Africa, N Iran, in several races. Northern birds migrate.
**Oman:** Regular passage migrant and winter visitor, locally in N Oman and Masirah, November–February, occasionally until April.

18cm/7in. A fairly robust sandy-brown lark with streaked breast and short crest, white outer tail-feathers, a dull white trailing-edge to the wing and chirruping call. The *juvenile* has pale edges to the feathers of the upper-parts. It differs from the **Woodlark** *Lullula arborea* [15cm/6in, breeds in W Eurasia south to W Iran, vagrant to Bahrain, not yet Oman] in that species' pale supercilium meeting across the nape, shorter tail, more contrasting plumage and *titloo-eet* call.

On coastal plains and foothills, amongst scrub vegetation and cultivation. Gregarious, usually in flocks. Not shy, but it crouches when alarmed. Normal flight is strong and undulating, but it has a more wavering flight when moving short distances. It perches on fences and low vegetation. It feeds on leaves, seeds and invertebrates amongst scrub and cultivation. Call, a rippling *chirrup*.

**[Small Skylark** (Lesser Skylark)   *Alauda gulgula*                              (Not illustrated)
Breeds in southern central Asia, SE Iran, India to SE Asia, in several races, sedentary and migratory; an unconfirmed report of five near Muscat, 6–11 November 1977. 17cm/6½in. Similar to Skylark, but smaller, paler, and more spotted and less streaked above; the tail is shorter with buff (not white) outer feathers. Its habits are broadly similar, the call is less rippling.]

**Short-toed Lark**   *Calandrella brachydactyla*

**World:** Breeds across S Eurasia, south to N Africa, Near East, Iraq, Iran, possibly Arabian Gulf, in several races. Migratory, reaching Africa, Arabia, India, Far East.
**Oman:** Regular and fairly common passage migrant, August–November and February–May, rarely in summer, occasionally over winter.

15cm/6in. A small sparrow-like lark, which requires care to distinguish it from Lesser Short-toed Lark. Sandy-buff above, streaked with dark brown, the crown often flat, the scapulars almost as long as the primaries and covering the folded wing-tip, and the dark centres to the median coverts appearing as a wing-bar; pale buffish-white below, with a black patch at the sides of the neck and upper breast (often concealed until the bird stretches its neck), the breast either plain or lightly streaked. It usually appears paler than the Lesser Short-toed Lark, and differs from the Singing Bush Lark (plate 81) in the lack of rufous on the wing and its stronger flight.

Widespread on sand and gravel with scrub, but rarely on saline areas (favoured by Lesser Short-toed). Usually in flocks, but may be overlooked on the ground. It feeds on seeds, vegetable matter and invertebrates, taken during a walk or run, with an occasional hop, or in a crouched position with tarsus on the ground. The flight is undulating, wheeling flocks showing the birds' pallid under-parts. The song is quite different from that of the Lesser Short-toed Lark, consisting of a simple phrase *tsee-tsik-si-wee-tsi-wichoo* repeated at regular intervals, and occasional single and mimicked notes, uttered in a high, deeply undulating song-flight. Calls, a soft *chirrup* or *chirrirup,* rather like a subdued Skylark.

**Lesser Short-toed Lark**   *Calandrella rufescens*

**World:** Breeds in Canaries, S Spain, N Africa to Near East, across S Asia, south to Iraq, Iran, central Arabia (Riyadh), in several races. Sedentary and migratory, reaching NE Africa, Arabia, India.
**Oman:** Regular passage migrant in small numbers, September–November and February–March, a few over winter; less common than Short-toed Lark.

15cm/6in. Very similar to Short-toed, but generally more strongly marked, darker and greyer, with the head similar to the mantle, and with a stubbier bill. Distinguished by call, having the tertials noticeably shorter than the wing-tip, a broad band of streaking across the breast usually extending to the flanks, and lack of black mark on the sides of the neck.

Prefers open country, particularly flat desert and saline areas, with or without scrub, usually in flocks, sometimes mixed with other larks. Feeds like Short-toed. The call is a diagnostic sharp, fairly loud rippling *prrrit* or *chirrik,* etc. The song is a musical jangle of call-notes, rattling and imitative phrases, uttered in climbing, hovering or circular flight with few undulations. The nest in Arabia is on the ground, a shallow scrape or cup similar to that of Short-toed.

Plate 83

## SWALLOWS and MARTINS: Hirundinidae                    Plates 84–85

**World:** 78 species. **Oman:** 7 species (2 breeding). Small bodied, fast, agile and graceful fliers, with long pointed wings, the tail of some species forked with long outer feathers. The bill is small and flattened with a wide gape; the neck and legs are short, the feet weak but with strong claws for clinging; they perch but stand less often. Mostly gregarious, particularly when not breeding. Some migrate long distances. All are insectivorous, catching small prey in flight; they drink mostly by swooping and pecking from the surface. They nest in natural holes, excavated burrows or in nests of mud collected in the bill, some colonially; see swifts (plate 77).

**Brown-throated Sand Martin** (Plain Sand Martin)    *Riparia paludicola*       Brown-throated
                                                                                                    Sand Martin A
**World:** Breeds in Africa, Madagascar, Afghanistan and nearby USSR to N India and Far East, in several races. Sedentary and migratory.
**Oman:** Vagrant (two seen, Masirah, 9 October 1975; one seen, Batinah, 10 September 1977).

12cm/4½in. Somewhat similar to Sand Martin, which it may accompany; but it is smaller, grey-brown from chin to lower breast with contrasting white lower belly and vent, and lacking the separate breast-band of that species and the white spots in the tail of crag martins.

Habits similar to those of Sand Martin.

**Sand Martin**    *Riparia riparia*                                              Sand Martin B
**World:** Breeds widely across N America and Eurasia south to Egypt, Iraq, Iran, N India, in several races. Mostly migratory, reaching Africa, Arabia, India.
**Oman:** Regular passage migrant, common in late August to October, less common November and March–April, a few to June.

13cm/5in. About the size of the Pale Crag Martin, but it has a grey-brown breast-band across the white under-parts, and is uniform and browner above and on the under-wing; it has no white spots in the slightly forked tail. The *immature* has pale fringes to the brown feathers. See Brown-throated Sand Martin, also Banded Martin (plate 85), which is darker, larger and heavier, with a white supercilium.

Feeds in low flight over water, cultivation, rubbish, etc., often in company with other hirundines. The flight is stronger and less graceful than that of Pale Crag Martin, with more irregular twisting bat-like movements and less gliding.

**Pale Crag Martin** (African Rock Martin)    *Ptyonoprogne fuligula*            Pale Crag Martin C
**World:** *P.f. obsoleta* Pale Crag Martin breeds in N and NE Africa, Near East, Socotra, S and E Arabia, Iraq, Iran, NW India. (Sometimes treated as a separate species, **Pale Crag Martin** *H. obsoleta.*)
**Oman:** Common breeding resident, also a common migrant and winter visitor August–February; occasionally on Masirah in winter.

13cm/5in. Smaller and more slender than Crag Martin. Uniform pale grey-brown above, except for darker flight-feathers and indistinct white spots on the slightly forked tail; the under-wings are very pale grey with contrasting dark linings, and the chin to breast is unspotted white, shading to pale brown on the under tail-coverts.

In very graceful, slow, gliding, soaring flight along cliff faces and tall buildings, usually in pairs, visiting water, cultivation, rubbish, etc.; on passage and over winter more often in groups and loose flocks at low altitudes. The nest, February–July, is a shallow oval cup of mud lined with feathers, etc., attached to the wall or sloping roof of an open cave, sometimes on a beam of a building. 2–3 eggs, whitish speckled purple-grey; it is probably double-brooded. Call, a dry *prrrt* and *kreee*.

**Crag Martin**    *Ptyonoprogne rupestris*                                       Crag Martin D
**World:** Breeds across S Eurasia to Manchuria, south to NW Africa, Jordan, N Iraq, N India. Northern birds migrate, reaching northern Africa, Arabia.
**Oman:** Scarce irregular passage migrant, September–October, March–May.

14cm/5½in. Like a large Pale Crag Martin, but much darker above and below, with less contrast between the mantle and wings, and much darker under-wings and vent. The chin is usually spotted brown, and the tail squarer-tipped, with clearer white sub-terminal spots.

Habits like those of other hirundines on passage, singly or in loose parties, sometimes with other species. Differs from Pale Crag Martin in its quicker heavier flight.

214

Plate 84

**House Martin**    *Delichon urbica*

**World:** *D.u. urbica* breeds in W and central Eurasia, south to NW Africa, Near East, N Iraq, Iran, N India; migratory, reaching S Africa, Arabia, India.
**Oman:** Sporadic passage migrant, in small numbers, February–April, late August to November, very occasionally in other months.

12.5cm/5in. Small and thickset; glossy blue-black except for a distinct white rump and pure white under-parts. The tail is less deeply forked than that of immature Swallow, and the legs are covered in white feathers. The *juvenile* has the dark parts tinged brown, a brown wash from chin to flanks and sometimes an incomplete brown breast-band like the Sand Martin (plate 84). Readily distinguished from Little Swift (plate 77) by the white under-parts.

Might occur anywhere at aerial insect food, and often together with similar species. Though parties of 20–30 sometimes occur it is more often seen in ones and twos. Call, a dry *chirrp* or *chichirrrp*.


**Red-rumped Swallow**    *Hirundo daurica*

**World:** *H.d. rufila* breeds in S Europe, NW Africa, Near East, Asia Minor to S Iran, NW India, north to central Asia; migratory, reaching Africa, Arabia, N India. Other races in Africa, SW Arabia, India, E and SE Asia.
**Oman:** Scarce and irregular passage migrant, February–April and August–September, rarely in May.

18cm/7in. Distinguished from the superficially similar Swallow by the pale rufous rump, face and hind-neck (the rump appearing whitish in some); it also lacks the black gorget and white tail-spots, and is buff or dull white below. It usually appears to be longer in the tail than the Swallow.

Occurs at aerial insect food, usually with similar species. Only reported in ones and twos. When feeding it flies with more graceful soaring and sweeping movements than the Swallow, frequently gliding and occasionally landing.


**Swallow** (Barn Swallow)    *Hirundo rustica*

**World:** *H.r. rustica* breeds in W and central Eurasia, south to NW Africa, Asia Minor, Iraq, Iran, Arabian Gulf, N India; migratory, reaching S Africa, Arabia, India. Other races in Near East, E Asia and N America.
**Oman:** Widespread passage migrant, July–December (peak September/October when very common) and February–May, a few in January: occasionally breeds in the Musandam region (first reported in 1980).

19cm/7½in. A familiar bird with slender build, long forked tail and a distinctive manner of hawking for insects. The *adult* has uniform blue-black upper-parts, white spots in the tail, chestnut throat and forehead, a dark breast-band, and pinkish to white under-parts (sometimes reddish). The *juvenile* is duller above, paler below, and has much shorter tail-streamers, reminiscent of martins. See Red-rumped Swallow.

In open country. Seen particularly over water, cultivation, rubbish-tips, marshes and beaches. Often low down, twisting irregularly in graceful hunting flight, occasionally gliding and snapping insects audibly from the air or from vegetation or the water-surface. Loosely gregarious, gathering at roosts. The nest, from February, is an open saucer of mud pellets reinforced by grass stems, lined with feathers, and fixed to the wall of a sheltered rock or on a ledge. 3–6 eggs, white with reddish-brown speckles. Call, *tswit*, often repeated as a twitter; the song is a more musical warbling twitter.


**[Banded Martin**    *Riparia cincta*

**World:** Breeds in E and S Africa; a local resident and migrant.
**Oman:** One unconfirmed sight record of one near Salalah, 29 May 1978; not previously known in Arabia.

16.5cm/6½in. Larger than the Sand Martin (plate 84), and more heavily built, with the broad brown breast-band usually extending down the centre of the breast, a white supercilium from the nostril, and whiter under wing-coverts. See Brown-throated Sand Martin (plate 84).

Widely distributed in Africa, often over grassy country; not common and not gregarious. Said to be rather sluggish for a martin, picking insects off grass tops and settling on the stems.]

Plate 85

217

# PIPITS and WAGTAILS: Motacillidae

Plates 86–88

**World:** 48 species. **Oman:** 11 species (1 breeding). Small to medium-sized terrestrial birds, usually with a long tail, all with slender bills and long claws. **Pipits** usually brownish and streaked, many confusingly similar. **Wagtails** are distinctly coloured, with comparatively longer tails, wagged more often. All walk and run, and favour open country, often grassy, sometimes wet. Actively hunt invertebrates, pecking off ground and vegetation, running and jumping up to catch them. Calls simple, repetitive. Nest is a lined cup on the ground.

## Tawny Pipit    *Anthus campestris*

Tawny Pipit  A

**World:** Breeds across S and central Eurasia to Mongolia, south to NW Africa, Palestine, N Iran. Migratory, reaching Africa, Arabia, India.

**Oman:** Fairly common passage migrant, occasionally over winter, September–April. *A.c. campestris* and *griseus* occur.

16.5cm/6½in. Tall, slim and the least streaked of the pipits. The *adults* vary from uniform pale sandy-brown to grey above, with a prominent row of black median wing-covert feathers edged with pale buff, and a pale supercilium; they are pale below except for the almost unstreaked buffish breast. The *juvenile* is more streaked above and the breast has bold dark brown streaks like the larger Richard's Pipit. The yellowish legs and pale-edged tail are fairly long.

Dry open ground and cultivation, singly or in small groups. Call, a loud *tzeep* or *chee-up*.

## Richard's Pipit    *Anthus novaeseelandiae*

Richard's Pipit  B

**World:** Breeds in E Asia, India, to Australasia, also Africa, in several races. Migratory, reaching India, SE Asia.

**Oman:** Vagrant or very uncommon passage migrant, late September to December, perhaps in spring.

18cm/7in. A large, long-legged and boldly marked pipit. Tawny-brown above, streaked darker, with a pale supercilium, and white outer tail-feathers; the breast is buff and heavily spotted, the belly pale; the legs are pale or brownish. The *juvenile* appears greyer with wide pale feather-fringes. It differs from the Tawny Pipit in having a conspicuous dark moustachial-streak and a more spotted breast and in being darker above.

Grass, scrub and cultivation; usually singly and very shy. It stands erect like Tawny and Long-billed Pipits. Flight-call is a loud harsh *rrreep*.

## Long-billed Pipit    *Anthus similis*

Long-billed Pipit  C

**World:** *A.s. arabicus* breeds in S and E Arabia; sedentary and at least partially migratory. Other races in Africa, Socotra, Near East, Iran, N India, Burma.

**Oman:** Widespread but local breeding resident, not on Masirah, with undefined winter movements.

20cm/8in. A large upright pale sandy-brown pipit, faintly mottled darker above with a broad pale supercilium; the throat is whitish, the breast faintly spotted, the belly buff. The long dark brown tail has pale buff outer feathers. Legs long and flesh-coloured. Differs from the rather similar Tawny Pipit in larger size, longer bill, lack of white in the tail, habits and song.

Breeds in the mountains and foothills amongst broken rock on steep hillsides with some trees and scrub, but also in the grass zone of Dhofar. In winter some occur briefly on low ground and islands. Usually seen singly, occasionally in parties in winter. Nest from February/March. 2–5 eggs, usually 3, greyish, heavily speckled brown. The song is distinctive, usually from a tree or rock, also in direct or gliding flight on broad wings, a long series of loud, deliberate 1-to-3-syllable notes, *e.g. tewchip tschirp tswee tsup tree tushree shree.*

218

Plate 86

**Tree Pipit**    *Anthus trivialis*

**World:** Breeds from Europe to central Siberia, south to N Iran, N India, in two races. Migratory, reaching Africa, Arabia, India.
**Oman:** Regular and fairly common passage migrant, August–November, February–April, occasionally to May; a few over winter.

15cm/6in. Closely similar to the less common Meadow Pipit. Brown above with darker streaks; pale below with a buffish-yellow breast lightly streaked brown; the tail is shorter than the larger Tawny and Long-billed Pipits (plate 86) and has white outer feathers visible in flight. The legs are brownish-flesh, pinker than those of the Meadow Pipit, from which it also differs in its stockier build, short hind-claw, habits and call. It differs from winter Red-throated Pipit in unstreaked rump and less bold streaks on upper-parts, breast and flanks.

Vegetation, often moist, but usually near trees, to which it flies if disturbed. Singly or in loose parties of up to 20, rather shy. The flight is jerky, rising and falling but not regularly undulating like Tawny Pipit (plate 86). Call, a rough *teez* or *pizzt,* alarm note *sip.*

**Meadow Pipit**    *Anthus pratensis*

**World:** Breeds from Greenland across W Eurasia to W Siberia in two races. Migratory, reaching N Africa, Near East, Arabia, Iraq, Iran, NW India.
**Oman:** Scarce passage migrant and winter visitor October–February.

14.5cm/5¾in. Closely resembles the more common Tree Pipit (see above), but has a whiter, less yellowish breast with smaller, more numerous streaks; the legs are more brownish and the rump is very faintly streaked. Differs from the Red-throated Pipit in the lack of orange-buff on the throat, and less conspicuous streaking, particularly on the upper-parts; and from Red-throated and Tree Pipits in its call.

In open country, and less dependent upon trees than Tree Pipit, but it will perch in them when present. Singly or in small loose parties. It flies like the Tree Pipit, but is more active on the ground. Call, a loud thin *tissip* or *psip*, similar to that of Water Pipit but less rasping and often uttered in threes; also an alarm note, *seep.*

**Water Pipit**    *Anthus spinoletta*

**World:** *A.s. coutellii* breeds in Caucasus, south to N Iran, and E Turkestan to Mongolia; migratory, reaching Near East, Arabia, N India, Far East. Other races (incl. **Rock Pipit)** N America, Europe, Far East.
**Oman:** Uncommon passage migrant and winter visitor, November–March.

16.5cm/6½in. The only black-legged pipit in Oman. *Adult (autumn)* is dark brown above, with faint darker streaks, a whitish supercilium and white outer tail-feathers; whitish below, the breast and flanks spotted and streaked with brown. In *spring* the breast is uniform pinkish. Differs in *winter* from Meadow Pipit (plate 87) in larger size, browner upper-parts, dark legs and call; in *spring* from Tawny Pipit in smaller size, darker upper-parts, etc.

Marshes, irrigated cultivation, wadi beds, pools. In small numbers, but occasionally in roosts of up to 50 birds. Perches freely on bushes, and roosts in reeds and rushes near water. Call, a fairly distinctive thin *tseep-eep* and a shorter *tsip.*

**Red-throated Pipit**    *Anthus cervinus*

**World:** Breeds in a narrow band across N Eurasia. Migratory, reaching northern Africa, Arabia, India, SE Asia.
**Oman:** Common passage migrant, some over winter, October–April, occasionally from September to May.

14.5cm/5¾in. In *autumn* and *winter* rather like Tree Pipit, but darker above and more boldly marked, the upper-parts including the rump heavily streaked black, and the breast and flanks heavily spotted and streaked black. From January/February the throat and supercilium become orange-buff or reddish, this colour sometimes extending to the breast. The legs are yellowish to brownish.

Open country with vegetation, irrigated cultivation, margins of water, often in small parties, occasionally in larger roosts of over 20. It feeds on a wide variety of invertebrates including small snails, also on seeds. Its gait and flight are like those of Tree Pipit. Call, a high squeaky *teee*, less rasping than that of Tree Pipit.

Tree Pipit    A

Meadow Pipit    B

Water Pipit    C

Red-throated Pipit

*winter*    E

*summer*    D

220

Plate 87

## Yellow Wagtail  *Motacilla flava*

**World:** Breeds across Eurasia, W Alaska, south to NW Africa, Near East, Iran, in many races. Mostly migratory.
**Oman:** Fairly common passage migrant mid-August to November, February–May, rarely June; some over winter.

16.5cm/6½in. The *males (breeding)* have olive-green back and rump (never grey as in Citrine Wagtail), yellow under-parts and white outer tail-feathers, but heads vary according to race: **Yellow Wagtail** *M.f. lutea*, most of head yellow to olive, no distinct supercilium (see Citrine); **Blue-headed** *M.f. flava*, crown, nape and ear-coverts blue-grey, white supercilium from base of bill, chin white, throat yellow; **Syke's** *M.f. beema* (not illustrated) similar to *flava* but much paler grey; **Black-headed** *M.f. feldegg*, whole head black except for a yellow chin; **Grey-headed** *M.f. thunbergi* (not illustrated), crown and nape grey, ear-coverts black, no supercilium, chin white or yellow. *Females* and *winter males* are browner above, paler below with less yellow (see Grey Wagtail). *Juveniles* have pale buff chin and throat and a dark bib (see White Wagtail).

Amongst vegetation, particularly if moist, associating with cattle, etc., and at rubbish. It walks and runs briskly after insects, moving the head back and forth, the tail constantly wagged up and down. Quite tame and very gregarious, particularly at roosts, to which they move before dusk in strongly undulating flight. The call is a harsh *tissweep*.

## Citrine Wagtail (Yellow-headed Wagtail)  *Motacilla citreola*

**World:** Breeds in central Asia, south to E Iran, NW India, in several races. Migratory, reaching E Arabia, India, SE Asia.
**Oman:** Uncommon passage migrant and winter visitor, September–April.

16.5cm/6½in. Usually seen in winter plumage when confusion with Yellow Wagtail is sometimes possible. *Male (summer)* has rich lemon-yellow head, neck and under-parts, diagnostic black collar, grey or black back, grey rump, and black tail with white sides. The *female* and *winter male* have greyish upper-parts, dull yellow supercilium and forehead, broad white edges to innermost secondaries and tips of coverts forming a conspicuous double wing-bar, yellow face and breast, breast tinted grey at the sides and rest of under-parts whitish, sometimes tinged with yellow. The *juvenile* is pale grey above with the conspicuous white wing-bars, and whitish below.

Marshy or moist vegetation, occasionally running streams (see Grey Wagtail). It can wade deeply and it perches readily. The call is a hard *tzeet* or *chizzit*, rather similar to that of the Yellow Wagtail.

## White Wagtail  *Motacilla alba*

**World:** Breeds from S Greenland across Eurasia, south to NW Africa, Lebanon, Iran, Himalayas, in several races. Migratory.
**Oman:** Fairly common passage migrant, fewer but varied numbers over winter; September–April, rarely May.

18cm/7in. The distinctive grey, black and white wagtail of winter. The *adult (summer)* has a white mask, framed by black on the crown, nape, chin, throat and breast, joined on the ear-coverts in some races; the mantle and rump are grey, the wings blackish-brown with white edges to the coverts, and the long tail black with white outer feathers; the belly is white. In *winter* the throat becomes white and the black of the breast is reduced to a crescent. The *juvenile* is browner above, the white parts tinged yellow in some, with a black bib.

Wander near habitation, water, farms, rubbish, etc., more widespread than other wagtails, otherwise with generally similar habits and undulating flight. The call is a rather harsh, shrill *chisseek*.

## Grey Wagtail  *Motacilla cinerea*

**World:** *M.c. cinerea* breeds in Europe and central Asia, south to NW Africa, Iran, N India; migratory, reaching Africa, Arabia, India.
**Oman:** Widespread passage migrant and winter visitor in small numbers, late August to March, occasionally to May.

18cm/7in. A very slender dainty wagtail, distinguished from the more bulky Yellow Wagtail by its blue-grey upper-parts, proportionately longer tail and darker wings; the rump is greenish-yellow (grey in Citrine). The sexes are generally alike; in *winter* the black of the throat is replaced by buff, and the under-parts are paler except for the yellow under tail-coverts. The *juvenile* is rather similar to *winter adults,* but is more brownish-grey above, with dark marks on the side of the buff throat; differs from young White Wagtail in yellow under tail-coverts and long tail.

It winters at water in mountain wadis, occasionally on the plains. Usually found singly, but it roosts with others if present. The long tail is wagged conspicuously. Call, a short *zitzi* or *chip*.

222

Yellow Wagtail

*M.f. lutea*
*male summer*  E
Blue-headed Wagtail
*male summer*  D
Black-headed Wagtail
*male summer*  C
Blue-headed Wagtail
*male winter*  A
*juvenile*  B

Citrine Wagtail

*male summer*  G
*female summer*  F

White Wagtail

*M.a personata*
*male summer*  J

*male winter*  H

Grey Wagtail

*male summer*  L

*male winter*  K

Plate 88

# BULBULS: Pycnonotidae

**World:** 120 species. **Oman:** 1 species (breeding). Dull-coloured birds, with loose soft plumage, often with brightly coloured under tail-coverts, and with marks on the head. Plumage of sexes is similar, immatures duller and paler. Bill short, small and notched, with rictal bristles. Wings short and rounded. Tail comparatively long. They occur in or near trees and bushes, often in small parties, and roost communally when not breeding. The food is mainly fruit, also seeds, insects and nectar.

**Yellow-vented Bulbul** (Black-capped Bulbul)  *Pycnonotus xanthopygos*      Yellow-vented Bulbul B

**World:** Breeds in Asia Minor, Syria, south to Sinai and Arabia. (Sometimes treated as a race of **Common Bulbul** *P. barbatus* of Africa.)
**Oman:** Common and widespread resident, not on Masirah.

10cm/7½in. One of the characteristic birds of trees in Oman. In flight the black head and dark tail contrast with the paler brown of the body and wings. The head, slight 'crest' and throat are black, the tail dark brown, the nape, back and wings brown; the under-parts are paler, and the ventral region and under tail-coverts are bright lemon-yellow. The *juvenile* is paler, and has a browner head. The wattle of bare skin round the orbit is whitish.

Amongst trees and bushes in open semi-desert, hillsides and wadis, and in gardens and other cultivation. A sociable bird, gregarious, inquisitive, noisy and cheery. It is tame near habitation, but shy elsewhere. It feeds on fruit, some leaves, seeds and occasionally nectar; also on insects, the latter often taken aerially, particularly at dusk, by a bee-eater-like swoop upwards from a tree perch or by pecking from the foliage, sometimes in a short hover. The nest, from February, is a neat cup of plant stems, lined with hair, wool, etc., in a tree or bush. The eggs, 3–5, are glossy pink, heavily spotted with brown and purple. The calls are staccato, fluty and varied, usually in phrases of two or three notes, and include a slow *krik krik* or *prip prup*, more rapid *tchink-tchink-tchink, kutchi-kutchi-kutchi, tiwink-tiwinktiwink* and a bubbling courtship-call.

[**White-cheeked Bulbul**  *Pycnonotus leucogenys*      White-cheeked Bulbul A

**World:** Breeds in S Iraq, S Iran, Bahrain and the mainland nearby, NW India. (Includes **White-eared Bulbul**, often treated as a distinct species *P. leucotis*.)
**Oman:** Has been reported very rarely, presumably as an escaped captive bird.

20cm/8in. Differs from Yellow-vented Bulbul in the conspicuous white cheek, white tips to tail-feathers below, paler under-parts and more musical calls.]

# WAXWINGS: Bombycillidae

**World:** 9 species. **Oman:** 1 species. Closely related birds in sub-families of which only one occurs in Arabia, Hypocoliinae, with the single species Hypocolius. [**Waxwing** *Bombycilla garrulus*, Bombycillinae, 18cm/7in, breeds across N Eurasia and has reached S Iran and NW India as a vagrant in winter. The family is noted for irregular breeding distributions and periodic irruptions.]

**Hypocolius**  *Hypocolius ampelinus*      Hypocolius

**World:** Breeds in SW Arabia(?), Iraq, S Iran. Migratory, but movements poorly understood; has occurred in UAE in spring.
**Oman:** Vagrant or scarce passage migrant (reported singly near Fasad, Dhofar, 25 March 1972; on Masirah, 7 November 1979; Wadi Andur, Dhofar, 20 November 1979).

23cm/9in. It resembles a long-tailed waxwing, shrike or bulbul at first glance. The *male* is mostly pale      *male* C
greyish with a buff forehead, but it has a black line from the bill to the black ear-coverts and half-collar, a contrasting wing-pattern of black primaries with white tips and a black trailing-edge to the under-wing, and a long grey tail with a broad black terminal band. The bill is dark, the legs yellowish. The *female* is duller, lacks the black on the head and has less black and white in the wings. The *juvenile* is pale sandy-brown and lacks other marks except a dark tip to the tail.

It prefers thick bushes and trees, where it feeds on berries, other fruits and invertebrates, usually in parties, and with furtive movements reminiscent of a babbler. On passage it is not easily found, tending to stay deep in cover and to 'freeze' if alarmed. The flight is direct, not undulating. Often silent on passage, otherwise noisy with various sonorous whistling notes *wheew, whee-di-du, di-di-du*, etc. (King).

Plate 89

## THRUSHES: Turdidae     Sub-family Turdinae            Plates 90–98

**World:** 310 species. **Oman:** 27 species (4 breeding). A large assemblage of closely related robins, redstarts, chats, wheatears and thrushes.

### Thrush Nightingale (Sprosser)     *Luscinia luscinia*          Thrush Nightingale A

**World:** Breeds from E Europe to central Asia. Migratory, reaching SE Africa, Arabia.
**Oman:** Scarcely seen passage migrant, reported in August and mid-May.

16.5cm/6½in. Very similar to Nightingale, but differs in darker, more olivaceous-brown upper-parts, darker and duller rufous-brown tail, paler chin and throat, and dull breast mottled with brown crescentic marks.

Very similar to Nightingale in habits. Song (heard on passage in May) is varied and louder than that of Nightingale, and includes a whistling *seetoo-seetoo-seetoo* and some mimicry.

### Nightingale     *Luscinia megarhynchos*          Nightingale B

**World:** *L.m. hafizi* and *L.m. africana* breed in Turkey, Syria, N and W Iran, NW Afghanistan, north to central Asia; migratory to Africa. A darker race in Europe.
**Oman:** Passage migrant, May and late August to October, scarce except in Dhofar in autumn.

16.5cm/6½in. Slightly smaller than a bulbul, and little noticed unless in song. It is uniform brown to pale grey-brown above with conspicuous rufous rump and tail; breast pale grey-brown, whiter on throat and belly.

Undergrowth, bushes, low trees, preferably moist. It tends to keep low in cover, often standing still and upright, the wings drooped, the tail occasionally strongly depressed and raised (not as high as with Rufous Bush Robin) or vigorously fanned and swung. Feeds on or near the ground on invertebrates and fruits. Song, heard in autumn, a rich variety of liquid bubbling and whistling notes, also distinct phrases *pee CHOOK, pree TUK TUK* and deep hard calls *krrk, tuc-tuc;* alarm note *swerz.*

### Rufous Bush Robin (Rufous Bush Chat)     *Cercotrichas galactotes*       Rufous Bush Robin D

**World:** *C.g. syriacus* and *C.g. familiaris* breed from the Balkans to NW India, north to central Asia, south to Gulf coast of Arabia; migratory, reaching Arabia, Africa.
**Oman:** Fairly common passage migrant, March–May (rarely February, June), August–October (rarely November); most autumn passage passes over N Oman.

15cm/6in. A slim grey-brown bush robin with a conspicuously long graduated rufous tail with black-and-white tips, a distinct pale supercilium, rufous rump, short pointed wings and whitish under-parts. Differs from other red-tailed species in its tail-tips, behaviour and call. [**Black Bush Robin** C. *podobe* 21cm/8½in, breeds eastwards to Hadhramaut and Riyadh, not yet recorded in Oman.]

Bushes, especially *Acacia* when on passage, perching low down, dropping to feed on invertebrates on the ground, occasionally in bushes and in the air. It frequently jerks the tail high over the back, occasionally fanning it and flicking the short drooping wings. Nest (not yet found in Oman) is from May, a small cup in a bed of plant material 1–2m up on a palm trunk or bush. 2–5 eggs, whitish flecked with brownish. Song, from an exposed perch, a sweet, thin, whistling warble; call on passage, a thin repeated *sseep* or *tseek,* also a short *zip* and *zerk.*

## ACCENTORS: Prunellidae

**World:** 12 species. **Oman:** 1 species. Dull plumaged, sparrow-sized and unobtrusive. Hop and creep on the ground and in low vegetation. Bill fine and slender. Sexes similar.

### Radde's Accentor     *Prunella ocularis*          Radde's Accentor C

**World:** Breeds in alpine SE Transcaucasia, NE Turkey, Iran, dispersing to lower altitudes in winter.
**Oman:** Vagrant (one confirmed record, on Masirah, 2–22 November 1976).

15cm/6in. Small and secretive. The head is blackish, sometimes slightly spotted paler, with a distinct buffish supercilium; the mantle is grey-brown with black streaks, the rump greyish, the tail brown with grey-buff outer edges and a slight notch; the under-parts are pale, except for a buff wash across the breast and brown streaks on the flanks.

It skulks in bushes and amongst rocks. Call, a 2- or 3-syllable trill.

Plate 90

**Bluethroat**   *Luscinia svecica*

**World:** Breeds across N Eurasia to W Alaska, south to Caucasus, N India, in several races. Migratory, reaching Africa, Arabia, India, SE Asia.
**Oman:** Regular passage migrant and winter visitor locally in small numbers, September–March.

15cm/6in. A small skulking chat, brown or grey-brown above, with a pale supercilium and bright chestnut patches at the base of the outer tail-feathers. The *male (in spring)* has a blue bib with or without a red or white spot and bordered below by varied bands of black, white and chestnut; from *autumn* the bib is pale. The *female* and *juvenile* resemble *winter males*, but may lack the blue and chestnut on the throat.

Fresh-water marshes, wadi reed-beds, damp cultivation. Shy and skulking, occasionally coming into view on stems, and on the ground where it bobs, hops and runs during searches for insects, snails, etc. It perches upright, wags and fans the tail, and occasionally gives a very sweet song in winter quarters from the top of a bush. Call, a harsh *turrk* or *tak*.

**Whinchat**   *Saxicola rubetra*

**World:** Breeds from W Europe to central Asia, south to NW Iran. Migratory to Africa.
**Oman:** Uncommon passage migrant, September–October, February–April.

13cm/5in. A small short-tailed bird, perching on bush tops like the Stonechat, from which *adult males* are easily distinguished, but with which *females* and *young* may be confused. *Adult male (summer)* is streaked brown above, with a dark cheek-patch bordered by a prominent white supercilium and a white moustachial-streak, a white patch on each side of the base of the tail, a broad white patch at the base of the wing and a small patch on the coverts; the chin to breast and flanks are rufous-buff, the belly white. *Male (winter)* is duller, *female* and *young* similar but less distinctly marked, though usually with a buff supercilium and always with white tail-patches; the young lack the white wing-patches.

Perches prominently on bushes, fences, etc., often still and silent. Unsociable. Bobs, flicks wings and tail and drops on to insects, etc., on the ground. Call, a short *tu-tek-tek*.

**Stonechat**   *Saxicola torquata*

**World:** Breeds across Eurasia, south to Iran, also in SW Arabia and Africa, in many races, some migratory.
**Oman:** Uncommon passage migrant, occasionally in winter, September–April.

13cm/5in. The *adult male (summer)* differs from the Whinchat in black head and throat, white neck-patch and white rump/base of tail (without white side-patches); the back is darker and the under-parts reddish (not buff); in *winter* it is duller, browner above. *Female (summer)* has a dusky throat, otherwise *female* and *young* are sometimes confused with the Whinchat, but they lack the pale supercilium and white tail-patches of the Whinchat and are usually more reddish below. There are racial variations; some birds in Oman have either more or less white or pink at the base of the tail.

It perches like the Whinchat, singly or in pairs. Restless, the wings and tail occasionally flicked open and the tail jerked up and down. The call, *wheet tzak-tzak*, is like two stones struck together.

**[Robin**   *Erithacus rubecula*

Breeds from W Europe to central Asia, south to NW Iran; a rare visitor in some winters to the lower Arabian Gulf, not yet recorded in Oman. 14cm/5½in.]

**White-throated Robin** (Persian Robin)   *Irania gutturalis*

**World:** Breeds in Turkey, Armenia to Turkestan, south to Palestine, Iran, Afghanistan. Migratory, crossing the Arabian Gulf, reaching E Africa.
**Oman:** Scarce passage migrant (two off Musandam, 30 April 1971).

16.5cm/6½in. The *adult male* is grey above, except for browner wings, rounded black tail, black sides of the head and neck and a faint supercilium; a white triangular throat-patch (when seen from the front) contrasts with chestnut breast and under-wings, and the belly and under tail-coverts are white. *Adult female* is brownish above, the breast greyish, the flanks and under-wing pale chestnut. The *immature male* has a black line under the white throat.

Usually keeps well under cover of thick bushes and low trees, searching the ground for invertebrates. It wags the tail slowly if alarmed.

Bluethroat

red-spotted race
male summer A
male winter B
white-spotted race
male summer C
female D

Whinchat

male E

female F

Stonechat

male G

female H

Robin J

White-throated Robin

male K

female L

Plate 91

**Blackstart**    *Cercomela melanura*

**World:** *C.m. erlangeri* breeds from SW Arabia to Aden, Hadhramaut and S Oman; sedentary. Other races in Africa, Near East, Arabia.
**Oman:** Common breeding resident in the Dhofar mountains.

15cm/6in. An upright grey bird with a black tail. The sexes are similar. The flight-feathers and ear-coverts are dark brown, and there is a black line from bill to eye and a slight white eye-ring; the chin is white in some birds, the breast and belly are pale grey to buffish and the wing-linings and under tail-coverts are white. The *juvenile* is browner.

Hills and valleys with trees and rocks. It perches on rocks and in and on trees. It feeds on berries and invertebrates, taking the latter by searching vegetation, occasionally hawking or hovering briefly, but usually by dropping on to prey on the ground. The tail is occasionally cocked and depressed, or flirted with a slight flick of the wings. The nest, from April, is a lined cup of grasses in a crevice or under a boulder. 3–4 eggs, white to pale blue, with reddish speckles. Song (one of the first in the spring dawn chorus), often from a treetop, a series of loud, well-spaced notes *chree chrew chitchoo chirrichiwi*, etc.; also a sweet warble and scolding noises.


**Redstart**    *Phoenicurus phoenicurus*

**World:** *P.p. phoenicurus* breeds from W Europe to central Asia; *P.p. samamisicus* breeds in Crimea across to Transcaucasia, south to Palestine, Iraq, Iran; both are migratory, reaching Arabia, Africa.
**Oman:** Scarce but regular passage migrant, March–April (occasionally February–May), October–November; spring passage follows main departure of Black Redstart.

14cm/5½in. The *adult male* differs from the more common Black Redstart (some of which are very similar) in its paler grey crown and back, white forehead and supercilium, black terminating on the lower throat, white belly and brighter orange-red tail; in *winter* it is browner above, fringes partly covering white of head and black of throat. The *female* is rather similar to female Black Redstart but paler brown, particularly below. In the *male samamisicus* there is a whitish wing-panel (fringes to the flight-feathers), but some birds are intermediates with only a trace of white.

Its habits are like those of the Black Redstart, but it is more arboreal and usually more shy and active.


**Black Redstart**    *Phoenicurus ochruros*

**World:** *P.o. phoenicuroides* breeds from Transcaspia to central Asia, south to Iran, N India; migratory: reaching Africa, Arabia, India. Other races across S Eurasia.
**Oman:** Widespread winter visitor October–March, usually fairly common but few in some years.

14cm/5½in. A familiar winter bird, but care is required to distinguish it from the Redstart (see dates of occurrence). The *adult male* is dark grey above, with a black forehead (occasionally tinged with white) and chestnut rump and tail, the brown central feathers giving the tail a darker appearance than in the Redstart; it is black from forehead to upper breast (fringed with greyish in *autumn*) and the rest of the under-parts and under-wing are chestnut. The *female* and *immature* are brown above with a pale eye-ring and tail like the *adult male;* the under-parts are reddish-brown, the under-wing tinged chestnut.

In winter quarters usually in the low open branches of trees such as *Acacia*, but will also perch on buildings, rocks, etc. It is solitary, and in winter males are more common than females. It shivers the tail and makes light, dancing flights round the tree, hovering briefly to take insects, more often pouncing upon them on the ground, then returning quickly to a perch. It roosts in holes. Call, *tuk* and *tuk-tuk*.


**Eversmann's Redstart** (Rufous-backed Redstart)    *Phoenicurus erythronotus*

**World:** Breeds in central Asia. Migratory to S Iran, N India, occasionally to Arabian Gulf States, etc.
**Oman:** Winter vagrant (one seen, Jabal Akhdar, 22 February 1977; one, Masirah, 19–24 November 1979).

16cm/6¼in. A large, brightly patterned redstart. The *adult male* has blue-grey forehead, crown and nape, black from ear-coverts down the sides of the neck, brick-red or brown mantle, black and brown wings with large white patches, orange-chestnut rump and tail with darker central and outer tail-feathers; the belly is white or pale grey and the rest of the under-parts chestnut. In *winter* there are brown fringes on the grey above, and whitish fringes on the chestnut below. The *female* is similar to the female Redstart, but shows white on the closed wing and has a more orange back.

Usually amongst trees. It has the behaviour of other redstarts, but deliberately jerks the tail upwards and does not vibrate it. The calls include a distinct growling rattle, *dr-r-r-r.*

Plate 92

A confusing group of small thrush-like birds of open country, mostly with conspicuous white rumps (except Red-tailed), and white sides to at least the base of the tail (except Desert and Red-tailed). They usually feed on invertebrates on the ground in brief sallies from an exposed perch on a rock or low shrub, where they are easily seen. Rather solitary, aggressive and intolerant of others; most species have a hard chacking call (hence 'chats'). Several may occur suddenly in an area as a 'fall' of migrants.

### Wheatear (Northern Wheatear)    *Oenanthe oenanthe*

Wheatear

**World:** *O. o. oenanthe* breeds across Eurasia, south to Mediterranean, Near East, Iran, N India; migratory to Africa.
**Oman:** Passage migrant in very small numbers, March–April (rarely May) and mid-August to November.

15cm/6in. The *male (in spring)* has a distinctive combination of grey crown, nape and mantle, black mask and wings, and white or pinkish under-parts. The *female* and *autumn male* closely resemble the Isabelline Wheatear, but are smaller and dumpier, with a less upright stance, blackish under-wings, a narrower black terminal tail-band and usually a more conspicuous eye-stripe. See Black-eared Wheatear (below) and Pied Wheatear (plate 95).

*male spring* B
*male winter* C
*male 1st winter* A

In open semi-desert or coastal scrub. It perches on rocks, fences and bushes more frequently than the Isabelline, and on the ground tends to hop rather than run.

### Black-eared Wheatear    *Oenanthe hispanica*

Black-eared Wheatear

**World:** *O. h. melanoleuca* breeds in SE Europe, Turkey, Transcaucasia, south to Palestine, Iran; migratory to Africa. Another race in S Europe, NW Africa.
**Oman:** Scarce passage migrant in September and October.

14.5cm/5¾in. The *male (in spring)* is strikingly creamy-white with black cheeks, chin and throat, black wings and black inverted T on the tail; an uncommon white-throated form is known. *Autumn males* have brown tips to the body-feathers, obscuring the pattern. The *female* is similar to the female Wheatear, but is smaller and slighter, with darker cheeks and wings and more white in the tail. See Pied Wheatear (plate 95).

*male* D

*female* E

Habitat is as Wheatear. It usually feeds in short shrike-like pounces from a bush or tree.

### Isabelline Wheatear    *Oenanthe isabellina*

Isabelline Wheatear  F

**World:** Breeds in SW and central Asia, south to Turkey, Palestine, Iraq, Iran, NW India. Migratory, reaching Africa, Arabia, NW India.
**Oman:** Passage migrant; a few from mid-July and August, in small numbers (perhaps fairly common in Dhofar) in September and October, locally over winter and in return passage March–April, occasionally to May.

16.5cm/6½in. A large drab wheatear of open country. Sexes are similar; pale uniform sandy-buff with a dark streak from bill to eye, pale ear-coverts, pale under-wings and a broad dark terminal tail-band giving a less well defined inverted T pattern than in Wheatear, and with longer bill and legs than that species.

Widespread, especially among desert scrub. Its stance is more upright than that of the Wheatear. It rarely perches, except on low scrub bushes, preferring to run to take its prey.

### Desert Wheatear    *Oenanthe deserti*

Desert Wheatear

**World:** Breeds in N Africa, Near East, NW Arabia, southern central Asia, Iran, NW India, in several races. Migratory, reaching NE Africa, Arabia, NW India.
**Oman:** Common passage migrant and fairly common winter visitor, August–April, occasionally to May. *O. d. atrogularis* or *oreophila* occur.

15cm/6in. Distinguished in all plumages by the almost completely black tail, with no white visible at the sides. The *male (in spring)* is creamy-buff or brown above, with black face, chin, throat and wings, white rump and a varied amount of white on the wing-coverts visible in flight and often showing as a line above the black on the folded wing. The *females* and *autumn males* are duller, with the black of the face, chin and throat obscured or absent, and the white of the rump variably tinged orange-buff. See black-throated phase of Black-eared Wheatear (above).

*male* H

*female* G

In open country with scattered scrub and other bushes, on which it perches. It drops on to prey like a shrike, returning quickly to a perch.

Plate 93

## Hume's Wheatear    *Oenanthe alboniger*

**World:** Breeds from NW India to Iran, south to Oman. Sedentary.
**Oman:** A fairly common breeding resident in N Oman.

16.5cm/6½in. The familiar black-and-white wheatear of the northern mountains. The sexes are alike. The *adults* are glossy black on the head, mantle, wings, under-wing and from chin to throat, and pure white on the lower back, base of the tail and rest of the under-parts. The *juvenile* is similar but dull blackish-brown instead of black, and with less black on the throat. It differs from the male **Eastern Pied Wheatear** *O. picata* [15.5cm/6in, breeds in Transcaspia, Iran to NW India, wintering southwards and could reach Arabia] in that species' slightly smaller size and slighter build, and with black reaching the upper breast and less white on the back; the female **Eastern Pied Wheatear** has the same pattern but with dark brown instead of black.

Mountains, foothills and rocky slopes down to sea-level. Not very shy, and often visiting habitation. It perches on rock ledges, trees, fences, etc., and flies up cliff-faces with a combination of fluttering and soaring upwards in the up-draught. In display it raises the white feathers of the back. The nest, from February, is a saucer or cup of plant stems, mud, etc., placed in a crevice in rock or deserted buildings. 3–4 eggs, rarely 5, pale blue, sometimes speckled red; double-brooded. Song, a varied, far-carrying *chiroochiri-chirrichiri*; calls include *triki-treek*, *trooti-trooti-tree*, etc.', also harsh chacks.

## White-crowned Black Wheatear    *Oenanthe leucopyga*

**World:** *O. l. ernesti* breeds in Near East and Arabia; mostly sedentary. Another race from Morocco to Sudan.
**Oman:** Status uncertain (three single birds reported in Fasad-Shisur area, May, June and October 1971).

17cm/6½in. A mostly black wheatear, with the white of the outer tail-feathers extending to the tip of the tail. The *adult* has a white crown, resembling the Hooded Wheatear. The *immature* has a completely black head, resembling that of Hume's, but can be distinguished by the black breast and belly.

A bird of the most desolate country, in desert or wadis, but has become attached to villages in part of its world range.

## Hooded Wheatear    *Oenanthe monacha*

**World:** Breeds very locally from NE Africa, Near East, Arabia, Iran to NW India. Partly migratory or wandering.
**Oman:** Breeding resident in Dhofar; has been reported in N Oman and Masirah between August and March, status uncertain.

17cm/6½in. The *male* differs from all other wheatears except the White-crowned Black in having outer tail-feathers which are mostly white with indistinct dark tips. It differs from the Mourning Wheatear (plate 95) in its larger size, its longer bill, the fact that the black of the throat extends to the breast, its white (not rusty) under tail-coverts and its completely black wings; and from the White-crowned Black in the white (not black) belly. The *female* is sandy-brown above with a pinkish-buff rump and outer tail-feathers, and is pale buffish-white below, paler than the female Mourning Wheatear in Dhofar.

Rocky slopes and broken desert country, often without vegetation. The nest is probably from March, like the Mourning Wheatear, the song is a medley of whistles and warbles.

## [Finsch's Wheatear    *Oenanthe finschii*                    (Not illustrated)

**World:** Breeds from Turkey to Transcaucasia, south to Palestine and Iran; sedentary and migratory.
**Oman:** Not confirmed.

13.5cm/5¼in. The *male (in spring)* is strikingly black-and-white, resembling the Black-eared Wheatear (plate 93), but with the white of the crown extending down the back to the rump, and the black of the face and throat joining the black of the scapulars and wings. In *autumn* the crown and mantle are isabelline. The *female* is similar to a female Wheatear (plate 93), but rather yellowish in tone.

On the borders of desert and cultivation. On alighting it characteristically bobs forward and flirts the tail.]

Plate 94

**Red-tailed Wheatear**     *Oenanthe xanthoprymna*

**World:** *O. x. chrysopygia* breeds from Armenia, Transcaspia to N Afghanistan, south to Iran and Baluchistan; migratory, reaching Arabia and NW India. Another race in SW Iran.
**Oman:** Locally common passage migrant and winter visitor between late August and April.

14cm/5½in. The only wheatear in Oman with a conspicuously orange rump (female Desert and Hooded Wheatears have paler orange-buff rumps). The sexes are generally similar; rather uniform sandy or greyish-brown, with pale throat and supercilium, a dark eye-stripe, and the tail showing deep orange at the base and sides above a dark terminal band. *Males (in spring)* are greyer, particularly on the upper-parts and breast, and the dark eye-stripe is more pronounced. The uncommon race in SW Iran, with a black throat and white sides to the tail, has not occurred in E Arabia. See female Black Redstart (plate 92).

*O.x. chrysopygia*
*female* B

*male* A

Widespread in or near hills, perching on bushes, trees and wires. Usually solitary. Rather a belligerent bird, but is usually seen off by Hume's, on whose territory many naturally occur.


**Pied Wheatear**     *Oenanthe pleschanka*

**World:** *O. p. pleschanka* breeds in southern central Asia from the Black Sea to China, south to Iran and N India; migratory, reaching E Africa. (It is the eastern equivalent of the Black-eared Wheatear *O. hispanica,* plate 93, of which it is sometimes considered a race and with which it hybridizes in N Iran. *O. leucomela* is a synonym of *O. pleschanka.*)
**Oman:** Passage migrant September to November and February to early April, most in March but in small numbers.

14.5cm/5¾in. Identical in size and shape to Black-eared Wheatear. *Male (in spring)* resembles male black-throated Black-eared Wheatear, but has a black (not white or buff) back, and the back of the mantle connects with the black of the throat. *Autumn males* in fresh plumage have the black of the mantle obscured with buff tips, and closely resemble autumn male Black-eared. The *females* and *immatures* are almost indistinguishable from female Black-eared in the field, but tend to be duller and darker, with pale earth-brown tips to the feathers of the mantle. Hybrids between Pied and Black-eared show a confusing variety of intermediate forms, with varied amounts of black on the throat, sides of neck and mantle, and can closely resemble Finsch's Wheatear (plate 94). See also Mourning Wheatear.

*O.p. pleschanka male* E

*male autumn* D
*female* C

Its habits are similar to those of the Black-eared Wheatear.


**Mourning Wheatear**     *Oenanthe lugens*

**World:** *O. l. boscaweni* breeds in SE Arabia from the Hadhramaut to S Oman; sedentary. Other races in N and E Africa, SW Arabia, Near East, S Iran.
**Oman:** Breeding resident in Dhofar.

13.5cm/5¼in. The *adult male* is very similar to the Pied Wheatear, but best distinguished by the rusty tinge on the under tail-coverts (though this is sometimes pale, restricted to the vent and difficult to see), the pale bases to the flight feathers visible in flight as a pale patch or 'window', and by narrow white tips to the broader black tail-band. The *female* has a similar tail-pattern but is otherwise very different, being grey-brown above, with the head tinged rufous and a pale patch in the open wing; paler grey-brown below, with some darker streaks on the throat, and dark brown under-wings; it is darker than the female Hooded Wheatear (plate 94), and in general colouration somewhat reminiscent of the Spotted Flycatcher (plate 107).

*male* G

*female* F

Rocky, almost bare hillsides, often sheltering in caves. It is usually in pairs, but the drab female may be overlooked. The nest and eggs have not yet been described, but are probably from February/March, in a rock cleft; it is probably double-brooded (young seen April–July). The song (from February) is a sweet warble, uttered from a rock or tree; when defending young it calls with a double staccato grating *krik-krik* or *chzak-chzak*, uttered with bowing, tail-raising and wing-flicking.

236

Plate 95

237

## ROCK THRUSHES: *Monticola*

Both species which occur in Oman resemble true thrushes, genus *Turdus*, but the wings are longer and the tail shorter; they are birds of open rocky country, with chat-like habits. The males have colourful plumage, the females are brown.

### Rock Thrush  *Monticola saxatilis*

Rock Thrush

**World:** Breeds in a narrow belt from NW Africa and S Europe across to China, south to Iran, Afghanistan and NW India. Migratory, reaching Africa and Arabia.

**Oman:** Fairly common but local passage migrant in September and October (numbers varying annually, and most missing northern N Oman), a few occasionally in winter, slight return passage mid-February to April (rarely in Dhofar), rarely in May.

19cm/7½in. A rather shy, stocky and short-tailed thrush of rocky hillsides. The *male (in spring)* is unmistakable, with bright blue head and throat, white back, blackish wings, and orange-rufous under-parts, rump and tail, with brown central tail-feathers. In *winter* generally browner above, the colours of the upper-parts, except for the orange-rufous upper tail-coverts and tail, partly obscured by black and pale tips to the feathers, and the wing-feathers have pale fringes; the chin and throat are pale, and the rest of the under-parts are bright orange-rufous, but with dark bars, spots and pale tips to the feathers. The *females* and *young males* are similar but much paler, with little trace of the blue and white of the male's upper-parts; they are readily distinguishable from the female Blue Rock Thrush by smaller size, paler under-parts and short orange-rufous tail.

*male* B

*male winter* A

*female* C

Typically a bird of rocky hillsides and crags, feeding on the ground amongst rocks, but on passage often in lowlands, sometimes perching on trees. As a rule it has an upright stance, but it is shy, wary, and usually solitary, and occasionally crouches. It has a chat-like habit of jerking up the tail.

### Blue Rock Thrush  *Monticola solitarius*

Blue Rock Thrush

**World:** *M. s. longirostris* breeds in Transcaspia, south to N Iraq, Iran, Afghanistan; migratory, reaching Africa, Arabia, NW India. Other races in NW Africa, Europe to Near East and Caucasus, and from N India to E and SE Asia.

**Oman:** Passage migrant and winter visitor, local and not very common, between September and March, more often seen from January.

20cm/8in. Slightly larger and longer-tailed than the Rock Thrush and more reminiscent of the typical thrushes (plates 97 and 98). The *male (in spring)* is dull blue, sometimes paler blue-grey, with brown or blackish wings and tail; in poor light it can appear black and resemble a male Blackbird (plate 97). In *autumn* it is duller, with pale fringes to the feathers above and below. The *females* and *immatures* are dark sooty-brown above with some faint mottling on head and mantle; paler brown below, with whitish mottling on the throat and heavy dark concentric marks on the breast, flanks and belly.

*male* D

*male winter* E
*female* F

Rocky hillsides, crags, gorges and old buildings down to sea-level; it occasionally perches on posts and trees. It bobs the head down and the tail up, and droops the wing-tips. It watches for invertebrate prey, then pounces on to the ground or makes short sallies to catch insects in flight; it will also come to fruiting trees in wadi-beds, sometimes with the Rock Thrush, though it is usually solitary. It is occasionally heard in sweet whistling sub-song from January.

Plate 96

## THRUSHES: *Turdus* Plates 97–98

Medium-sized, upstanding song-birds, with fairly slim bills and ample, square-ended tails. Many are brown above and spotted below. They feed on invertebrates, particularly earthworms and snails, but most will take berries and fruit when available. On the ground they have a ponderous hopping gait. Many species flock in winter and have distinct flight-calls.

### [Blackbird *Turdus merula* Blackbird

**World:** Breeds on Atlantic Islands, in NW Africa, Europe to W Asia, and from Turkey to China, south to Iran and India, in several races. Sedentary and migratory; occurs occasionally in the Arabian Gulf in winter, once in Fujairah (UAE) on 29 October 1970.
**Oman:** A potential winter vagrant, not yet reported.

25cm/10in. The *adult male* is uniform jet-black, with a bright orange-yellow bill and eye-ring; the *immature male* is duller, with blackish-brown wings and a dark bill. The *female* is uniform dark brown above, paler below with a whitish chin, and obscure speckling and dark streaking on the breast. *male* B / *female* A

In thickets, date-groves and cultivation, feeding on the ground or in fruiting trees. It is very shy, quickly retreating into cover when alarmed, and is usually silent. If numerous it can be noisy, particularly when going to roost at dusk. Calls, a loud *chuck chuck* or *chink chink* and a high-pitched *tsee.*]

### Ring Ouzel *Turdus torquatus* Ring Ouzel

**World:** Breeds locally in Europe, Turkey, Caucasia, Transcaspia to N Iran, in several races. Partially migratory, reaching N Africa, Near East, Iraq, Iran; a vagrant further south.
**Oman:** Winter vagrant (one 11 December 1977 and one 10 February 1978; both in the Dhofar mountains).

24cm/9½in. The *adult male* resembles a male Blackbird, but has a broad white crescent or gorget across the upper breast, a duller bill, and greyish edges to the secondaries and coverts showing as a grey patch in the closed wing. In *winter* it is more scaly above and below, with pale feather-edges. The *female* is browner, and has a duller crescent on the breast. The *juvenile* has no white crescent, and is grey-brown, mottled below like a young Blackbird, but with the pale wing-patch. Rare albinistic (white-marked) Blackbirds with white on the breast can cause confusion. *male summer* C / *male winter* D

Prefers high open ground and lightly wooded slopes, but in winter also on low ground in the cover of bushes, rocks, etc. It is shy and has a rapid, dodging flight; unlike the Blackbird, it often flies high and far when flushed. It feeds on fruit and invertebrates, in vegetation and on the ground. Call, a hard *tchak* or *tak*, quite unlike that of the Blackbird.

### Black-throated Thrush *Turdus ruficollis* Black-throated Thrush

**World:** Black-throated Thrush *T. r. atrogularis* breeds in W Siberia (to the west of **Red-throated Thrush** *T. r. ruficollis*); migratory, reaching Iran, northern India, Burma, occasionally Iraq and Arabia.
**Oman:** Irregular winter visitor in some years between November and March, in small or very small numbers.

23.5cm/9¼in. A rather greyish thrush, with unstreaked whitish lower breast and belly. The *male (in spring)* is distinctive, with greyish upper-parts, black face, throat and upper breast, and white belly. The *winter* and *immature males* are duller, with brown tips to the black feathers of the face and throat. The *female* is greyish-brown above, and whitish below with a well-defined gorget of dark spots and streaking on the upper breast. Both sexes show pale rufous wing-linings in flight. *male spring* F / *male winter* E

In date-groves and large gardens, often in small loose flocks and usually rather shy. It feeds on the ground or in trees, on invertebrates, berries and other small fruit. Call, *chuck* or *chuck-chuck-chuck*, harder than that of Blackbird.

240

Plate 97

**[Mistle Thrush**  *Turdus viscivorus*

**World:** Breeds from Europe to central Asia, south to NW Africa, Lebanon, N Iran, northern India, in several races. Resident and partial migrant, occasionally to Arabian Gulf States in cold weather.
**Oman:** Not yet reported.

27cm/10½in. A large thrush, uniform greyish-brown above, and buffish-white below with profuse round black spots from chin to lower belly, and a dusky crescent on the cheek; the whitish tips of the outer tail-feathers and the white wing-linings are both conspicuous in flight. The sexes are similar.

Habits similar to those of Black-throated Thrush. The usual call is a distinctive grating chatter.]

**[Redwing**  *Turdus iliacus*

**World:** *T. i. iliacus* breeds across N Eurasia to E Siberia; migratory, reaching latitude of the Mediterranean and Iran, rarely to Arabian Gulf States and NW India.
**Oman:** Not yet reported.

21cm/8¼in. A small dark thrush, rather like a Song Thrush but with a conspicuous creamy-buff supercilium and bright orange-rufous wing-linings and flanks, the latter visible when the bird is perched. The sexes are similar. Readily distinguished from Eye-browed Thrush by the extensive streaking on the under-parts.

Habits similar to those of Song Thrush. The usual call is a thin, high-pitched *seeh*.]

**[Fieldfare**  *Turdus pilaris*

**World:** Breeds from S Greenland, N and central Europe to Siberia. Migratory, reaching the latitude of the Mediterranean and Iran, occasionally to Arabian Gulf States and NW India.
**Oman:** Not yet reported.

25.5cm/10in. A large and attractive thrush, readily distinguished by the combination of grey crown and nape, dark chestnut mantle, rich buff breast boldly streaked with black, white wing-linings, grey rump and black tail. The sexes are similar.

Habits similar to those of Black-throated Thrush. The usual call is *chak-chak-chak*, rather like some calls of the Black-throated (plate 97).]

**Song Thrush**  *Turdus philomelos*

**World:** Breeds across Europe to Lake Baikal (central Asia), south to Turkey and N Iran, in several races. Sedentary or migratory, reaching northern Africa, Arabia, SW Asia.
**Oman:** Passage migrant and winter visitor between November and March, in very small numbers, varying annually; fairly regular in N Oman and Masirah, reported less often in Dhofar.

23cm/9in. The commonest thrush in Oman; uniform warm brown above and whitish below, with a buff tinge on the breast and conspicuous black spotting from the sides of the throat to the lower breast and flanks. The sexes are similar. Distinguished from the similar-sized Redwing by the pale eye-ring, lack of conspicuous supercilium and absence of chestnut on the flanks; from the Mistle Thrush by warmer brown upper-parts, less evenly spotted under-parts and lack of white in the tail; and from both by buff wing-linings.

In thickets, date-groves, cultivation and gardens; rather shy and secretive. It usually feeds on the ground, in thick cover, on invertebrates, particularly snails. The usual call is a thin *sip* or *seep*, shorter and less penetrating than that of the Redwing.

**Eye-browed Thrush**  *Turdus obscurus*

**World:** Breeds in central and E Asia. Migratory to SE Asia; stragglers have reached Europe. (Sometimes treated as the western race of **Pale Thrush** *T. pallidus*.)
**Oman:** Vagrant (one male, Masirah, 26 September 1974, the first for Arabia).

19cm/7½in. A small and distinctive thrush. The *male* has a grey head and throat, olive-brown upper-parts, conspicuous white supercilium, white patch from below the eye to the chin, whitish throat, grey upper breast, and unstreaked orange-buff lower-breast and flanks contrasting with the white belly. The *female* is duller, with an olive-brown head, the white throat streaked with brown. It resembles a small, pale Redwing, but is readily distinguished by the complete absence of spotting and streaking on the under-parts.

Habits similar to those of Song Thrush. Call, a thin *zip-zip*.

Mistle Thrush A

Redwing B

Fieldfare C

Song Thrush D

Eye-browed Thrush

*male* F

*female* E

242

Plate 98

## WARBLERS: Sylviidae

Plates 99–106 and Appendix 2

**World:** 339 species. **Oman:** 33 species. Small to very small rather solitary birds, with plain colours and fine pointed bills. Often rather similar, best identified by voice and habits. Sexes usually similar. Feed on invertebrates, occasionally fruit, in trees, bushes or low vegetation.

**Graceful Warbler** (Graceful Prinia)  *Prinia gracilis*

Graceful Warbler A

**World:** Breeds in NE and E Africa, Near East, Arabia, Turkey, Iraq, S Iran to N India, in several races. Sedentary.
**Oman:** Common and widespread breeding resident.

13cm/5in incl. tail. A very small, restless, brown warbler with small wings and a long tail. The Oman races are mouse-brown above with faint dark streaks on crown and mantle; pale whitish, buff or greyish below, the under-side of each feather of the graduated tail having a white tip and a black spot sub-terminally. The yellow-brown bill and mouth become black when *breeding*. The *juvenile* is paler, more buffish, with pale fringes to feathers above, and no noticeable tail-spots. See Scrub Warbler.

In or near cultivation or thick vegetation. Often skulks in low vegetation, but will perch on trees and low scrub, twitching the tail and body sideways and occasionally cocking the tail to reveal the black and white spots on the under-side. The flight is uneven. In display the male makes a triple wing-snapping *brrrp-brrrp-brrrp*. The nest, January–October, is a lined, domed ovoid of grass, down, hairs, gossamer, etc., with a side entrance, built in low plants or up to 3m high in creepers and low trees. The 3–5 eggs are varied pinkish-brown with darker marks; double- or triple-brooded. The song is a loud succession of double notes, *az-zeek az-zeek az-zeek*; call note, *breep* or *rrrp*; alarm note, a rapid *trrt-trrt-trrr*.

**Scrub Warbler** (Streaked Scrub Warbler)  *Scotocerca inquieta*

Scrub Warbler B

**World:** Breeds from N Africa through Arabia, Iran, Transcaspia, Turkestan to NW India, in several races. Sedentary.
**Oman:** Breeding resident, very local and widely dispersed.

10cm/4in. A very small plump warbler with short wings and long blackish tail. Grey-brown above, heavily streaked on the crown and much less so on the mantle; it has a pale supercilium, a dark stripe through the eye, slight dark streaks on the pale throat and upper breast, and the belly and flanks variably tinged pinkish to pale chestnut. The tail is blackish with pale tips to the outer feathers below. It differs from the Graceful Warbler in habitat, behaviour, voice and plump shape; the head often appears larger, and the tail is much darker and not so conspicuously spotted below.

Desolate hillsides and semi-desert wadis with some bushes, from near sea-level to over 2,500m. A delightful, confiding and inquisitive bird, in pairs or family parties, often feeding on the open ground amongst rocks. It has a springing jump, and the tail is frequently cocked over the back and waved from side to side. The nest, from March, is a small lined ovoid with a side entrance, usually low down in a hillside bush. The 4–5 eggs are whitish to pinkish, sometimes speckled reddish; double-brooded. Song, a high-pitched distinctive whistle *psee-eee* or *p'yee*, the notes very often ending with a 'sad' deflection, *pseeyoo*, sometimes preceded by *tip* or *tissip* and ending with a *pipiprr*; calls include a rapid *tit-tit-priwiwiwi*.

**[Cetti's Warbler**  *Cettia cetti*

Cetti's Warbler C

**World:** Breeds in N Africa, S Europe, Asia Minor to Iran, in several races; migratory in the east, reaching Iraq, Kuwait, Iran, NW India
**Oman:** May occur as an irregular winter visitor (one report), but confirmation is lacking.

14cm/5½in. Dark rufous-brown above, with short greyish supercilium and noticeably rounded tail, pale greyish below with whitish chin and throat, brownish flanks and white fringes to long under tail-coverts. Best distinguished from other species in the field by darker colouration, more rounded dark tail (10, not 8, feathers) and greyish under-parts. A very secretive warbler of dense vegetation.]

**Grasshopper Warbler**  *Locustella naevia*

Grasshopper Warbler D

**World:** Breeds from UK to central Asia, in several races. Migratory, reaching N Africa, India, occasionally Arabian Gulf.
**Oman:** Vagrant or scarce passage migrant (reported near Muscat, September 1978).

13cm/5in. A dull-coloured warbler with a graduated tail. Olive-brown above, with black streaks and spots and an indistinct supercilium; whitish or buffish below, with indistinct streaks on the throat and mottled under tail-coverts.

Very secretive, in thick low vegetation, often near water. Call, a short hard *tik*.

Plate 99

MARSH and REED WARBLERS: *Locustella* and *Acrocephalus*

Plates 99–101 and Appendix 2

A very confusing group of medium to large warblers of thick vegetation near and over water, mostly uniform brownish above and buffish-white below; best identified by song, though this is seldom heard in Oman. Field identification of several species is nearly impossible and knowledge of their status in Oman is incomplete. *Locustella* warblers are very secretive, usually keeping low down in tangled vegetation. They have rather long, broad and well-graduated tails. They often feed on the ground, where they have a distinctive running gait, with the tail held high. *Acrocephalus* warblers have shorter, more rounded tails, are generally more confiding and show a preference for reed-beds and other emergent aquatic vegetation.

**Sedge Warbler**    *Acrocephalus schoenobaenus*    Sedge Warbler A

**World:** Breeds in NW Africa, Europe to central Asia, south to NW Iran. Migratory to Africa.
**Oman:** Uncommon passage migrant, September to October, perhaps November, and April to early June.

13cm/5in. Distinguished from other warblers except the Moustached Warbler by conspicuous creamy-white supercilium, heavily streaked crown, nape and mantle, unstreaked rufous-brown rump and whitish under-parts. Very similar to Moustached, but paler, particularly on the crown and cheeks, with the supercilium tapering behind the eye (not square-ended), and the mantle less rufous; the tail is seldom cocked like that of Moustached.

Mangroves, cultivation and other low vegetation when marshy vegetation is not available. Usually rather secretive, creeping among the stems of vegetation, sometimes on the ground. The flight is erratic and jerky. Song, occasionally heard in spring, is a prolonged medley of sweet notes, interrupted by harsh chattering. Calls, a grating *chirr* and a harsh *tuk-tuk*.

**Moustached Warbler**    *Lusciniola melanopogon* (Syn. *Acrocephalus melanopogon*)    Moustached Warbler B

**World:** *L. melanopogon mimica* breeds in SW Russia, south to Iraq, Iran, locally in NW India; partial migrant, reaching Iraq, Iran, NW India, occasionally NE Arabia. Another race in S Europe and Mediterranean.
**Oman:** Vagrant or scarce passage migrant (one reported, Batinah, 12–14 October 1977; one, Dhofar, 4 July to 8 September 1978).

13cm/5in. Very similar to Sedge Warbler, but a perkier and more robust bird, with the rounded tail often flirted or cocked. It also differs in having a darker, almost blackish crown, a prominent white supercilium ending squarely behind the eye, dark brown cheeks contrasting with the clean white throat, and a richer rufous tinge to the nape and mantle.

In similar situations to Sedge Warbler, but more commonly in reed-beds, where it often feeds just above the water-level. Calls, a soft *churr* and a harsh *chick*.

**Savi's Warbler**    *Locustella luscinioides*    Savi's Warbler C

**World:** *L.l. fusca* breeds in southern central Asia; sedentary and migratory, reaching Near East and E Africa, very occasionally to W Arabian Gulf. Another race in NW Africa and W Eurasia.
**Oman:** Vagrant or scarce passage migrant (reported on Batinah, 16 May 1976; in Dhofar, 16 April and 13 and 26 September 1978).

14cm/5½in. Superficially resembles several of the *Acrocephalus* warblers, but is darker, with longer, broader and well-graduated tail, often with faint barring. The upper-parts are uniform dark rufous-brown; the under-parts are brownish-white, with a conspicuous white chin and a rufous tinge on the flanks; the supercilium is short and indistinct, and the under tail-coverts have indistinct buff tips. Distinguished from the Grasshopper Warbler (plate 99) by larger size and unstreaked upper-parts; from the River Warbler by more rufous upper-parts and lack of streaking on breast.

Amongst reeds, mangroves and other vegetation. Less secretive than Grasshopper Warbler, occasionally coming into view on high stems. Call, a scolding *tswik*.

**River Warbler**    *Locustella fluviatilis*    River Warbler D

**World:** Breeds in E Europe and W Asia. Migratory, reaching SE Africa, occasionally Near East, Iraq, Arabia.
**Oman:** Vagrant (one reported found dead in Dhofar, 15 September 1978).

13cm/5in. Rather similar to Savi's Warbler, but with paler, earth-brown upper-parts and obscure streaking on the dull greyish breast. The long under tail-coverts reach the tip of the tail, and are buffish-brown, broadly tipped white (tipped buffish in Savi's).

Marshy and dry vegetation, bushes, trees and cultivation. It keeps closely to cover, but will run mouse-like on the ground through tangled vegetation. Call, a distinctive *pink*.

Plate 100

## Reed Warbler    *Acrocephalus scirpaceus*

Reed Warbler B

**World:** *A. s. fuscus* breeds in southern central Asia, south to Turkey, Palestine, Iran; migratory, reaching E Africa, Arabia, NW India. Another race from Europe to W Asia.
**Oman:** Fairly common passage migrant August–October and February–May; locally over winter and summer.

13cm/5in. The commonest unstreaked *Acrocephalus* warbler in Oman; uniform olive-brown upper-parts lightly tinged rufous, especially on the rump, short pale supercilium, creamy-white chin and throat, and whitish under-parts tinged buff on the flanks. The legs are usually dark. Indistinguishable in the field from the Marsh Warbler, and separable in the hand only with difficulty, by the wing formula.

Prefers reed-beds, but on passage also in thick bushes and cultivation. It is rather skulking, but occasionally leaves cover to sidle up grass stems, or fly for a short distance, with tail fanned and depressed. The alarm note is a low grating *churr*, and a frog-like croak.

## Blyth's Reed Warbler    *Acrocephalus dumetorum*

Blyth's Reed Warbler A

**World:** Breeds in central Eurasia, south to E Iran, N Afghanistan. Migratory SE to India, at least occasionally to E Africa, E Arabia. (Sometimes treated as a race of **African Reed Warbler** *A. baeticatus.*)
**Oman:** Vagrant or passage migrant, scarce or overlooked (birds examined at Bahla, 14–15 March 1979).

13cm/5in. Virtually indistinguishable in the field from Reed and Marsh Warblers, but is paler olive-brown above, has shorter, more rounded wings and appears to have a longer tail and a longer, finer bill. The well-rounded tail is occasionally flicked. See Olivaceous Warbler (plate 102).

Damp and dry vegetation, including reeds, bushes, trees and cultivation.

## Marsh Warbler    *Acrocephalus palustris*

Marsh Warbler C

**World:** Breeds from Europe to W Asia, south to Caspian region. Migratory to SE Africa.
**Oman:** Passage migrant, scarce or overlooked (specimens examined March–May, and October).

13cm/5in. Probably indistinguishable in the field from the race *fuscus* of the Reed Warbler; the legs are usually pale, and in spring the upper-parts are more olive, less brown, but these differences are not reliable.

Habits as Reed Warbler, but more frequently in dry vegetation, and usually less skulking.

## Great Reed Warbler    *Acrocephalus arundinaceus*

Great Reed Warbler D

**World:** Breeds in Eurasia, south to NW Africa, Palestine, Iraq, NW Iran, in several races. Migratory, reaching Africa and Far East.
**Oman:** Uncommon passage migrant, August–October and March–May; often confused with the more common Clamorous Reed Warbler.

19cm/7½in. Rather similar to Reed Warbler, but much larger and chunkier, with heavy thrush-like bill and more conspicuous pale supercilium. See Clamorous Reed Warbler.

Reeds, mangroves and bushes, not always near water on passage. Habits similar to Reed Warbler's, but its movements are heavier, and it is rather less skulking. Call, a deep *chuk* or *gurk*.

## Clamorous Reed Warbler (Southern Great Reed Warbler)    *Acrocephalus stentoreus*

Clamorous Reed Warbler E

**World:** *A. s. brunnescens* breeds in SW Russia, south to Iran, Afghanistan, India; sedentary and migratory, reaching Arabia, India, occasionally E Africa. Other races from Near East to Australia.
**Oman:** Fairly common passage migrant and local winter visitor between July and May; breeding migrant on N Batinah in small numbers.

18cm/7¼in. The commoner of the two large reed warblers in Oman; differing from Great Reed in its paler and less rufous upper-parts, white under-parts lacking the rusty tinge on the flanks, longer and slimmer bill, less conspicuous supercilium and relatively longer tail and shorter wings. The overall impression is of a paler, longer and slimmer bird than the chunky Great Reed Warbler.

In mangroves and reeds, occasionally in bushes near water. The nest, from April, is a deep lined cup of stems, leaves, etc., attached to mangrove or reed stems. The eggs, 3–5, are pale blue-green with bold brownish marks. The song is a series of varied pleasing notes, interspersed with harsh, guttural notes; often uttered from an exposed perch. Calls, like Great Reed Warbler.

Plate 101

## WARBLERS: *Hippolais*

*Hippolais* warblers are rather nondescript, with relatively long broad bills; superficially similar to *Acrocephalus* warblers, but with square-ended tails and more arboreal habits.

### Olivaceous Warbler    *Hippolais pallida*

Olivaceous Warbler A

**World:** *H. p. elaeica* breeds in SE Europe, Turkey, Palestine to Iraq, Arabian Gulf, Iran, north to Aral Sea; migratory, reaching Africa, S Arabia. Other races in Spain, northern Africa.
**Oman:** Fairly common passage migrant, August–October and February–May, occasionally over summer; in N Oman in song from March and might breed occasionally.

13.5cm/5¼in. A medium-sized greyish warbler with a flat forehead, large bill and long blue-grey or grey-brown legs. Uniform grey-brown tinged olive above, with darker wings and tail, and a pale face with an indistinct supercilium; white tinged with buff below, the tail with whitish on the outer webs and tips of the outer feathers. Very similar to a large Booted Warbler, and best identified by song. It differs from Upcher's Warbler in that species' larger size and more pronounced tail-movements; from the Garden Warbler (plate 105) in head and bill shape, and more conspicuous supercilium.

Trees and bushes, especially near water. It is rather restless, and occasionally wags its tail up and down, faster than Upcher's. The nest is a strong cup laced to a sheltered outer twig or branch. The eggs, usually 3–4, are pinkish-lilac with dark speckles; it is double-brooded. The song is a rather soft warbling, with a basic and repeated phrase but many harsh notes and much chattering; it is usually uttered from a perch in cover; call, a sharp *chack*.

### Booted Warbler    *Hippolais caligata*

Booted Warbler B

**World:** Breeds in central Asia, south to Iran, N Oman, NW India, in two races. Migratory, reaching India, Arabia.
**Oman:** Uncommon passage migrant and winter visitor, probably overlooked; a migrant breeder to N Batinah.

11.5cm/4½in. Like a small version of Olivaceous Warbler, best identified by song. Usually somewhat paler than Olivaceous, particularly on the under-parts, and has a finer bill and more rounded head, recalling Willow Warbler (plate 106). The legs are usually pale brown tinged with blue-grey.

Mangroves, bushes, trees and cultivation. Usually rather shy and skulking. The nest, from March, is a small lined cup in a low bush. The eggs, 4–6, are pale pinkish with dark marks. The song is faster and more chattering than that of the Olivaceous Warbler, and lacks the basic theme; it is often uttered from a high perch in the inner branches of a tree or bush. Calls, *chrek-chrek* or *churr*.

### Upcher's Warbler    *Hippolais languida*

Upcher's Warbler C

**World:** Breeds in Near East from Palestine, north to Transcaucasia and Aral Sea, south to Iran, Afghanistan, NW India. Migratory to E Africa.
**Oman:** Fairly common passage migrant July–October, March–May, rarely in June.

14cm/5½in. Rather similar to a large Olivaceous Warbler, but with a more pronounced pale supercilium and a darker tail which is slowly depressed and raised or waved from side to side. In *spring* it often shows a pale panel on the wing formed by pale edges to the secondaries, and can then be confused with the very similar **Olive-tree Warbler** *Hippolais olivetorum* [15cm/6in; breeds in SE Europe and Near East; migratory to Africa; reported but not yet confirmed in Oman], which is larger, with a conspicuously long and dagger-like bill and blue-grey, not brownish, legs.

Semi-desert bushes and trees, on plains and in wadis in mountains. Rarely skulks, and often stands rather upright in an open position, moving its tail. Calls, *chak-chak* or *tit*.

### Icterine Warbler    *Hippolais icterina*

Icterine Warbler D

**World:** Breeds from central Europe to central Asia and N Iran. Migratory to southern Africa.
**Oman:** Scarce or overlooked passage migrant, August–September, one report in March.

13.5cm/5¼in. Similar in shape to Olivaceous Warbler, and in plumage to a large Willow Warbler (plate 106). In *spring* olive-brown above and yellow below, with a short yellow supercilium. In *autumn* much paler below, with the yellow restricted to the throat and upper-breast. Distinguished from Willow Warbler by heavier dagger-like bill, steep forehead, bluish-grey legs, and pale panel in the closed wing formed by pale fringes to the secondaries and tertials (obscure in *adults* in *autumn*).

Habits on migration are similar to those of Olivaceous Warbler.

Plate 102

Round-headed warblers of bushes and trees; sexes often dissimilar.

**Orphean Warbler**    *Sylvia hortensis*                    Orphean Warbler  A

**World:** Breeds in N Africa, S Europe, Turkey to Turkestan, south to Palestine, Iran, NW India in several races. Migratory to Africa, Arabia, India.
**Oman:** Passage migrant and winter visitor in small numbers between August and March, occasionally to May.

15cm/6in. A large, stout and rather long-billed warbler; greyish-brown above and whitish tinged with buff below, with a rather long black tail with white outer-feathers and white tips to all the feathers except the central pair. The *male* has black lores and ear-coverts and blackish crown, contrasting with a white throat; the *female's* head is duller and browner. The iris is usually a distinctive yellowish-white, but may be dark. (See Blanford's Warbler; also Barred Warbler, plate 104.)

In bushes and trees, feeding on invertebrates and fruit. It is larger, with slower and more deliberate movements, than other black-capped warblers. Occasionally heard in a sweet sustained warbling sub-song; call, a hard *tak* or *tik* and a *trrr*.

**Blanford's Warbler** (Arabian Warbler)    *Sylvia leucomelaena*        Blanford's Warbler  B

**World:** *S. l. leucomelaena* breeds from NW Saudi Arabia to S Yemen, east to S Oman; probably sedentary.
**Oman:** Uncommon breeding visitor or resident in Dhofar (reported between March and October).

15cm/6in. Very similar to Orphean, but slightly smaller, with a smaller bill, rounder forehead and a white eye-rim; the tail appears all black from above, but has white tips on the outer feathers visible from below. The *male's* black cap is normally clearly defined as in Orphean, the *female's* cap is dull black or brown. The iris is brown, sometimes with a paler outer ring (but many Orpheans also have brown eyes).

On hillsides and in mountain wadis. Rather solitary and seldom seen. More active than Orphean; the tail is moved up and down more often. The nest, probably from early April, is a cup placed in a bush or tree. The song is a loud rich musical warble, uttered from cover.

**Ménétries' Warbler**    *Sylvia mystacea*                    Ménétries' Warbler

**World:** Breeds in southern central Asia, south to Palestine, Iraq, Iran, N Afghanistan. Migratory, reaching NE Africa, S Arabia. (Sometimes treated as a race of **Subalpine Warbler** *S. cantillans*, or of **Sardinian Warbler** *S. melanocephala,* which do not occur in Oman.)
**Oman:** Passage migrant in small numbers, September–November and February–April, occasionally to May and over winter.

13.5cm/5¼in. A small warbler with a habit of waving its blackish tail. The *adult male* is distinctive,     *male*  C
with dull-black head merging into the grey of the back, grey-brown wings, and rounded blackish tail with much white on the outer feathers and on some tips; the under-parts are whitish or pinkish to chestnut. The legs and eye-ring are pale yellow to orange, but in *autumn* become paler and inconspicuous. The *female* and *immature* are nondescript greyish olive-brown above and whitish below,     *female*  D
with contrasting blackish tail with white in the outer feathers; they differ from Lesser Whitethroat (plate 104) in paler lores and ear-coverts, and darker tail.

On plains and in desert wadis. It is rather restless, flitting to the top of a bush, working quickly downward with much waving of the tail and later flying out to the top of the next bush.

**Desert Warbler**    *Sylvia nana*                    Desert Warbler  E

**World:** Breeds in the Sahara, and from N Caspian to NE China, south to Iran, NW India, in several races. Sedentary and migratory, reaching NE Africa, Arabia, NW India.
**Oman:** Regular passage migrant and winter visitor in small numbers, between September and March; *S. n. nana* occurs.

11.5cm/4½in. A small pale sandy-brown or greyish-brown warbler, the sexes alike, with pale rufous rump, upper tail-coverts and central tail-feathers, the rest of the tail dark brown with conspicuous white edges; it is creamy-white below. Iris golden-yellow, legs orange-yellow.

Coastal and desert scrub, also in wadis and mountains. Singly, sometimes in pairs, searching low scrub and bushes and the ground around them. It will deliberately and repeatedly follow wheatears from bush to bush, feeding near and below them, hopping around with cocked tail. Occasionally in song in winter, a sweet tinkling warble, usually from inside cover; calls, *chichi-chrrr, pee-prrr* and a grating *tzerrrk,* somewhat resembling that of Scrub Warbler (plate 99).

Plate 103

**Barred Warbler**  *Sylvia nisoria*

**World:** Breeds from central Europe to central Asia, in two races. Migratory to E Africa, occasionally SW Arabia.

**Oman:** Scarce passage migrant, reported near Muscat twice (28 August and 7 May 1971), but on Masirah about three immatures reported each year between September and October.

15cm/6in. A very large and robust greyish warbler, with stout bill, and longish tail with white fringes and tips to the outer feathers. The *adult* is unmistakable, with conspicuous grey barring on the whitish under-parts (less extensive in the *female* than in the *male*), two white wing-bars and a pale yellow iris. The *immature* is sandy grey-brown above and whitish below, with pale tips to the wing-coverts forming a distinct wing-bar, and usually some faint barring on the under tail-coverts and lower flanks; it is paler and greyer than the rather similar immature Orphean Warbler, and shows less white in the paler tail.

In bushes and trees. It is usually shy, skulking in cover, and often rather restless. It takes invertebrates and fruit. It is generally silent on passage.

**Lesser Whitethroat**  *Sylvia curruca*

**World:** Breeds from W Europe to E Asia (Gobi), south to Near East, Iran, NW India, in several races. Migratory, reaching central Africa, Arabia, SE Iran, India. (**Desert Lesser Whitethroat** *S. c. minula* and **Hume's Lesser Whitethroat** *S. c. althaea* are often treated as separate species.)

**Oman:** Common and widespread passage migrant and winter visitor between September and April, occasionally August–May; most are *minula,* but some *curruca* occur on passage.

**Desert Lesser Whitethroat** *S. c. minula* 13.5cm/5¼in. It is sandy-grey above, greyer on the crown and with contrasting blackish-brown lores and ear-coverts, and some birds showing a faint pale super-cilium; the tail is only slightly darker than the rest of the upper-parts and has extensive white on the outer feathers; the under-parts are whitish, tinged with buff on the flanks. The bill is usually rather pale with a dark tip, and the legs are dark. It can be confused with some Ménétries' Warblers, but has darker ear-coverts and a paler tail. **Lesser Whitethroat** *S. c. curruca* is generally greyer above, and has a slate-grey crown and blackish lores and ear-coverts, giving a more pronounced masked effect; the throat is a purer white, and the bill is darker, with only a little pale at the base of the lower mandible.

In bushes and trees. In winter particularly in semi-desert *Acacia,* moving from tree to tree, restlessly searching for small invertebrate food, even before sunrise, and frequently calling. Sub-song, a delicate monotonous warble, is heard occasionally from January. The calls of the two sub-species are quite different; *minula* has a loud staccato buzzing *tz-tz-tz-tz, tre-ter-zz-zz-zz,* while *curruca* gives a hard *tek . . . tek,* or *tak . . . tak.*

**Whitethroat**  *Sylvia communis*

**World:** *S. c. icterops* (incl. *rubicola*) breeds from E Mediterranean across central Asia to NW China, south to Iran and Baluchistan. Other races in Europe and Asia. All are migratory to Africa.

**Oman:** Common and widespread passage migrant, August–November, occasionally December, and April–May.

14cm/5½in. A grey-brown warbler with a white or whitish throat, often puffed out, conspicuous reddish or sandy-brown in the wings, and a rather long tail with the outer feathers edged white. The *male* in good plumage has a grey head contrasting with white lower cheeks and throat, and a pinkish breast. The *female* and *immature* have a brown head, and are duller below. It differs from Lesser and Desert Lesser Whitethroats in larger size and brown wing-patch; from Garden Warbler (plate 105) in slimmer build, white throat, wing-patch and white in the outer tail-feathers.

Bushes and trees, where it moves about less secretively than many warblers. The call note is a sharp *chack*; also a noisy *sweerz* or *churr.*

254

Barred Warbler

*adult summer* A

*immature* B

Desert Lesser
Whitethroat D

Lesser Whitethroat C

Whitethroat

*male* E

*female* F

Plate 104

**Blackcap**   *Sylvia atricapilla*

**World:** Breeds in N Africa, Europe to central Asia, south to N Iran, in several races. Migratory, reaching S Europe and Africa.
**Oman:** Scarce passage migrant, October–November (one report each) and March–May (six seen).

14cm/5½in. Similar in size and shape to Garden Warbler, but the *male* is greyer, with jet-black forehead and crown when *adult*, blackish-brown when *immature*. The *female* is darker above, with chestnut-brown forehead and crown. The *male* is distinguished from other black-capped warblers by its grey lores and ear-coverts, and by lack of white in the tail.

Bushes and trees. Fairly active, feeding in cover on invertebrates and fruit; rarely on the ground. Call, a hard *tak, tak* and a *churr*.

**Garden Warbler**   *Sylvia borin*

**World:** Breeds from Europe to central Asia, south to Armenia, in two races. Migratory to Africa.
**Oman:** Scarce autumn passage migrant, September–October (5 or 6 occasions) and possibly February–March (unconfirmed).

14cm/5½in. A very uniform brownish warbler with paler under-parts, best identified by its rather plump shape, rounded head, short and stubby bill and lack of plumage features; virtually no supercilium or eye-stripe, and no white in the tail. The rather stout legs are greyish-brown. Readily distinguished from similarly coloured *Hippolais* warblers (plate 102) by head and bill shape.

Bushes and trees. Its habits and calls are very similar to those of the Blackcap, but it is usually more secretive.

## LEAF WARBLERS: *Phylloscopus*                    Plates 105–106

A confusing genus of small to very small olive-brown warblers, often with some yellow; in bushes and trees, hunting restlessly for insects, occasionally flirting the wings and tail and sometimes pursuing prey like a flycatcher. The sexes are alike.

**Green Warbler** (Bright Green Leaf Warbler)   *Phylloscopus nitidus*

**World:** Breeds in a narrow belt from E Turkey across Caucasia, Transcaspia, N Iran to NW Afghanistan. Migratory south-east to India, Sri Lanka. (Sometimes treated as a race of **Greenish Warbler** *P. trochiloides* and often confused with it in Oman.)
**Oman:** Vagrant or scarce autumn passage migrant in some years between October and November.

11cm/4¼in. A small warbler, bright olive-green above, with a conspicuous white to yellowish wing-bar, a yellow supercilium and a dark streak through the eye; yellowish below, paler or whitish on the belly; see Wood Warbler (plate 106). The legs are dark. In *autumn* it is paler and greyer, with less yellow in the plumage, and then confusingly similar to Greenish Warbler, but the wing-bar is usually more conspicuous.

In trees and bushes, restlessly searching for small invertebrates, sometimes in parties with other species, occasionally flicking the wings and hovering briefly to capture prey. Call when feeding, a loud *che-wee* (rarely heard in Oman).

**[Greenish Warbler**   *Phylloscopus trochiloides*

**World:** Breeds from the Baltic to China, south to N India, in several races. Migratory to India and SE Asia.
**Oman:** Possible vagrant, but confirmation is necessary.

11cm/4¼in. Rather similar to Green Warbler, and often confused with it, but it is duller, with greyer upper-parts, paler supercilium, less distinct wing-bar, whitish under-parts faintly streaked yellow, with a greyish tinge on the flanks. Worn *adults* in *autumn* may appear very grey, and the wing-bar is often indistinct or absent; confusion is then possible with pale Chiffchaffs (plate 106) which can show an indistinct wing-bar.

Habits and call are similar to those of Green Warbler.]

Blackcap

*male* B
*female* A

Garden Warbler C

Green Warbler D

Greenish Warbler E

Plate 105

**Yellow-browed Warbler**   *Phylloscopus inornatus*

**World:** *P. i. humei* breeds from central Asia, south-westwards to NE Afghanistan and W Himalayas; migratory to SE Iran, E Arabia, India.
**Oman:** Scarce passage migrant and winter visitor, between September and March.

*P.i. humei* A

10cm/4in. A very small warbler, smaller than the Chiffchaff but with a relatively larger head and shorter tail; olive-brown above with two buffish-white wing-bars (the lower bar large and distinct, the upper bar indistinct or absent), and a long conspicuous whitish supercilium above a dark eye-stripe; whitish below, the flanks tinged brownish. Bill and legs usually very dark. Differs from Green and Greenish Warblers in smaller size, duller plumage and longer supercilium extending to the sides of the nape.

Very active, foraging rapidly for small insects, also taken in brief hovering and chases. Call, a loud *chiwee*.

**Willow Warbler**   *Phylloscopus trochilus*

**World:** Breeds from Europe to E Siberia, in several races. Migratory to Africa.
**Oman:** Uncommon passage migrant, September–October and April–May, often confused with Chiffchaff.

*P.t. acredula* B

11cm/4¼in. Very similar to Chiffchaff, but usually appears larger and has longer, more pointed wings. Olive-brown above with a yellowish-green tinge; whitish below, usually with a more conspicuous yellow supercilium and more extensive yellow suffusion on the breast than Chiffchaff. *Young in autumn* have dull yellow under-parts; compare larger Icterine Warbler (plate 102). Legs usually pale brown, but in some birds dark as in Chiffchaff. Bright individuals are easily confused with Wood Warbler, but are less green above and less clear white on the lower breast and belly.

Habits are very similar to those of the more common Chiffchaff. Call, a soft, almost disyllabic *hooeet*.

**Chiffchaff**   *Phylloscopus collybita*

**World:** Breeds in Canaries, N Africa, Europe to E Siberia, south to N Iran, in several races. Migratory, reaching northern Africa, Arabia, India.
**Oman:** Common passage migrant, a few over winter, between October and March, occasionally early April; *P. c. abietinus* and *P. c. tristis* occur.

*P.c. tristis* C

11cm/4¼in. The commonest leaf warbler in Oman. Olive to grey-brown above, with a short buffish-white supercilium above a dark eye-stripe; dull white below, with buffish flanks and usually some faint yellowish streaks on the breast; under wing-coverts and bend of wing yellowish. Legs very dark. Some individuals in *autumn* show a faint wing-bar; see Greenish Warbler (plate 105).

Trees, cultivation, reeds, etc., hunting restlessly for small insects, sometimes caught in quick sallies. Song, sometimes heard in winter and spring, a distinctive *chiff-chaff-chaff-chiff*, etc.; call of *tristis*, a loud plaintive *seep*; of other races, *wheet*, rather like Willow Warbler.

**Plain Leaf Warbler** (Plain Willow Warbler)   *Phylloscopus neglectus*

**World:** Breeds in Iran and neighbouring Russia, Afghanistan, NW India. Migrates to lower altitudes in winter, occasionally to Arabia.
**Oman:** Vagrant or scarce winter visitor (one from near Sohar, December 1925; two reported, Thamarit, November 1978); probably overlooked.

10cm/4in. A very small warbler, superficially similar to a small drab Chiffchaff, but plumper, with a noticeably more rounded head, finer bill, indistinct supercilium, and dull greyish olive-brown and buffish-white plumage with no trace of green or yellow.

Junipers, acacias, tamarisks, etc., rarely in cultivation. More active than Chiffchaff and hovers more frequently. The call is distinctive, a harsh *churr* or *chiip*.

**Wood Warbler**   *Phylloscopus sibilatrix*

**World:** Breeds in Europe and W Asia, south to Caucasus. Migratory to tropical Africa.
**Oman:** Scarce passage migrant, reported September–October (to December occasionally on Masirah) and March–May.

12.5cm/5in. A large leaf warbler, with relatively long pointed wings and short tail. Best distinguished from others of the genus by its greener upper-parts, and pale lemon throat and upper breast contrasting sharply with the pure-white lower breast and belly.

Bushes and trees, usually fairly high up. It does not flick the wings and tail like most other leaf warblers, but occasionally droops the wing-tips. Call, *peeu*.

Plate 106

259

# FLYCATCHERS: Muscicapidae

**World:** About 113 species. **Oman:** 3 species. 'Typical' flycatchers of the Old World. Small, short-legged birds of wooded regions, they feed by catching flying insects, normally in repeated short sorties from an exposed perch, returning to that or another perch. Some take invertebrates from vegetation, very occasionally from the ground. The bill is broad at the base, with bristles at the gape. Other families include the monarch or paradise flycatchers (plate 108).


**Spotted Flycatcher**   *Muscicapa striata*                                         Spotted Flycatcher  A

**World:** Breeds from W Europe to central Asia, south to NW Africa, Palestine, Iran, NW India, in several races. Migratory, reaching S Africa.
**Oman:** Passage migrant, common from mid-August to October, occasionally to December; less common in April–May; rarely March and July. *M. s. neumanni* occurs.

14cm/5½in. A smallish grey-brown bird with distinctive behaviour. It is dull grey-brown above, with dark spots on the pale forehead, distinct pale fringes to the darker flight-feathers and dark tail; the under-parts are whitish with dark streaks from the sides of the neck to the breast and flanks. The *immature* is similar but has broader pale fringes to the secondaries and pale tips to the coverts. It differs from the **Brown Flycatcher** *M. latirostris* [12cm/4¾in, breeds in E Asia to Japan, also in parts of India, sedentary and migratory, reported but not confirmed in Oman] in that species' smaller size, conspicuous whitish eye-ring, more uniform upper-parts except for pale fringes on the secondaries, only very faint spots and streaks on the under-parts, more wing-flicking and more crepuscular habits.

Among trees, usually on an exposed lower branch, fence, etc. It stands rather upright and stationary, rarely flicking wings or tail, but frequently darting out briefly in erratic, swooping, twisting flight to snap up flying insects, returning to the same or another perch. Singly, not gregarious, but several occur in proximity in passage, when they call with a sharp *zik*.


**Red-breasted Flycatcher**   *Ficedula parva*                                        Red-breasted Flycatcher

**World:** *F. p. parva* breeds from N and E Europe to central Asia, also Caucasus to Iran; migratory to W India (some reach W Africa). Another race across E Asia.
**Oman:** Scarce autumn passage migrant, between September and December, under 10 a year.

11.5cm/4½in. A small warbler-like flycatcher. Uniform grey-brown above and buffish-white below,    *male* B
with a conspicuous pale eye-ring and broad white patches at either side of the base of the dark tail. The *adult male* has a greyish head and bright orange-red throat and upper breast. The *female* and   *female* C
*immature* have little or no orange on the under-parts, and the *immature* has buff tips to the secondaries and upper wing-coverts.

Under shady trees, in gardens or on open scrub, stationary on low branches or restlessly pursuing insects in short flight, also taking them among foliage and from the ground. Occurs singly or in small parties. The wings are frequently flicked and the tail jerked upwards, revealing the white at the sides. Calls, a harsh chatter and a quiet *chik*.


**Semi-collared Flycatcher** (Eastern Collared Flycatcher)   *Ficedula semitorquata*   Semi-collared Flycatcher

**World:** Breeds in Greece, Turkey, Palestine, Caucasus, N Iran. Migratory to E Africa. (Sometimes treated as the south-eastern race of **Collared Flycatcher** *F. albicollis*, or of **Pied Flycatcher** *F. hypoleucos*, and, except for males in breeding plumage, very similar in appearance.)
**Oman:** Scarce passage migrant in N Oman between March and April (perhaps May) in some years (based on records of 'Collared' and 'Pied' which have been confused with Semi-collared in the past).

12.7cm/5in. A typical flycatcher. The *male (breeding)* is strikingly pied; deep black above and white   *male* D
below, with white forehead, half-collar (sides of neck), wing-patches and edges of tail, and greyish rump. The *female*, *winter male* and *immature* are olive-brown above and buffish-white below; they   *female* E
differ from the Spotted Flycatcher in lacking the streaking, and having fairly conspicuous white wing-patches and white edges to the outer tail-feathers; *males* may show some white on the forehead, and *females* may show a faint half-collar. All except *spring males* are indistinguishable in the field from Pied and Collared. Spring male Collared Flycatcher has complete white collar and white rump, while spring male Pied has less white on the sides of the neck than Semi-collared, and glossy black rump.

Its habits are similar to those of Spotted except that it rarely returns to the same perch; it hovers, and more often feeds on the ground; it flicks the wings and wags the tail more, and perches deeper in cover. The call is a short *tik* or *zrr*.

260

Plate 107

# MONARCH or PARADISE FLYCATCHERS: Monarchidae

**World:** 92 species. **Oman:** 1 species.

**African Paradise Flycatcher**  *Terpsiphone viridis*

**World:** *T. v. harterti* breeds in SW Saudi Arabia, Yemen, S Yemen to S Oman. Other races in Africa.
**Oman:** Small numbers occur in Dhofar in all months, presumably residents.

African
Paradise Flycatcher

*male non-breeding* B

*male breeding* A

20cm/8in, excl. tail-streamers. A distinctive, graceful bird of woodland, with a colourful combination of glossy blue-black from head to nape and breast or belly, bright orange-chestnut mantle and tail, black wings, warm blue-grey under-parts and whitish under tail-coverts. There is considerable individual variation; some are more black, some have a green sheen on the head, and some have white or chestnut fringes on the wing-coverts and secondaries. The *breeding males* have the central pair of tail-feathers elongated to ribbon-like streamers, which are sometimes white. The *female* and *immature* have a paler abdomen and lack the tail-streamers.

On and near wooded hillsides and valleys, a few to coastal gardens in winter. Usually seen singly or in small parties in and around trees, cliff-side bushes, reeds, etc., searching amongst the foliage for insects, occasionally pursuing them in flight. It comes down to water to drink and bathe, also to catch insects. The nest (from February, near Aden) is a tiny deep cup of moss and lichen high up in the fork of a thick bush or tree, often near water. Eggs, 3, are creamy-white, spotted red and lilac. Song, a short rippling musical *wheeo wheeo-wip-wip-wip*; the calls include a loud rasping *skwee* or *skweech* and *sississi*.

# PENDULINE TITS: Remizidae

**World:** 8–9 species. **Oman:** 1 species.

**Penduline Tit**  *Remiz pendulinus*

**World:** Breeds very locally from S and E Europe to China, south to Iran (*macronyx* group), in many races. Sedentary, migratory and irruptive; has visited Kuwait and Bahrain in winter and spring.
**Oman:** Vagrant or accidental (one near Muscat, 29 March 1971).

Penduline Tit

*male* C

*female* D

*R. p. macronyx* 10cm/4in. A small grey-and-brown bird with black on the head. The crown is whitish or chestnut; there is a black band from the bill and eyes which meets round the nape and often extends to the whole head; the throat is blackish, the mantle chestnut, and the wings and longish tail grey-and-white; the under-parts are whitish-buff, with rufous on the breast and flanks. The *female* usually has the black restricted to a patch from bill to cheeks.

In reeds, mangroves or bushes near water, where it normally feeds in active parties, acrobatically taking insects from vegetation in a manner resembling warblers or white-eyes; it also takes seeds. The contact call is a thin drawn-out *swee, swee*.

# BABBLERS: Timaliidae

**World:** 230 species. **Oman:** 1 species (resident). A varied group, often placed amongst the thrushes and warblers. The genus *Turdoides* occurs from N Africa to India.

**Arabian Babbler** (Brown Babbler)  *Turdoides squamiceps*

**World:** Breeds in Palestine, Sinai, Arabia, in several races.
**Oman:** Widespread but local and not very common breeding resident; *T. s. muscatensis* occurs.

Arabian Babbler E

28.5cm/11in. A grey-brown thrush-like bird with a long graduated tail, short, rounded and loosely held wings and distinctive habits. The flat forehead and crown are slightly mottled; the breast and belly are buffish-grey, the rest of the under-parts whitish. The legs are strong and covered with protective overlapping scales. The bill is strong, decurved and yellowish-horn, brighter yellow with a dark tip in *young birds*. The iris is dark grey in *juveniles*, changing to whitish *(males)* and brown *(females)*.

Amongst small trees and thickets, between sea-level and 2,000m, and from coast to interior semi-desert, in inquisitive territorial groups of 2–15 individuals. They search for invertebrates, fruit and seeds in cover and on the ground nearby, at least one bird keeping watch. The group flies and glides low down out of a tree, one by one. One nest is built co-operatively by each group in March/April, a large loose cup, sometimes domed, 1–7m up inside cover. Eggs, 2–4, laid by one female (unusually up to 9 by two birds); all group members 'help' feed, guard and care for the young, which remain with the group. Noisy when excited, flicking the wings, 'stirring' the tail vigorously or jumping along the ground. Song, a prolonged sibilant trill, *tsee-tsee-trrrrr* or *sississirrr*; call, a ringing whistle *psee-oo, psee-oo*; alarm, a thin whistling *pseeep*.

262

Plate 108

## SUNBIRDS: Nectariniidae

**World:** 105 species. **Oman:** 3 species (breeding).

**Purple Sunbird**   *Nectarinia asiatica*

**World:** *N. a. brevirostris* breeds in UAE, Oman, SE Iran to NW India; sedentary and locally migratory.
**Oman:** Common resident in N Oman, some wander south to the latitude of Masirah in winter.

10cm/4in. *Male (breeding)* appears almost black at a distance, but is glossed metallic blue to purple on head and mantle and dark purple and green below, sometimes with an inconspicuous blue or copper breast-band. The *female* is olive-brown above, with a darker brown tail and pale yellowish or whitish under-parts. *Male (non-breeding)* is similar, but has darker wings and tail, and brighter yellow under-parts with a varied black stripe from chin to belly. Like most sunbirds, has yellow-red pectoral tufts, erected only during display.

Amongst trees and bushes from sea-level to mountains, frequently in parties searching for insects, nectar and fruit, also in swift and jerky flight. The nest, from January, is an untidy purse, suspended from the inner branch of a tree or bush. 2–3 eggs, whitish, tinged green to brown, slightly speckled; double-brooded. Song, *sisisi-sew-sew-sew*; calls, *sweep* (rising) and *zik*.

**Palestine Sunbird** (Northern Orange-tufted Sunbird)   *Nectarinia osea*

**World:** *N. o. osea* breeds from Syria to SW Arabia and S Oman. Another race in central Africa.
**Oman:** Fairly common breeding resident in Dhofar, with seasonal movements.

11.5cm/4½in. A small sunbird, sometimes mistaken for Purple Sunbird (not found in Dhofar). The *male (breeding)* differs from Abyssinian in smaller size and in having nape, neck and mantle metallic bluish-green; forehead and chin blue, shading into violet on upper breast, rarely with any scarlet. *Female* and *young* are grey-brown above, paler and tinged yellow below;the tail is dark with pale under tail-coverts. *Male (non-breeding)* shows traces of breeding plumage.

Trees and bushes from sea-level to hills, flocking and wandering after breeding, and reaching semi-desert in searches for food and water. Nests from February/March. 2–3 eggs. Song, a sibilant warble; calls include *tchew* and *twee* repeated rapidly in a medley.

**Abyssinian Sunbird** (Shining Sunbird)   *Nectarinia habessinica*

**World:** *N. habessinica hellmayri* breeds in Yemen to S Oman. Other races in W Saudi Arabia and E Africa.
**Oman:** Fairly common resident in Dhofar, with seasonal movements.

12.5cm/5in. The *adult male* differs from Palestine Sunbird in its larger size, more green or yellowish-green gloss from nape to mantle, broad scarlet breast-band with an indistinct narrow blue band above it, and different song. The *female* is dark brown above, and brown below with the under tail-coverts occasionally fringed white; the *immature male* has a blackish throat.

Amongst trees and flowering plants, in hills and coastal cultivation, but less gregarious than Palestine Sunbird. Nests from February/March. 2 eggs. Song, a loud bubbling trill (diagnostic), sometimes interspersed with *keeyipipip*, or *wee-ee-ee* or *tchew-chip*.

## WHITE-EYES: Zosteropidae

**World:** 85 species. **Oman:** 1 species (breeding).

**White-breasted White-eye**   *Zosterops abyssinica*

**World:** *Z. abyssinica arabs* breeds from W Saudi Arabia to S Oman. Other races in E Africa and Socotra.
**Oman:** Fairly common resident in Dhofar, with seasonal movements.

11.5cm/4½in. Olive-green above, with a distinct white eye-ring of small feathers, the forehead often yellow with pollen; the chin, throat and under tail-coverts are pale yellow, the breast and belly buffish-white to grey.

In trees and bushes in mountains and valleys, wandering more widely in winter. Usually in pairs or active, agile, noisy foraging parties, sometimes with sunbirds. Appears to feed mainly on insects, taken in vegetation and on the ground. The flight is fast and bobbing. Nest (not yet described in Arabia) is probably from April/May, a flimsy cup of mosses, etc., in a fork of a bush or tree. Song, a sibilant trill; calls, a rapid high-pitched *tsee-tsee-tsee*, or *tsseeup*.

Purple Sunbird

*male* C
*female* B
*male non-breeding* D

Palestine Sunbird

*male* E

*female* F

Abyssinian Sunbird

*male* G
*female* H

White-breasted
White-eye A

Plate 109

265

# ORIOLES: Oriolidae

**World:** 28 species. **Oman:** 1 species.

## Golden Oriole  *Oriolus oriolus*

**World:** *O. o. oriolus* breeds from continental Europe to central Asia, south to NW Africa, NW Iran; migratory to Africa.
**Oman:** Regular passage migrant in small numbers, August–October, and May.

24cm/9½in. The *adult male* is usually brilliant yellow, with black lores, wings and tail, a yellow patch on the wings and broad yellow tips to the outer tail-feathers. The *female* and *immature* are yellowish-green, the wings and tail somewhat darker, and the under-parts pale greyish to white, occasionally yellowish, with fine grey-brown streaks. The bill is reddish or brown.

In trees, where it may be overlooked. The flight is rapid and undulating, characteristically ending in an upward swoop into cover. It feeds on invertebrates and fruit, occasionally taken in large hops on the ground. It comes to water if available.

## SHRIKES: Laniidae                                    Plates 110–111

**World:** 72 species. **Oman:** 8 species (2 breeding). Mostly aggressive carnivorous non-gregarious birds, with strong hooked bill, strong legs and toes, and needle-sharp claws. They hunt invertebrates and small vertebrates, usually in a sudden dash or swoop from an exposed perch, or (in some species) pursuing them amongst vegetation or on the ground; they fly low with glides, swooping up to perch.

## Isabelline Shrike (Red-tailed Shrike)  *Lanius isabellinus*

**World:** Breeds in S central Asia, south to Iran, NW India, in several races. Migratory, reaching Africa, Arabia, India. (Includes **'Rufous Shrike'** *L. i. phoenicuroides*. Sometimes considered as races of Red-backed Shrike *L. collurio* or **Brown Shrike** *L. cristatus*.)
**Oman:** Common and widespread passage migrant, some from July, most from late August; a few over winter; less common on spring passage, February–May.

17cm/6¾in. Rather varied; pale sandy or darker grey-brown above, and whitish below, with an isabelline or rufous crown and nape, a broad dark eye-stripe, a pale supercilium and a rufous tail (often looking dark when closed); some birds have a small white wing-patch. *Female* and *immature* are paler, with inconspicuous brown crescentic marks on the under-parts, and a duller tail.

Amongst scattered trees and bushes, singly but many may occur in the same area on passage; it is more skulking in winter. It will seize food on the ground and occasionally in flight.

## Red-backed Shrike  *Lanius collurio*

**World:** Breeds from W Europe to central Asia, south to Turkey, NW Iran, in several races. Migratory to Africa.
**Oman:** Uncommon passage migrant late August to November; scarce February to May; rarely in other months.

17cm/6¾in. The *male* is distinctive, with blue-grey crown, nape and rump, chestnut mantle, dark flight-feathers without a white patch, a black tail with white sides, and a white supercilium above a broad black eye-stripe; under-parts whitish, tinged with pink. The *female* is uniform rufous-brown above, with less distinct facial marks, the tail dark brown edged with white, and dark crescentic marks on the whitish under-parts. The *immature* is similar, but with the mantle often barred. See Bay-backed Shrike (plate 111).

Amongst scattered trees and bushes, with habits similar to those of Isabelline Shrike.

## Black-headed Bush Shrike  *Tchagra senegala*

**World:** *T. s. percivali* breeds in S Arabia. Other races in Africa.
**Oman:** Fairly common resident in Dhofar.

20cm/8in. Distinctively marked, with a black stripe over the crown from forehead to nape, another through the eye, and a contrasting long bold whitish supercilium; the mantle of soft feathers is dull grey-brown, the wing-coverts and outer primaries chestnut, the rest of the flight-feathers blackish; the tail is long, black, and tipped with white in some individuals; the under-parts are dull greyish.

Skulks in low bushes and trees on mountainsides from near sea-level, occasionally emerging to feed amongst vegetation or on the ground, on fruit, insects, etc. The nest, from May, is a small roughly lined cup of vegetable stems in the fork of a low tree. 2–3 eggs, whitish, blotched reddish or brown. Usually heard before seen, it has a wide variety of loud prolonged whistles, *chreeo-chreeo-chreeo* or *tsuke-tsuke-tsuke* and *vichree-vichree-vichree*, etc., also a low swearing alarm.

Plate 110

### Lesser Grey Shrike    *Lanius minor*

**World:** *L. m. turanicus* breeds in central Asia, south to N and W Iran; migratory, probably to S Africa. Another race in W Eurasia.

**Oman:** Scarce and irregular passage migrant between July and November, rarely March–June.

20cm/8in. The *adult male* differs from the Great Grey Shrike in smaller size, black forehead, lack of pale supercilium, broader white wing-bar and pinkish tinge on white under-parts. The *female* and the buffish-grey *immature* lack a fully developed black forehead and resemble Great Grey, but have relatively longer wings, a shorter tail and stouter bill.

Habitat similar to Great Grey. Perches prominently, pouncing on invertebrate prey, but rarely pursuing it.

### Great Grey Shrike    *Lanius excubitor*

**World:** Breeds in N America, Eurasia, northern Africa, Arabia, northern India, in many races. Sedentary or migratory.

**Oman:** Common breeding resident *(L. e. aucheri)*; passage migrant and winter visitor between July and March *(aucheri, pallidirostris* and *lahtora)*.

*L. e. aucheri* 24cm/9½in. A large shrike with pale grey upper-parts and white under-parts tinged with grey; the forehead is grey and there is a narrow white supercilium above the black mask (compare Lesser Grey Shrike). The wings are black with a prominent white wing-bar (appearing as two patches on the closed wing), and the long graduated tail is black with white outer-feathers. The *immature* is pale grey tinged with isabelline above, and creamy-white below; it has dark brown ear-coverts, pale edges to the wing-feathers and a brownish bill.

Trees in open semi-desert or edges of cultivation or copses, singly or in pairs. Widespread, wary but perching prominently, flying low down and swooping up to perch again, or dropping on or chasing prey. The nest, from January, is a lined cup in a larger mass of twigs in a bush or tree. Eggs 3–6, mostly pale greenish with brown blotches. Song, a medley of warblings and harsher notes; call, a hard ringing double note *trip-trip* or *tew-dew*, etc.

### Bay-backed Shrike    *Lanius vittatus*

**World:** Breeds in SE Iran, Afghanistan, India. Sedentary, locally migratory, occasionally to UAE.

**Oman:** Vagrant (one seen, Batinah, 29 April 1979).

18cm/7in. More colourful than Red-backed, with pale grey head and nape, white forehead, black band across lower forehead to ear-coverts, chestnut-maroon mantle, whitish or greyish rump, the wings and tail blackish with a white wing-patch, and white outer tail-feathers; the under-parts whitish, with pinkish on breast and flanks. The *immature* is greyer, with a reddish tail.

Habits similar to those of Great Grey Shrike.

### Woodchat Shrike    *Lanius senator*

**World:** *L. s. niloticus* breeds in E Asia Minor and Transcaspia, south from Palestine to Iran; migratory to Africa.

**Oman:** Irregular passage migrant in small numbers, between February and April in some years.

17cm/6¾in. A distinctive black-and-white shrike with chestnut crown and nape, black from forehead to ear-coverts and on the back, wings and tail, white scapulars forming a V on the back, a white wing-patch and a white rump; it is creamy-white below. The *female* is duller, with paler chestnut crown and nape and often some white on the forehead. The *immature* is browner and barred.

In and on trees, fences, etc., at cultivation.

### Masked Shrike    *Lanius nubicus*

**World:** Breeds from SE Europe, Turkey to Palestine, Iraq, W Iran. Migratory to Africa.

**Oman:** Scarce passage migrant between March and May (seven records from 1967).

17cm/6¾in. A slim black-and-white shrike, with broad white forehead and supercilium, orange-rufous flanks and black rump (white in Woodchat). The *female* is browner above.

Keeps more to cover in or under trees than Woodchat, taking insects in flight and on the ground.

Lesser Grey Shrike

*adult male* A

*immature* B

Great Grey Shrike C

Bay-backed Shrike D

Woodchat Shrike

*adult male* G

*immature* H

Masked Shrike

*male* F
*female* E

Plate 111                                                                                                269

# CROWS: Corvidae

**World:** 116 species. **Oman:** 3 species (resident). Quite large, highly intelligent birds, including typical crows, jays, magpies, nutcrackers and choughs, distributed almost worldwide. Typical crows are mostly black, some glossed or with pale marks, the sexes similar. The bills are fairly long and stout, often with a hooked tip, the nostrils protected by bristles. The legs and toes are strong, and they can walk well. Very versatile feeders, foraging mainly on the ground, and mostly omnivorous, taking carrion, other birds and eggs, grain, fruit, invertebrates, etc. Most drink daily. The flight is strong, and some often soar. Most are gregarious, and some nest colonially and roost communally. The nest is a large twig structure on a tree, cliff or artifact. The food is carried in the throat to the incubating female and to young. Many appear to mate for life. Their vocabulary is extensive.

## House Crow     *Corvus splendens*

House Crow  A

**World:** Breeds from India to SE Asia, in several races; introduced to parts of Arabian Gulf, Arabia, Africa, Malay peninsula. Sedentary, with some cold-weather movements.
**Oman:** Common resident in parts of Musandam, along Batinah to Muscat, and at Qurayat, occasionally to Masirah; most resemble *C. s. zugmayeri* or intergrades with *C. s. splendens*.

43cm/17in. A medium-sized crow with large glossy black mask (from crown to lower throat in some), black wings and tail, blackish back and belly, and contrasting pale pinkish-grey from nape and hind-neck to lower breast. The *immature* has the pale parts darker and black parts browner. It differs from the Brown-necked Raven in its habits, broader and rounder wings, shorter and more square-ended tail and black feet.

Around human habitation and trees nearby, in large, noisy and inquisitive throngs, but in places singly and skulking; always very wary. They visit rubbish, fresh water and beaches, stand on and search camels, etc., for parasites, and harry smaller creatures. Some may have come from India on the rigging of ships (reliably witnessed elsewhere). The flight looks laboured and they seldom soar. The nest, from March, is usually in a fairly large tree, including mangroves, often near others. The eggs, 3–5, are greeny-blue with some olive spots; single-brooded, but many replace losses up to midsummer. Call, a monotonous *caaa*, occasionally high-pitched.

## Fan-tailed Raven     *Corvus rhipidurus*

Fan-tailed Raven  B

**World:** Breeds in S Sahara, E Africa, Near East, Arabia.
**Oman:** Common resident in Dhofar.

47cm/18½in. All-black, with blue to purple sheen, tinged brown with wear. It differs from Brown-necked in smaller size, much broader wings, and shorter tail fanned almost to reach the wings when soaring, turning or landing, with distinctive silhouette. The feet appear pale in flight.

Mountain cliffs, wandering early to feed at rubbish, around habitation, cattle, etc. Will perch on cattle, etc., and have been seen to catch and eat locusts in flight. Fond of soaring; some roost in trees by day on the coast. The nest, from December/January, rarely to June, is on a cliff ledge or in a crevice, singly or colonially. Eggs, 2–4, are similar to those of Brown-necked. Calls include a rather high-pitched, resonant *cruk-cruk*.

## Brown-necked Raven     *Corvus ruficollis*

Brown-necked Raven  C

**World:** *C. r. ruficollis* breeds from Cape Verde Islands, deserts of N and E Africa, Sinai, Palestine, Arabia, S Iran, NW India, north to Transcaspia, Turkestan; sedentary.
**Oman:** Widespread and fairly common resident.

50cm/19½in. All-black except for a blue-and-purple sheen which fades, and a brownish tinge from nape to upper back which becomes more noticeable with wear and is not a reliable character. *Juveniles* lack the brown tinge. The legs are black, appearing pallid in flight. Differs from House Crow in habits, longer, narrower, pointed wings (appearing falcon-like in swift glides), longer graduated tail; from Fan-tailed also in size and tail.

Desert interior, and from coast and inshore islands to mountain-tops, also into marginal cultivation. Often singly and in pairs, it will fly long distances to scavenge and drink, when congregations of hundreds occur locally; it will stand on camels, etc., like other corvids. It soars freely and has acrobatic displays. Nest from February, rarely to June, singly on desert trees and cliffs. Eggs, 2–4, blue to greenish, covered with brownish speckles. Calls include far-reaching resonant *curlowk-curlowk*, short *cruk-cruk*, deep growling *kurark-kurark* and varied conversational notes.

Plate 112

# STARLINGS: Sturnidae

**World:** 110 species. **Oman:** 4 species (1 resident). Medium-sized robust birds with strong bill and legs. Mostly dark and glossy, some are colourful or have head-wattles. Very gregarious. They walk and run, and the flight is distinctive, with frequent glides. They whistle and mimic sounds.

**Starling**     *Sturnus vulgaris*

Starling

**World:** Breeds from Europe to central Asia, south to Azores, Turkey, Iran, NW India, in many races. Migratory, reaching N Africa, Arabia, northern India. Introduced to N America, S Africa, Australasia.
**Oman:** Passage migrant and winter visitor in most years, in irregular numbers October–March, rarely August and April.

21.5cm/8½in. Dark, with a short square tail, longish bill and short pointed wings. *Adult (summer)* is blackish, glossed green to purple, with a yellow bill. In *autumn* rather spotted (buff tips to feathers), the bill darker.

*summer* B<br>*S.v. poltaratskyi winter* A

Widespread and shy, visiting rubbish, cultivation, water and trees, in small parties and flocks. Calls, mostly at communal roosts, a grating *cheerr*, whistles and clicks.

**Wattled Starling**     *Creatophora cineracea*

Wattled Starling

**World:** Breeds in S and E Africa. An irregular or irruptive local migrant, which has occurred in S Arabia.
**Oman:** Irregular visitor to Dhofar and Masirah, occasionally into desert, in small numbers, between June and January.

21.5cm/8½in. It is grey-brown above, with a whitish rump and sandy-buff below, with a paler belly. *Male (breeding)* has contrasting glossy black flight-feathers and tail, a varied white wing-patch (primary coverts), the head bare and black with black wattles on head and throat, and yellow skin from the eyes to the hind-crown. In *autumn* the head becomes feathered. *Female* and *immature* are browner; they lack the wing-patch but have a whiter rump.

*adult male* C<br>*immature* D

Short grass and scrub, perching on trees. Often in shy restless flocks, usually following locusts, but will take other invertebrates, fruit, etc. Rather silent, but has a squeaky whistle.

**Rose-coloured Starling**     *Sturnus roseus*

Rose-coloured Starling

**World:** Breeds in SE Europe to SW Asia, south to Turkey, Lebanon, Iran. Migratory to India.
**Oman:** Passage migrant and winter visitor between August and April in small irregular numbers.

21.5cm/8½in. The distinctive pale rose body contrasts with glossy blue-black head, crest and neck, black wings and tail. The *immature* is dull brown above, and buffish below with a streaked breast; it differs from the Starling in its paler colours, from the Wattled Starling in the lack of a pale rump.

*adult* E<br>*immature* F

In trees, grass and cultivation, feeding on locusts, fruit, etc. It has a chattering and warbling song.

**Tristram's Grackle**     *Onychognathus tristramii*

Tristram's Grackle

**World:** Breeds from Palestine and Jordan, south to Sinai, S Yemen, S Oman.
**Oman:** Fairly common resident in Dhofar; once reported near Muscat, 4 May 1972.

28cm/11in. A dark starling, with a pale chestnut patch in the pointed wings (inner primaries) visible as a narrow bar at rest. The *male* is black with a violet-blue gloss. The *female* and *immature* have less gloss, and the head and neck to upper breast greyish and streaked. See Blackbird (plate 97).

*adult* G<br>*immature* H

Bare mountain and coastal cliffs, wandering widely amongst vegetation, cattle and rubbish, down to coastal plains and desert margin. Usually in pairs or flocks, sometimes quite tame. It feeds mostly on fruit and invertebrates. The nest, from February, is of twigs, rubbish, hair, etc., sparsely lined, in a crevice or cave, or on a ledge, singly or near others. Eggs, 3–4, are pale blue with reddish speckles. Call, a loud musical whistle *sweee-to* and *tsoowheeo*.

[**Brahminy Mynah**     *Sturnus pagodarum*                    (Not illustrated)

Breeds in India, mainly resident but has marked seasonal movements. One near Muscat 17 November to 2 December 1977, probably an escape. 22cm/8½in. Grey above except for glossy black from forehead to crest at nape; rounded black wings, brown tail edged with white; reddish-pink or fawn below, with white wing-linings; yellow legs and tip of bill. Open trees and gardens. It has an undulating flight.]

[**Common Mynah**     *Acridotheres tristis*                    (Not illustrated)

Breeds from Turkestan, SE Iran, to Far East; introduced widely into southern hemisphere; said to occur as a naturalized escape at Al Ain, UAE. 23cm/9in. Dark brown, with glossy black head and a white wing-patch, conspicuous in flight; yellow orbital skin, bill and legs.]

Plate 113

# SPARROWS: Passeridae

**World:** 37 species. **Oman:** 4 species (2 breeding). Small, thick-billed, mostly gregarious birds, widespread in the world and sometimes introduced. Most species are drab, some with black, white or yellow, the males usually brighter, but not as bright as some superficially similar weavers (Ploceidae) and weaver-finches (Estrildidae) (plate 115).

## Yellow-throated Sparrow    *Petronia xanthocollis*

Yellow-throated Sparrow A

**World:** Breeds from S Iraq, S Iran, eastern UAE, N Oman to India, in two races. Sedentary and migratory.
**Oman:** Breeding summer visitor and passage migrant in N Oman, March–October, widespread in small numbers (*P. x. transfuga* from NW India); on Masirah a few regularly on passage, September–November and March–April, once August; also seen at Ra's al Hadd in September (race?).

14cm/5½in. An unstreaked sandy-brown sparrow, somewhat similar to the Pale Rock Sparrow, but with a chestnut wing-patch and double white wing-bar, pale throat with an indistinct yellow patch and, when *breeding*, a black bill. The *female* has a paler throat, indistinct wing-markings and a brownish bill. The *immature* has a pale pinkish bill. See House Sparrow.

Old trees in semi-desert, occasionally in cultivation. It is sometimes difficult to see in cover unless it calls, and it can be overlooked as House Sparrow, with which it roosts. It feeds on seeds, invertebrates and nectar. It migrates in small flocks, dispersing to nest rather locally, from April, in holes in trees. The eggs, 3–4, are pale, variably marked with brown. The song is more mellow and pleasant than that of House Sparrow, a loud repeated *chilp-chalp*, which is distinctive when known.

## Spanish Sparrow    *Passer hispaniolensis*

Spanish Sparrow B

**World:** *P. h. transcaspicus* breeds in Turkey, Caucasus, Iran, Transcaspia to Turkestan, Afghanistan; sedentary and migratory. Another race in Mediterranean region.
**Oman:** Vagrant or very irregular winter visitor to N Oman and Masirah, between November and March in very small numbers (reported four times between 1963 and 1979).

14.5cm/5¾in. The *male* differs from the House Sparrow in the bright chestnut crown and nape, darker back, more extensive black bib reaching the breast, and boldly streaked flanks. The *females* and *young* are very similar to House Sparrow, but have darker backs and indistinct streaks below.

Habits similar to those of House Sparrow, with which it occasionally associates.

## House Sparrow    *Passer domesticus*

House Sparrow

**World:** Breeds in Eurasia, S to northern Africa, Arabia, Iran, India, in many races. Sedentary and migratory. Introduced into many other parts of the world.
**Oman:** Locally common resident in Oman, apparently absent from south of Sur to E Hadhramaut.

*P. d. indicus* (=*hufufae*), 14.5cm/5¾in. The *male* has a grey crown, brown sides to the nape, white face, black throat (partly concealed in winter), grey rump, white wing-bar; dull greyish under-parts. The *female* and *young* are duller brown above, with a pale supercilium, and they lack the grey, black and white.

*male* C

*female* D

Near habitation, cultivation and rubbish. In parties, flocking at roosts and after breeding. A cheeky, wary companion. Perches in trees, etc., hops along the ground, and takes seeds, insects, etc., there and from crops. The nest, from February (sometimes earlier), is an untidy ball of straw, string, etc., often close to others, in trees, pylons, buildings and rock crevices. Eggs, 3–4, pale, variably marked with brown. It has a chirruping *chee-ip* and a monotonous series of chirps and cheeps.

## Pale Rock Sparrow    *Petronia brachydactyla*

Pale Rock Sparrow E

**World:** Breeds in Lebanon, Syria, Armenia, Transcaspia, Iran. Migratory, reaching E Africa.
**Oman:** Passage migrant, late August to October, and February to early April, not uncommon, probably regular and overlooked.

14cm/5½in. A plain sandy-brown sparrow, with pale fringes on the wing-feathers, a pale supercilium, and white spots on the tips of the outer tail-feathers, visible when spread; the under-parts are pale to whitish.

Open grassy and stony semi-desert, sometimes with bushes, visiting crops and water. One report of an incomplete straw nest built in Dhofar on 28 February 1979. The best character is its call, a soft purr or trill; the song (heard from birds on the ground at Salalah on 13 March 1978) is a whistle and cicada-like trill, *tee-zeeze*.

Plate 114

# WEAVERS: Ploceidae

**World:** 91 species. **Oman:** 1 species (resident). Stocky, sparrow-like birds, with coloured or black plumage in breeding males. They build strong domed nests, and have elaborate displays.

**Rüppell's Weaver**    *Ploceus galbula*

Rüppell's Weaver

**World:** Breeds in E Africa, SW Arabia to S Oman.
**Oman:** Very local breeding resident in Dhofar, with local movements.

*male breeding* A
*female* B

14cm/5½in. The *male (breeding)* is unmistakable. The *female, young* and *male after breeding* are olive-brown above, with dark streaks and mostly yellow fringes to wings and tail, the under-parts are buff and white, the bill brown; in this plumage they have been confused with sparrows.

Coastal cultivation and hills, with trees. Usually in parties, but in large roosts after breeding. The nest, March–September, singly or colonially, is of straw and strips of leaf neatly woven into globular shapes with side or bottom entrance, suspended from or attached to a branch, leaf or another nest; part-nests may be built by the male at any season, accompanied by wing-shivering displays. Eggs, 2–4, usually 3, pinkish, green or blue marked with brown, some replaced by Didric Cuckoo (plate 73). Song, a prolonged wheezy *tzeeeg* and varied rattling noises, one like paper tearing; calls, a harsh *tzig*, *zwik* and a sibilant chatter.

# WEAVER-FINCHES: Estrildidae

**World:** 125 species. **Oman:** 2 species (resident). Small to very small finch-like seed-eaters, mostly very social. Often brightly coloured; munias are duller. Build a fixed ball-nest of fine grasses, cotton, feathers, etc., with a side entrance, for the 4–6 white eggs, or for roosting.

**African Silverbill**    *Euodice cantans*

African Silverbill C

**World:** *E. c. orientalis* breeds in E Africa and S Arabia. Another race from W Africa to Sudan. (Sometimes placed in genus *Lonchura* and treated as a race of *malabarica*).
**Oman:** Common breeding resident in Dhofar, with irregular and seasonal movements.

10cm/4in. A very small and rather dull seed-eater. The upper-parts are brown with faint dark vermiculations, the darker primaries form a dark line with the tail when closed, the rump, upper tail-coverts and tail are very dark brown (but occasionally tinged white, pink or cinnamon), the tail graduated to a point; the cheeks and under-parts are creamy-white with slight dark spots on the chin; the bill is metallic grey. The *juvenile* has pale feather-fringes and a shorter tail.

Coastal and semi-desert trees and cultivation. Gregarious and not shy, it roams in pairs and parties, feeding on small seeds and invertebrates, and congregates in roosts which are large in autumn. The nest, April–October, is in a tree, 2–4m above ground, occasionally in an old weaver nest. The song is a high-pitched trill of rapidly repeated single then double notes, descending then rising in each phrase; the calls are somewhat similar to those of Indian Silverbill.

**Indian Silverbill** (White-throated Munia)    *Euodice malabarica*

Indian Silverbill D

**World:** Breeds in E Arabia, SE Iran to India, Sri Lanka.
**Oman:** Fairly common and widespread in N Oman (not Masirah), with irregular and seasonal movements.

10cm/4in. It differs from African Silverbill in its white rump and upper tail-coverts and in its usual lack of vermiculations and chin-spots.

In semi-desert trees and cultivation, from coast to 2,000m, with behaviour similar to that of African Silverbill. It nests from February in widely dispersed localities. The song is a short trill; the calls, a rapid high-pitched *chirrup* sounding like *zip*, repeated in flight, also a harsh *tchwit* (alarm), an excited *trititit* and conversational *seesip seesip*.

**[Arabian Waxbill**    *Estrilda rufibarba*    (Not illustrated)

Breeds in SW Arabia, E to the Hadhramaut and may wander to Dhofar; it could be confused with escaped caged birds of other species. 10cm/4in. Grey-brown above and buff below, with fine dark bars and a crimson line from bill to behind ear; the wings and graduated tail are dark. A shy, gregarious species.]

Plate 115

# FINCHES: Fringillidae                                    Plates 116 and 117

**World:** 125 species. **Oman:** 5 species. Arboreal birds with notched tail, and strong, stout grooved bill of varied shapes for extracting, holding and crushing hard seeds and shelling them with the aid of the tongue. Many species are colourful, particularly the males. Often gregarious, with undulating flight and well developed flight-call. Sub-family Fringillinae (chaffinches and Brambling) have no crop. The Carduelinae (122 species) include serins, grosbeaks, goldfinches, siskins, linnets, trumpeter finches, rosefinches, etc., some of which occur or might occur in Oman, and care is required in identifying them.

## [Siskin    *Carduelis spinus*                                        Siskin

**World:** Breeds erratically in W Eurasia, south to N Iran and in E Asia. Nomadic in winter, irregular and occasionally irruptive; a winter vagrant to Arabian Gulf.
**Oman:** Not yet reported.

12cm/4¾in. A small yellow-green finch. The *male* has a black crown and chin, and yellow rump, wing-bar and sides of tail. The *female* and *young* are duller, greyer, less yellow, and have streaked under-parts; they differ from serins in having yellow sides to the tail.

*adult male* B
*immature* A

It feeds in trees on seeds and berries.]

## Goldfinch    *Carduelis carduelis*                                Goldfinch C

**World:** Breeds from Azores and Europe to central Asia, south to the Canaries, northern Africa, Near East, Iran, in several races. Partial migrant, reaching N Sinai, Iraq, Kuwait, S Iran; vagrant to Bahrain.
**Oman:** Vagrant (one reported, Batinah, 26 April 1979).

12cm/4¾in. The *adults* have a distinctive pattern and call, with a striking head-pattern of red, white and black (western races), or red and grey (eastern races), black wings with a broad yellow wing-bar, black tail with white tips, and a pale rump and under-parts. The *immature* is similar but has buff tips to the wing-feathers and tail. The slender and pointed bill is pale with a dark tip.

It feeds on the seed-heads of low plants, and perches on trees. Its flight is more buoyant and undulating than that of most finches; the flight-call is a distinctive, rapid and liquid *tswitt-witt-witt.*

## Brambling    *Fringilla montifringilla*                              Brambling

**World:** Breeds from Norway across Eurasia. Highly migratory, reaching Mediterranean region, Iran, NW India, SE Asia, E Arabia.
**Oman:** Winter vagrant to N Oman (seen singly 28 November 1976, 16 December 1977, 1 February 1980), and Masirah (about four between 24 November and 8 December 1975).

14.5cm/5¾in. Sparrow-sized, the *male (breeding)* has a glossy black head and mantle, bright orange-buff shoulder-patches and breast, a white rump (distinctive in flight), and white and orange-buff wing-bars. The autumn *male*, *female* and *young* have a mottled brown head and mantle. It is the northern representative of the **Chaffinch** *F. coelebs* [15cm/6in, breeds from W Europe to central Asia, south to northern Africa, N Iran; northern birds migrate and have straggled to the Arabian Gulf, not Oman], and it differs from that species in its black or brown head, white rump, orange-buff markings and more distinctly notched black tail.

*male spring* E
*female winter* D

It feeds on seeds on the ground (like the Chaffinch), flying into trees if disturbed. Flight-call, a harsh *tsweek* and a soft *chuk-chuk-chuk.*

Plate 116

**Golden-winged Grosbeak**    *Rhyncostruthus socotranus*

Golden-winged Grosbeak

**World:** A monotypic genus. *R. s. percivali* (incl. *yemenensis*) breeds from SW Arabia to S Oman. Other races in Somalia and Socotra.
**Oman:** Uncommon breeding resident in Dhofar.

14cm/5½in. A distinctive, robust finch of the mountains. The *adult male's* crown is chocolate brown, shading to the brown or isabelline of the mantle and the grey rump; there is some black round the bill (forehead, lores, throat) and a contrasting white cheek-patch; the wings and tail are black with bright yellow fringes; the breast is chestnut, the rest of the under-parts greyish. The *female* is similar, but smaller and duller, and lacks the black forehead. The *immature* is streaked.

*male spring* A

*immature* B

Wooded and rocky hillsides and ravines, singly, in pairs and in roaming winter parties. It perches sparrow-like on the tops of trees and bushes, yet is surprisingly unobtrusive. It feeds on buds, fruit and seeds. In flight it appears robust, with a short tail. The nest and eggs of the species are undescribed. Song, from late February and March, a jingle of liquid notes and *kwink kwink kwink*, interspersed with clear fluty notes, from a tree-top and in occasional gliding flight; calls include a distinct fluty *booo-peep* (one or the other note pitched much higher), *seed-loo*, *wheep*, a trill and a chirp.

**Scarlet Rosefinch** (Scarlet Grosbeak or Common Rosefinch)    *Carpodacus erythrinus*

Scarlet Rosefinch

**World:** Breeds from NE Europe across Asia, south to Caucasus, N Iran, Afghanistan, Himalayas, Mongolia, in several races. Migratory to India, SE Asia, also reaching E Arabia.
**Oman:** Autumn passage migrant in very small numbers, September–November, occasionally December; *C. e. kubanensis* has been provisionally identified from Masirah.

14.5cm/5¾in. The *adult males* have the head, rump and breast crimson of varied intensity, the tail and wings browner with pinkish fringes, and two pale wing-bars (tips of coverts); the rest of the under-parts are whitish, and the legs and stubby bill are brown. The *female* and *young* are very dull, being brownish, with a streaked throat, heavily streaked breast, pale belly, a double pale wing-bar and a black beady eye.

*male* C

*female* D

In open scrub desert, trees, bushes and cultivation. Call, a distinctive *whee-ee* or *too-ee*.

**Trumpeter Finch**    *Bucanetes githagineus*

Trumpeter Finch

**World:** *B. g. crassirostris* breeds in Sinai, Palestine, N and central Arabia, southern Transcaspia, Iran to NW India; sedentary and locally migratory. Other races in the Canaries, NW and NE Africa, S Spain. (Sometimes placed in the genus *Rhodopechys*).
**Oman:** Status uncertain; reported very occasionally in N Oman, not Masirah, between October and March, once in May and July; probably a breeding resident and a possible winter visitor.

12.5cm/5in. The *male (breeding)* is tinged rosy, with a greyish head, grey-brown mantle and rosy fringes to the black wing- and tail-feathers; pale rosy under-parts, and a stout scarlet or orange bill. In *autumn* the *male* becomes less rosy and the bill becomes dull yellow. The *female* lacks the grey on the head and is less rosy, particularly in *winter*.

*male* E

*female* F

Arid hills, plateaux, rocky slopes and ravines, coming to water in the morning and evening. Normally in pairs or small parties, occasionally singly. It feeds on the ground and perches upright on rocks. The nest (in SW Arabia) is a cup of grass in a rock crevice, under rocks, or in the shelter of bushes. The call is a high-pitched nasal bray *zaa-aaa*, like a child's trumpet; the song is a buzzing note with occasional twittering.

Plate 117

## BUNTINGS: Emberizidae, sub-family Emberizinae                    Plates 118–120

**World:** 278 species. **Oman:** At least 8 species (2 resident). A large varied group of small Old World buntings (40 species) and American sparrows. The males are usually brighter-coloured than the females, which are often drab and difficult to identify. Most differ from finches in their longer tail and slighter build. The bill is short and stout for cracking small seeds, obtained mainly on the ground; berries are also eaten, and like many granivorous species they feed insects to the young. The flight is strongly undulating. Strictly territorial when nesting, they are gregarious at other times. Northern species are migratory, and mixed winter flocks may roam widely. The nest is cup-shaped, sometimes domed, and is placed on or near the ground.

**House Bunting** (Striped Bunting)    *Emberiza striolata*                    House Bunting

**World:** *E. s. striolata* breeds in N Sudan, Sinai, Arabia, SE Iran, northern India. Other races in N and E Africa.
**Oman:** Local breeding resident with seasonal movements; also a scarce autumn migrant and winter visitor.

14cm/5½in. A small unobtrusive bunting, with a striped head and uniform chestnut shoulder-patch.    *male* A
The *adult male's* head is dark, usually streaked white or buff at the sides, the mantle is tawny with dark streaks, the wing-coverts and fringes of the flight-feathers are chestnut, and the tail is dark with tawny    *female* B
outer edges; the chin, throat and upper breast are grey-brown with greyish-white mottling, the rest of the under-parts are tawny chestnut. The *female* and *young* are duller grey-brown with dark streaks and indistinct head-streaks. It differs from the Cinnamon-breasted Rock Bunting (of Dhofar) in the uniform chestnut shoulder-patch and call, also in the lack of a pale streak in the centre of the *male's* crown.

Breeds on arid rocky hillsides from sea-level to 2,500m, wandering in parties on plains when not breeding. Not very shy, it perches occasionally in small trees, and it comes frequently to water. The nest, from late January to June (to October on high ground), is in a rock crevice. Eggs, 2–3, white to pale blue-green, spotted red or brownish. Song, a loud *tsee skwitchi witchi wee*; the flight-call is a quiet *terze*.

**Cinnamon-breasted Rock Bunting**    *Emberiza tahapisi*                    Cinnamon-breasted
Rock Bunting

**World:** *E. t. arabica* breeds from SW Arabia to S Oman. Other races in Africa and Socotra.
**Oman:** Common local breeding resident in Dhofar, with seasonal movements.

14cm/5½in. A small dark bunting. The *adult male* is distinctive, with black-and-white striped head,    *male* C
dark-streaked mantle, black wings with tawny feather-fringes, and black tail; it has a black or blue-grey bib, and the rest of the under-parts are deep cinnamon-chestnut; in flight the head appears pale,    *female* D
the body dark and the tail black. The *female* is duller, and the head is brown with buffish stripes (absent in *immatures*). It differs from the House Bunting (whose range partly overlaps in Dhofar) in its calls, bolder colours of the *male*, and the lack of a uniform chestnut shoulder-patch. [**Rock Bunting** *E. cia* is much larger, 16cm/6¼in, and is not known south of Lebanon or Iran.]

Rocky hillsides, often with much vegetation and trees; it occasionally wanders to the plains, and comes to water frequently during the day. It feeds in loose parties on open ground like the House Bunting, but in less arid situations. Not shy, but if disturbed will fly to a bare rock. The nest, from February/March and again from September, is a frail lined cup of grasses under cover of boulders or very low in a bush. The 2–4 eggs are very similar to those of House Bunting. Song, mostly February–April and August–November, is a reedy *tistisTEWstiziki* or *tititita-pisi*, from tree-top or rock; the contact note is a distinctive soft mewing *crurwaow*, also *tzi-wer-wer*.

**[Cinereous Bunting**    *Emberiza cineracea*                    (Not illustrated)

**World:** Breeds in Turkey, also SW Iran. A scarce and little-known migrant, reaching E Africa, SW Arabia, Arabian Gulf E to the Tunb Islands (rarely).
**Oman:** A possible vagrant, not yet reported.

*E. c. semenowi* (in Iran). 16.5cm/6½in. The *male* is greyish, with a dark olive-yellow head, pale yellow eye-ring, and a bright yellow throat when *breeding;* the rest of the upper-parts are olive-grey with dark streaks, and there is white on the outer tail-feathers; it is pale yellow below, with darker olive breast and flanks. The *female* is tinged olive, with browner head and dark-streaked breast.

Usually found on broken rocky ground with short vegetation.]

Plate 118

**Rustic Bunting**   *Emberiza rustica*

**World:** *E. r. rustica* breeds across N Eurasia; migratory to Japan and E China, vagrant to Turkey, W Europe, E Arabia. Another race in extreme NE Asia.
**Oman:** Vagrant (singles seen on Masirah, 26 October 1975, 15 November 1974, 14 November 1979).

14.5cm/5¾in. A small restless bunting, with very white under-parts with rusty spots; the crown-feathers are often raised to give a slightly crested effect. The *male (breeding)* has a black head (compare Reed Bunting), broad white eye-stripe and white throat; the rest of the upper-parts are chestnut-brown with dark streaks, and the outer tail-feathers are white; it is very white below, with large rusty spots across the breast and on the flanks. The *female* and *winter male* have mottled brown instead of black on the head; they differ from the Reed Bunting in the rusty spots on the under-parts.

Trees or open country. Call, a sharp *tic, tic* or *tsit, tsit.*

**Little Bunting**   *Emberiza pusilla*

**World:** Breeds from NE Europe across N Eurasia. Migratory to SE Asia, E India; vagrant to W Europe, Near East, Iran, Arabian Gulf.
**Oman:** Vagrant (single birds seen on Masirah, 19 October and 3–6 November 1975).

13.5cm/5¼in. A very small dull bunting, reminiscent of a small compact short-legged female Reed Bunting. The *male* differs in the rufous-chestnut cheeks and centre of the crown, the latter bordered by dark stripes, and in duller under-parts with finer black (not rusty) streaks. The *female* and *young* differ in dull chestnut cheeks and the fact that the olive-brown lesser wing-coverts lack any trace of chestnut.

It feeds mainly on the ground and has a sharp *zik* or *pwik* call.

**[Reed Bunting**   *Emberiza schoeniclus*   (Not illustrated)

**World:** Breeds across Eurasia, south to Syria, N Iran (irregularly). Sedentary and migratory, reaching Iran, NW India, vagrant to Arabian Gulf.
**Oman:** Not reported.

15cm/6in. The *male (breeding)* has a black head and throat, white collar, moustachial-streak and outer tail-feathers, and greyish-white under-parts; in *winter* the crown is like the mantle, rufous-brown with black streaks. The *female* and *young* are brown like the *winter male,* with bright chestnut lesser wing-coverts, pale buff supercilium and black-and-white moustachial-streaks; the under-parts are buffish, with narrow black and brown streaks on the sides of the breast and flanks.

Marshes, cultivation, etc. Calls include a sharp *chink* and a shrill *tseep.*]

**Ortolan Bunting**   *Emberiza hortulana*

**World:** Breeds from Europe to central Asia, south to Palestine, N Iran. Migratory, reaching W, N and E Africa and Arabia.
**Oman:** Passage migrant in very small numbers, April (rarely February), and September to early November.

15.5cm/6½in. The *adult male (breeding)* is distinguished by the combination of yellow throat and buffish-chestnut under-parts; it has a grey-green head and breast-band, a boldly streaked mantle, a yellow throat with an olive moustachial-stripe at the sides, and a yellowish eye-ring; the lower breast and belly are buffish-chestnut, and the bill and legs are orange. The *female* is browner, with streaking on the head, a paler throat, and streaked breast without the grey-green band. The *immature* is more heavily streaked on head and mantle (blackish feather-centres), the moustachial-streak and eye-ring are present but indistinct, the throat is buffish-white spotted with brown, the breast is heavily streaked and the belly is very pale chestnut; the bill and legs are pale pinkish.

Open desert, hillsides, edges of cultivation. It feeds on the ground, usually in small parties. Calls, a sharp *tsip*, *twick* or *tsee-ip*, and a liquid *pwit* given in flight.

Plate 119

**Yellow-breasted Bunting**  *Emberiza aureola*

**World:** *E. a. aureola* breeds from NE Europe across northern Eurasia; migratory, reaching N and E India, SE Asia, and has occurred in Iraq, Iran, Arabian Gulf. Another race in Far East.
**Oman:** Vagrant or accidental (4, Batinah, 10 August 1977; on Masirah, the first records in Arabia, a total of 5 between 11 September and 16 December 1974. Other reports of 'Yellowhammer' may have been this species).

14cm/5½in. The smallest bunting with yellow under-parts in Oman. The *male (breeding)* has a black mask, rich chestnut upper-parts, white wing-patch (sometimes also a bar) and a diagnostic narrow dark chestnut breast-band; there are some chestnut streaks on the flanks and some white on the outer tail-feathers; in *winter* the mask is browner and the back paler tawny. The *female* and *young* are tawny-brown above, heavily streaked with black, with a white wing-bar in flight, bold brown crown-stripes with a pale centre, pale supercilium and brown face; the under-parts plain yellowish except for the buff and dark-streaked flanks and sides of breast; they differ from **Yellowhammer** *E. citrinella* [16.5cm/6½in, breeds from Europe to S Asia; partly migratory, reaching Iraq not Arabia] in that species' larger size, bold chestnut rump, indistinct yellowish head-pattern, heavily streaked breast and flanks, lack of white wing-bar and more conspicuous white outer tail-feathers.

*adult male* B

*first winter* A

In open country with scrub, singly or in parties. Call, a short quiet *zi(p)*.


**Corn Bunting**  *Miliaria calandra*

Corn Bunting C

**World:** *E. c. buturlini* breeds from Syria, N Iraq to Turkestan, south to Iran: sedentary and migratory, reaching Sinai, Arabian Gulf, N & E Arabia. Another race west to Europe and the Mediterranean.
**Oman:** Uncommon passage migrant and winter visitor between November and February; rarely into summer.

18cm/7in. The sexes are similar, and though lacking outstanding features it is noticeably large and stocky, with a large round head and stubby bill; it has dull grey-brown plumage with a dark face, and no white outer tail-feathers.

It perches on trees, fences, wires, etc., near scrub and cultivation, usually in parties; and it flies down with dangling legs to feed and hop on the ground. The calls include a long *kwit* or *pit* or *kwit-it-it*; the song (very rarely heard in winter) is like the rattling of a bunch of keys.


**Black-headed Bunting**  *Emberiza melanocephala*

Black-headed Bunting

**World:** Breeds from SE Europe to SW Russia (Volga and Caucasus), south to Palestine, and to Iran, where it hybridizes with **Red-headed Bunting** *E. bruniceps* in the east. Migratory to India, and occurs in Arabian Gulf.
**Oman:** Passage migrant, from August (rarely July) to October (rarely December), and in April; scarce except on Masirah where it is sometimes fairly common.

16.5cm/6½in. A fairly large bunting with yellow under-parts. The *male (breeding)* has a black head, narrow yellow collar, chestnut mantle and sides of breast and rump, darker white-fringed wings and dark tail without white. In *winter* the head is brown, the feathers of the upper-parts with paler fringes, the yellow under-parts less bright. The *female* and *young* are brown above with dark streaks; the under-parts are pale buffish, yellower on the *female's* under tail-coverts. The *male* lacks the breast-band and white outer tail-feathers of Yellow-breasted Bunting and the *female* differs in its paler unstreaked under-parts.

*adult male* D

*female* E

In trees, cultivation and scrub. Call, *zitt* or *zee*.

286

Plate 120

287

# Check List of the birds of Oman

All species at present admitted to the Oman List are listed here, including naturalised escaped species. Alternative English names have been omitted.

The presently known status of each species is indicated thus:

BR = breeding resident (often with local seasonal movements)

MB = migrant breeder, breeding visitor

PM = passage migrant

SV = summer visitor (not breeding)

WV = winter visitor (not breeding)

(S) = a few or occasional in summer (not breeding)

(W) = a few or occasional in winter (not breeding)

V = vagrant, scarce visitor

? = query, or status uncertain.

The sequence and scientific nomenclature generally follow K. H. Voous, *List of Recent Holarctic Bird Species*, London: Academic Press for British Ornithologists' Union, 1977.

# NON-PASSERIFORMES

## Podicipedidae

| | | |
|---|---|---|
| *Tachybaptus ruficollis* | Little Grebe | BR PM WV |
| *Podiceps cristatus* | Great Crested Grebe | WV |
| *Podiceps nigricollis* | Black-necked Grebe | PM WV |

## Procellariidae

| | | |
|---|---|---|
| *Bulweria fallax* | Jouanin's Petrel | BR? |
| *Puffinus carneipes* | Pale-footed Shearwater | SV |
| *Puffinus pacificus* | Wedge-tailed Shearwater | SV? |
| *Puffinus lherminieri persicus* | Persian Shearwater | BR? |

## Hydrobatidae

| | | |
|---|---|---|
| *Oceanites oceanicus* | Wilson's Storm-petrel | SV |
| *Pelagodroma marina* | White-faced Storm-petrel | SV |
| *Fregetta tropica* | Black-bellied Storm-petrel | SV |

## Phaethontidae

| | | |
|---|---|---|
| *Phaethon aethereus* | Red-billed Tropicbird | BR |

## Sulidae

| | | |
|---|---|---|
| *Sula dactylatra* | Masked Booby | BR |
| *Sula leucogaster* | Brown Booby | V |

## Phalacrocoracidae

| | | |
|---|---|---|
| *Phalacrocorax carbo* | Great Cormorant | WV |
| *Phalacrocorax nigrogularis* | Socotra Cormorant | BR SV |

## Pelecanidae

| | | |
|---|---|---|
| *Pelecanus onocrotalus* | White Pelican | V |

## Ardeidae

| | | |
|---|---|---|
| *Botaurus stellaris* | Bittern | PM WV |
| *Ixobrychus minutus* | Little Bittern | PM (W) BR? |
| *Nycticorax nycticorax* | Night Heron | PM WV |
| *Butorides striatus* | Little Green Heron | BR PM |
| *Ardeola ralloides* | Squacco Heron | PM WV |
| *Ardeola grayii* | Indian Pond Heron | PM WV |
| *Bubulcus ibis* | Cattle Egret | V or SV WV |
| *Egretta gularis* | Western Reef Heron | BR PM WV |
| *Egretta garzetta* | Little Egret | PM WV (S) |
| *Egretta alba* | Great White Egret | WV (S) |
| *Ardea cinerea* | Grey Heron | PM WV (S) |
| *Ardea purpurea* | Purple Heron | PM WV |
| *Ardea goliath* | Goliath Heron | V or WV |
| *Ardea melanocephala* | Black-headed Heron | V |

## Ciconiidae

| | | |
|---|---|---|
| *Ciconia abdimii* | Abdim's Stork | V |
| *Ciconia ciconia* | White Stork | PM (W) |

## Threskiornithidae

| | | |
|---|---|---|
| *Plegadis falcinellus* | Glossy Ibis | PM WV (S) |
| *Threskiornis aethiopicus* | Sacred Ibis | V |
| *Platalea leucorodia* | Spoonbill | PM WV (S) |

## Phoenicopteridae

| | | |
|---|---|---|
| *Phoenicopterus ruber* | Greater Flamingo | PM WV (S) |

## Anatidae

| | | |
|---|---|---|
| *Cygnus columbianus bewickii* | Bewick's Swan | V |
| *Anser albifrons* | White-fronted Goose | V |
| *Anser anser* | Greylag Goose | V |
| *Tadorna ferruginea* | Ruddy Shelduck | PM WV |

| | | |
|---|---|---|
| *Tadorna tadorna* | Shelduck | PM WV |
| *Nettapus coromandelianus* | Cotton Teal | WV (S) |
| *Anas penelope* | Wigeon | PM WV |
| *Anas strepera* | Gadwall | PM WV |
| *Anas crecca* | Teal | PM WV |
| *Anas platyrhynchos* | Mallard | PM WV |
| *Anas acuta* | Pintail | PM WV |
| *Anas querquedula* | Garganey | PM WV |
| *Anas clypeata* | Shoveler | PM WV |
| *Marmaronetta angustirostris* | Marbled Teal | V |
| *Netta rufina* | Red-crested Pochard | V |
| *Aythya ferina* | Pochard | PM WV |
| *Aythya nyroca* | Ferruginous Duck | PM WV |
| *Aythya fuligula* | Tufted Duck | PM WV |

### Accipitridae

| | | |
|---|---|---|
| *Pernis apivorus* | Honey Buzzard | V or PM |
| *Milvus migrans* | Black Kite | PM WV BR? |
| *Neophron percnopterus* | Egyptian Vulture | BR PM WV |
| *Gyps fulvus* | Griffon Vulture | PM WV |
| *Torgos tracheliotus* | Lappet-faced Vulture | WV BR? |
| *Aegypius monachus* | Black Vulture | PM WV BR |
| *Circaetus gallicus* | Short-toed Eagle | PM WV BR? |
| *Circus aeruginosus* | Marsh Harrier | PM WV |
| *Circus cyaneus* | Hen Harrier | PM (W) |
| *Circus macrourus* | Pallid Harrier | PM (W) |
| *Circus pygargus* | Montagu's Harrier | PM (W) |
| *Accipiter gentilis* | Goshawk | V |
| *Accipiter nisus* | Sparrowhawk | PM WV |
| *Buteo buteo* | Buzzard | PM (W) |
| *Buteo rufinus* | Long-legged Buzzard | BR PM WV |
| *Aquila pomarina* | Lesser Spotted Eagle | V |
| *Aquila clanga* | Spotted Eagle | PM WV |
| *Aquila rapax (or nipalensis)* | Steppe Eagle | PM WV (S) |
| *Aquila heliaca* | Imperial Eagle | PM WV |
| *Aquila chrysaetos* | Golden Eagle | WV |
| *Aquila verreauxii* | Verreaux's Eagle | BR |
| *Hieraaetus pennatus* | Booted Eagle | PM (W) |
| *Hieraaetus fasciatus* | Bonelli's Eagle | BR PM WV |

### Pandionidae

| | | |
|---|---|---|
| *Pandion haliaetus* | Osprey | BR PM WV |

### Falconidae

| | | |
|---|---|---|
| *Falco naumanni* | Lesser Kestrel | PM (W) |
| *Falco tinnunculus* | Kestrel | BR PM WV |
| *Falco amurensis* | Manchurian Red-footed Falcon | PM |
| *Falco subbuteo* | Hobby | PM (S) |
| *Falco concolor* | Sooty Falcon | MB PM (W) |
| *Falco biarmicus* | Lanner | ? |
| *Falco cherrug* | Saker | PM WV (S) |
| *Falco peregrinus* | Peregrine | PM WV BR? |
| *Falco pelegrinoides* | Barbary Falcon | BR PM? |

### Phasianidae

| | | |
|---|---|---|
| *Alectoris chukar* | Chukar | BR |
| *Alectoris melanocephala* | Arabian Red-legged Partridge | BR |
| *Ammoperdix heyi* | Sand Partridge | BR |
| *Francolinus pondicerianus* | Grey Francolin | BR |
| *Coturnix coturnix* | Common Quail | PM (W) |

### Rallidae

| | | |
|---|---|---|
| *Rallus aquaticus* | Water Rail | PM (W) |
| *Porzana porzana* | Spotted Crake | PM WV |
| *Porzana parva* | Little Crake | PM WV |
| *Porzana pusilla* | Baillon's Crake | PM WV |
| *Crex crex* | Corncrake | PM |
| *Amaurornis phoenicurus* | White-breasted Waterhen | V |
| *Gallinula chloropus* | Moorhen | BR PM WV |
| *Fulica atra* | Coot | PM WV (S) |

### Gruidae

| | | |
|---|---|---|
| *Grus grus* | Common Crane | V |
| *Anthropoides virgo* | Demoiselle Crane | V |

### Otidae

| | | |
|---|---|---|
| *Tetrax tetrax* | Little Bustard | V |
| *Chlamydotis undulata* | Houbara | BR PM WV |

### Jacanidae

| | | |
|---|---|---|
| *Hydrophasianus chirurgus* | Pheasant-tailed Jacana | WV (S) |

### Haematopodidae

| | | |
|---|---|---|
| *Haematopus ostralegus* | Oystercatcher | PM WV (S) |

### Recurvirostridae

| | | |
|---|---|---|
| *Himantopus himantopus* | Black-winged Stilt | PM WV (S) |
| *Recurvirostra avosetta* | Avocet | PM WV (S) |

### Dromadidae

| | | |
|---|---|---|
| *Dromas ardeola* | Crab Plover | MB PM WV |

### Burhinidae

| | | |
|---|---|---|
| *Burhinus oedicnemus* | Stone Curlew | PM WV |
| *Burhinus capensis* | Spotted Thick-knee | BR? |

### Glareolidae

| | | |
|---|---|---|
| *Cursorius cursor* | Cream-coloured Courser | PM WV |
| *Glareola pratincola* | Pratincole | PM (W) |
| *Glareola nordmanni* | Black-winged Pratincole | V or PM |
| *Glareola lactea* | Little Pratincole | V or PM WV |

### Charadriidae

| | | |
|---|---|---|
| *Charadrius dubius* | Little Ringed Plover | MB PM WV |
| *Charadrius hiaticula* | Ringed Plover | PM WV (S) |
| *Charadrius alexandrinus* | Kentish Plover | MB PM WV(S) |
| *Charadrius mongolus* | Lesser Sand Plover | PM WV (S) |
| *Charadrius leschenaultii* | Greater Sand Plover | PM WV (S) |
| *Charadrius asiaticus* | Caspian Plover | PM |
| *Charadrius morinellus* | Dotterel | V |
| *Pluvialis dominica* | Lesser Golden Plover | PM WV (S) |
| *Pluvialis apricaria* | Golden Plover | V or PM WV |
| *Pluvialis squatarola* | Grey Plover | PM WV (S) |
| *Hoplopterus spinosus* | Spur-winged Lapwing | V |
| *Hoplopterus indicus* | Red-wattled Lapwing | BR |
| *Chettusia gregaria* | Sociable Lapwing | V |
| *Chettusia leucura* | White-tailed Lapwing | PM WV |
| *Vanellus vanellus* | Lapwing | V or WV |

### Scolopacidae

| | | |
|---|---|---|
| *Calidris alba* | Sanderling | PM WV (S) |
| *Calidris minuta* | Little Stint | PM WV (S) |
| *Calidris temminckii* | Temminck's Stint | PM WV |
| *Calidris subminuta* | Long-toed Stint | PM WV |
| *Calidris ferruginea* | Curlew Sandpiper | PM WV (S) |
| *Calidris alpina* | Dunlin | PM WV (S) |
| *Limicola falcinellus* | Broad-billed Sandpiper | PM WV |
| *Philomachus pugnax* | Ruff | PM WV (S) |
| *Lymnocryptes minimus* | Jack Snipe | PM WV |
| *Gallinago gallinago* | Common Snipe | PM WV (S) |
| *Gallinago media* | Great Snipe | V or PM |
| *Gallinago stenura* | Pintail Snipe | V or PM WV |

| | | |
|---|---|---|
| *Limosa limosa* | Black-tailed Godwit | PM WV (S) |
| *Limosa lapponica* | Bar-tailed Godwit | PM WV |
| *Numenius phaeopus* | Whimbrel | PM (W) |
| *Numenius tenuirostris* | Slender-billed Curlew | V |
| *Numenius arquata* | Curlew | PM WV (S) |
| *Tringa erythropus* | Spotted Redshank | PM WV |
| *Tringa totanus* | Redshank | PM WV (S) |
| *Tringa stagnatilis* | Marsh Sandpiper | PM WV (S) |
| *Tringa nebularia* | Greenshank | PM WV (S) |
| *Tringa ochropus* | Green Sandpiper | PM WV (S) |
| *Tringa glareola* | Wood Sandpiper | PM (W) |
| *Xenus cinereus* | Terek Sandpiper | PM WV (S) |
| *Actitis hypoleucos* | Common Sandpiper | PM WV (S) |
| *Arenaria interpres* | Turnstone | PM WV (S) |
| *Phalaropus lobatus* | Red-necked Phalarope | PM WV |
| *Phalaropus fulicarius* | Grey Phalarope | PM? WV? |

## Stercorariidae

| | | |
|---|---|---|
| *Stercorarius pomarinus* | Pomarine Skua | PM WV |
| *Stercorarius parasiticus* | Arctic Skua | PM WV |
| *Stercorarius longicaudus* | Long-tailed Skua | V |
| *Stercorarius skua* | Great Skua | SV (W) |

## Laridae

| | | |
|---|---|---|
| *Larus hemprichii* | Sooty Gull | BR MB PM |
| *Larus leucophthalmus* | White-eyed Gull | V |
| *Larus ichthyaetus* | Great Black-headed Gull | PM WV (S) |
| *Larus ridibundus* | Black-headed Gull | PM WV (S) |
| *Larus genei* | Slender-billed Gull | PM WV (S) |
| *Larus canus* | Common Gull | V or WV |
| *Larus fuscus* | Lesser Black-backed Gull | PM WV (S) |
| *Larus argentatus* | Herring Gull | PM WV (S) |

## Sternidae

| | | |
|---|---|---|
| *Gelochelidon nilotica* | Gull-billed Tern | PM WV (S) |
| *Sterna caspia* | Caspian Tern | PM WV (S) |
| *Sterna bergii* | Crested Tern | BR MB PM |
| *Sterna bengalensis* | Lesser Crested Tern | PM (S) (W) |
| *Sterna sandvicensis* | Sandwich Tern | PM SV WV |
| *Sterna dougallii* | Roseate Tern | MB |
| *Sterna hirundo* | Common Tern | PM (S) (W) |
| *Sterna repressa* | White-cheeked Tern | MB PM (W) |
| *Sterna anaethetus* | Bridled Tern | MB PM (W) |
| *Sterna fuscata* | Sooty Tern | V |
| *Sterna albifrons* | Little Tern | PM? |
| *Sterna saundersi* | Saunders' Little Tern | MB PM |
| *Chlidonias hybrida* | Whiskered Tern | PM (S) (W) |
| *Chlidonias niger* | Black Tern | V |
| *Chlidonias leucopterus* | White-winged Black Tern | PM WV |
| *Anous tenuirostris* | Lesser Noddy | SV |
| *Anous stolidus* | Common Noddy | MB |

## Rynchopidae

| | | |
|---|---|---|
| *Rynchops albicollis* | Indian Skimmer | V |

## Pteroclididae

| | | |
|---|---|---|
| *Pterocles lichtensteinii* | Lichtenstein's Sandgrouse | BR |
| *Pterocles coronatus* | Coronetted Sandgrouse | BR |
| *Pterocles senegallus* | Spotted Sandgrouse | BR |
| *Pterocles exustus* | Chestnut-bellied Sandgrouse | BR |

## Columbidae

| | | |
|---|---|---|
| *Columba livia* | Rock Dove | BR |
| *Columba oenas* | Stock Dove | V |
| *Columba palumbus* | Woodpigeon | BR |
| *Streptopelia decaocto* | Collared Dove | BR PM WV |
| *Streptopelia tranquebarica* | Red Turtle Dove | V |
| *Streptopelia turtur* | Turtle Dove | MB PM |
| *Streptopelia orientalis* | Rufous Turtle Dove | PM |
| *Streptopelia senegalensis* | Palm Dove | BR PM |
| *Oena capensis* | Namaqua Dove | V |
| *Treron waalia* | Yellow-bellied Green Pigeon | MB? |

## Psittacidae

| | | |
|---|---|---|
| *Psittacula krameri* | Rose-ringed Parakeet | BR V |

## Cuculidae

| | | |
|---|---|---|
| *Clamator jacobinus* | Jacobin Cuckoo | V or PM |
| *Chrysococcyx caprius* | Didric Cuckoo | MB |
| *Cuculus canorus* | Cuckoo | PM |
| *Eudynamys scolopacea* | Koel | V |

## Tytonidae

| | | |
|---|---|---|
| *Tyto alba* | Barn Owl | BR |

## Strigidae

| | | |
|---|---|---|
| *Otus sunia* | Oriental Scops Owl | BR |
| *Otus brucei* | Bruce's Scops Owl | MB or BR |
| *Otus scops* | Scops Owl | PM |
| *Bubo bubo* | Eagle Owl | BR |
| *Bubo africanus* | Spotted Eagle Owl | BR |
| *Athene noctua* | Little Owl | BR |
| *Asio otus* | Long-eared Owl | V |
| *Asio flammeus* | Short-eared Owl | PM |

## Caprimulgidae

| | | |
|---|---|---|
| *Caprimulgus nubicus* | Nubian Nightjar | PM? |
| *Caprimulgus europaeus* | Nightjar | PM (W) |
| *Caprimulgus aegyptius* | Egyptian Nightjar | PM (W) |

## Apodidae

| | | |
|---|---|---|
| *Apus apus* | Swift | PM (S?) |
| *Apus pallidus* | Pallid Swift | MB PM (W) |
| *Apus melba* | Alpine Swift | PM |
| *Apus affinis* | Little Swift | V |

## Alcedinidae

| | | |
|---|---|---|
| *Halcyon leucocephala* | Grey-headed Kingfisher | MB |
| *Halcyon chloris* | White-collared Kingfisher | BR |
| *Alcedo atthis* | Kingfisher | PM WV |

## Meropidae

| | | |
|---|---|---|
| *Merops orientalis* | Little Green Bee-eater | BR |
| *Merops superciliosus* | Blue-cheeked Bee-eater | MB PM |
| *Merops apiaster* | Bee-eater | MB PM |

## Coraciidae

| | | |
|---|---|---|
| *Coracias garrulus* | Roller | PM |
| *Coracias benghalensis* | Indian Roller | BR PM WV |

## Upupidae

| | | |
|---|---|---|
| *Upupa epops* | Hoopoe | MB BR? PM (W) |

## Picidae

| | | |
|---|---|---|
| *Jynx torquilla* | Wryneck | PM (W) |

291

# PASSERIFORMES

## Alaudidae

| | | |
|---|---|---|
| *Mirafra cantillans* | Singing Bush Lark | MB (W) |
| *Eremopterix nigriceps* | Black-crowned Finch Lark | BR PM WV |
| *Eremalauda dunni* | Dunn's Lark | BR |
| *Ammomanes cincturus* | Bar-tailed Desert Lark | BR |
| *Ammomanes deserti* | Desert Lark | BR |
| *Alaemon alaudipes* | Hoopoe Lark | BR |
| *Melanocorypha bimaculata* | Bimaculated Lark | PM WV |
| *Calandrella brachydactyla* | Short-toed Lark | PM (W) (S) |
| *Calandrella rufescens* | Lesser Short-toed Lark | PM WV |
| *Galerida cristata* | Crested Lark | BR |
| *Alauda arvensis* | Skylark | PM WV |

## Hirundinidae

| | | |
|---|---|---|
| *Riparia paludicola* | Brown-throated Sand Martin | V |
| *Riparia riparia* | Sand Martin | PM (W) |
| *Ptyonoprogne fuligula obsoleta* | Pale Crag Martin | BR PM WV |
| *Ptyonoprogne rupestris* | Crag Martin | PM |
| *Hirundo rustica* | Swallow | MB PM |
| *Hirundo daurica* | Red-rumped Swallow | PM |
| *Delichon urbica* | House Martin | PM |

## Motacillidae

| | | |
|---|---|---|
| *Anthus novaeseelandiae* | Richard's Pipit | V |
| *Anthus campestris* | Tawny Pipit | PM (W) |
| *Anthus similis* | Long-billed Pipit | BR |
| *Anthus trivialis* | Tree Pipit | PM (W) |
| *Anthus pratensis* | Meadow Pipit | PM (W) |
| *Anthus cervinus* | Red-throated Pipit | PM (W) |
| *Anthus spinoletta* | Water Pipit | PM WV |
| *Motacilla flava* | Yellow Wagtail | PM (W) |
| *Motacilla citreola* | Citrine Wagtail | PM WV |
| *Motacilla cinerea* | Grey Wagtail | PM WV |
| *Motacilla alba* | White Wagtail | PM WV |

## Pycnonotidae

| | | |
|---|---|---|
| *Pycnonotus xanthopygos* | Yellow-vented Bulbul | BR |

## Bombycillidae

| | | |
|---|---|---|
| *Hypocolius ampelinus* | Hypocolius | V or PM |

## Prunellidae

| | | |
|---|---|---|
| *Prunella ocularis* | Radde's Accentor | V |

## Turdidae

| | | |
|---|---|---|
| *Cercotrichas galactotes* | Rufous Bush Robin | PM |
| *Luscinia luscinia* | Thrush Nightingale | PM |
| *Luscinia megarhynchos* | Nightingale | PM |
| *Luscinia svecica* | Bluethroat | PM WV |
| *Irania gutturalis* | White-throated Robin | PM |
| *Phoenicurus erythronotus* | Eversmann's Redstart | V |
| *Phoenicurus ochruros* | Black Redstart | PM WV |
| *Phoenicurus phoenicurus* | Redstart | PM |
| *Cercomela melanura* | Blackstart | BR |
| *Saxicola rubetra* | Whinchat | PM |
| *Saxicola torquata* | Stonechat | PM (W) |
| *Oenanthe isabellina* | Isabelline Wheatear | PM WV |
| *Oenanthe oenanthe* | Wheatear | PM |
| *Oenanthe pleschanka* | Pied Wheatear | PM |
| *Oenanthe hispanica* | Black-eared Wheatear | PM |
| *Oenanthe deserti* | Desert Wheatear | PM WV |
| *Oenanthe xanthoprymna* | Red-tailed Wheatear | PM WV |
| *Oenanthe lugens* | Mourning Wheatear | BR |
| *Oenanthe monacha* | Hooded Wheatear | BR WV? |
| *Oenanthe alboniger* | Hume's Wheatear | BR |
| *Oenanthe leucopyga* | White-crowned Black Wheatear | ? |
| *Monticola saxatilis* | Rock Thrush | PM (W) |
| *Monticola solitarius* | Blue Rock Thrush | PM WV |
| *Turdus torquatus* | Ring Ouzel | V |
| *Turdus obscurus* | Eye-browed Thrush | V |
| *Turdus ruficollis atrogularis* | Black-throated Thrush | WV |
| *Turdus philomelos* | Song Thrush | WV |

## Sylviidae

| | | |
|---|---|---|
| *Cisticola juncidis* | Fan-tailed Warbler | ? |
| *Prinia gracilis* | Graceful Warbler | BR |
| *Scotocerca inquieta* | Scrub Warbler | BR |
| *Locustella naevia* | Grasshopper Warbler | V or PM |
| *Locustella fluviatilis* | River Warbler | V |
| *Locustella luscinioides* | Savi's Warbler | V or PM |
| *Acrocephalus melanopogon* | Moustached Warbler | V or PM |
| *Acrocephalus schoenobaenus* | Sedge Warbler | PM |
| *Acrocephalus agricola* | Paddyfield Warbler | V or PM |
| *Acrocephalus dumetorum* | Blyth's Reed Warbler | V or PM |
| *Acrocephalus palustris* | Marsh Warbler | PM |
| *Acrocephalus scirpaceus* | Reed Warbler | PM (W) (S) |
| *Acrocephalus stentoreus* | Clamorous Reed Warbler | MB PM WV |
| *Acrocephalus arundinaceus* | Great Reed Warbler | PM |
| *Hippolais pallida* | Olivaceous Warbler | PM (S) |
| *Hippolais caligata* | Booted Warbler | MB PM WV |
| *Hippolais languida* | Upcher's Warbler | PM |
| *Hippolais icterina* | Icterine Warbler | PM |
| *Sylvia mystacea* | Ménétries' Warbler | PM (W) |
| *Sylvia nana* | Desert Warbler | PM WV |
| *Sylvia leucomelaena* | Blanford's Warbler | BR or MB |
| *Sylvia hortensis* | Orphean Warbler | PM WV |
| *Sylvia nisoria* | Barred Warbler | PM |
| *Sylvia curruca* (incl. *minula*) | Lesser Whitethroat (incl. Desert Lesser Whitethroat) | PM WV |
| *Sylvia communis* | Whitethroat | PM |
| *Sylvia borin* | Garden Warbler | PM |
| *Sylvia atricapilla* | Blackcap | PM |
| *Phylloscopus nitidus* | Green Warbler | PM |
| *Phylloscopus inornatus* | Yellow-browed Warbler | PM WV |
| *Phylloscopus sibilatrix* | Wood Warbler | PM |
| *Phylloscopus neglectus* | Plain Leaf Warbler | V or WV |
| *Phylloscopus collybita* | Chiffchaff | PM (W) |
| *Phylloscopus trochilus* | Willow Warbler | PM |

## Muscicapidae

| | | |
|---|---|---|
| *Muscicapa striata* | Spotted Flycatcher | PM |
| *Ficedula parva* | Red-breasted Flycatcher | PM |
| *Ficedula semitorquata* | Semi-collared Flycatcher | PM |

## Monarchidae

| | | |
|---|---|---|
| *Terpsiphone viridis* | African Paradise Flycatcher | BR? |

## Timaliidae

| | | |
|---|---|---|
| *Turdoides squamiceps* | Arabian Babbler | BR |

**Remizidae**

| | | |
|---|---|---|
| *Remiz pendulinus* | Penduline Tit | V |

**Nectariniidae**

| | | |
|---|---|---|
| *Nectarinia asiatica* | Purple Sunbird | BR |
| *Nectarinia habessinica* | Abyssinian Sunbird | BR |
| *Nectarinia osea* | Palestine Sunbird | BR |

**Zosteropidae**

| | | |
|---|---|---|
| *Zosterops abyssinica* | White-breasted White-eye | BR |

**Oriolidae**

| | | |
|---|---|---|
| *Oriolus oriolus* | Golden Oriole | PM |

**Laniidae**

| | | |
|---|---|---|
| *Tchagra senegala* | Black-headed Bush Shrike | BR |
| *Lanius isabellinus* | Isabelline Shrike | PM (W) |
| *Lanius collurio* | Red-backed Shrike | PM |
| *Lanius vittatus* | Bay-backed Shrike | V |
| *Lanius minor* | Lesser Grey Shrike | PM |
| *Lanius excubitor* | Great Grey Shrike | BR PM WV |
| *Lanius senator* | Woodchat Shrike | PM |
| *Lanius nubicus* | Masked Shrike | PM |

**Corvidae**

| | | |
|---|---|---|
| *Corvus splendens* | House Crow | BR |
| *Corvus ruficollis* | Brown-necked Raven | BR |
| *Corvus rhipidurus* | Fan-tailed Raven | BR |

**Sturnidae**

| | | |
|---|---|---|
| *Onychognathus tristramii* | Tristram's Grackle | BR |
| *Sturnus vulgaris* | Starling | PM WV |
| *Sturnus roseus* | Rose-coloured Starling | PM (W) |
| *Creatophora cineracea* | Wattled Starling | V |

**Passeridae**

| | | |
|---|---|---|
| *Passer domesticus* | House Sparrow | BR |
| *Passer hispaniolensis* | Spanish Sparrow | V or WV |
| *Petronia brachydactyla* | Pale Rock Sparrow | PM |
| *Petronia xanthocollis* | Yellow-throated Sparrow | MB PM |

**Ploceidae**

| | | |
|---|---|---|
| *Ploceus galbula* | Rüppell's Weaver | BR |

**Estrildidae**

| | | |
|---|---|---|
| *Euodice malabarica* | Indian Silverbill | BR |
| *Euodice cantans* | African Silverbill | BR |

**Fringillidae**

| | | |
|---|---|---|
| *Fringilla montifringilla* | Brambling | V |
| *Rhynchostruthus socotranus* | Golden-winged Grosbeak | BR |
| *Carduelis carduelis* | Goldfinch | V |
| *Bucanetes githagineus* | Trumpeter Finch | BR? |
| *Carpodacus erythrinus* | Scarlet Rosefinch | PM |

**Emberizidae**

| | | |
|---|---|---|
| *Emberiza striolata* | House Bunting | BR PM WV |
| *Emberiza tahapisi* | Cinnamon-breasted Rock Bunting | BR |
| *Emberiza hortulana* | Ortolan Bunting | PM |
| *Emberiza rustica* | Rustic Bunting | V |
| *Emberiza pusilla* | Little Bunting | V |
| *Emberiza aureola* | Yellow-breasted Bunting | V |
| *Emberiza melanocephala* | Black-headed Bunting | PM |
| *Miliaria calandra* | Corn Bunting | PM WV |

# Appendix 2

## Additional species

Details of species found in Oman since the main text was completed.


**Fan-tailed Warbler**    *Cisticola juncidis*    (Not illustrated)    See also plate 99

**World:** Breeds across S Eurasia, south to Africa, Palestine, S Arabia, India to N Australia, in several races. *C. j. uropygialis* breeds from W to E Africa and S Arabia. Sedentary.
**Oman:** Status uncertain (one seen, Salalah, 1 June 1980).

10cm/4in. A very small dark streaked warbler, with a short rounded tail. It is pale chestnut to sandy above, heavily streaked darker brown (feather centres), with a tawny rump, no supercilium, and a dark brown tail with sub-terminal black spots and white tips; it is whitish below, tinged pale brown on the breast and flanks. It lacks the long tail of Graceful Warbler (plate 99), and the pale supercilium of Sedge and Moustached Warblers (plate 100).

Lowland vegetation, particularly cultivation, where it hunts insects restlessly on or near the ground. It is very excitable when nesting, leaping into the air. The nest (from March near Aden) is bottle shaped, made of grass, gossamer etc., with a top opening. Usually 3 pale blue eggs. Song, in undulating flight, *zeep-zeep-zeep*, one note to each undulation; call, *tew*.


**Paddyfield Warbler**    *Acrocephalus agricola*    (Not illustrated)    See also plate 100

**World:** Breeds in Crimean region, in southern central Asia south to NE Iran, NW India, and in Manchuria, in several races. Migratory, reaching SE Iran, India, SE Asia.
**Oman:** Vagrant or scarce passage migrant (one found on Masirah, 6 November 1979).

13cm/5in. The most richly coloured of the unstreaked *Acrocephalus* warblers; warm rufous-brown above, with a conspicuous creamy supercilium and a dark streak through the eye; pale buff below, suffused with rusty on the flanks and under tail-coverts. The bill is relatively short and stout, the wings short and rounded, and the tail long and often slightly cocked.

Thick low vegetation and bushes near water, occasionally on wet ground in the open.

## Species requiring confirmation

The species listed here have been published as having occurred in Oman, but the reports have been omitted from the Oman Check List, either because the evidence at present available is inconclusive, or because in a few cases it is clear that an error was made.

| | | | |
|---|---|---|---|
| *Bulweria bulwerii* | Bulwer's Petrel | *Calidris maritima* | Purple Sandpiper |
| *Fregetta grallaria* | White-bellied Storm-petrel | *Larus marinus* | Great Black-backed Gull |
| *Phaethon lepturus* | White-tailed Tropicbird | *Clamator glandarius* | Great Spotted Cuckoo |
| | (Yellow-billed Tropicbird) | *Otus bakkamoena* | Collared Scops Owl |
| *Fregata* species | Frigatebird species | *Merops albicollis* | White-throated Bee-eater |
| *Geronticus eremita* | Bald Ibis (Hermit Ibis) | *Coracias abyssinicus* | Abyssinian Roller |
| *Phoenicopterus minor* | Lesser Flamingo | *Alauda gulgula* | Small Skylark (Lesser Skylark) |
| *Plectropterus gambensis* | Spur-winged Goose | *Riparia cincta* | Banded Martin |
| *Anas formosa* | Baikal Teal | *Hirundo smithii* | Wire-tailed Swallow |
| *Melanitta nigra* | Common Scoter | *Oenanthe finschii* | Finsch's Wheatear |
| *Elanus caeruleus* | Black-winged Kite | *Oenanthe moesta* | Red-rumped Wheatear |
| *Milvus milvus* | Red Kite | *Turdus olivaceus menachensis* | 'Olive Thrush' |
| *Haliaeetus albicilla* | White-tailed Eagle | *Cettia cetti* | Cetti's Warbler |
| *Gyps rueppellii* | Rüppell's Vulture | *Hippolais olivetorum* | Olive-tree Warbler |
| *Melierax metabates* | Dark Chanting Goshawk | *Phylloscopus trochiloides* | Greenish Warbler |
| *Numida meleagris* | Helmeted Guineafowl | *Corvus corax* | Raven |
| *Calidris canutus* | Knot (Red Knot) | *Estrilda rufibarba* | Arabian Waxbill |
| *Calidris ruficollis* | Red-necked Stint | | |
| | (Rufous-necked Sandpiper) | | |

## Escapes

Birds reported in Oman and thought to be escaped captives.

| | | | |
|---|---|---|---|
| *Mycteria leucocephala* | Painted Stork | *Pycnonotus leucogenys* | White-cheeked Bulbul |
| *Melopsittacus undulatus* | Budgerigar | *Sturnus pagodarum* | Brahminy Mynah |
| *Psittacula eupatria* | Large Indian Parakeet | *Lonchura punctulata* | Spotted Munia |
| *Psittacula krameri* | Rose-ringed Parakeet (also a | | |
| | naturalised resident) | | |

## Appendix 5

### Ringed birds recovered in Oman

#### Key to sequence, symbols and terms

Species
○ = Ringing details (age on ringing is indicated by 'Pullus' = nestling or chick not yet flying, or 'Juvenile' = young, in first true feathers)
● = Recovery details
Sources of information

BTO = British Trust for Ornithology

---

**White Stork**    *Ciconia ciconia*
○ Helgoland 208.615. Pullus. 21 June 1931 (text reads '21.IV.31', presumably in error). Near Sulau, Militsch, German Silesia, 51°30′N. 17°11′E (now Milicz, Wroclaw, Poland).
● 14 September 1931. Near Saham, Batinah, 24°10′N. 56°50′E. (Caught.)
(R. Drost, *Vogelzug*, 1932, 3(1): 39; BTO.)

○ Budapest 5205. Pullus. June 1912. Bellye, Hungary, 45°36′N. 18°45′E (now Belje, near Osijek, Jugoslavia).
● Approx. 10 October 1912. 'Muscat'.
(F. Haverschmidt, *The Life of the White Stork*, 1949, p.68; BTO.)

○ Helgoland 217.116. Pullus. 23 June 1936. Odisheim, Niedersachsen, West Germany, 53°42′N. 8°55′E.
● 'During the Second World War, Mudherib, Muscat' ( = Al Mudayrib, SE of Ibra), 22°36′N. 58°40′E.
(*Auspicium*,1961, 1(4): 305; BTO.)

○ Rossitten BB 6605. Pullus. June/July 1936. Norkitten, Insterburg, E Prussia, 54°38′N. 21°48′E (now Chernyakhovsk (Kaliningrad), USSR).
● Approx. 16 September 1936. Buraimi, 24°14′N. 55°47′E.
(*Vogelzug*, 1937, 8(4): 204; BTO.)

○ Radolfzell BB 16810. Pullus. 1 July 1961. Grenz, Brandenburg, East Germany, 53°20′N. 14°02′E.
● 15 June 1963. Suma'il, approx. 23°19′N. 58°00′E.
(*Auspicium*, 1964, 2(1): 51; BTO.)

○ Gdansk V 1293. Pullus. 30 June 1976. Grabowiec, Bialystok, Poland, 52°38′N. 23°24′E.
● August 1976. Al Hoata, Rakhyut, Dhofar, approx. 16°44′N. 53°25′E.
(BTO.)

○ (No details.) Bulgaria.
● July (No details) Oman.
(M. Paspaleva, *Fragmenta Balcanica, Musei Macedonici Scientiarum Naturalium*, 1962, 4(14): 107–12, without further details; BTO.)

○ Moskwa A 51886. Juvenile. 11 July 1959. Near Chernobilsk, Kiev District, USSR ( = Chernobyl'), 51°17′N. 30°15′E.
● August 1959. '60 miles SE Ibra, Province Dhahira' (location uncertain, but probably near 'Ibri, Dhahira district, 23°14′N. 56°30′E).
(L. Cornwallis; Amotz Zahavi.)

○ Zagreb OD 118.866. Pullus. 23 June 1978. Centa (Vojvodina), Jugoslavia, 45°07′N. 20°23′E.
● 25 March 1979. Jabal Qara, Dhofar, 17°17′N. 54°05′E. (Found dead at roadside.)
(Mother of Salim Khosey Amoosh; T. Henry; BTO.)

**Greater Flamingo**    *Phoenicopterus ruber*
○ Tehran LL 1921. Pullus. 8 August 1971. Lake Rezaiyeh, Azerbaijan, Iran, 37°25′N. 45°30′E.
● 12 November 1971. 'Muscat'.
(Dr D.A. Scott; BTO.)

○ Tehran LL 5580. Pullus. 23 August 1974. Ashk (Eshek) Island, Lake Rezaiyeh, Azerbaijan, Iran, 37°23′N. 45°30′E.
● 4 November 1974. Jazirat Ma'awil, near Khawr Barr al Hikman, 20°43′N. 58°42′E. (Found recently dead.)
(C.I. Griffiths and T.D. Rogers; Dr D.A. Scott; BTO.)

○ Tehran LL 5710. Pullus. 24 August 1974. Lake Rezaiyeh, Azerbaijan, Iran.
● 15 November 1974. 10km from Sohar, 24°22′N. 56°45′E.
(Dr D.A. Scott; BTO.)

## Sooty (Hemprich's) Gull   *Larus hemprichii*
○ London EH 24.488. Pullus. 22 October 1976. Jazirat Shaghaf, off Masirah Island, 20°27′N. 58°45′E.
● 14 July 1977. Muscat, 23°37′N. 58°36′E.
(Mohsin al-Jabri; Royal Air Force Ornithological Society; BTO.)

○ London EB 89.035. Pullus. 22 October 1976. Jazirat Shaghaf, off Masirah Island, 20°27′N. 58°45′E.
● Spring 1977. Near Matrah, 23°37′N. 58°34′E. (Caught alive in fish-net.)
(Helal Badr; Royal Air Force Ornithological Society; BTO.)

## Slender-billed Gull   *Larus genei*
○ Moskwa M 271.608. Juvenile. 9 June 1976. Astrakhan Reserve, Volga delta, USSR, 46°14′N. 49°00′E.
● 21 January 1977. Off Jazirat Ghanem, Musandam region, 26°22′N. 56°22′E. (Caught on fishing-line.)
(Sultan of Oman's Navy; BTO.)

## Caspian Tern   *Sterna caspia*
○ Moskwa M 264.907. Pullus. 22 June 1975. Alakol' Lake (Kurgan), Kazakhstan, USSR, 46°00′N. 82°00′E.
● 20 January 1976. Sur Masirah, Masirah Island, 20°26′N. 58°43′E. (Found recently dead.)
(C.I. Griffiths; BTO.)

## Sandwich Tern   *Sterna sandvicensis*
○ Moskwa P 567.985. Juvenile. 8 July 1978. Astrakhan Reserve, Volga delta, USSR, 46°14′N. 49°02′E.
● 25 January 1980. Sidab, near Muscat, 23°36′N. 58°36′E. (Found dead.)
(Mrs A. L. Watts; BTO.)

○ Moskwa P 432.451. (Details awaited).
● 23 July 1979. Jazirat Shinzi, off Masirah Island, 20°35′N. 58°56′E. (Moulting, trapped, ring removed, re-ringed with BTO ring London EH 77002 and released.)
(J. Oddos; Dr C. J. Feare.)

## Marsh Warbler   *Acrocephalus palustris*
○ (No details). December. Tsavo, Kenya, 2°59′S. 38°28′E.
● 'August (three years later). Oman.'
(G. Zink, *The Ring*, 1979, 100: 44, without more details; BTO.)

## Note
The study of the movements and longevity of birds will be assisted greatly if anyone finding a bird with a numbered ring on its leg would, *if the bird is dead*, remove the ring, or the leg with the ring; *if the bird is alive*, write down the details imprinted on the ring, then release the bird; and send the details of when, where and by whom it was found, plus the ring number, or the ring if removed, to:

or direct to:

Adviser for the Conservation of the Environment
PO Box 246                                    British Trust for Ornithology
MUSCAT                                        Beech Grove
Sultanate of Oman                             TRING  Herts  HP23 5NR England

# Bibliography

This bibliography includes most of the references which directly concern the ornithology of the Sultanate of Oman, but it omits the references which appear in Appendix 5. It also includes works of wider interest (marked*).

ABDULALI, H. 1968-continuing. A catalogue of the birds in the collection of the Bombay Natural History Society. *J. Bombay nat. Hist. Soc.* 65-.

ALEXANDER, H. G. 1929. Some birds seen in the Indian Ocean and the Mediterranean. *Ibis* (12)5: 41-53.

ALEXANDER, H. G. 1931. Shearwaters in the Arabian Sea. *Ibis* (13)1: 579-581.

ALEXANDER, W. B. 1954. Notes on *Pterodroma aterrima*. *Ibis* 96: 489-491.

ALLEN, M. 1980. *Falconry in Arabia.* London: Orbis.

*ANDERSON, J. 1896. *A Contribution to the Herpetology of Arabia.* London: Porter.

BAILEY, N. and BOURNE, W. R. P. 1963. Some records of petrels handled in the northern Indian Ocean. *J. Bombay nat. Hist. Soc.* 60: 256-258.

BAILEY, R. S. 1965. Cruise of RRS *Discovery* in the Indian Ocean. *Sea Swallow* 17: 52-56.

BAILEY, R. S. 1966. The sea-birds of the southeast coast of Arabia. *Ibis* 108: 224-264.

BAILEY, R. S. 1966. Migrant land-birds in the Mediterranean and Red Seas and the Indian Ocean. *Ibis* 108: 421-422.

BAILEY, R. S. 1967. Migrant waders in the Indian Ocean. *Ibis* 109: 437-439.

BAILEY, R. S. 1968. The pelagic distribution of sea-birds in the western Indian Ocean. *Ibis* 110: 493-519.

BAILEY, R. S. 1974. The effects of seasonal changes on the seabirds of the western Indian Ocean. *J.mar.biol.Assoc.India* 14(1972) (2): 628-642.

BATES, G. L. (1940). *Birds of Arabia.* (Unpublished typescript. Copies in the British Museum (Natural History), London and Tring, and at the library of Aramco, Dhahran, Saudi Arabia.)

BENT, J. T. 1895. Exploration of the frankincense country, southern Arabia. *Geogrl. J.* 6: 109-134, map p.204.

BENT, J. T. 1895. The land of frankincense and myrrh. *Nineteenth Century* 38: 595-613.

BENT, T. and BENT, M.V.A. 1900. *Southern Arabia.* London: Smith, Elder.

BERLIOZ, J. 1955. Capture d'un nouveau *Bulweria fallax* Jouanin en mer d'Oman. *Oiseau Revue fr. Orn.* 25: 312-313.

BLANFORD, W. T. 1876. *Eastern Persia, an Account of the Journeys of the Persian Boundary Commission 1870-71-72. Vol II. The Zoology and Geology.* London: Macmillan.

BOURNE, W. R. P. 1960. The petrels of the Indian Ocean. *Sea Swallow* 13: 26-39.

BOURNE, W. R. P. 1961. Concentrations of birds off the coasts of Somaliland and Oman. *Sea Swallow* 14: 27.

BOURNE, W. R. P. 1963. A review of oceanic studies of the biology of seabirds. *Proc. XIII Int.Orn.Congr.Ithaca, 1962*: 831-854.

BOURNE, W. R. P. 1965. The missing petrels. *Bull.Br.Orn.Club* 85: 97-105.

BOURNE, W. R. P. 1974. Survey of ornithological work in the Indian Ocean. *J.mar.biol.Assoc.India* 14(1972)(2): 609-627.

BROWNE, P. W. P. 1950. Notes on birds observed in South Arabia. *Ibis* 92: 52-65.

BROWNE, P. W. P. 1955. Records of birds in Arabia. *Ibis* 97: 373-375.

BROWNE, P. W. P. 1955. Asiatic Golden Plovers in Arabia. *Br. Birds* 48: 230-232.

BRUIJNS, W. F. J. Mörzer and BRUIJNS, M. F. Mörzer. 1957. Waarnemingen van de Grauwe Franjepoot, *Phalaropus lobatus* (L.) in de Indische Oceaan. *Ardea* 45: 72-84.

BRUYNS, W. F. J. Mörzer and VOOUS, K. H. 1965. Great Skuas *(Stercorarius skua)* in northern Indian Ocean. *Ardea* 53: 80-81.

BUNDY, G and WARR, E. (In press). A check-list of the birds of the Arabian Gulf States. *Sandgrouse* 1.

BURTON, A. R. 1918. Close-barred Sandgrouse at Muscat. *J. Bombay nat.Hist.Soc.* 25: 751-752.

BUTLER, E. A. 1877. Astola, a summer cruise in the Gulf of Oman. *Stray Feathers* 5: 283-304.

*BUXTON, P. A. 1923. *Animal life in deserts.* London: Arnold.

CHILMAN, P. W. G. 1970. White-bellied Storm-petrels *Fregetta grallaria* in North Indian Ocean and Arabian Sea in the summer. *Sea Swallow* 20: 41-42.

*CLOUDSLEY-THOMPSON, J. R. and CHADWICK, M. J. 1964. *Life in Deserts.* London: Foulis.

COWLES, G. S. 1980. A new sub-species of *Halcyon chloris* from an isolated population in eastern Arabia. *Bull. Br.Orn.Club* 101: (in press).

COX, P. Z. 1925. Some excursions in Oman. *Geogrl. J.* 66: 193-227, map p. 288.

CRAMP, S. and SIMMONS, K. E. L. 1977 – continuing. *Handbook of the Birds of Europe, the Middle East, and North Africa: the Birds of the Western Palearctic.* Vol 1 –  . Oxford: Oxford University Press.

DAVID, A. C. F. 1956. Further notes from the Kuria Muria Islands – coast of Oman. *Sea Swallow* 9: 17.

FISKEN, W. L. N. 1962. *IN* Phalaropes and Wilson's Storm Petrels in Arabian Sea. *Sea Swallow* 15: 34.

GALLAGHER, M. D. 1974. On the occurrence of the Great White Egret *Egretta alba* in the Persian Gulf region. *Bull.Br.Orn.Club* 94: 122-126.

GALLAGHER, M. D. 1977. Birds of Jabal Akhdar. *IN* The Scientific Results of the Oman Flora and Fauna Survey 1975. *J. Oman Stud. Spec.Rep.* 1: 27-58.

GALLAGHER, M. D. 1977. Cyclone hits Masirah. *RAF Orn.Soc.Newsl.* 29: 3-4.

GALLAGHER, M. D. 1980. The Sooty Falcon in Oman. *1979/80 Hawk Trust Annual Report*: (in press).

GALLAGHER, M. D. and FEARE, C. J. 1980. Ticks and terns. *RAF Orn.Soc.Newsl.* 34: 8-10.

GALLAGHER M. D. and ROGERS, T. D. 1980. On some birds of Dhofar and other parts of Oman. *IN* The Scientific Results of the Oman Flora and Fauna Survey 1977 (Dhofar). *J. Oman Stud.Spec.Rep.* 2: (in press).

GIBSON-HILL, C. A. 1948. The storm-petrels occurring in the northern Indian Ocean and adjacent seas. *J. Bombay nat. Hist. Soc.* 47: 443-449.

GIBSON-HILL, C. A. 1952. The tropic-birds occurring in the Indian Ocean and adjacent seas. *J. Bombay nat. Hist.Soc.* 49: 67-80.

GILL, F. B. 1967. Observations on the pelagic distribution of seabirds in the western Indian Ocean. *Proc.U.S.Nat.Mus.* 123(3605): 1-33.

GREEN, C. 1949. The Black-shouldered Kite on Masira, Oman. *Ibis* 91: 459-464.

GRIFFITHS, C. I. 1976. Some recent visits to Salalah. *RAF Orn.Soc.Newsl.* 25: 21-23.

GRIFFITHS, C. I. and ROGERS, T. D. 1975. *An interim list of the birds of Masirah Island, Oman.* (Duplicated typescript. Copy at the British Museum (Natural History), Tring. Revised typescript issued privately in 1976.)

GRIFFITHS, W. A. C. 1975. A Bibliography of the avifauna of the Arabian Peninsula, the Levant and Mesopotamia. *Army Bird-watching Soc.Periodic Publ.* No. 2. (Addendum No. 1 dated 1978, and No. 2 dated 1979, published by Orn.Soc.Middle East.)

GRIMWOOD, I. R. 1963. Notes on birds seen in eastern Aden Protectorate. *Bull.Br.Orn.Club* 83: 50-51.

GUICHARD, K. M. and GOODWIN, D. 1952. Notes on birds collected and observed in Oman and Hadhramaut. *Ibis* 94: 294-305.

GULF BIRD-WATCHERS' NEWSLETTER. 1969-1971. 24 parts. Ed. M. D. Gallagher. (Duplicated typescript. Copies at the British Museum (Natural History). Tring, and at Edward Grey Institute, Oxford).

HAINES, S. B. 1857. The Kooria Mooria Islands. *Naut.Mag.* 26: 385-389.

HARRISON, D. L. 1959. *Footsteps in the Sand.* London: Benn.

HARRISON, J. M. 1956. On a collection of birds made by Flight Lieutenant David L. Harrison in Oman, Arabia. *Bull.Br.Orn.Club* 76: 34-36 & 46-51.

HAY, R. 1947. The Kuria Muria Islands. *Geogrl. J.* 109: 279-281.

HEKSTRA, G. P. 1973. Scops and screech owls. Ch.6 IN *Owls of the World.* Ed. J. A. Burton. Netherlands: Peter Lowe.

HEUGLIN, T.von. 1859. List of birds observed and collected during a voyage in the Red Sea. Ed. and translated by Dr G Hartlaub. *Ibis* 1859: 337-352.

HEUGLIN, M. T. von. 1869-1873 (-1875). *Ornithologie Nordost-Afrikas, der Nilquellen und Küsten-Gebiete des Rothen Meeres und des nördlichen Somal-Landes.* 57 parts. Cassel: Theodor Fischer.

HONEYWELL, R. A. and HONEYWELL, G. E. 1976. *Birds of the Batinah of Oman.* (Published privately; PO Box 4668, Ruwi, Oman.)

HOOGSTRAAL, H. 1969. *Ornithodoros (Alectorobius) muesebecki,* N.sp., a parasite of the Blue-faced Booby *(Sula dactylatra melanops)* on Hasikiya Island, Arabian Sea. *Proc.ent.Soc.Wash.* 71: 368-374.

HULTON, J. G. 1839-1840. Notice on the Curia Muria Islands. *Trans. Bombay geog.Soc.* 3-5: 183-197.

HULTON, J. G. 1841. An account of the Curia Muria Isles near the south-eastern coast of Arabia. *Jl.R.geog.Soc.* 11: 156-164.

HUME, A. O. 1872. *Puffinus persicus* sp. nov. *Stray Feathers* 1: 5-7.

HUME, A. O. 1872-1873. Contributions to the ornithology of India – Sindh. *Stray Feathers* 1: 44-49, 91-289.

HUTCHINSON, G. E. 1950. The biochemistry of vertebrate excretion. *Bull.Am.Mus.nat.Hist.* 96: 1-554.

JENNINGS, M. 1980. RAFOS Masirah Expedition 1979. *Bull.Orn.Soc.Middle East* 4: 5-7.

JONES, M. E. 1964. Storm petrels in the Arabian Sea. *Sea Swallow* 16: 67-68.

JOUANIN, C. 1955. Une nouvelle espèce de Procellariidé. *Oiseau Revue fr.Orn.* 25: 155-161.

JOUANIN, C. 1957. Les Procellariidés mélaniques signalés en Mer d'Oman. *Oiseau Revue fr.Orn.* 27: 12-27.

KINNEAR, N. B. 1927. (A note on the collection of G. M. Lees, with a description of a new race of sandgrouse, *Pterocles coronatus saturatus).* *Bull.Br.Orn.Club* 48: 11-12.

KINNEAR, N. B. 1931. On some birds from central South Arabia. *Ibis* (13) 1: 698-701.

LATHAM, J. J. 1967. Bird notes of Aden Protectorate, Salalah and Habilayn. *J.RAF Orn.Soc.* 3: 8-12.

LEES, G. M. 1928. The physical geography of S. E. Arabia. *Geogrl. J.* 71: 441-470.

LØPPENTHIN, B. 1951. Sea birds of the Persian Gulf. *Proc.X. Int. Orn.Congr. 1950:* 603-610.

*LORIMER, J. G. 1908-1915. *Gazetteer of the Persian Gulf, Oman and Central Arabia.* 2 vols. in 6 parts. Calcutta: Government Printers. (Reprinted in 1970; Farnborough: Gregg).

LOW, G. C. 1937. Grey and Red-necked Phalaropes in Arabian Sea. *Ibis* (14) 1:866.

MEINERTZHAGEN, R. 1925. The distribution of the phalaropes. *Ibis* 12(1): 325-344.

MEINERTZHAGEN, R. 1937. Grey and Red-necked Phalaropes in Arabian Sea. *Ibis* (14) 1: 667.

MEINERTZHAGEN, R. 1954. *Birds of Arabia.* Edinburgh, London: Oliver and Boyd. (Reprint, in press; London: Sotheran).

MEYER de SCHAUENSEE, R. and RIPLEY S. D. 1953. Birds of Oman and Muscat. *Proc.Acad.nat.Sci.Philadelphia* 105: 71-90.

MILES, S. B. 1901. Across the Green Mountains of Oman. *Geogrl. J.* 18: 465-498.

MILES, S. B. 1910. On the border of the Great Desert; a journey in Oman. *Geogrl. J.* 36: 159-178; map p.248; 405-425.

MILES, S. B. 1919. *The Countries and Tribes of the Persian Gulf.* 2 vols. London: Harrison. (Reprinted in 1966 in 1 vol; London: Frank Cass.)

MOREAU, R. E. 1938. Bird migration over the north-western part of the Indian Ocean, the Red Sea and the Mediterranean. *Proc.zool.Soc.Lond.* (A) 108: 1-26.

MOREAU, R. E. 1952. The place of Africa in the Palaearctic migration system. *J. anim.Ecol.* 21: 250-271.

MOREAU, R. E. 1966. *The Bird Faunas of Africa and its islands.* London, New York: Academic Press.

MOREAU, R. E. 1969. The Sooty Falcon. *Bull.Br.Orn.Club* 89: 62-67.

*MOREAU, R. E. 1972. *The Palaearctic-African Bird Migration Systems.* London, New York: Academic Press.

OWEN, W. F. W. 1833. *Narrative of voyages to explore the shores of Africa, Arabia and Madagascar.* 2 vols. London: Bentley.

OWEN, W. F. W. 1857. The coast of Arabia Felix from the Journal of Capt. W. F. W. Owen, of HMS *Leven. Naut.Mag.*: 180-191.

PAIGE, J. P. 1960. Bird notes from Aden and Oman. *Ibis* 102: 520-525.

*READE, D. G. 1980. Development of the water resources of Oman for agriculture. *FAO Field Document* No. 14. Muscat: Food and Agriculture Organisation of the United Nations, and Water Resources Department, Ministry of Agriculture and Fisheries.

RIPLEY, S. D. 1951. Three birds from the mountains of Muscat. *Postilla* 10: 1-2.

RIPLEY, S. D. 1954. Comments on the biogeography of Arabia with particular reference to birds. *J. Bombay nat.Hist.Soc.* 52: 241-248.

*Royal Air Force Ornithological Society's Expedition to Masirah Island 6-26 October 1976.* 1978. Ed. A. C. Curry. (Printed privately by RAF Orn.Soc. Copy at the British Museum (Natural History), Tring. Reprinted in *J.RAF Orn.Soc.* 1980.)

*Royal Air Force Ornithological Society's 1979 Masirah Island Expedition.* (In Prep.) Ed. C. A. Pomeroy.

SEA SWALLOW. 1947-continuing. The Annual Report of the Royal Navy Bird Watching Society. (Contains many reports of birds off Oman; for some titles see in Griffiths, 1975.)

*SERVENTY, D. L. 1971. Biology of desert birds. IN *Avian Biology* 1: 287-339. London, New York: Academic Press.

SETON-BROWNE, C. and HARRISON, J. 1968. Observations on wildfowl on the Batinah coast, Muscat and Oman, south-east Arabia, 1962-1967. *Bull.Br.Orn.Club* 88: 59-73.

SETON-BROWNE, C. J. 1968. Bird Watching in Oman. *Adjutant* 1: 4-7.

SHARPE, R. B. 1886. On a collection of birds from the vicinity of Muscat. *Ibis* (5) 4: 162-168.

SILSBY, J. 1980. *Inland Birds of Saudi Arabia.* London, Jeddah: Immel.

SMITH, P. A. 1969. Observations from the interior of Muscat and Oman during 1966-67. *Bull.Br.Orn.Club* 89: 52-60.

STANFORD, W. 1973. A note on the birds of Oman and the Trucial States 1954-1968. *Army Bird-watching Soc. Periodic Publication* No. 1.

STRICKLAND, M. J. 1974. Masira Island: doubts on the Black-shouldered Kite. *Ibis* 116: 94.

THESIGER, W. 1959. *Arabian Sands.* London: Longmans, Green.

THOMAS, B. 1931. A journey into Rub' al Khali – the Southern Arabian Desert. *Geogrl. J.* 77: 1-37.

THOMAS, B. 1931. A camel journey across the Rub' al Khali. *Geogrl. J.* 78: 209-242.

300

THOMAS, B. 1932. *Arabia Felix: Across the 'Empty Quarter' of Arabia*. London, New York: Jonathan Cape.

TICEHURST, C. B. 1924. *Phalaropus lobatus IN* The birds of Sind. *Ibis* 1924: 126.

TICEHURST, C. B., with CHEESMAN, R. E. and Cox, P. Z. 1925. Birds of the Persian Gulf Islands. *J. Bombay nat.Hist.Soc.* 30: 725-733.

TUCK, G. S. 1974. Seabirds of the Persian Gulf (the Gulf) and Gulf of Oman. A survey (1958-1973). *Sea Swallow* 23: 7-21.

UDVARDY, M. D. F. 1965. A Classification of the Biogeographical Provinces of the World. *IUCN Occasional Paper* No. 18. Morges, Switzerland.

VAURIE, C. 1959 & 1965. *The Birds of the Palearctic Fauna*. 2 vols. London: Witherby.

VOOUS, K. H. 1977. *List of recent Holarctic bird species*. London: Academic Press for British Ornithologists' Union. (Reprinted, with amendments, from *Ibis* 115 (1973): 612-638; *Ibis* 119(1977): 223-250, 376-406.)

WALKER, F. J. (In press). Notes on the birds of northern Oman. *Sandgrouse* 2.

WALKER, F. J. (In press). Notes on the birds of Dhofar, Sultanate of Oman. *Sand-grouse* 2.

WALTER, H. (In prep.). The Sooty Falcon *Falco concolor* Temminck in Oman: Result of a breeding survey. *J. Oman. Stud.*

WARR, F. E. 1973. *Birds recorded in the Dhofar Province of the Sultanate of Oman.* (Duplicated typescript, revised 1976; photocopy in the British Museum (Natural History), Tring.)

WARR, F. E. 1976. *Birds recorded in the Sultanate of Oman (excluding Dhofar, Masirah Island and the Musandam Peninsula)*. (Duplicated typescript; copy in the British Museum (Natural History), Tring.)

WHISH, R. W. 1860. Descriptive sketch of the Island of Jibleea, Kuria Muria Bay. *Trans. Bombay geogr.Soc.* 15: 38-40.

## FURTHER READING

ALI, S. and RIPLEY, S. D. 1968-1974. *Handbook of the birds of India and Pakistan.* 10 vols. Bombay, London, New York: Oxford University Press.

ARCHER, G. and GODMAN, E. M. 1937-1961. *The Birds of British Somaliland and the Gulf of Aden*. Vols 1-2, London: Gurney and Jackson; vols 3-4, London, Edinburgh: Oliver and Boyd.

BOVEY, D. and MANDAVILLE, Jr., J. P. 1978. *Wild Flowers of Northern Oman*. Muscat: Government of Oman.

CAMERON, A. D. and HARRISON, C. J. O. 1978. *Bird Families of the World*. Oxford: Elsevier-Phaidon.

HUE, F. and ETCHECOPAR, R. D. 1970. *Les Oiseaux du Proche et du Moyen orient, de la Mediterranée aux contrefort de l'Himalaya*. Paris: Boubée.

MACKWORTH-PRAED, C. W. and GRANT, C. H. B. 1952, 1955. Birds of Eastern and North-eastern Africa. 2 vols. London: Longmans, Green. (Reprinted in 1980.)

PORTER, R. F. *et al.* 1976. *Flight Identification of European Raptors*. 2nd ed. Berkhamstead: T. & A. D. Poyser.

The Scientific Results of the Oman Flora and Fauna Survey 1975. 1977. Ed. Harrison, D. L. *J. Oman. Stud. Spec. Rep.* 1.

The Scientific Results of the Oman Flora and Fauna Survey 1977 (Dhofar). 1980. Ed. Sale, J. B. *et al. J. Oman Stud. Spec. Rep.* 2.

TURNER ETTLINGER, D. M. (Ed.). 1974. *Natural History Photography*. London, New York: Academic Press.

VOOUS, K. H. 1960. *Atlas of European Birds*. London: Nelson.

# Index

Figures in bold type against the main
entries indicate the relevant colour plates.

306

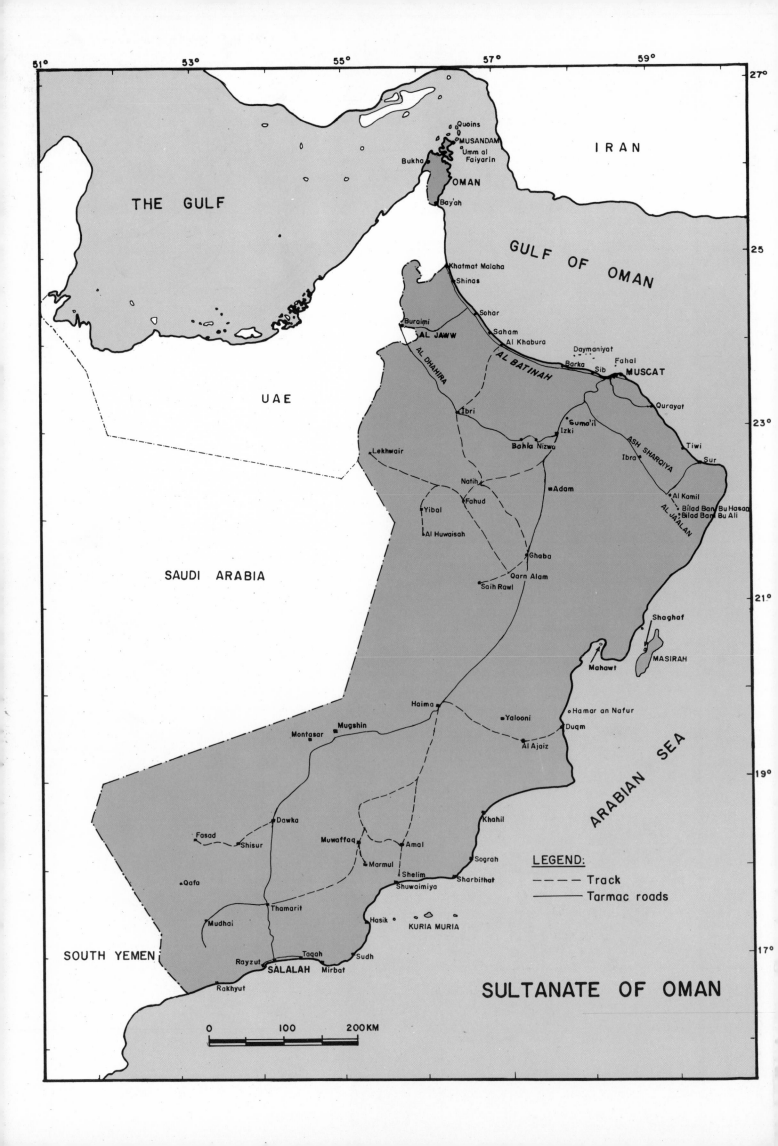